NONPROFIT GOVERNANCE

The Executive's Guide

Victor Futter, General Editor

George W. Overton, Managing Editor

Published by the American Society of Corporate Secretaries
and The American Bar Association Section of Business Law

The materials contained herein represent the opinions of the authors and editors and should not be construed to be the action of the American Bar Association or the Section of Business Law unless adopted pursuant to the bylaws of the Association.

Nothing contained in this book is to be considered as the rendering of legal advice for specific cases, and readers are responsible for obtaining such advice from their own legal counsel. This book is intended for educational and informational purposes only.

©1997 by the American Bar Association and the American Society of Corporate Secretaries.
All rights reserved.
Printed in the United States of America.

Library of Congress Catalog Card Number 96-79908
ISBN 1-57073-422-4

Cover design by Emily Friel

Discounts are available for books ordered in bulk. Special consideration is given to state and local bars, CLE programs, and other bar-related organizations. Inquire at Publications Planning & Marketing, American Bar Association, 750 North Lake Shore Drive, Chicago, Illinois 60611.

01 00 99 98 97   5 4 3 2 1

Table of Contents

Preface

Currently there are over one million nonprofit[1] organizations in the United States covering an enormous array of institutions including, among others, religious organizations, colleges and universities, foundations, symphonies, museums and other cultural organizations, hospitals, trade associations, consumer "watch-dog" and advocacy groups, social service agencies, and sports leagues. These organizations run the gamut from substantial bodies and large public universities to a plethora of small, community-based, self-help development organizations.

Nonprofits join the private sector and the government sector as the third major leg of the national economy with aggregate annual revenues exceeding $750 billion, or about fifteen percent of the nation's gross national product. Eighty million people spend three hours per week or more working for nonprofits; another eleven million people work full-time for nonprofits. Together these two groups constitute a larger number than those engaged in the for-profit field. In addition, millions of people make financial contributions to nonprofits, with eighty-eight cents of every dollar raised for the nonprofit sector coming from individuals. Nonprofits are thus a vital, essential, and significant portion of the national scene.

As Peter F. Drucker has written:[2]

> Indeed, the most noteworthy feature of the American nonprofit institution is not its size. It is the explosive growth in the scope of nonprofit work and the parallel growth in the demands placed on the competence of the nonprofit institution. These demands go way beyond what good intentions and generosity can supply. Increasingly, *they demand professionalism of a high order*. The more a nonprofit institution relies on volunteers, the *more professional its management has to be*. An organization has far too many things to do for it to be able to operate without professional, full-time staff. Furthermore, if performance standards are to have any results, they must be coupled with executive accountability.[3]

This book is addressed primarily to the managers of the nonprofit organization, in contrast to the directors of such an entity, or to the public interests that may surround it. The Section of Business Law of the American Bar Association (ABA) and the American Society of Corporate Secretaries (ASCS), in preparing and publishing this work, join many voices heard today in recognizing the important role nonprofits play in American life, in predicting a still larger role for them in the near future, and in sharing a concern that many such organizations need more conscious attention to their internal procedures as they assume broader and larger responsibilities. We do not think it is helpful to discuss these challenges in the abstract. Therefore, we have assembled the thinking of experienced men and women, each of whom has written on a specific topic, and invite the reader—the staff of a nonprofit—to think about how her or his organization could benefit from their suggestions.

Our writers sometimes overlap with their counsel, but where there is repetition, it may emphasize the importance of an area that calls for scrutiny. An example might be the role of a nominating committee, the importance of which is emphasized by more than one of our authors.

The strengthening of the structure of a nonprofit requires that more conscious attention be placed on the role of the board, and that the nonprofit executive director and his or her staff appreciate that, in addition to performing the vital function contained in their mission, they have an *essential and active management role to play*. The precise division of responsibilities between the board of directors (policy matters) and staff (management matters) of a nonprofit will vary among different types of organizations; but we state unequivocally that, while in the past an executive director may have been able to neglect the management responsibility of his or her position, in today's environment doing so puts one's job, and the entire organization, at risk. The key to making a board effective is to organize its work, and that is the CEO's responsibility. It is the staff that will make the management of an organization strong and effective, which will make the board and management function together as an effective team, and which will make the organization's dreams a promise, and the promise a reality. We hope this book will help staff achieve this.

This book is intended to assist the executive director and other individuals in the nonprofit world who handle the various aspects of what, in the corporate for-profit arena, is called the corporate secretary's office. We recognize that, with an almost infinite variety of nonprofit organizations, the tasks described will be performed in a variety of ways and may be assigned to several people. Some of the functions may be carried out by the executive director, the assistant to the executive director, an administrative assistant, other staff members, or by the secretary. Some of the organizations will have a secretary who is a paid staff member. In others, the secretary may be an unpaid board member, with staff members carrying out the various duties. For ease of reference, we have blanketed all of these activities and titles under the simple heading "secretary's office"; and when we refer to the secretary, we mean to cover all the persons who handle a part of the secretary's job. While the tasks may be carried out in a variety of ways, the substance of the fundamental tasks remains the same. It is this we hope to describe and elucidate. It is our view that the executive director, assisted by the secretary, must serve as the nonprofit's manager, caretaker, and provider. Some of the functions described below must be performed even if the nonprofit is too small to have a separate office assigned to them.

This book necessarily, from time to time, addresses directors' duties and responsibilities, because only if the staff understands them can it do an adequate job in supporting and informing directors. In addition, directors will benefit from reading this book in order to understand their relation to staff and how a well-organized staff should operate.

Because of the wide variation in size, structure, nature, and mission in the huge nonprofit world, the material and suggestions set forth in the chapters that follow are obviously not applicable in their entirety to all organizations. Rather, each organization should select the items applicable to it and helpful in its operations. We hope that each of you will find many such valuable items. Additional assistance may be found in the various publications cited in the bibliographies at the end of many chapters.

Whether nonprofit entities are large or small, however, they face many similar problems. A number of these problems bear remarkable similarity to those faced in commercial, for-profit enterprises.

Depending on the size, structure, nature, and mission of the organization, the nonprofit's secretary's office may be concerned with:

- Preparation for and organization of board meetings;
- Recording, reviewing, and editing of minutes;
- Corporate governance;
- Accountability and responsibility;
- The fiduciary duties of directors;
- Board and committee structure and effectiveness;
- What ethical and other policies (e.g. conflicts of interest) to adopt and what procedures to adopt to ensure the highest level of ethical leadership and to prohibit self-dealing by board and staff;
- Bylaws;
- Selection and retention of board members;
- Records retention;
- The functions and operations of audit, compensation, executive, nominating, and other committees;
- Tax exemption questions and filings;
- Appropriate insurance coverage and risk management techniques to mitigate institutional risk;
- Liability to third parties;
- What lobbying activities, if any, may be engaged in;
- Compliance with federal and state laws and regulations;
- Protection of directors through indemnification, insurance, and exoneration; and
- Protection of the organization's intangible assets.

The secretary's office of a nonprofit can play an enormously beneficial role by being vigilant concerning those matters that facilitate the operations of the organization's board and management as well as those matters that arise from the conduct of activities that could adversely affect the organization (e.g., self dealing, prohibited political contributions) or place the organization's tax-exempt status at risk. In most nonprofit organizations, revocation of tax-exempt status would dictate dissolution.

We recognize that most executive directors (and probably most secretaries) are far too busy and overburdened to sit down and read this guidebook. We trust, however, that they will assign the reading of it to a member of their staff and that this staff member will bring applicable portions to their attention. While the nonprofit field is flooded with literature, we view this book as unique because its one volume covers, with forms and checklists, the preponderant portion of the management problems a nonprofit will face. Further, its practical advice is based on the experience of those who have faced and are familiar with board organization and management problems.

Nonprofit organizations, like their for-profit siblings, are governed by state law with respect to their organization, operation and existence, and by the Internal Revenue Code.[4] A majority of the substantial states in the nation have adopted annual registration reporting requirements for charitable organizations which raise funds and/or conduct programs.

Where a specific state law is used as a model we have referred to it, but in general we have used as a reference the Model Nonprofit Corporation Act.[5] These references basically refer to corporate organization and maintenance, and the reader is encouraged to research separately the statutes of the state under whose laws the organization is formed and charitable registration/fundraising statutes or consumer protection statutes where appropriate.

The ASCS has been a preeminent leader in developing educational tools and information for its corporate members. Many directors and senior officers of for-profit corporations, who are also directors of nonprofit organizations, bring expectations of high performance to such nonprofit entities in what might be called the corporate governance area. At the same time, as noted above, a large number of nonprofits, while receiving high grades on motivation and dedication, may not have the expertise to deal with all the matters previously listed and may need training in general management. Hence, the ASCS decided to undertake the mission of developing a set of educational programs and tools for secretaries in the nonprofit field, a number of whom are members of the ASCS.

Similarly, the ABA's Section of Business Law has maintained continuing scrutiny in nonprofit matters through its Committee on Nonprofit Corporations. Its *Guidebook for Directors of Nonprofit Corporations* is a recent product of that mission. It is the hope and expectation of both the ABA and the ASCS that many organizations will benefit from the cumulative base of knowledge collected in this work. By adding its expertise to that of the ASCS in this venture, the ABA is continuing, and hopefully expanding, the assistance readily available to those who give of their time to serve the worthwhile causes of the nonprofit.

This is the ABA's second book and the ASCS's first for the nonprofit community. Accordingly, we welcome the suggestions of our readers. The book covers several of the secretary's essential tasks. We plan to supplement it from time to time with additional monographs or with revised versions of existing chapters. We welcome suggestions for additional topics as well as any criticism, instruction, thoughts, and insights which will improve our product. We particularly welcome any forms or checklists which we might add to future editions. By working together, we will be able in time to produce a guidebook that truly answers all the questions and problems with which the secretary's office is faced in the nonprofit arena.

Please address any communication to us as follows.

> Nonprofit Committee
> American Society of Corporate Secretaries
> 521 Fifth Avenue
> New York, NY 10175

or

American Bar Association
Section of Business Law
Committee on Nonprofit Corporations
750 North Lake Shore Drive
Chicago, IL 60611

or

Telephone:

Victor Futter	(201) 643-5083
George W. Overton	(312) 201-2000
David M. Bardsley	(212) 708-2256
Lynn A. Howell	(813) 345-1121
David W. Smith	(212) 681-2012

We hope this information will serve you well and we look forward to hearing from you.

Victor Futter

Notes

1. The terms "nonprofit" and "not-for-profit" are interchangeable. Thus the Model Act is called the *Model Nonprofit Corporation Act*, while the New York statute uses the term "not-for-profit." We have opted to use "nonprofit." *See* "A Warning on Words," page xviii.

2. Peter F. Drucker, *Managing for the Future: The 1990s and Beyond* (New York: Truman/Talley Books/Dutton, 1992).

3. Ibid. (emphasis added).

4. 26 I.R.C. (1994).

5. Model Nonprofit Corp. Act (1987).

Acknowledgments

While each chapter is shown to have an individual author, generally the draft for each chapter was reviewed by five commentators and was the subject of discussion at two meetings of the Nonprofit Committee of the ASCS. Hence the ultimate product is very much of a collegial product, and each of the ASCS members whose name is listed below has made a significant contribution to this work.

In addition, following the completion of this work by the ASCS, the ABA's Section of Business Law made a detailed review of each chapter leading to further revisions. Finally, the work was reviewed and commented upon by the Corporate Laws Committee of the Section.

The preceding two paragraphs do not apply to the chapter by William G. Bowen (which was originally in the form of a speech at a national conference of the ASCS) or to the chapter by Professor Regina E. Herzlinger, because it is a reprint from the *Harvard Business Review*. These two pieces are intended as "thought provokers" and are obviously not statements of legal principles.

We would be remiss indeed if particular expressions of thanks were not made to several individuals.

First, to Thomas L. Ambro, co-chair of the Business Law Section's Committee on Publications. Without him, it would have been impossible to put together this first cooperative venture between the ABA and the ASCS. Throughout, he has had a sound vision of the project and directed it with wise counsel. Similarly, Linda C. Hayman, the other co-chair of the Section's Committee on Publications, has given us wise and staunch support.

Second, to Lisa A. Runquist, who was chair of the Section's Nonprofit Corporations Committee for most of this project. She not only gave this project her firm support, but carefully reviewed and commented upon the manuscript prior to its publication. Similar words of thanks also go to Lynn A. Howell, Lisa's successor.

Thanks, too, go to Donald A. Scott for his careful review on behalf of the Corporate Law Committee of the Section and to William Anselm Humenuk for his careful review on behalf of the Section's Committee on Nonprofit Corporations, Legal Guidebook Subcommittee.

But above all, thanks go to George W. Overton, our managing editor, for his many significant contributions during our committee meetings and for his prodigious undertaking in carefully editing and reorganizing the manuscripts for this book. It was a herculean task indeed to bring some uniformity and provide a sense of organization to an exceedingly diverse group of individual chapters. George brought imagination to this work, conceived and constructed design and layout, and gave to this book the same care and attention to detail that characterized his work in editing the Section's companion volume, *Guidebook for Directors of Nonprofit Corporations*.

On the side of the ASCS, particular thanks go to David W. Smith, its president, for his unstinting assistance and continuous encouragement for this project. He has been a tower of strength to us all. Similarly, we have benefitted from the sustenance and advocacy by successive chairmen of the ASCS: Jack Goetsch, Stephen P. Norman, G. Penn Holsenbeck, and Sigurd Ueland, Jr., all of whom, from the time this project started, gave us the courage and perseverance to complete it. Cheryl A. Sorokin, chair of the Corporate Practices Committee, pitched in by giving the manuscript a careful reading, raising many questions, and providing us with the benefit of her reflections.

Note must also be made of the fact that the early vision for this book came from two of the first vice chairs of the ASCS Nonprofit Committee, Philip A. Faix, Jr. and David M. Bardsley, during a meeting of E. Alan Klobasa's Education Committee. Phil and David were the early sparkplugs and contributors and significantly aided in getting this project off the ground and completed. We are also grateful for Alan's encouragement throughout this project.

Thanks also to Carol A. Strickland and her successor, Rebecca R. Morris, as chair of the ASCS Publications Oversight Committee, for their unstinting support and endorsement.

We would be derelict indeed if we did not thank Jacqueline M. Odes at the ABA, who was in fact the true editor of this work, and Sandy Eitel, also at the ABA, who did an outstanding job of marketing and promoting the book. Our appreciation also goes to Tami Howie, Jason McCullough, E. Keith Eckloff, and Laura Downes, staff of *The Business Lawyer*, University of Maryland School of Law, for their assistance.

Finally, thanks to Mike Goodman in the national office of the ASCS for his help on various aspects of this publication.

Victor Futter

Committee Membership

Nonprofit Committee
American Society of Corporate Secretaries

Victor Futter, chair

Archie M. Bankston
David M. Bardsley, vice chair
Carol M. Barker, vice chair
Lucy S. Binder
Robert W. Bishop, vice chair
Paula Bowen
James E. Buck
Alfrieda S. Burke
George J. Casper III
Patricia Conway
Martin A. Coyle
Ann Marie Plubell Czulowski
Joan Dubinsky
Frank W. Evans
Philip A. Faix, Jr., vice chair
Susan Sommer Futter
Terence J. Gallagher
Cynthia Gordon
Carl T. Hagberg
John B. Hicks
Michael Hone
Lynn R. Isaacs
Gilbert H. Jacobson
E. Alan Klobasa
Kenneth P. Kopelman

Robert Kornreich
Matthew A. Landy
William Lehr, Jr.
Linda Listoe
Michael P. Maloney
Albert P. Mauro
Carmelita M. Montesa
Theodore J. Mortensen
George W. Overton
Rosalyn Owen
John K. Notz, Jr.
Leonard M. Polisar
David B. Rigney
Henry J. Scarfo
Edward R. Schmidt
Jean M. Schmidt
Robert L. Seaman
Peter Swords
Sally P. Trabulsi
Robert Vanni
Cherry S. White
J. Warren Wood
J. Taylor Woodward III
David W. Smith, ex-officio
Michael E. Goodman, ex-officio

The Committee on Nonprofit Corporations
Section of Business Law
American Bar Association

Lynn A. Howell, chair
Lisa A. Runquist, immediate past chair

Victor Futter
Michael Hone
William A. Humenuk
Joseph Lunin

John K. Notz, Jr.
George W. Overton
Donald Kramer

Resources

Listed below are organizations which publish a number of items of interest to the nonprofit community.

1. Section of Business Law
   American Bar Association
   750 Lake Shore Drive
   Chicago, IL 60611

2. American Society of Corporate Secretaries
   521 Fifth Avenue
   New York, NY 10175

3. Association of Governing Boards
   of Universities and Colleges
   1 DuPont Circle
   Washington, DC 20036

4. The Independent Sector
   1828 L Street, N.W.
   Washington, DC 20036

5. The National Center for Nonprofit Boards
   2000 L Street, N.W.
   Suite 510
   Washington, DC 20036

6. Jossey-Bass Publishers
   350 Sansome Street
   San Francisco, CA 94104

General Bibliography

American Bar Association, Section of Business Law. *Guidebook for Directors of Nonprofit Corporations.* Chicago, 1993.

American Society of Corporate Secretaries. *Annual Meeting of Shareholders: A Guidebook.* 3d ed. New York, 1991.

————. *Corporate Minutes: A Monograph for the Corporate Secretary.* New York, 1996.

————. *The Corporate Secretary and the Board of Directors: A Comprehensive Guidebook.* New York, 1987.

————. *Meetings of the Board of Directors and its Committees: A Guidebook.* New York, 1985.

————. *Nominating Committee Practices and Procedures.* New York, 1981.

————. *Records Retention.* Reprint. New York, 1985.

————. *Varying Approaches to Problem Areas in Preparing Minutes—A Syllabus.* New York, 1983.

Bader, Barry S. *Planning Successful Board Retreats.* Washington, D.C.: National Center for Nonprofit Boards, 1991.

Baughman, James C. *Trustees, Trusteeship and the Public Good.* New York: Quorum Books, 1987.

Bowen, William G. *Inside the Boardroom.* New York: John Wiley & Sons, Inc., 1994.

————, Thomas I. Nygren, Sarah E. Turner and Elizabeth A. Duffy. *The Charitable Nonprofits: An Analysis of Institutional Dynamics & Characteristics.* San Francisco: Jossey-Bass, 1994.

Bryce, Herrington J. *Financial and Strategic Management for Nonprofit Organizations.* 2d ed. Englewood Cliffs, NJ: Prentice-Hall, 1992.

Carver, John. *Boards That Make A Difference.* San Francisco: Jossey-Bass, 1990.

Dalsimer, John Paul. *Understanding Nonprofit Financial Statements A Primer for Board Members.* Washington, D.C.: National Center for Nonprofit Boards, 1991.

Drucker, Peter F. *Managing for the Future: The 1990s and Beyond.* New York: Truman Talley Books/Dutton, 1992.

————. "The Age of Social Transformation." *Harper's,* 1994.

The Peter F. Drucker Foundation for Nonprofit Management. *The Drucker Foundation Self-Assessment Tool for Nonprofit Organizations.* San Francisco: Jossey-Bass, 1993.

Edie, John A. *Directors and Officers Liability Insurance and Indemnification.* Washington, D.C.: Council on Foundations, 1988.

Guthrie, Kevin M. *The New York Historical Society—Lessons Learned from One Nonprofit's Long Term Struggle for Survival.* San Francisco: Jossey-Bass, 1996.

Houle, Cyril O. *Governing Boards: Their Nature and Nurture.* San Francisco: Jossey-Bass, 1989.

Howe, Fisher. *What Every Board Member Should Know About Fund Raising.* San Francisco: Jossey-Bass, 1991.

————. *Welcome to the Board: Your Guide to Effective Participation.* San Francisco: Jossey-Bass, 1995.

Ingram, Richard T. *Ten Basic Responsibilities of Nonprofit Boards.* Washington, D.C.: National Center for Nonprofit Boards, 1993.

Kurtz, Daniel L. *Board Liability: Guide for Nonprofit Directors.* Mt. Kisco, NY: Moyer Bell Limited, 1988.

Lord, James Gregory. *The Raising of Money: Thirty-Five Essentials Every Trustee Should Know.* Cleveland: Third Sector Press, 1983.

Milaro, Marie. *A Handbook For Museum Directors.* Washington, D.C.: Smithsonian Institute.

Nelson, Judith Grummon. *Six Tips to Recruiting, Operating and Involving Nonprofit Board Members.* Washington, D.C.: National Center for Nonprofit Boards, 1991.

A Warning on Words

Anyone writing for a nonprofit audience must face a problem unique to this field: an exasperating ambiguity of titles and terms for the various players in our field. In this work, we will use the following terms with only the following definitions, and we, for these pages, exclude other meanings for these words.

Board or **Board of Directors** shall refer to the governing body of a nonprofit organization (as defined under applicable state law). In a given case, this entity may have a name such as "Governing Committee," "Board of Trustees," "House of Delegates," "Board of Governors," etc. We shall use only the words set forth above in bold face.

Chair shall refer to the person who presides over or convenes the **Board of Directors**, and who is usually not an employee and not engaged full time in the organization's service, although in a few cases, the **Chair** and the **Executive Director** may be the same person.

Executive Director shall refer to the chief staff officer of the organization, who may, in any given case, be called the "president" or some other title. By "executive director" we refer, of course, to a man or woman who will be the principal individual responsible for the organization; if it is large he or she will usually be a full-time paid employee; often, in small nonprofits, the only such employee, a part-time employee, or a volunteer.

The reader will note that we avoid the word "president," which could mean either a paid executive (**Executive Director**) or the man or woman who presides over the Board of Directors (**Chair**).

Secretary shall refer either to a staff person who, in a large organization, has general charge of corporate records, procedures and continuity, or to the secretary's office (*see* Preface). We generally do not use this word to mean a noncompensated, or volunteer, board member simply bearing that title who does not bear these responsibilities.

Member shall refer to any person having voting rights of any kind (usually including the right to elect directors) in the corporate frame of governance. We do not refer to "members" where the word is used simply to describe donors without such rights, or persons simply entitled to use a facility, such as entry to a museum.

Lastly, although much of what follows is applicable to nonprofit entities of any legal variety (corporations, unincorporated associations, trusts, etc.), we are generally describing the rights, duties, opportunities, and challenges of a nonprofit corporation. Because, however, the teaching of our authors usually reaches beyond corporate structures, we use *organization* as the general term for the entities we describe, unless a specific reference to corporate law is intended.

We recognize also that certain organizations or categories thereof (e.g., religious groups) will have special rules applicable only to them. These are not covered here. By and large we have endeavored to deal with problems or suggestions applicable across the board to all nonprofits.

INTRODUCTION
A View of Our Universe

We begin our analysis with William Bowen's reminiscent commentary. Although it speaks to his experience with boards of directors (business and nonprofit), he also is concerned with the interplay of board and staff and all the various problems that are addressed in this volume. This piece thus provides an essential background for the problems treated herein.

Inside the Boardroom: A Reprise

William G. Bowen[1]

This chapter discusses the role of the board of directors, as seen by someone who has served on both business and nonprofit boards.

Introduction

As I can attest from personal experience, the leading corporate secretaries are often the unsung heroes of corporate governance. Here, I want to take a somewhat broader perspective and comment about the work of boards in both the for-profit and nonprofit sectors. There is, in my view, much to be learned by comparing the two sectors.

This is a topic that I have, if you will, "grown up with," and the comments I make here, and the much more extensive discussion contained in my book on this subject, are based on an amalgam of study of the relevant literature and an odd array of intense personal experiences. My wife is convinced that I am a "virus"; wherever I go, there is trouble. Be that as it may, I have enjoyed a rich variety of opportunities to learn, and the presumptive norms contained in my book grow out of that experience.

Do Boards Matter? What Do They Do?

Let me begin at the beginning, with the fundamental question of whether boards matter at all. It would be easy, and quite wrong, to exaggerate their importance. As we all know, external forces, including the march of technology and the workings of markets, constrain actions and often determine outcomes. I doubt that any board, however talented and far-seeing, could have spared IBM the agonies associated with the shift to distributed processing. As a wise commentator, Charles Exley, former chairman and CEO of NCR, put it, "[w]hen you make the best milk bottle in town . . . , and someone discovers milk cartons . . . , you confront one huge problem to which there are no easy solutions" (Bowen, p. 27).

Nonprofit boards face severe constraints of their own. These are often looser, however, than those that dictate business corporate behavior, and for that reason, and because of the existence in the nonprofit sector of multiple objectives, nonprofit boards frequently have more room to maneuver. Thus, while all boards matter, I believe that nonprofit boards often matter more than for-profit boards. Market sanctions, takeovers, mergers, and purchases and sales of assets provide powerful mechanisms for resolving questions about the future of for-profit entities; some nonprofits, in contrast, may simply drift along, living lives that are simultaneously undistinguished and largely unnoticed—until some disaster strikes. One challenge, I believe, is to find better ways of encouraging "death with dignity" within the nonprofit sector; but that is a topic all its own.

What do boards do? Contrary to much accepted lore, boards almost never "make policy" in any thoroughgoing way. Rather, they raise questions, debate options, and eventually adopt (or not) recommendations brought to them by the executive director. As Nicholas Katzenbach has reminded me insistently, the very thought of a board actually making policy, from scratch, is frightening in the extreme. Chaos would surely result.

Boards do serve other important functions. All boards share certain responsibilities: (1) to select, advise, evaluate, and, if need be, replace the executive director; (2) to establish and review strategic directions and to approve specific objectives; (3) to ensure, to the extent possible, that the resources needed to accomplish the objectives are in hand; (4) to monitor the performance of management; (5) to ensure that the organization operates responsibly (ethically) as well as effectively; and (6) to establish and carry out an effective system of governance at the board level.

This list of common functions, while useful in some respects, obscures rather than clarifies major differences between the for-profit and nonprofit sectors. There is, most important of all, a fundamental distinction related to mission. Whereas for-profit boards concentrate on enhancing shareholder values—and may, in pursuit of that objective, enter entirely new businesses and abandon long-established ones—nonprofit boards are much more committed to the established missions of their organizations, with all that follows from that simple statement. As John Whitehead, now chairman of AEA Investors and formerly co-managing partner of Goldman Sachs and Deputy Secretary of State, puts it, "A for-profit board has an obligation to *get out* of a bad business while a nonprofit board may have an obligation to *stay in*, if it is to be true to its mission" (Bowen, p. 23). Another special characteristic of many nonprofits is that their boards must devote a great deal of time and energy to mobilizing volunteers and raising money.

Board Size and Composition

In my view, for-profit boards should normally have no more than ten to fifteen members. Many nonprofit boards need to be larger, primarily because of the twin needs to represent more diverse constituencies and to raise money.

Boards can be, and often are, too big to function effectively. Beyond some limit, interaction is difficult and individual accountability is lost. As Taylor Reveley, an attorney with extensive experience on nonprofit boards, has observed:

> [T]he sheer size of the board erodes its effectiveness. Members can shelter poor attendance, lack of preparation, avoidance of difficult issues and failing to do anything significant amid the heaving mass of the board (Bowen, p. 42).

Overly large boards are an especially serious problem in much of the nonprofit sector, though there are ways to minimize the disadvantages. Recently, I saw a story in the *New York Times* on the financial and other troubles of the National Rifle Association, which noted that the board of the organization had seventy-six members and that it did not seem to have provided good oversight. No surprise in that!

Selection of outstanding individuals is obviously of paramount importance to the composition of a board. The right people can make any structure work, and no structure can be so brilliantly conceived that it will compensate for the inadequacies of individuals.

I have little to add to the usual catalog of virtues to be sought in selecting board members. Integrity, competence, insight, and dedication to the cause are obviously required, as is the ability to work with colleagues in settings in which collective decision making is required. I will, however, advance one proposition in which I have come to believe strongly: *courage and the will to act are often the attributes in scarcest supply*. In my experience, after some amount of time and discussion (frequently too much time and too much discussion, to be sure) it usually becomes fairly clear what should be done. The trick is marshalling the energy—and especially the courage—to act. It is so much easier simply to wait a little longer for events to unfold. If there were more time, it would be instructive to consider the factors that inhibit directors from acting courageously, or from acting at all.

In the case of nonprofit boards, there is another key attribute that is sometimes overlooked or undervalued in choosing board members: *a genuine understanding of the mission of the organization, combined with empathy and commitment*. Boards may include individuals who simply "don't get it" (i.e., who fail to understand how a ballet company functions, how graduate education relates to undergraduate education, and so on). Ron Daniel, the former managing director of McKinsey and an active trustee of nonprofits, said bluntly: "Such a person will never be of any use" (Bowen, p. 51), and, in fact, may be quite harmful, especially if the individual feels the need to be heard (repeatedly!).

Diversity, properly understood, is also very important in composing any board. Members should complement one another by contributing a variety of backgrounds, experiences, and perspectives. Genuine diversity is an excellent antidote to "groupthink," which is one of the most dangerous maladies that can afflict a board. The New Era debacle reminds all of us of what can happen when individuals are too inclined to follow someone else's lead.

For many boards today, no organizational problem is more difficult than finding the best way of including members of previously excluded groups, especially racial minorities. It can be tempting to adopt the easy approach and earmark positions, but this seems to me both patronizing and an inadequate response to the *opportunity* to enrich a board by recruiting outstanding individuals of varied backgrounds and persuasions.

Let me advance a related proposition: it is undesirable for a board to be limited to "one of anything," even though practical constraints on size preclude giving full effect to this "Noah's Ark" principle. It is much easier, for example, for women and members of minority groups to address the full range of issues presented to a board from their individual perspectives if the board is not expecting a single woman, or a single member of a minority group, somehow to present *the* perspective of women or minorities, as if any such thing as a single perspective existed in the first place.

We should reject categorically any notion that individual board members are meant to represent particular constituencies. The case for diversity should not be construed in this way. If individuals believe that they are on a board to represent a defined group, or a particular point of view, they will not be what Quakers call "weighty" members. It is too easy to dismiss their arguments as special pleading. To have influence, individuals must be perceived as concerned about the best interests of the organization as a whole.

The next norm I want to mention pertains to independence. In selecting board members, care should be taken to avoid even the appearance of "incestuous" relationships. It is unwise, in my view, for CEOs to serve on one another's boards, never mind compensation committees. Also, I am opposed to allowing board members to serve simultaneously as consultants to the same company. Individuals should be either board members or consultants, never both at the same time. Of course, independence is ultimately a matter of attitude and integrity; it cannot be guaranteed by rules, and overly rigid proscriptions will do more harm than good. One of the greatest risks is that subtle pressures, including a desire to "stay a member of the club," will inhibit candor. As Mike Blumenthal, now at Lazard Freres and formerly chairman and CEO of UNISYS and Secretary of the Treasury, commented: "It's tough to be the skunk at the garden party (I know!)" (Bowen, p. 61).

Another precept concerns the role of former CEOs. In my view, a former CEO should not continue to serve on the board, except in rare cases and, at most, for a short period of time. The obvious advantages of continuity and experience notwithstanding, the presence of a former CEO has major drawbacks: it makes it harder for the new CEO to be truly in charge, and to be perceived as in charge, and it can also inhibit discussion and make it harder to change policies and move in new directions. With the best will in the world, it is difficult for any former CEO to be entirely objective about decisions made on his or her watch. Moreover, friends of the former CEO and others who do not want to hurt feelings or give offense, will inevitably find it more difficult to modify earlier judgments if their architect, for whom one has both affection and respect, is sitting right across the table. A former CEO said that, in retrospect, he had

> made a big mistake in staying on the board after stepping down as CEO. . . . The discussions were painful, I never knew when I should comment or when I should stay quiet, and it was just not a good idea to stay there. If people wanted my views, they could obtain them in other ways (Bowen, p. 65).

This proposition applies in both the nonprofit and for-profit sectors. When I first became president of Princeton, I could not understand why it made sense to deprive the board, and me, of the wisdom of my illustrious predecessor, Bob Goheen. He would have been a fine board member and a source of help rather than difficulty for me but he did not want to stay on. I now believe that the members of the Princeton Board, who (in company with President Goheen) thought it better for me to start off on my own, were right. As I have had occasion more recently to remark, when someone has wanted me to do something or other at Princeton, "One president at a time is enough, maybe more than enough!"

The Relationship Between the Executive Director and the Board

In the for-profit world, the over-arching issue of governance is how to achieve a sensible balance between mechanisms that encourage crisp executive decision making and mechanisms that encourage the right kind of oversight by the governing board. In my view, this balance is often tilted too much in the direction of the executive director. The situation in the nonprofit world is usually quite different.

I would like to emphasize that I do not believe that the right way to address the problem of balance in the corporate world is by setting out to "defang" the executive director. Executive directors need to be powerful and to feel that they are powerful. They should come to clear conclusions and act. It would be counterproductive to encourage executive directors to be less aggressive, to hang back, to be in any way "wimp-like." We want executive directors to be strong leaders. It is the other side of the equation that requires attention if a better balance in the distribution of authority and responsibility is to be achieved. The real need is for boards to be less supine, so that they can be reliable sources of constructive skepticism. Board members need to be good critics as well as compatriots. Strong executive directors and strong boards can complement each other in any number of ways, and both are necessary for a company to function at its best. A healthy, friendly tension is appropriate.

Experiences in the nonprofit sector convince me that more of a partnership approach would benefit companies and their executive directors. In the business corporate world, the CEO is commonly the chairman of the board as well and a number of people have suggested dividing the two functions and electing a separate chairman from among the outside directors. Dissatisfaction has been expressed with what has seemed to many to be an excessive concentration of power in the hands of a single person. In John Whitehead's words, "One-man rule is a bad idea. A single CEO-chairman can do great damage before being reined in—often when it is too late, or almost too late" (Bowen, p. 83).

Still, whatever the force of the abstract arguments, I am persuaded that the notion of a separate chairman for business boards is not an idea whose time has come. It continues to have an aura of the unseemly about it. An empirical reality is that in almost all cases in which for-profit entities have elected separate chairmen, they have done so only for transitional periods, usually in the aftermath of upheavals. American Express and Westinghouse have now recombined the positions of chairman and CEO. General Motors still has a separate chairman, but this is, as far as I am aware, the only extant large-company case of its kind. Whatever the merits, as long as the concept of a separate chairman is so rarely embraced by the corporate world in America, it will inevitably have more than a slight hint of the unseemly about it.

It is impossible to know if resistance to the idea of a separate chairman will diminish over time. At this juncture, the wise course is to see if there are less contentious, and less disruptive, ways of achieving agreed-upon objectives. I believe there are. Bestowing the title of "chairman" on an outside director is by no means the only approach. My own view is that the best first step that can be taken now is to establish a strong board "committee on governance," or "committee on the board," to be chaired by an outside director and to be given at least some of the responsibilities that might otherwise be entrusted to a separate chairman. Another approach is the formal designation of a "lead director," but this idea has difficulties of its own.

This approach locates core responsibilities for governance in a defined place, which is very important, because in time of trouble board members need to have somewhere to go, without seeming disloyal, while preserving the collective character of board decision making. It would not be as unsettling as the appointment of a separate chairman or lead director. It would surely not appear to be as revolutionary a step, but it could prove to be a deceptively powerful, and useful, instrument of effective governance, depending of course on the capacities of its members and on how it is viewed by the CEO.

In the nonprofit world, I fear that we sometimes confront the opposite problem of balance—too little respect for the executive director. For example, I am amazed by the fact that people debate actively the question of whether the executive director should even be a member of the board, or whether the executive director should have a vote. My answer to both of these questions is: Absolutely! The executive director needs to feel that he or she is much more than a hired hand, and that board members are peers, not superior beings. That is essential if a real partnership is to be formed and is to work.

Let me now step back for a moment and call attention to a broader question more historical in character: what accounts for the fact that the separate chairman model, which is so unusual in the for-profit world, has been dominant in the nonprofit sector for years? A large part of the answer, I believe, lies in the long-recognized needs of most nonprofits for generous patrons and unpaid volunteers, combined with widespread skepticism about the capacity of idealistic staff members and presidents to run nonprofits effectively without the active involvement of lawyers, investors, and other practical-minded people from the business world. Also, the special missions of nonprofits, their collegial character, and an ingrained distrust of concentrations of power encourage a less hierarchical structure and more checks and balances.

Business Leaders on Nonprofit Boards

Having just made at least part of the case for the active involvement of business leaders on nonprofit boards, I want now to make what may seem to be a contradictory assertion: well-regarded representatives of the business world are often surprisingly ineffective as members of nonprofit boards, somehow seeming to have checked their analytical apparatus and their "toughness" at the door. Lest you think that this is an idiosyncratic view of mine, I should report that this harsh-sounding proposition is widely shared by, among others, a number of individuals from the business world.

Needless to say, there are also many instances in which this proposition about the performance of business executives on nonprofit boards does *not* hold. One commentator observed that in her experience "[business] CEOs tend to be the *best* board members; they are more likely than others to understand how complex organizations function" (Bowen, p. 133). I agree. My conclusion is that the range of performance by business executives is very wide indeed, extending from "extremely disappointing" all the way up to "very best."

I cannot attempt to provide any full account of what I believe leads to such a surprisingly large number of disappointing experiences with business executives on nonprofit boards. I will, however, suggest, to provoke thought, that explanations include motives for joining boards, including the sometime desire to have a "vacation from the bottom line," reluctance to be perceived as an axe-wielding barbarian, and the failure of the staffs of many nonprofits—sometimes the intentional failure—to take full advantage of what well-intentioned, well-prepared executives can contribute to the process of making hard choices.

Also, nonprofits labor under the handicap of having to cope with the mysteries of fund accounting. The problems created by this impenetrable mode of record keeping constitute a separate subject, worthy of far more attention than it usually receives. It is relevant in this context because it helps explain why competent business executives often fail to see impending difficulties. The method of accounting makes it hard to know what is really going on and those versed in the ways of business may be especially reluctant (embarrassed?) to admit that even they cannot read the financial statements.

Conclusion

It is a challenge to be a good director of any enterprise, whether in the for-profit or nonprofit sector. Needed are not only competence and dedication, but also courage and empathy, open-mindedness, and a capacity to work in organizational settings in which the distribution of authority is ambiguous and personal relationships are complex. Managing an organization is generally much easier.

In my view, it is especially hard to be an effective director of a nonprofit organization. The very mission of the enterprise can be difficult to define with precision and subject to intense debate. It is often seen differently by various influential participants and supporters. Relevant data and analyses are frequently either unavailable or, if available, tricky to interpret. Performance often defies easy assessment and lack-luster leadership can go unnoticed, or at least uncorrected, for considerable periods of time. Resources are almost always scarce, and problems often appear intractable. Creative solutions can be elusive and, if identified, hard to put into effect—in part because of the lack of ready access to the kind of "buy-sell" mechanisms provided by markets.

The obverse side of these last observations is that nonprofit boards are tremendously important. In stressing the challenges that confront a conscientious trustee, I am not seeking to convey anything like a message of despair. One of the hallmarks of our country is the number and vitality of nonprofit entities. In their own ways, they have much to teach their profit-making relatives about the marshalling of resources, how to do much with little, and the advantages of forms of collegial decision making.

The continuing success of the institutions that comprise this "third sector" depends in no small measure on the willingness of talented people to work diligently on their behalf as directors or trustees. We can be grateful that so many people seem genuinely to believe that working hard for a good cause is its own highest reward and a privilege. That is, let me say emphatically, my own view.

Notes

1. This chapter is adapted from material in my book, William G. Bowen, *Inside the Boardroom: Governance by Directors and Trustees*, New York: John Wiley & Sons, 1994. It has been adapted with the permission of John Wiley & Sons, Inc. To order copies of this title please call 1-800-CALL WILEY.

One of the book's distinguishing characteristics is that it is concerned with both for-profit and nonprofit boards. Each has lessons to teach the other, and there is more than a little room for improved performance all around. Much of the raw material for the book consists of lessons I have learned while serving on a reasonably wide variety of corporate and nonprofit boards. These include, in the for-profit sector, American Express, Merck, NCR (before it was taken over by AT&T), Readers Digest, and the Rockefeller Group, Inc. (the owner of Rockefeller Center); in the nonprofit sector, Denison University, the Center for Advanced

Study in the Behavioral Sciences, the Public Broadcast Laboratory, the Smithsonian Institution, the Sloan Foundation, Princeton University, and the Andrew W. Mellon Foundation. I mention these associations in the spirit of full disclosure, so that the reader will know, as it were, "where I have been," and, just as important, "where I have not been." I am fully aware of the gaps in my experience. A second source of material has been extensive conversations and exchanges of correspondence with colleagues and friends who have had their own experiences on boards of many kinds. The views of these "commentators" are cited repeatedly in the book and occasionally in this chapter.

PART I
The Board of Directors and Its Committees

*The executive director and the corporate secretary of a nonprofit corpo-
ration are partners (we choose that word deliberately) with the board in
the fulfillment of the corporate mission. To carry out that role in the
partnership, the staff must fully understand how effective boards are
created, how they work best, and how and why they need staff support
to achieve optimum performance.*

*The reader will note that several of our authors devote detailed atten-
tion to the nominating committee. Here is an area where a decision is
not that of the staff, but where staff research, staff communication, and
staff continuity may make all the difference. This is illustrative of the
many areas where the input and service of both the corporate secretary
and staff service would add to effective maximization of a nonprofit's
mission.*

Effective Oversight: A Guide for Nonprofit Directors

Regina E. Herzlinger[1]

We discuss here the role of the nonprofit in a period of change and the responsibility of directors to identify the changes in roles and resources.

More than ever, the public is looking to the nonprofit sector to address the social problems that are hobbling the United States—problems that business and government have failed to solve. Nonprofit organizations hold more promise than businesses do, because they are relatively free of the unrelenting need to increase profits, which so often results in a compromised quality of services. And, unlike government agencies, nonprofits are directly accountable to their boards of directors and to the contributors on whose support they depend. But to flourish in an economy that demands increased organizational efficiency and in a society that demands increased accountability, nonprofits need powerful and proactive boards of directors to provide oversight. And those boards need to devise systems of measurement and control.

Nonprofits have a record of promoting literacy, providing health care, supporting the arts, and offering a safety net for the poor that neither business nor government can match. New York City even recruited the nonprofit Salvation Army to run some of its shelters for the homeless—shelters the homeless cite for efficient operations and compassionate workers. But nonprofits can also stumble, as recent revelations about abuses of funds and organizational inefficiency suggest.

Some organizations have rewarded executives with the kind of salaries and perks once reserved for corporate heavyweights. The public was shocked, for example, by the 1992 disclosure that the president of the United Way earned $463,000 per year—while the average U.S. family got by on $36,000. Meanwhile, tuition at nonprofit colleges grew by more than twice the general rate of inflation between 1980 and 1990. And then there was the well-publicized attempt by the Christian Science Church to diversify, resulting in a $325 million loss and prompting some constituents to call for the resignation of the board.

Other nonprofits, such as hospitals, have been charged with providing too few services, particularly to the poor, who should be their primary concern. A 1987 *Harvard Business Review* article concluded that the nonprofit hospital chains studied did not provide sufficient charity care to warrant their exemption from paying income taxes. Indeed, the poor would have benefitted more if the considerable profits earned by those so-called nonprofit hospitals had been taxed and the proceeds used to pay for their hospital care. In 1989, a General Accounting Office study confirmed this controversial conclusion when it reported that 57% of the nonprofit hospitals it examined provided charity care whose value was less than the tax benefits they received. And today, state and local governments are likely to sue nonprofit hospitals for tax payments when they provide inadequate levels of charity care.

As a result of such revelations about some nonprofits, *all* nonprofits face increased scrutiny from both benefactors and government regulators. And the role of the board member has become that much more critical. Most board members take seriously their legal responsibility to act with care and good faith, but they don't always know how to translate their life experiences into effective oversight of these unique organizations. Traditional measures of corporate performance, such as profits or return on investment, are hardly relevant.

Nonprofits lack the guidance the market provides corporations. The reactions of clients to the products and services that nonprofits offer are not as revealing as the responses of customers to the products and services sold by a for-profit company. Because nonprofits are usually subsidized and their services are frequently free, clients are more likely to forgive poor quality and ignore inefficiency. Consequently, board members cannot rely on a key indicator of corporate success—the value of services sold—to evaluate their organization's performance. Market signals may also mislead when nonprofits provide innovative services that are intended to shape public opinion rather than appeal to the masses. If patrons fail to throng to an avant-garde art exhibition but critics find it provocative, a museum may well have accomplished its goal.

Board members of nonprofits may also be perplexed about their appropriate roles. Some are so intimidated by the talent and professional expertise of the organization's employees that they abandon their oversight role. How can I tell a symphony orchestra to play Beethoven? they ask themselves. How can I tell a doctor how to operate? At the opposite end of the spectrum are the enthusiastic amateurs who become excessively involved in the organization's work. Such board members may give unsolicited—and unwanted—counsel on orchestra programs, museum exhibitions, educational curricula, surgical and diagnostic protocols, or social service intervention strategies. Other overseers pour themselves into fund-raising, perceiving their mission solely in terms of securing the organization's financial welfare. Finally, some board members use their appointment to add a notch on their social-climbing belt. Events planned ostensibly to help the organization are actually vehicles for enhancing a board member's status.

But the role of a director is neither to counsel conductors nor to climb on their coattails. Goals like fund-raising are important but ultimately secondary to the primary mission of overseeing the organization. If the board of a nonprofit is to be effective, it must assume the roles that owners and the market play in business. The board must ensure that the nonprofit's mission is appropriate to its charitable orientation and that it accomplishes that mission efficiently. In the absence of concrete measures and market signals about mission, quality, and efficiency, that is no easy task. Consequently, the board must devise its own system of measurement and control.

Based on studies of hundreds of nonprofit organizations during the last 25 years, I have developed four questions that can help board members create such a system:

1. Are the organization's goals consistent with its financial resources?
2. Is the organization practicing intergenerational equity?
3. Are the sources and uses of funds appropriately matched?
4. Is the organization sustainable?

Together these questions can offer a framework to help board members provide the critical oversight that nonprofit organizations need in order to survive.

When the former executive director of the Girl Scouts of the U.S.A., Frances Hesselbein, assumed her position in 1976, she found an organization with substantial strengths: membership in the millions; a devoted, skilled executive staff and volunteers, most of whom had been Scouts in their youth; and numerous camp properties. The Girl Scouts' historic mission of providing girls with opportunities to define their identities, bond with other females, and identify more closely with nature was consistent with the emerging feminist and environmental movements of the time.

But the organization was also showing signs of strain: membership was declining; some individual councils were operating with small but steady losses; some camps were underutilized and poorly maintained; and the organization was increasingly dependent on the sale of its famous cookies as a source of revenue. Hesselbein realized that the trend of steady, small losses would ultimately deny Girl Scout services to future generations of girls, that an excessive investment in camping properties would reduce the councils' ability to provide other kinds of services, and that over-reliance on cookie sales as a source of revenue would expose the councils to great financial risk if sales declined. Her observations form the heart of the four questions.

When asked whether there were too many camps, she was questioning whether the councils' *goals and financial resources were consistent.* For example, if only 10% of a council's middle-class members attended a camp, should the council devote a larger percentage of its expenses and assets to subsidizing them? In many cases, the councils concluded that the answer was no and reluctantly dispatched camping properties that had been the source of fond memories for many of their adult members but were no longer an appropriate use of the organization's resources.

When the councils lost money in their yearly operations, they were most likely depriving future Girl Scouts of the benefits received by the present generation. That kind of loss results in a lack of *intergenerational equity*—a jaw-breaking term that means "fairness in dealing with future generations." Because many of the people who served on the boards of the councils were former Scouts, they found this issue compelling. At Hesselbein's urging, they acted to reverse their losses, insisting that their councils break even or generate profits.

When some councils analyzed their activities, they found that although most of their expenses were fixed, such as those of operating the camps and paying their executive staffs, a sizable portion of their revenues was variable and outside their control. The amount of a United Way grant to a local council, for example, could not be anticipated. Furthermore, the revenues the councils did control, such as those from membership and camping fees, did not cover their fixed expenses. It was hardly surprising that some camp properties were rundown. Hesselbein saw that there was a clear *mismatch between the sources and uses of funds.* Some councils corrected the mismatch by increasing their fixed revenues and the proportion of the variable expenses. They increased membership and hired temporary employees, for example, if fixed revenues were not available to match the fixed expenses of permanent staff.

Hesselbein observed that councils that concentrated a large proportion of their resources in any one activity put their *sustainability* in jeopardy. For example, a council that derived the bulk of its revenues from cookie sales would be in serious trouble if cookie sales declined. (One year, sales did plummet after unsubstantiated reports circulated that some cookies contained pins.) Similarly, the future of a council whose assets were invested primarily in camping properties would be in jeopardy if camping waned in popularity or if the areas abutting camps were turned into dumping grounds. The many councils that acted to diversify their activities greatly increased their chances of survival.

Although nonprofit organizations lack many of the concrete measures and market signals that for-profit corporations enjoy, there are key indicators on which boards of directors can rely. Answering the four questions can help nonprofits develop such measures.

Are the organization's goals consistent with its financial resources? Many organizations have excessively modest goals relative to their resources. Nonprofit charitable foundations control vast assets of approximately $120 billion. But their assets have grown much faster than the amounts they give away. For example, while the Robert Wood Johnson Foundation's investment holdings have tripled since 1981, its grants have grown by only 9%. In 1990, with assets of $2.6 billion, it spent $130 million—but only $66 million of that was in grants, according to Gilbert M. Gaul and Neill A. Borowski's "Warehouses of Wealth: The Tax-Free Economy" (*Philadelphia Inquirer*, April 24, 1993).

Conversely, some nonprofits have overly ambitious goals given their resources. For example, the directors of the Christian Science Church invested $325 million in a variety of nonprint media in an effort to bring the *Christian Science Monitor* into the age of electronic journalism. The cable television venture ended in 1992, although the shortwave and radio ventures continue. Some contend that the church severely strained its resources by pumping so much money into cable.

Two ratios help measure the consistency between goals and financial resources. The asset turnover ratio measures the relationship between sales revenues and assets, and provides an indication of how much service activity (as measured in sales revenues) the assets generate. Organizations with high asset turnover are probably generating more service activity than those with low asset turnover. Low-turnover organizations are more likely to be investing their assets to earn income than to provide services. The liquidity ratio measures the relationship between assets and liabilities and also helps to determine the consistency of goals and resources. A highly liquid organization usually has overly modest social goals, whereas an organization with low liquidity may be excessively ambitious.

Both ratios must be carefully computed and cautiously interpreted. For example, neither should include assets whose use has been restricted by donors or the revenues those assets generate. For such restricted resources, the ratios should be computed separately. Similarly, the sales revenues included in the turnover ratio should be valued at their market price if prices have been discounted for indigent users.

There is no absolute right level for these ratios just as there is no one right body temperature. Ratios are meaningful only if they are interpreted in the context of similar organizations. (Industry groups publish comparative data.) A comparison of dissimilar nonprofit organizations cannot provide useful information for oversight purposes. The fact that a social service agency has an asset turnover ratio of 4, for example, while a hospital has a ratio of 1 is not particularly illuminating, because the hospital cannot achieve the ratio of the social service agency any more than an elephant can achieve the speed of a sparrow. But it is useful for directors to know that their hospital has an asset turnover ratio of 0.8 while the average for hospitals its size is 1. In this context it is not only appropriate but also useful to ask, Why is our elephant at the rear of the herd?

Directors should determine the social and demographic characteristics of the users who generate the sales revenues to ensure that the organization is serving the truly needy and the other groups it intends to serve. A hospital should track its charity patients, a school its scholarship recipients, and a museum its visitors to make sure that they are not inadvertently serving only the well-to-do.

Sometimes financial resources are not well matched with goals because they are derived or used in ways that are inconsistent with the organization's mission. When nonprofit organizations invest in subsidiary activities whose sole purpose is to generate funds to support the organization's charitable mission, such as museums that run gift shops or religious organizations that sponsor rummage sales, those activities can take on a life of their own and dominate the agenda of the organization. In the case of one prominent museum, the revenues earned from merchandising sales were reportedly 17 times higher than the revenues from admissions—an imbalance that could cause a museum to focus more on merchandising than on art.

Other fund-raising activities may also be inappropriate given the stated goals of an organization. The driving force of a nonprofit should be a desire to do good, not to serve commercial interests.

One can question, for example, the appropriateness of a public broadcasting station's airing a long statement of gratitude to a corporate sponsor. After all, the nonprofit station exists solely to provide commercial-free broadcasting, and the statement of gratitude may serve the same function as a commercial. And is it appropriate for nonprofit, tax-exempt universities to create subsidiaries like those that sell computer equipment and software, and compete with taxpaying businesses primarily on the basis of lower costs due to their tax-exempt status? Nonprofit organizations certainly were not given their tax-free status to gain an advantage in competing with taxpaying businesses.

Further problems arise when nonprofits spend money on activities and gifts that appear extravagant to the public. Some Blue Cross-Blue Shield plans—nonprofit health insurance organizations once known for their charity—are a case in point. Last year, the *New York Times* reported that while insurance rates skyrocketed, the Maryland Blue Cross-Blue Shield plan bought a $300,000 skybox at a baseball park and the New York State plan spent $15,000 on a gift of silver punch bowls for board members—the very people responsible for making sure funds are used to advance the nonprofit's social goals.

The distribution of expenses is another important indicator of the match between resources and goals. The bulk of a nonprofit's expenses should be used to provide services, unless the organization is undertaking a massive fund drive or unusual administrative work. Too often, administrators become self-serving, permitting administrative expenses to grow while the expenses of the service component shrink. A landmark national survey by James Cook, "Charity Checklist" (*Forbes*, October 28, 1991), indicated that expenses for program services as a percentage of all nonprofit expenses averaged 76% and ranged from a high of 99% (for the Jewish Communal Fund of New York) to a low of 2%. The percentage of contributions spent on fund-raising averaged 18% and ranged from 0% (for the Jewish Communal Fund) to 90%.

Selected Indicators for Answering the Four Questions

Questions

1. Consistency between goals and financial resources	2. Intergenerational equity	3. Match between sources and uses of funds	4. Sustainability

Indicators

1. Asset turnover; liquidity; socio-demographic characteristics of clients; distribution of expenses	2. Inflation-adjusted balance sheet	3. Analysis of controllability of fund sources and uses	4. Integrated financial and strategic plan; dispersion measures

---

Comparative surveys can provide nonprofits with some guidance on how much to spend on administration, but, again, no magic formulas exist. While a start-up may well spend all its money on administration, a mature organization should not. Oversight of this issue requires board members to understand the costs of providing different services and the accounting methods used to compute them.

Such data are easily misunderstood, as the Girl Scouts of the U.S.A. discovered when an irate volunteer alleged that her local council was spending too much money on administration and not enough on program services. She failed to understand that the administrative expenses included salaries for people engaged directly in designing services for the Girl Scouts—from programs to teach wilderness survival skills to campaigns to promote responsible sexual practices—and in recruiting a diverse population of girls and volunteers. In fact, the program expenses for the Girl Scouts in 1992 represented 75.5% of revenues—a figure solidly within the average range for all nonprofits.

Nonprofits Should Not Sacrifice Present Generations of Users for the Benefit of Future Generations

Is the organization practicing intergenerational equity? In general, nonprofits should not sacrifice present generations of users for the benefit of future ones and vice versa. When a charity saves an excessively large proportion of its resources to help future users, it denies benefits to present users. Conversely, when it consumes virtually all its assets to serve present users, it denies the benefits of the organization's services to future users.

Barring extraordinary circumstances, an established nonprofit organization whose financial resources are well matched with its goals should practice intergenerational equity by conserving its capital so that present and future generations have equivalent opportunities to benefit from its resources. (This measure excludes organizations that were created to accomplish a time-limited goal. For example, an organization created to bring benches into a city park should be dissolved when its goals are achieved and need not be concerned about intergenerational equity.)

An inflation-adjusted balance sheet provides a good financial measure of whether the goal of intergenerational equity has been achieved. If the fund balance account on the current period's balance sheet carries the same value as the previous period's inflation-adjusted account, the total capital available to the users of the organization's services (the fund balance) has neither increased nor decreased and intergenerational equity has been achieved. (Of course, new or rapidly expanding nonprofits cannot follow this principle: by their very nature, they are investing now—decreasing the resources available to present users—to benefit future users.) Maintaining intergenerational equity usually requires that the organization earn a profit sufficient to permit it to replace its net assets. In this case, *profit* is not a return to the owners but an allowance for the replacement of depleted capital.

Some people in business and government question the value of an inflation-adjusted balance sheet. They contend that it is rendered useless by the dubious assumptions it requires about replacement values. I disagree. After all, conventional financial statements are filled with assumptions about items such as pensions, depreciation, and amortization. And market values are readily available for measuring the inflation-adjusted values of monetary assets and liabilities. Of course, the replacement values assigned to real assets may be somewhat crude at times. But the valuable information that inflation accounting provides more than compensates for that.

Are the sources and uses of funds appropriately matched? Some expenses incurred by nonprofits are fixed in the sense that they are exceedingly difficult to reverse. The compensation of a tenured professor at a college is a fixed expense, as is that of a noted conductor of a symphony orchestra. Mandated expenses that cannot be controlled by the organization are also fixed, such as the obligation to provide certain kinds of retirement benefits. Other expenses are more readily reversible. Generally, those expenses are controllable and represent resources that can be easily purchased or not as the organization sees fit.

Poor Matching of Variable Revenues and Fixed Expenses Caused Columbia and Yale to Downsize— and Provoked Student Protests

Fixed expenses should be funded by sources that can be readily controlled and that yield a fairly even stream of income over time—for example, the income from endowment capital invested in a well-diversified portfolio that, on average, yields roughly the same return over a long period of time. Uncontrollable, variable sources of capital are not a good way to fund fixed expenses.

To assess the match between sources and uses of funds, each must first be categorized as fixed or variable. The ideal match is between fixed revenues and all of an organization's expenses. If such a match is not possible, as is often the case, fixed expenses should be matched with fixed revenues and variable expenses with variable revenues.

Despite the rather obvious nature of these observations, they are frequently ignored. For example, many colleges and universities match the expense of compensating tenured professors with revenues earned from research grants. This combination of fixed expenses and variable revenues creates an unsustainable financial situation. Such poor matching caused students at Columbia and Yale to protest—with good reason—the unexpected downsizing of their universities. Similarly, a public broadcasting station that had matched the cost of building a large production complex with foundation funds that would be provided only if viewers matched them found itself near bankruptcy. Another public broadcasting station that had grown more cautiously, hiring staff only for given new production and dismissing them if the production was not renewed for another season, was far more successful.

Is the organization sustainable? If the answers to the first three questions are satisfactory, the status quo of the organization can be sustained if it is maintained on an inflation-adjusted constant value. To accomplish this goal, management should prepare a strategic plan and pro forma financial statements to demonstrate that continuation of the present policies will enable to organization to survive. If the organization is planning new programs, management should present a plan that discusses the separable financial consequences of each of the programs and their combined effects on the organization. The very discipline of creating a plan that integrates strategic and financial planning often identifies some activities whose impact has not yet been fully considered.

A major impediment to the sustainability of any organization is an excessive concentration on any one item—revenue sources, objects of expense, assets, or liabilities. It is startling to note how few nonprofits disperse their financial resources adequately. They become entranced with one person or project and concentrate their resources in one place. Concentration greatly increases the organization's risk. For example, revenues derived primarily from endowments invested in equities are vulnerable to stock market cycles; expenses concentrated in any one person—say, a "star" curator—are captive to that person's escalating demands; assets excessively concentrated in one category, such as a downtown campus, are subject to deterioration in value; and liabilities too heavily derived from one source—say, a savings and loan—risk the collapse of the funding resource. Dispersion in all financial categories will enhance an organization's sustainability.

If the entire board were to address all four questions, they would find the process time-consuming and unwieldy. Subcommittees provide the best forum for tackling the questions and determining relevant measures and systems of control—as long as their members have the necessary credentials and experience.

Unfortunately, some nonprofit organizations place people on boards simply because they're professionals, they're wealthy, or they represent a particular group—woefully inadequate criteria for board participation. Ideally, board members should have "footprints"—a record of productive involvement with the boards of other organizations and a personal history of social service. Potential members can be screened and trained by serving on other committees of the organization.

Board members should be willing to commit the substantial time needed to serve effectively. They should be broadly familiar with the type of industry in which the nonprofit operates or have operating experience at the top levels of management. For example, a top-level executive from a company that operates budget hotels would be a good candidate for the board of a nonprofit shelter for the homeless.

Professionals in the actual field of endeavor of the organization might seem like the best candidates for the board. But many of them lack crucial managerial experience, and they may be tempted to spend too much time second-guessing the work of the nonprofits' professionals—a role beyond the purview of the board. Professionals who are also managers, however, are often exceptional board members. A teacher who has served as a headmaster or a physician who was a hospital CEO may combine oversight experience with a special sensitivity to the mission of the organization. In general, board members who have track records of mentoring and development are less likely to cross the line from oversight to overmanagement.

Balance and diversity are particularly important to staffing subcommittees. The board, which should consist of 8 to 12 members regardless of the organization's size, should bring together people qualified to serve on the four most important committees: planning, compensation, auditing, and regulatory compliance. Detail-oriented financial executives should serve on the auditing committee. The compensation committee requires managers who are used to evaluating employees. And the planning committee needs creative visionaries.

The planning committee is key to answering the four questions. To ensure intellectual discipline, the planning process should be integrated with the budgeting process so that plans do not deteriorate into vague or extravagant statements of purpose. This subcommittee should include the most original thinkers on the board, those who are most likely to challenge the status quo. They are the people who can best articulate the organization's mission and determine whether its resources are fulfilling that mission.

Members of the compensation committee perform a particularly critical role as public scrutiny of salaries at nonprofits heightens. Although compensation committees usually perform their reviews by comparing the levels of compensation in their organization to those in other comparable nonprofit or business organizations, this process is not always sufficient. Clearly the public's opinion is that executives of nonprofit organizations should *not* earn the same compensation as equivalent business executives. The public has spoken with its purse and reduced its charitable donations to nonprofits whose executives earned what they viewed as excessive compensation. While the public probably does not expect nonprofit executives to take vows of poverty, it also does not expect them to receive lavish perks and earn salaries more than ten times the average U.S. family income of $36,000 per year, as many currently do.

Still, some board members believe that executives should earn an amount equivalent to what they could earn in the private sector. They argue strongly that nonprofits must compete for managerial talent on a level playing field with for-profit organizations. But this argument is somewhat undercut by the fact that many professionals employed by nonprofits accept salaries lower than they would receive in for-profit organizations. Kenneth Hodder, the national commander of the $1.3 billion Salvation Army, widely admired for its managerial excellence, receives cash compensation of about $25,000 per year.

Compensation committee members should evaluate openly and honestly whether the organization's public constituency may find the compensation of its executives excessive. They should avoid the practices of some compensation committees, which engage in considerable subterfuge, hiding portions of their executives' compensation in bonuses and other perks or in unconsolidated subsidiaries to avoid clear disclosure of the total amount. Committee members should be prepared to explain publicly why they pay the salaries they do. A good way to check on their comfort with compensation levels is to ask how they would feel if their names appeared in a front-page story in the local newspaper about nonprofit executive compensation.

The auditing committee should supervise the organization's external and internal auditors, if they exist; oversee the preparation of its annual financial statements; and, most important, report the results to the other board members. Nonprofit accounting usually relies on fund accounting, a measurement system that greatly multiplies the complexities of the financial report. Because most board members are not familiar with this method of accounting, they may ignore the important information contained in the financial statements. An auditing committee's report that consists of a mind-numbing trip through these foreign-sounding statements is generally useless. Instead, the committee's presentation should explain how the financial statements answer the four questions discussed above. It should also include a review of the social and demographic characteristics of the organization's clients.

The regulatory compliance committee, which oversees the work of the organization's internal auditing staff and monitors the organization's adherence to the requirements of key government agencies, may prove helpful to heavily regulated nonprofits, heading off potentially serious problems. MIT, Harvard, and Stanford were among the research universities whose accounting for overhead expenses was challenged by the federal government. The expenses of Stanford University's yacht were allegedly among the inappropriate overhead expenses billed to the government. The challenges ultimately resulted in the return of substantial funds to the government and in considerable embarrassment to the institutions.

To prevent such problems, this committee would spell out the policies governing compliance and audit their implementation. At its best, it could inspire adherence to the spirit and not merely to the letter of the law. Outside compliance auditors, when they are used, should report to this committee.

To a limited extent, the members of these subcommittees should overlap, so that they are familiar with one another's work. But as overlapping membership increases, the ability of each committee to provide checks and balances on the others' work diminishes. If feasible, these committees should be supported by appropriate staff people, such as the top-level executives in the planning, financial, controllership, and human resource functions.

Nonprofit boards frequently ask too much or too little of their members. Some boards deluge their members with information about every event and hold weekly meetings, while others may send out a two-line agenda for an annual meeting that reads: "Item 1: Approval of Prior Meeting's Minutes. Item 2: New Business." Clearly neither approach is useful. Instead, board members should be asked to meet as frequently as necessary. The boards of small or entrepreneurial nonprofits should generally meet more frequently than those of larger, well-established ones. Organizations in crisis must meet more often than stable ones. A calendar of three to seven meetings a year is usually a good starting point.

Open communication is crucial to making the four questions work. They will remain a theoretical exercise unless all board members understand them and are well versed in their measures. The board of directors of Bowdoin College in Brunswick, Maine, provides a good example of how to disseminate information effectively. All its members receive a thorough introductory grounding in their responsibilities on the board and in the measures associated with their work, as well as continuing education in issues relevant to the college. At each meeting, the chair of each subcommittee gives a full report, which is followed by an open debate. The voices of recent graduates are as welcome as those of more experienced board members, such as Leon Gorman, president of L.L. Bean.

Some Girl Scout councils take this process one step further, reporting results to the public as well. At a recent gathering of a Girl Scout council in Worcester, Massachusetts, administrators and board members hosted a public discussion about the organization's use of funds. One Girl Scout council had just been criticized on a national newsmagazine show, "Eye to Eye," which suggested that the council's staff members were hoarding most of the profits from cookie sales instead of using them to provide services for local troops. Rather than becoming defensive, the council discussed its revenue sources before an audience of nearly 200, consisting of Girl Scouts, volunteers, staff, and board members, and outlined how it used those funds to develop programs, maintain camps, and so on—the kind of full disclosure benefitting an organization with an ethical agenda. Most important, the council solicited open debate on how best to use its resources.

This kind of debate is critical to finding the best answers to the four questions—solutions that will allow board members to oversee productive organizations. Nonprofits form the backbone of the U.S. system for providing higher education, health care, and culture. And they represent the best hope for creating a more humane, literate society. But without effective oversight, nonprofits can easily lose sight of their mission, misusing funds or focusing on tangential issues. Only an informed and proactive board can ensure that an organization will fulfill its function, providing useful services for generations to come.

Notes

1. Regina E. Herzlinger is the Nancy R. McPherson Professor of Business Administration at the Harvard Business School in Boston, Massachusetts, and the senior author of *Financial Accounting and Managerial Control for Nonprofit Organizations*, Cincinnati: South-Western, 1993. This chapter is a reprint of an article in the July-August 1994 issue of the *Harvard Business Review*, and is reproduced here with the permission of the *Harvard Business Review*.

Building an Effective Board

Robert L. Seaman

This chapter provides a number of suggestions, based on the author's experiences, of the steps that might be taken by a nonprofit organization to build an effectively functioning board of directors.

Introduction

What does one think of when one conceives of an effective board of directors for a nonprofit? What mental image does this thought produce? One probably sees in one's mind hard working, enthusiastic, cooperative, and financially generous directors, all imbued with the sense of mission of the organization and working productively with a motivated executive director.

The short of it is that good leadership will build a good board. In contrast, poor leadership will never build a good board.

Let us assume, for purposes of discussion, that we have an established nonprofit, which has been operating successfully for many years, has made contributions, but may have lost its spark or perhaps its sense of direction. Usually change, or the seed of change, will emanate from the influence of one or two people on the board. Let us also assume that those two people have emerged and have begun to discuss between themselves what should be done to promote the future of the organization. The best advice one could give those individuals would be to seek to inspire the board with new leadership. Even before they can hope to do that, which usually involves persuading the existing leadership that it needs to change, they would want to persuade the board to prepare a profile of itself—a critical look to see where it currently stands.

The next step in the process will, hopefully, be a change in leadership. The leadership change might mean the replacement of the chair or the president, or it might bring a new executive director into the organization. Once a new executive director is in place, or if the board determines that the current executive director is effective, the board must also ask whether the chair is the right person for the position. Is he or she a leader? Can he or she control the board? Can he or she work effectively with the executive director? Can he or she play a major role in fund-raising? If not, the first task may be to find a new chair who can do all of the foregoing.

Having accomplished these changes, the next steps, in order of sequence, would likely be:

(1) the formation of a nominating committee, or the reconstitution of the existing one, and the initiation of an effective nominating process;
(2) the identification of board candidates;
(3) the orientation and education of the candidates who have been persuaded to join the board;

(4) the development of appropriate information flow between the organization itself and the board of directors because good information flow not only builds trust, but it also enables the organization to make better use of the talents of the exceptional people it has brought on its board;

(5) the review and reemphasis, and perhaps restatement, of the mission of the organization (Directors should be reminded that they must always put the interest of the organization first and must subordinate their egos and self-interest to that of the organization. Stressing a positive focus on the mission of the organization has the effect of building a cooperative and collegial atmosphere among directors.);

(6) the establishment of appropriate criteria and rules of proceeding for directors (This insures that capable directors will feel essential to the organization but do not overstep their bounds and infringe on management. It also enhances the satisfaction directors feel in their position by being able to see the effective implementation of the actions which they have recommended or authorized.); and,

(7) the periodic evaluation of the board of directors as a whole and of the individual directors who comprise it.

This process, coupled with appropriate board of director criteria and, possibly, term limits on membership, will tend to insure constant renewal of the spirit and energy of the board of directors. Each of the points outlined above will be discussed in more detail later in this chapter.

Preparation of a Confidential Profile of the Board of Directors

It is amazing how few boards have developed board profiles. The purpose of the confidential profile is to allow the board of directors to take a snapshot of itself. Who are its members? What backgrounds do they have? What expertise do they have? How old are they and how active is their participation on the board? What is their cultural and gender diversity? What recent financial contributions have they made to the organization? Do they represent adequately the constituencies that the organization serves? Where are they located geographically? What is their record of attendance at meetings?

Armed with a profile, which details this vital information for each director, the board is in a position to examine itself and to decide whether its members fill all of the board's needs. For example, a large university with several locations discovered recently that, contrary to university policy, the board included no graduate of one of its major campuses. This oversight was soon corrected, but might not have been, if the board had not been willing to take a close look at itself.

Sometimes the very critical review following a board profile will convince many of the directors that the organization has lapsed into a dearth of leadership. When several directors become convinced of this, it is incumbent upon them to take action necessary to correct the deficit. The directors have two choices. They can seek to replace or enhance the role of the chair, or they can focus on the leadership by the executive director. Whichever one is deemed most suitable for replacement, the board should focus on that individual and instigate change. The new leader would then be charged directly with the mission of revitalizing the board. The first step in this process would be the formation, careful selection, and orientation of an active nominating committee.

The Role of the Nominating Committee in Building or Revitalizing the Board

Most organizations already have a nominating committee; however, it may not be functioning effectively. This is usually the case after a period of declining board leadership. The nominating committee can be revitalized by refining its own charter, at the direction of the chair or executive director. This refinement and review would focus the committee on what it is supposed to do. It may, however, also be necessary to secure a change in the composition of the committee.

This can be done most easily by the chair if, under applicable law, he or she has the power to reconstitute committees and change their leadership without further consultation. Having been infused with new energy, the nominating committee should then build, with the help of the chair and others, a pool of candidates who might be interested in joining the board. The executive director should play a major role in this process because his or her success may well depend upon the caliber of the board selected.

This will be the beginning, but clearly not the end, of the arduous process of introducing new board members to the organization, inspiring them to lend their energy and their support—financial and otherwise—to the organization with the goal of producing a dynamic, enthusiastic group of directors who will serve the organization effectively.

Assuming that several potential candidates have been identified, the next step to be undertaken is that of setting up a formal procedure for introducing the candidates to the organization and orienting them in a thorough fashion to the organization's mission. This will also be the role of the nominating committee (see p. 83).

Orientation and Education of Directors Concerning the Function of the Organization

Most individuals, when first elected to join a board of directors, really don't know what the organization does. Really knowing what an organization does is very much a function of one's actual experience in working with the organization. Many people think they know what an organization does, but the fact of the matter is that they really do not. To impart this knowledge one must decide what board members should know about the operations of the organization and then plan a continuous program of ongoing education concerning the nature and accomplishments of the organization.

All programs work better if there is a plan with a desired outcome. The secretary should design an educational program which is intended to inform directors as fully as possible concerning the nature of the organization. As with most educational programs, it should begin with informative reading materials. These would include basic documents such as the organization's mission statement, articles of incorporation, bylaws and the resolutions creating the principal committees, as well as any other information generally published by the organization to describe its function.

Following this, actual "classroom" or "seminar" sessions should be scheduled with new and existing directors. These could involve a combination of a lecture by the executive director and other leaders of the organization, question and answer sessions in which directors interact among themselves, and meetings with those persons within the organization who deliver the organization's service or product. All effective educational efforts require "kicking the tires." That is, directors must visit the organization. They must walk through, talk to people at all levels of the organization, and see the organization actually in the process of delivering its service or product. Then there should be follow-up one-on-one sessions with the executive director and other executives in the organization to answer more questions from board members in order to bring the entire process together. This last step can often be best performed at a board retreat where one has the undivided attention of directors, and perhaps their spouses as well, for a specified period of time (see pp. 35 and 51).

Assuring Appropriate Information Flow to and from the Board of Directors

Quality, but not necessarily quantity, of information is essential to the effective functioning of an organization. The board of directors and its individual members are often one of the organization's greatest resources. If they are to perform at capacity, they will have to be kept informed. Also, effective decision making requires full and fair communication of information regarding the issues on which decisions are to be made. This involves a well-understood board meeting schedule with appropriate notices of meetings, an agenda, and backup materials for each important agenda item. It also requires that the board be constantly informed as to the principal activities in which the organization is involved and the nature of the constituencies it serves. Perhaps most important, good decision making requires the existence of a trust between the board and the providers of information from within the organization that the information received is full, fair, and complete (see p. 181).

Board procedures cover the manner of conducting board meetings, including, of course, requirements with respect to notices of meetings and agendas. Most importantly, such procedures cover the type of follow-up needed to assure that board decisions are appropriately implemented by the staff of the organization and results are reported back to the board. Here again, the secretary of the nonprofit will be a key participant. A board which meets, and after much deliberation, reaches a conclusion on a matter only to have the decision lie unimplemented by management, rapidly loses enthusiasm for taking action. It is, therefore, critical that the organization put in place an effective procedure for implementing the actions of its board and making sure that, not only are those actions implemented, but the results of those actions are reported back to the board.

An issue that often arises in the context of board information flow is what kind of communication there should be between an individual member of the board and the executive director or other highly placed persons in the organization. A corollary question is how much discussion and informal decision making should take place within small groups of directors outside of scheduled board and committee meetings. The writer is a proponent of the view that there should be substantial informal communication among directors and persons at the top level of the organization. This is often structured by the executive director so that major agenda items are thoroughly discussed with directors in advance of the meeting and their questions and concerns addressed. Other questions by directors might well be channeled through the secretary who can direct them to the proper staff person and also keep the executive director and chair informed if the matter is significant.

There will also inevitably be informal discussions between directors when they see one another on different occasions (cocktail parties, events at other organizations, etc.). This is all to the good and serves to build interest in the organization as well as an *esprit de corps*.

Problems, however, can arise where these informal communications lead either to politicking within the board itself by persons who have become part of a "power group of directors" or by directors seeking to advance their own agendas. Again, leadership is, without a doubt, the key to maintaining the appropriate balance. A balanced and complete flow of information to all directors also goes a long way toward maintaining fairness and participation and eliminating the potential dangers.

Developing and Refining the Mission of the Organization

The mission of the organization is why everybody is there. It is really the most exciting part of what the organization does. Developing the mission statement and refining it focuses the attention of board members on what the organization is all about. It is the time when good leadership from the chair or the executive director can infuse enthusiasm into the board and generate the kind of total participation that will really help to make the organization a success. From the other side, it is also a time when perceptive leadership can ascertain which directors are really interested in the organization and which are not. When faced with the issue of mission definition, some directors will just not warm up to the occasion. Some will protest and see no reason for the organization to reexamine its role. These will be times when the leadership of the nonprofit will have the opportunity to assess the character and the likely level of contribution, including financial, of members of the board. It may be the first leading indicator of when it is time for a board member to step down.

Because the topic here is building an effective board, the writer will not explore in depth the steps one might follow in producing an appropriate mission statement (see p. 157), but rather how the development of such a statement can be used to enhance the effective operation of the board itself. One should note in passing that the crafting of an effective mission statement really depends upon and goes with the continuing board education process mentioned above. Without real familiarity with the organization, directors are not in a position to participate in the mission formulation process, and often that lack of familiarity reveals itself most strikingly in a director's inability or unwillingness to be part of the process.

There are any number of ways to develop a mission statement. In its initial stages, the work is probably best assigned to a committee of the board, very often the nominating committee. The committee could begin its work by assembling a sampling of other mission statements from similar nonprofits. Then it should work up a first draft of a statement to be used by its own organization. Representatives of all of the organization's constituencies and levels of management should be engaged in the process either by being asked to review the draft statement prepared by the committee or by being asked to contribute their own suggestions for such a statement. All of the contributions can then be brought to the attention of the full board and sifted and sorted so that ideas flow back and forth in great profusion. It is desirable to maintain adequate notes of the process and this is usually done by the secretary of the board or the chair of the committee charged with preparing the statement. Once all ideas have been harvested from the many participants, the final work of crafting the statement is usually left to a small committee.

As one can see, directors of a nonprofit can be energized by becoming adequately informed about the organization, and receiving an enthusiastic welcome to the flow of ideas that this education engenders. This process can significantly enhance their contributions to the organization. It is a marvelous process which, if used by effective leadership, can really build an organization and its board of directors.

Building a Collegial and Effective Board of Directors

When a board of directors is made up of persons of accomplishment who are successful in their fields, those persons often bring to the board a strong sense of themselves and a belief in the correctness of the points of view which they articulate. While very helpful and energizing to the board if properly directed, this element of board interaction can easily lead to turf battles and other displays of egotism that will severely diminish the effectiveness of the board as a whole. Here, again, the leadership of an effective chair or executive director is key to maintaining the balance. Enthusiasm, of course, must never be discouraged. Displays of egotism, however, must be detected immediately and effectively neutralized. If necessary, directors continuing to display such attitudes will have to be asked to leave the board. Because one hopes that this will never happen, how does one protect against such a development? First, of course, are appropriate board selection procedures. Second, board education and emphasis on a mission statement will focus directors on the goals of the organization and develop a board culture which discourages directors from using the board as a forum for self-aggrandizing practices. The third means of protection would be to have strong leadership counsel noncollegial directors through the application of both pressure and persuasion. Finally, criteria for board membership that will permit "problem directors" to be moved off the board, if necessary, should be in place. This leads to the next topic, which has to do with the establishment of appropriate director criteria and procedural rules for meetings.

Director Criteria and Board Procedures

The establishment of director criteria really means who we want to have on the board and what kind of qualifications that person should have, both as a candidate for board selection and as a continuing member of the board. At the outset, a board might decide that it wishes to have people of a certain standing in the community, certainly of good character (the most important qualification for board membership), of sufficient means to assist the nonprofit financially, and who have the time and willingness to work for the goals of the organization. While these general criteria can work very well for identifying candidates for directors, the board should establish additional criteria with respect to the qualifications for selection and continuation as a director. These could involve such matters as requirements for attendance at board and committee meetings and at other functions of the organization. There may even be an informal or formal understanding concerning the level of financial contributions. Certainly there should be an understanding that all board members will make an annual contribution to the organization because full board participation is often crucial in obtaining support from outside funding sources.

Evaluation of the Board and of Individual Directors

Although left to last in this presentation, probably the most important step in building an effective board is putting in place a fair, impartial, and effective method of evaluating directors on a continuing basis. No board of directors will operate well if board members perceive that many of their fellows are really not pulling their weight. This perception will bring board and committee action to a standstill, discourage and perhaps eliminate enthusiasm, and, if not corrected, ultimately bring the nonprofit to its knees.

The evaluation of directors can be conducted on a periodic basis most effectively by a committee of the board. To best accomplish this function, the committee must establish a method for evaluating the performance of the director against the criteria previously adopted for selection and continuation as a member of the board. The best interval for evaluation is annual. While methods differ, peer evaluation is probably the most effective and involves confidential questionnaires by all board members of the performance of themselves and of other board members. The questionnaires should be returned to the committee charged with conducting the evaluation process. In the event of a complete failure to perform, which is rare, the committee is in a position to recommend either that the director not be renominated or, if a director has a continuing term, to approach the director and suggest his or her resignation from the board. This is often made easier if the nonprofit has in place an advisory committee or some other body where the director can continue to feel involved and be of assistance to the organization. It should be noted that very often a director's financial contribution continues after he or she has lost the energy to work for the organization, and an advisory committee provides a vehicle for continued involvement and for recognition of the financial contribution.

In the event the evaluations indicate that a director is showing signs of diminished enthusiasm, the committee is in a position to approach the director and inquire of his or her continuing desire to serve (or perhaps to ascertain the reason for the decline in interest). The counseling process can often turn a declining director whose difficulty is limited in scope (i.e., there is a particular problem with the board, the organization, or another director) into a board member with renewed enthusiasm. Hopefully, also, the evaluation process will serve to elicit comments from directors underlining their belief in the organization and its activities. In addition, it may provide a forum for directors to indicate their lack of agreement with the leadership or direction of the organization and the reasons for their dissatisfaction.

The process of evaluation and renewal of the board can often be made easier by establishing term limits on board membership. While term limits, which require one to stand off the board for a year (perhaps after six to nine years as a director), may result in the loss of a capable, long-term director, the greater benefit may lie in the circumstance of helping the board rid itself of a nonperforming member who wishes to hang on to a board position when he or she no longer merits one. The problem of losing effective directors can sometimes be solved by providing that term limitations do not apply to service in certain capacities (one could serve as a director, then as a vice-chair, then as a senior vice chair, etc.) and may also be mitigated by allowing directors to move to an advisory committee.

Limitation on the Terms of Directors and Board Officers

As the ending of the previous section of this chapter indicates, considerable thought has been devoted in recent years to whether term limitations are an effective means for maintaining the vitality of boards of directors of nonprofits. As also discussed above, term limitations have both pros and cons. In many local organizations, there is a tendency to ignore the need to bring new voices to the board and in such situations the issue must at least be evaluated.

Having the board of directors divided into three classes, where one-third of the board runs for reelection each year, produces some revitalization of the board through the election of new directors each year. The issue of the longevity of a director's effective service, however, really remains a case-by-case issue. Some directors tend to lose interest early, while others seem to find increasing vitality the longer they serve. Consequently, there really is no general answer and whatever standards are imposed will not be the best for all situations. The best compromise would probably require at least one year off the board after serving two consecutive three-year terms. One year is really not a long time and, if the director has a sincere interest in the organization, he or she will probably be available for renewed service in the future. Also, as indicated above, there are means of assigning "preferred positions" to essential directors which will allow them to bridge a mandatory break in board service.

This is accomplished by providing in the bylaws that certain officers of the board and perhaps the chairs of key committees can extend their terms beyond the normal limits of board service. Because this exception could be abused by strong and entrenched board leadership it would probably then be a good idea to include an overall limit of the total terms as a member of the board and as an officer.

Officerships of the board have similarly been the subject of tenure concerns. Certainly a board officer who remains in a position for many, many years may grow tired in the job. It usually takes at least one or two years, however, to come to know the position well and to be able to perform capably in the role. Therefore, one-year terms are really not long enough, whereas six-year terms are perhaps too long. A three- to four-year term for board officer positions might be most appropriate.

One wonders whether here, as in many situations, "bad cases make bad law." Do the limitations imposed to enable the board to be free of long-term entanglement with nonperforming and perhaps obstreperous persons, who are generally few in number when compared to the board as a whole, really cause the exception to dictate the rule? They probably do. On the other hand, the author has seen a previously superb board become paralyzed by the obstreperous actions of one or two powerful individuals, the expiration of whose tenures was eagerly awaited.

Several authoritative sources have begun to question the validity of *per se* board and officer limits. They recommend that the focus should be on contribution instead of mere length of service. As more sophisticated techniques are developed for rating the effectiveness of directors, this approach begins to make sense, particularly if the evaluation system requires an increasingly greater contribution to the board with longer service.

The positive side of term limitations is enhanced by the knowledge that periodically directors must be replaced. This promotes a culture or expectation of change on the board with the result that all those associated with the organization not only come to welcome change, but see the infusion of new directors and board officers as an additional area where they can make a contribution. By implementing term limits, the organization is almost self-impelled into a posture of greater outreach as it continually seeks new directors and board officers.

Here, as in so many other situations, leadership becomes critical. Legislation in terms of board limits is really most necessary when the board lacks effective leadership or, in the case where dominant leadership seeks to perpetuate itself, the board lacks an intelligent and effective opposition.

As one can see, there are many considerations and differing points of view on this subject. For example, it can further be argued that too much board turnover diminishes the role that the board can play and enhances the position of long-term staff persons. On the other hand, there are those who urge boards to adopt term limits to enhance outside perceptions of fairness and proper dealing. There are also those who advocate a more complex formula taking into account the average age of board members, the distribution of ages and the average length of service, and that these considerations be the background against which a contribution-based evaluation is then conducted.

While the current trend still seems to favor reasonable term limits in most cases, the General Motors Board's guidelines for corporate governance provide a flexible approach, which many nonprofits may wish to consider:

Term Limits

The Board does not believe it should establish term limits. While term limits could help insure that there are fresh ideas and viewpoints available to the Board, they hold the disadvantage of losing the contribution of Directors who have been able to develop, over a period of time, increasing insight into the Company and its operations and, therefore, provide an increasing contribution to the Board as a whole.

As an alternative to term limits, the Committee on Director Affairs, in consultation with the Chief Executive Officer and the Chairman of the Board, will review each director's continuation on the board every five years. This will also allow each director the opportunity to conveniently confirm his/her desire to continue as a member of the board (reprinted with the permission of General Motors Corporation).

Finally, it must be noted that, while term limits might be undesirable for a given organization at one point in time, they may be appropriate at another point in the organization's history.

Conclusion

The foregoing presentation has outlined a number of the considerations in building an effective board, many of which are well understood and others of which are continually evolving. It remains understood, however, that the single most important element in building an effective nonprofit board is strong leadership, either in the position of chair or the position of the executive director. Good leadership will almost inevitably build a good board. Poor or mediocre leadership will cause the board to struggle. While the programs outlined above may be helpful in all situations, they are more necessary when there is a lack of strong leadership. Strong leadership tends to build its own enthusiasm and, assuming the absence of caprice, will usually result in a strong board of directors. Where lack of leadership exists, the programs outlined above may facilitate a change of leadership, which can then, in turn, implement change in the board.

The New Director's Orientation

Kenneth P. Kopelman

This chapter summarizes the orientation process which all nonprofit organizations should conduct for new directors.

A new director joining the board of a nonprofit organization should receive more than a warm handshake and a slap on the back. An effective orientation serves a number of purposes. It makes the new director feel welcome, important, and involved in the organization. It equips the director with the knowledge needed to be a productive participant in the management of the organization. The orientation also often serves as a "first impression" and introduction to the "back office" of the organization. Accordingly, care should be taken in the planning and implementation of the director's orientation and the preparation of the orientation package. The secretary should play a leading role in designing, preparing for, and executing all the steps which are described below.

The orientation may be conducted by one or more of the executive director, the chair, the chair of the nominating committee, or the secretary. Who conducts the meeting should be primarily determined by the organization's perception of the role that the new director will play. If a director was selected because of the level of expertise in the organization's program areas, then perhaps the executive director, as the chief program officer, should conduct the orientation. If, on the other hand, the director was chosen primarily for the ability to donate and raise funds, then to avoid placing the chief program officer in the position of begging for operating funds, the chair should probably conduct the meeting, perhaps with the assistance of the director of development. In any event, it is the secretary's responsibility to schedule the orientation, line up the participants, and pull together the materials that comprise the orientation package.

The timing of the orientation is another issue to be considered. For example, if the director has to travel a great distance, it may be more convenient to schedule the orientation to coincide with the board meeting following the director's election. On the other hand, putting the orientation off until the next board meeting may prevent the new director from fully participating for as much as a quarter of a year. Moreover, convenience may dictate that a single orientation be conducted for a number of newly elected directors, in which case the timing will be determined by the participants' various schedules. Inasmuch as the orientation should be conducted at the organization's headquarters, another consideration is the organization's own schedule. Conducting the orientation at a time when the office is buzzing with program work or the launching of a major fundraising campaign, rather than at a time when much of the staff is on vacation, retreat, or traveling for business, should be considered.

At least two weeks prior to the date of the orientation, each new director should receive an orientation package, the contents of which are described in Exhibit 1.

During the orientation, the new director should be welcomed and given a brief overview of the organization's history, mission (see p. 157), and current programs. The orientation leader should take the new director through the orientation package, briefly describing the general duties of the directors (see p. 91). Certain sections of the orientation package should be specially highlighted during the orientation, including the directors' manual, the schedule of meetings for the next year, and the schedule of major fundraising events. If time permits, a brief walk through of the agenda of the most recent meeting would be helpful. This might also be an appropriate time to discuss committee assignments.

The orientation should include a tour of the organization's principal physical plant. The tour gives the new director a sense of the size of the staff and helps to humanize the staff for the director and vice versa. On the tour, the new director should be introduced to key program and development staff, each of whom should say a few words about his or her duties. If time permits, half-hour meetings should be scheduled with the heads of various departments, who should be encouraged to discuss the substantive issues and challenges with respect to their programs. Even more importantly, the director should be introduced to key support staff, such as the administrative assistant to the executive director, the director of development, and the secretary, as these are likely to be the persons at the organization with whom the new director will have the most frequent contact. They can also be very helpful when the new director needs support services while in pursuit of his or her duties.

The secretary should be present during all phases of the orientation process, some parts of which he or she will perform, to insure that the director is correctly guided and to strengthen his or her relationship with the new director.

It is also worth mentioning that many organizations have implemented mentoring programs for new directors. Under such a system, the new director is assigned a "buddy" who has been on the board for a number of years. It is the mentor's responsibility to personally invite the new director to fundraising events, to call to remind the new director of upcoming meetings and to generally nurture the new director's interest in the organization. If such a program is adopted, then the mentor should also participate in the orientation.

Because every organization is different, each orientation should be tailored to serve the director's needs, while keeping in mind the organization's budget.

Bibliography

American Hospital Association. *The Guide to Governance for Hospital Trustees.*

"The Care and Feeding of the Board," *Directors and Boards.* Vol. 17, No. 3 (Spring 1993).

Jennings, Harry H. and Paul B. Hood. *The Non-Profit Guide to Creating an Effective Governing Board.*

KPMG Peat Marwick. *A Practical Guide for the Corporate Director.* Washington, D.C.: National Association of Corporate Directors, 1990.

Nelson, Judith Grummon. *A Guide to Building Your Board: Six Keys to Recruiting, Orienting and Involving your Non-Profit Board Members.* Washington, D.C.: National Center for Nonprofit Boards, 1991.

Welcome to the Board: An Orientation Kit for Trustees. Washington, D.C.: National Center for Nonprofit Boards, 1994.

Exhibit 1
The Director's Manual and Orientation Packet
An Outline

Kenneth P. Kopelman and Cherry S. White

A director's manual provides a compendium of facts useful to all members of the board. The information offered varies from organization to organization. In preparing a manual for a specific organization, the secretary may wish to select from the items listed below and, in some cases, add to them. If the manual is prepared in looseleaf form, it provides an opportunity for the corporate secretary to update information on a regular basis.

Organization
1. Mission Statement
2. History of Organization
3. Organization Chart and Management Structure
4. Strategic Short and Long Term Plans
5. Projects Currently Underway with Implementation Schedules
6. Annual Report
7. Financial Statements
8. Capital and Operating Budgets
9. Fund Raising Activities
10. List of the Largest Contributors
11. Recent Press Clippings that Highlight the Organization's Work
12. Recent Books, Articles or Brochures that Have Been Published by the Organization
13. Results of Recent Membership or Customer Surveys
14. List of Other Nonprofit Organizations in the Same General Field

Meeting Material
1. Board and Committee Meeting Calendar and Attendance Requirements
2. Schedule of all Major Fundraising Events for the Upcoming Year
3. Copies of the Agenda and Minutes of the Board Meetings for the Last Year
4. List and Description of all Board Committees, and the most recent agenda for each committee

Board and Staff
1. List of Directors, including their titles, names of spouses, home and work addresses and telephone numbers (including any fax numbers), and committees on which each director serves

2. List of Key Staff Having Interface with the Board, including their titles, department or program assignments, home addresses and telephone numbers, and names of spouses
3. Names, Address, and Phone Numbers (including fax numbers) of Outside Professionals, such as independent auditors and counsel

Code of Ethics and Conflict of Interest Policies

1. Policy Manual or similar document(s), including Code of Ethics, and any Policies adopted by the Organization (e.g., regarding conflicts of interest, lobbying, electioneering, political contributions, etc.)
2. Description of Committee Structure, including current membership listing of standing Committees
3. Fee and Expense Reimbursement Policies for Directors, including description of any compensation or benefits
4. Excerpts of Relevant Statutes and/or Governmental Regulations
5. Description of Material Litigation, together with recent status report

Core Information

1. Articles of Incorporation (or Charter)
2. Bylaws (including description of term of office and rotation of board members)
3. Memorandum regarding Directors' Fiduciary Duties
4. Discussion of Indemnification: what it is and how it works
5. Summary of Directors' and Officers' Insurance Policies
6. Information regarding Tax-Exempt Status of the Organization

Composition and Operations of the Board of Directors

David M. Bardsley

This chapter summarizes the basic issues regarding board composition and operations, agendas, notices, meetings, resolutions, and minutes. Throughout the chapter, attention is drawn to certain issues that should be addressed explicitly in the bylaws, which are easier to change than the articles of incorporation.

Age Requirements and Minimum Number of Directors

Generally, each state requires a minimum number of directors that must serve on the board of a nonprofit organization and some states impose a minimum age. Either the bylaws may fix the number of board members or the number may be fixed in the articles of incorporation. Remember, however, that if the articles fix a specific number, and not a range of minimum to maximum, an amendment to the articles of incorporation will have to be filed with the state in order to increase or decrease the number of board members; however, amendments to the bylaws do not have to be filed with the state. Because they are easier to amend, the bylaws are the better place to address most of the issues raised in this chapter.

Terms and Classes

If the length of term for a director is not specified in the bylaws or articles of incorporation, state statutes usually fix a term at one year. If there is no statutory limit to the number of terms a director may serve, the bylaws may fix a limit (see p. 25). The directors may also be divided into classes, two or three being the most popular. Usually, the classes have to be uniform to the extent possible and a minimum number of classes may be fixed by state law.

Vacancies and increases usually may be filled by an affirmative vote of the directors. In most states, if the number of directors is less than a quorum, a vote of a majority of the remaining directors may fill the vacancies.

Bylaws should deal with the number of directors. They should also mention the length and number of the terms and classes, who elects the directors, and should provide for a manner of filling vacancies.

Notice

It is a matter of individual state law whether or not a minimum period of time must pass between when notice is given or received and the time of a meeting. If there is no requirement, it presumably could be a relatively short time, provided, of course, that a quorum can be obtained.

It is prudent to have the bylaws state a time between notice and a meeting even if state law does not require one.

In most cases a board meets on a regular basis, for example, the second Tuesday of each month, and the schedule for the following year is usually announced and approved at a meeting sometime in the last two months of the current year. This usually constitutes sufficient legal notice, and legally, nothing else need be done.

We all know, however, that if nothing else were to be done, no one would ever show up. Therefore, the usual practice is to send out a notice before each meeting as a reminder, even if the meetings are held regularly and are approved each year. When permissible by law, oral notice by telephone, confirmed in writing, can be quick and effective. Some corporate secretaries use the agenda as notice and do not send out a separate notice; others send out the notice, proposed agenda, and board materials all at the same time.

Under some state laws, the purpose of any regular meeting need not be specified in the notice, or waiver of notice, unless the certificate or bylaws provide otherwise. In some states, notice of purpose may be required for special meetings, even if it is not required for regular meetings.

Even if there is no requirement for notice to state the purpose of a special meeting, the better practice for special meetings is to have the bylaws require that notice must be given and a purpose must be stated. A notice of meeting requirement is also good practice for regular meetings.

Waiver of Notice

Most states recognize a waiver of notice of a meeting by a director whether that waiver is signed before, during or after a meeting. If a director appears at a meeting, he or she automatically waives notice unless he or she protests the lack of notice before the meeting or when it begins.

Waiver of notice is used when there is no time to give proper notice of a meeting, as with a hastily called emergency meeting. It is probably the more common practice to get signed waivers only from those directors who do not attend the meeting, because presence at the meeting constitutes a waiver unless the director objects to lack of notice.

In meetings not properly noticed and held, the actions taken are null and void. If, however, a sufficient number of waivers of notice are gathered from board members, the actions taken by the board at such a meeting will not be deemed null and void, even if the meeting was not properly noticed and held. The signed waivers should be placed in the minute book along with the minutes of the meeting (see Exhibit 1).

Action by Unanimous Consent Without a Meeting

Most states allow an action without a meeting only if all—not a majority, not a quorum—of the directors consent in writing to the adoption of a resolution. The resolution and consents must be filed with the minutes (see Exhibits 2 and 3).

Board Meetings

Directors cannot act individually, they may only act as a board. For the board to be able to act there must be a quorum of directors. If the bylaws require a specific number of directors rather than a minimum and maximum, vacancies must be counted when calculating the quorum. Therefore, if a board consists of twelve members and two seats are vacant, the quorum is calculated based on twelve members, not ten.

What constitutes a quorum is a matter of state law. In New York, for example, a quorum is a majority unless the bylaws or certificate of incorporation state a lesser number.[1] Most state law does not permit the bylaws or the certificate to authorize a quorum of less than one-third of the board.

In some states, once a quorum is obtained, the meeting may continue, if not challenged, even if a sufficient number of directors leave the meeting so that a quorum no longer exists. This is not true, however, in New York.[2]

Under some state nonprofit laws, if a director leaves the room and a vote is taken, a quorum must exist without the director who has left the room, even if that director will return. Statutes should be checked to see how the organization's state law addresses this issue.

Bylaws should address not only the size of the board—the minimum and maximum number—but also what constitutes a quorum. If they do not, state statutes will govern. Check state law and bylaws to see how they handle a vote at a meeting which has dropped below a quorum. Also, check to see how the organization's state law handles votes and quorums.

Telephone Meetings

Most states will allow a director to appear at a meeting by telephone provided that all members may hear each other.

The bylaws should state explicitly whether or not participation by telephone at board meetings is permissible.

Agendas

Notice may be given by way of the agenda. Most agendas include in the heading the time, date, place, and type of meeting. Presumably, this would suffice as notice, even if the bylaws required stating the purpose of the meeting, because the body of the agenda would do just that.

In some cases, the agenda is sent out with the necessary materials approximately one week in advance and usually is the only notice of a regular meeting sent to the directors. The secretary generally prepares the initial draft of the agenda. It is then floated to the necessary organization officers and finally to the executive director and chair of the board.

Many secretaries use a solicitation memo to gather the information used in compiling the agenda. A solicitation memo is simply a memo from the secretary to every department head, committee chair, and officer requesting agenda items that they wish to have the board address. Whatever method of contact is used, each committee chair should also be queried for possible agenda items. If the secretary is not the one preparing any resolutions that may be needed, arrangements should be made in advance with the person involved, concerning how and by whom the resolutions are to be prepared and when they will be delivered to the secretary for inclusion in the board materials.

If there are changes to the agenda after the mailing, an updated agenda may be sent to the directors if there is time; otherwise, the changes may be announced at the beginning of the meeting or as they appear during the course of the meeting. If the agenda has been revised but not mailed, the revised agenda should be distributed at the beginning of the meeting; this practice, however, should be avoided unless absolutely necessary.

Agendas differ in their physical structure, but a complete agenda would include in its heading the name of the organization, the title "Board of Directors Meeting," and the place, date, and time of the meeting.

Some agendas list the call to order, which occurs after the secretary has informed the chair that a quorum exists, as the first item. The second item on the agenda would then be the approval of the minutes from the last meeting. Because the directors should have received the minutes before the meeting and have had time to review them, reading of the minutes is not necessary. The minutes are then approved as presented. If there are corrections, the minutes may be corrected and approved as corrected or the corrections may appear in the minutes of the current meeting.

The next item is usually the treasurer's report or some other financial report. If foundation grants and other funding information is not included in this report, these items should be a separate agenda entry. The remaining items of the agenda are dictated by the meeting. Some agendas include, at the item number, the person who will be presenting that item. Some agendas even include the time allocated to each item.

If an item needs action and a proposed resolution needs to be voted upon, the proposed resolution, sometimes labeled as such, should have been sent with the agenda in the package mailed to the directors and should be referenced on the agenda next to its item number with words such as "action requested on Proposed Resolution #_____" (see Exhibit 4).

The next-to-last item on an agenda usually refers to a discussion of whatever additional items the directors feel should be discussed, or last minute items that have arisen since the agenda was prepared and mailed. This item is usually labeled "New Business" or "Other Business."

The last item is usually a reminder of the date, time, and place of the next meeting. Some agendas actually end with an item labeled adjournment. If nothing else, it serves as a reminder to the secretary to note the time the meeting ended as a matter of good corporate practice.

It is important to remember that, although the agenda is developed by the organization which has control over it, the agenda is essentially a communications document. It should list every significant item that will be discussed (see Exhibit 5). The directors should not be surprised by off-agenda items of which they have not been advised.

Personal or private matters, or any matter requiring confidentiality, are usually dealt with in an executive session where only board members are present. Check the organization's state statutes for so-called sunshine laws, and what can and cannot be discussed in an executive session.

Whether the directors are asked to bring the package that was mailed to them to the meeting or they are given the same materials again at the meeting is a matter of organizational history or the personal choice of the chair. The former saves a lot of unnecessary work, although the secretary should still bring a few extra copies of the materials to the meeting. In any event, the secretary should keep a copy of the package mailed to the directors in the secretary's office.

Minutes

At the extremes, minutes are of two types: (1) so-called long or narrative form and (2) the so-called short or abbreviated form.

Long or narrative minutes are detailed descriptions of what was said. The short or abbreviated form, also sometimes called action or result minutes, report only the actions taken or the briefest of discussion. Most minutes fall somewhere in between and detail is usually dictated by importance. There is no standard form and the organization's history, the personality of the chair, or the nature of the issue will dictate what is done. It is important, however, that the minutes accurately and carefully reflect the various items presented at the meeting and the actions, if any, that were taken.

Minutes kept in the long form may offer some protection to the directors. They can be used to show that the directors performed their fiduciary duty by fully exploring an issue (in legal terms this is called "due diligence"). The long form of minutes, however, may open up areas of cross examination in the event of litigation.

Generally, the minutes should cover each item on the agenda and any other substantive discussions. Minutes should not attempt to fill voids or correct mistakes. If an action was inadvertently not taken, the minutes should not reflect that it was, unless the addition is specifically brought to the attention of the directors before the minutes are approved.

Most items that the minutes might include (see Exhibit 6) are self-evident, such as the time of the start and finish of the meeting, but it would be beneficial to include (1) the time a director either leaves or enters the meeting after it has begun and (2) the quorum count.

Some states require a quorum for a vote. If a director or officer leaves during a meeting, it should be noted and the director named, but it should also be noted whether or not a quorum is still present. If the director returns to the meeting, this should also be noted. If a vote was taken while the director was not in the room, he or she should be briefed on any significant action after the meeting.

If the secretary is asked to leave the meeting, this also should be noted and a summary should be provided by the secretary *pro-tem*, most probably the chair; that person should probably also sign the minutes.

If state law requires a quorum at each vote, it is important to know if a quorum is present when a vote is taken. It might be desirable to state in the minutes that a quorum exists if a director leaves or abstains. One example would be "Upon motion duly made and seconded with a quorum still existing . . . ."

When the agenda calls for a resolution, the resolution is best set out in full in the minutes. It is also a good idea to include a separate index to the resolutions in the index to the minutes. If the resolution is not set forth in the body of the minutes, it should be attached as an exhibit or appendix along with all of the reports for that meeting. The type of index, whether index cards or computer, will naturally depend on the size of the organization and the budget.

Notes and Drafts

There is a debate among corporate secretaries whether it is better to retain or destroy your notes and drafts after the minutes have been approved. Some think that notes and drafts are helpful to refresh their recollection of what happened if asked at some future time. Others believe that they may confuse matters reported in the minutes or that this retention may inhibit full and frank discussion among the directors. There is also a concern that these notes and drafts are subject to subpoena in legal proceedings because the privilege against self-incrimination under the Fifth Amendment[3] does not apply to corporations, corporate documents, or corporate agents.

If notes and drafts are kept, remember that destroying them for one particular meeting or even several particular meetings may raise a suspicion. Clearly, notes should not be destroyed after a subpoena has been served. It may be unlawful to destroy notes and drafts in matters that are currently subject to investigation or litigation, even if such notes and drafts are routinely destroyed.

There is, however, no debate regarding how long the organization should retain the official minutes: forever. Organization minute books are specifically excluded from the provisions of the Uniform Preservation of Private Business Records Act[4] which permits the destruction of business records after the expiration of three years from their making.[5]

It is the secretary's responsibility to gather all information necessary for a meeting as well as having everything approved, copied, and sent to the directors before the meeting. It is also equally the responsibility of the secretary, after the meeting, to distribute information or communicate decisions made to those who are affected. This is particularly true if there will be a delay between the time of the meeting and the issuance of the minutes. If actions taken at the meeting are likely to receive publicity, the secretary should confer with the chair to determine who should call the absent directors to inform them of the action before they read about it in the papers.

Notes

1. N.Y. Bus. Corp. Law § 707 (McKinney 1986).
2. N.Y. Bus. Corp. Law § 708(d) (McKinney 1986).
3. U.S. Const. amend. V.
4. Unif. Preservation of Private Business Records Act (1995).
5. *Id.* § 2.

Exhibit 1
Waiver of Notice of Meeting by Directors

The undersigned, a director of [name of organization], an organization organized under the laws of the State of _____, does hereby waive, pursuant to section _____ of the bylaws, notice of the time, place and purpose of the (*insert date*) meeting of the directors of said organization, and does hereby consent that the meeting be held at _____ Street, City of _____, County of _____, State of _____, on the ____ day of _____, 19__, at _____ o'clock __.M. (*insert Time Zone*), and does further consent to the transaction thereat of any and all business that may properly come before said meeting.

Dated: _____, 19__

[Signature]

_____

[Type Name]
Director

COMMENT

A signed waiver may be executed before or after the meeting. A waiver of the notice of a meeting of the board of directors need not specify the purpose of any regular or special meeting, unless required by the bylaws. The form may readily be adapted to provide for waiver by more than one, or all, directors, by the same instrument.

Exhibit 2
Consent of Members of Board of Directors
for Action without a Meeting

The undersigned, being all the members of the Board of Directors of [name of organization], do hereby consent pursuant to section ___ of the [by-laws or certificate of incorporation] to the adoption of the following resolution authorizing [set forth action to be taken], without a meeting on written consent.

[Set forth resolution authorizing the action].

Dated: _____, 19__

[Signature]

_____

[Type Name]
Director
[continue as needed with signatures]

COMMENT

All signatures may appear on one consent form or there may be separate consent forms for each director or some forms signed by different directors. Nonetheless, all directors must sign one of the forms.

Exhibit 3
Certificate of Secretary

I, _____, Secretary of _____, an organization duly organized under the laws of the State of _____, do hereby certify that I have compared the foregoing with a resolution adopted by the Board of Directors of _____ by unanimous written consent without a meeting, said resolution and the written consents thereto being filed with the minutes of the proceedings of the said Board, on page _____ thereof, and I hereby further certify that the same is a true, correct, complete copy thereof, and that the said resolution has not been rescinded, amended, or modified, and is in full force and effect as of the date hereof.

IN WITNESS WHEREOF, I have hereunto set my hand this _____ day of _____, 19__, and affixed the organization's seal by authority of the Board of Directors.

[L.S.]

[Signature]

_____
[Type Name]
Secretary, [Name of organization]

COMMENT

If there is no organization seal, eliminate the words "and affixed the organization's seal by authority by the Board of Directors" after the date in the last line of the certificate.

The secretary's certificate may be required by third parties to confirm directors' resolutions made at a meeting or by written consent.

The secretary's certificate that a resolution was duly adopted and remains in force binds the organization to third persons who may rely on the certificate and need not inquire into the question whether all organizational formalities were followed. This conclusion is usually placed on the ground of actual, implied, or apparent authority, or estoppel.

Exhibit 4
Resolutions

Although there are no absolute rules, and state laws differ, formal resolutions are generally considered to be either required or appropriate for the following matters.

1. Any matter required to be covered by a resolution according to statute, charter, or the organization's bylaws
2. If a certificate of the secretary or of some other officer of the corporation is required to be filed or furnished, or is likely to be required to be filed or furnished at some future date, indicating the granting of authority by the board or appropriate committee of the board to perform a certain act (almost all banking activities from checking accounts to safety deposit boxes need a resolution)
3. When the matter regulates the management of the organization and is meant to be permanent until changed
4. Establishment of board committees, the number of members, authority, and responsibilities, including quorum counts if different from bylaws
5. Large financial expenditures or acquisitions
6. Real estate matters
7. If the matter pertains to an amendment to either the articles of incorporation or the bylaws of the organization
8. In response to the request of a third party that the action taken be evidenced by a formal resolution
9. Any other substantial, significant, or material matter

Exhibit 5
Agenda

Board of Directors Meeting
One Million Big Bucks Avenue
Moneytown, N.Y. 10003
Board room - Tenth Floor
Friday, January 8, 1999
4:30 p.m.

I.   Call to Order   (name), Chair

II.   Approval of Minutes   (name), Chair
      Exhibit A
      (Board action required)

III. Treasurer's Report   (name), Treasurer
      Exhibit B
      (Board acceptance required)

IV.   Committee Reports

      A Communications   (name), Committee Chair
         Exhibit C
         (Board action required on
         proposed resolution)
      B. Education   (name), Committee Chair
      C. Community outreach   (name), Committee Chair
         Exhibit D
      E. Benefit   (name), Committee Co-chair
         Exhibit E
         (Board action required)
      F. Grants and Foundations   (name), Committee member

V.   Request for participation in   (name), Committee Chair
      combined program with . . .

VI.   New Business

VII. Next meeting
      February 12, 1999

VIII. Adjournment

Exhibit 6
Minutes

It is usually appropriate for the minutes to include the following items.

1. The time the meeting was called to order
2. The names of the directors who were present at the beginning of the meeting and which directors were absent from the meeting
3. The names and titles of other persons present at the meeting, and if outside the organization, their affiliation
4. Some organizations include the names of the various movers, and the seconds, of resolutions adopted at the meeting. This may be done on all occasions or only on important votes or resolutions.
5. The times at which various persons entered and left the meeting room
6. The names of the individuals who made presentations or reports during the meeting; a summary of the presentation if of sufficient importance or a note that the report appears at "Exhibit or Appendix __"
7. The names of directors voting against an item (The general rule is that directors who are present and not noted as voting against an item have voted for that item.)
8. The names of any directors who abstained from the discussion or the vote on any matter brought before the meeting
9. Each agreement or consensus arrived at during the meeting, even though such agreement or consensus was not necessarily evidenced by a formal resolution of the board
10. Each other matter upon which the directors focused at the meeting, such as the receipt of a report
11. The time the meeting adjourned

Board Retreats

Victor Futter

This chapter describes the purpose of a board retreat, the planning involved, matters which might be considered, attendance, and time requirements.

The object of a board retreat is to have a large block of uninterrupted time to discuss the organization's objectives and problems. It is an occasion when directors can really learn whom the organization serves or whom it represents. It enables board members to get to know each other and to share ideas in a way board meetings do not provide. It also provides a means for board members to come away with a sense of collective purpose. It is a means to build an effective board (see p. 25). Properly handled, it can be a watershed event.

Retreats should not be boondoggles or solely, or even primarily, concerned with social events. They provide an opportunity to get busy people away from their offices and their own problems and instead to focus on the organization's problems. It is an occasion for the board to step back from its routine business and take an in-depth look at the organization's direction.

While, if long enough, a retreat can be coupled with a board meeting, it should not be viewed as a board meeting nor as a means for dealing with action items. Nonetheless, it must have a purpose and an objective or it will become a hot-air discussion, which will turn directors off. Hence, the emphasis on focusing on long-term policy issues that should be addressed over time.

There should also be some time for social events. It provides an opportunity for the directors to get to know one another better and to meet and appraise senior staff.

A retreat, then, is a gathering of the directors for a meeting which, depending upon the organization, can be for one day or less, a weekend, or five days. Generally, it is held at a resort or an executive conference center, but it can also be held at an organization's headquarters or some other suitable location.

Among the prime matters to be considered at a retreat is the organization's mission (see p. 157). This gives the directors an opportunity to focus on and discuss the direction of the organization. Strategic planning or total quality management (see p. 279) are also suitable topics for a retreat.

It is suggested that such a discussion be preceded by a recital of the history of the organization and a description of its activities. Following such an introduction, the executive director might continue by giving his or her views of the future and the long range plans for the organization; this will shape and direct the directors' discussion. Retreats are a wonderful opportunity to educate directors, particularly new directors, and to build up their enthusiasm and *esprit de corps*.

In addition to the mission and long range plans, a retreat might consider any one or more of a number of other problems:

(1) a serious financial problem;

(2) a new fund-raising event;

(3) the operation and organization of the board;

(4) an accreditation report;

(5) staffing problems and considerations;

(6) staff compensation; or

(7) risk analysis, insurance, and catastrophe planning.

The important thing is to keep the retreat focused on a particular problem or set of problems. A meeting like this requires careful preparation. The demand on the secretary's or the staff's time will be considerable, but the dividend and rewards from the project should make it all worthwhile.

A week before the retreat, each director should receive a bound volume containing the materials for the meeting. This will have been prepared by the secretary and approved by the executive director and the board chair. In other words, for there to be an intelligent discussion, the directors must have an opportunity to review and reflect upon the topics to be considered.

In addition, visual aids should be prepared to help the directors absorb the oral presentations (as a general rule, people only absorb twenty-five percent, if that much, of what they hear and fifty percent of what they see).

Workshops are an essential part of a retreat. The directors might be separated into small groups of five to eight people, each to discuss a particular topic and to come back and report or make recommendations to the entire board. Here, again, the organization is building up the interrelationships between the directors and giving them a feeling of participation and contribution. This is what excites a director's enthusiasm.

Social events are an important part of a retreat. In a one-day event, this is probably limited to breakfast, lunch, and a reception at the end of the day. Depending on the state of the organization's treasury, dinner or even a dinner dance might be included. In more elaborate retreats, golf, tennis, or sailing can be part of the occasion. Retreats also provide the opportunity to honor retiring directors or officers.

A question which often arises in connection with a retreat is: should staff attend? if so, which staff members should be included?

The first time an organization holds a retreat, it might not wish to have any staff other than the executive director and secretary attend. At subsequent retreats, a few very senior staff might be asked to attend the entire retreat and a limited number of other staff members might be invited to attend particular portions of the program, where their knowledge and insights might be helpful. Because a primary function of a retreat is usually long-range planning, members of the staff who deal with planning and finances are often asked to participate. To the extent staff are invited, it provides the directors with an opportunity to judge the depth of management and the wisdom of any proposed management succession plans.

Another question is whether spouses or "significant others" should attend. This will depend on the size and type of organization and length of the retreat. All other things being equal, it is desirable to have spouses and "significant others" attend to assist in building up board relationships and cohesion. If they do attend, it will be necessary to plan events for them during the times when the board is engaged in business activities.

Organizations subject to sunshine, or open meeting, laws should carefully check those laws to determine what type of meetings, or portions of meetings, may be excepted so that open and frank board discussion is not inhibited.

Depending upon the nature of the discussion, some organizations find it helpful to bring in an outsider who may add expertise to the matter under consideration. Depending upon the expert's nature and relation to the organization, the expert may be asked to stay for all or only part of the retreat.

Some organizations find it helpful to hire paid professional facilitators to conduct the retreat, not only because of their skills, but because they are more convenient targets for difficult questions or matters likely to arouse a dichotomy of emotional board viewpoints. Others believe this is a waste of money and, to some extent, time, and that current board members, other than the chair or executive director, are better equipped to conduct the discussion and to get to the heart of the matter.

The objection is sometimes made that board members will be reluctant to devote a considerable portion of time to such an occasion. This is not so; board members will be delighted to do so, provided the program is carefully thought through, informative, and helpful to them and the organization. Indeed, a retreat is an event that will effectively energize a board about the organization and its leadership responsibilities.

One word of caution; for a retreat to be successful, it must be enthusiastically endorsed and supported by the chair and the executive director. They must be involved in the planning process, and the input of all board members should be sought in advance of the retreat. Finally, a date must be set sufficiently in advance so that most, if not all, board members will be available. At the close of the retreat, each attendee may be asked for any parting comments.

Bibliography

Bader, Barry S. *Planning Successful Board Retreats: A Guide for Board Members and Chief Executives.* Washington: National Center for Nonprofit Boards, 1991.

Committees

David M. Bardsley

This chapter discusses the role of committees of a nonprofit board, and the relationship of staff to them.

Introduction

At the outset, it should be recognized that a sound operating committee structure is vital to the successful operation of a board and of the organization as a whole. It is here that the real work of the board begins. It is in the framework of committee meetings that directors are able to meet and discuss matters in depth in small groups. It is here that they get to know one another and to operate as a team. It is here that they are able to become acquainted with and judge staff who are invited to participate in committee meetings.

The entire board should give considerable thought to:

(1) the desired committee structure in light of both the immediate and long-range plans of the organization;

(2) what the executive director wants each committee to do; and

(3) the selection of the members of the committee, particularly the chair of each committee, because the operation and success of each committee will depend on its chair.

The types of committees an organization may have are often found in its bylaws, but these may be modified from time to time or supplemented by board resolutions. The committee structure and duties will, in the first instance, be reviewed by the chair and/or the nominating committee and then will be submitted to the board for final approval. The selection of the members of the committees is usually the province of the chair, subject to the approval of the board. But the executive director's recommendations to the chair and/or the nominating committee with respect to both of these matters will often be followed, and while exercising tact, the executive director should not be reticent because his or her success may well depend on how well the board's committees perform.

One possible or desirable approach to enhancing the appropriate consideration of committee structure, functions, and selection is for the secretary of the organization, after consultation with and approval by the executive director, to submit annually a proposed committee structure. The proposal should include a description of committee functions and suggested appointments. This should not be viewed as a routine matter or a "cut-and-paste" project, but rather the committees, their functions, operations, membership, and chairs should be analyzed critically in light of the organization's needs. If the job is done well by the secretary, it should simplify the task of the executive director who, after reviewing and discussing it with the secretary and adding the executive director's input and insights, should be thoroughly prepared to discuss the matter with the chair. Following that discussion and a subsequent consultation with the chair of the nominating committee, the suggestions would then be discussed with the nominating committee as a whole. Following committee approval, with such changes as the committee cares to make, the suggestions would be submitted to the board for approval.

In addition, during any year of operations, the secretary should be alert—and should not hesitate to suggest to the executive director—any changes or modifications which should be made in committee structure, functions, operations, or membership to serve better the needs of the organization. While the executive director has general overall responsibility for the organization and will, of course, need to be intimately involved in anything affecting the board, the secretary, with the approval of the executive director, should consider that the immediate responsibility for oversight of the committee structure lies with him or herself.

With this in mind, let us consider the various aspects of board committees.

This chapter will review the major committees that are common to most boards and give a brief description of their functions. All committees listed need not be part of every organization and committees essential to an organization may not be among those discussed here. This is just a broad-based attempt to familiarize the reader with the more common committees found in nonprofit organizations.

Formation

Committees are not usually required by statute, but rather are provided for in the bylaws or by resolution.

Authority

The board may delegate any duty that is not required by statute or the bylaws to be performed by the full board. Some states, for example, prohibit a committee from presenting an issue directly to the members for a vote; filling a vacancy on the board or on a committee; fixing compensation of a board member or officer; amending or repealing the bylaws; adopting new bylaws; or amending or repealing resolutions unless the resolution specifically allows for such committee action.

Generally, boards approve a bylaw or resolution detailing the committee's authority and responsibility so that these are clearly understood. In lieu of this, the committee may draft its own statement for approval by the board. The committee does the necessary research and study, compiles data, gathers information and facts, and makes recommendations or gives advice to the board on the issue in question.

The board may also wish to consider an occasional grant of authority to a committee to undertake specific additional responsibilities within the scope of the committee's primary function.

Number of Members

A minimum number of members of a committee may be fixed by state statute, bylaws, or resolution. It may also be appropriate to state a maximum and a quorum in the bylaws or resolution.

Conduct of Meeting

In conducting a committee meeting, the same rules that govern board meetings generally apply regarding notice, waiver, quorum, agendas, minutes, telephone meetings, unanimous consent, and other procedural matters.

Scheduling of Meetings

Schedule meetings at a time convenient for the committee members. This may be right before or after a board meeting, first thing in the morning, or at the end of the day. Avoid scheduling meetings for the middle of the morning or middle of the afternoon, as such schedules materially interfere with a director's other duties.

Responsibility

The board may delegate responsibility to a committee, but it may not abdicate it. The board still maintains oversight responsibility and the committee should report to the board at the next meeting or some other agreed-upon interval. The minutes and schedule of the committee should be kept in the secretary's office and be open to inspection by board members as may be necessary.

In its annual review, the board should be careful to consider that the committee's duties and work are consistent with its mandate.

Types of Committees

Executive

An executive committee is essentially a mini-board which does most of the work of the organization between board meetings.

When there are large boards—e.g., thirty to fifty directors—it is not uncommon to delegate considerable authority to the executive committee in order to facilitate operations. Boards should avoid creating two classes of directors, in which only those on the executive committee have full participation as directors. Directors in the second category may not feel involved and this may lead to their resignations.

On the other hand, for large boards that meet infrequently (four to six times a year) a committee such as this, which can meet frequently and on relatively short notice, is essential in order to get the organization's work done. Such a committee should also be concerned with strategic planning, policy formation, and long term goals. This committee functions essentially as a think tank. Under these circumstances, the members of such a committee will be the more active members of the board. The point is that there must be an effective body to help discharge the board's oversight responsibilities, to plan for board meetings, and to handle routine and other matters between meetings of the board.

In smaller boards, the powers of the executive committee may be considerably circumscribed so that it is only authorized to act when necessary between meetings of the board, and thus exists essentially for emergencies.

Permanent or Standing

These committees, such as the audit, compensation, development/fund-raising, nominating and personnel committees, usually provide a periodic overview of the regular ongoing functions of the organization or of the board; others, such as finance, community relations, and long-range planning, make frequent periodic reports to the board.

Ad Hoc

Usually organized to perform a specific task, ad hoc committees may organize a special event, building acquisition, or create plans to meet a specific goal. This type of committee is usually disbanded when its task is finished.

Typical Committees

Organizations can have a variety of committees. Described below are those believed to be the most common.

Audit Committee

The functions of the audit committee include recommending the appointment of independent auditors, reviewing the audit report and management letter, and consulting with the independent auditors with regard to the adequacy of internal controls (see p. 63).

Budget Committee

This function may be included in the audit or finance committee if it is not given to a separate committee.

The function of the budget committee is to provide cost projections for the programs and goals of the organization over a certain time period, usually one year. This committee is also responsible for overseeing the actual day-to-day expenditures of the organization and conferring with the budget staff, if one exists.

It should be recognized that a budget is more than a financial document. It sets forth a picture of the organization's priorities and areas of emphasis. In addition, when the budget is approved, it gives the staff the ability to function, within its guidelines, without requiring board approval for every expenditure.

Nominating Committee

The function of the nominating committee is to recommend to the full board individuals to fill board vacancies. It is the function of its members to review the background of potential candidates and to approach and interview them for candidacy. This committee usually solicits recommendations for candidates from other board members as well as senior executive officers.

This committee should also develop specifications for board needs, such as particular expertise in the areas of real estate, law, finance, and public relations, as determined by the organization's particular mission.

The nominating committee should make recommendations for criteria to evaluate directors continuing on the board; experience, attendance, committee service and number of hours or dollars donated, length of service, background, diversity, and particular expertise may be criteria used. The committee should review those appointments according to the established criteria.

This committee should also review the operations of the board to assure that they comply with legal requirements (see p. 83 for more detail on the nominating committee).

Compensation or Personnel Committee

Although it is usually thought to be a creature of the for-profit world, the compensation committee is becoming especially important in the nonprofit sector in discharging the board's oversight responsibilities, especially in light of recent media attention to abuse in the area of executive compensation in nonprofit organizations.

The compensation committee is responsible for developing a compensation philosophy and guidelines for the entire executive and managerial group and for the development and succession plans for management. Members of the committee should be directors who are not involved with the management.

The committee should obtain and study the compensation practices and guidelines for other organizations in similar fields, and other organizations comparable in size and funding. It should review the role and performance of the executive director and recommend future compensation (including perquisites, if any) usually on an annual basis.

This committee reviews and comments on the CEO's recommendations for compensation for others in the managerial group, and is also responsible for reviewing any health, retirement, incentive compensation, or other personnel plans of the organization, as well as insurance for the management and board. These duties may be divided between a separate personnel committee or may be handled by a personnel subcommittee. This committee may also be the group that hears employee grievance appeals (see p. 69).

Planning Committee

Concerned with the organization's overall mission, long-term objectives, and key organizational strategies and structure, the planning committee may develop these items, review management proposals, or both.

This committee considers the introduction of new projects or programs, monitors ongoing projects and programs, and reviews the long-term needs of the community served by the organization and the organization's plans to meet those needs.

Membership Committee

For membership organizations, this committee is responsible for recruiting members and, if appropriate, reviewing the qualifications of a candidate for membership. The committee should propose and review all categories of membership, recommend membership criteria, and oversee the effectiveness and compliance with these criteria.

This committee should conduct ongoing membership communications and be responsible for the continuing dialogue a member has with the organization. It should be the first depository of complaints, comments, suggestions, and recommendations and may or may not be in charge of some sort of written communication on a periodic or as-needed basis.

In addition to these duties, the membership committee may be responsible for fund-raising among the members in conjunction with the development/fund-raising committee.

Development/Fund-raising Committee

This committee deals with two aspects of fund raising: annual giving and capital campaigns. Both aspects may be handled by the same committee, although a capital campaign has unique qualities that make a separate committee desirable.

The annual giving campaign should solicit annual contributions for the organization. The committee may accomplish this by holding special events on a periodic basis, such as benefits and fund-raisers, or through different types of fund-raising events such as banquets and planned giving (see p. 249).

A capital campaign raises funds for capital programs such as buildings or creating or increasing an endowment. This committee might work in conjunction with the membership committee to increase membership or to increase giving from membership. It may also work with the budget/planning committee.

The committee for a capital campaign may provide guidance to and review the fund-raising staff or an outside organization, if either exists. It may make decisions about the methods used, such as direct mail telemarketing or other methods of fund raising. A very helpful reference explaining the director's and organization's role in fund raising is *The Board Member's Guide to Fund Raising,* by Fisher Howe (1991).

Finance or Investment Committee

This committee develops financing plans for the future, watches cash flow, and, in general, seeks to assure the financial health of the organization. The finance committee oversees the investments of the organization to be sure that its endowment and other income are wisely and prudently invested, and that the terms of any restrictions on funds or endowments are recognized.

External Relations Committee

The purpose of this committee is to plan, organize, and approve all external relations material and events. The committee may perform these functions itself or it may hire and oversee an outside organization. If staff fulfills this function, this committee should oversee the staff. This committee may work in close contact with events, development/fund-raising, and/or planning committees.

Conclusion

Each organization should develop its own list of special issues and determine which committee will handle each. These special issues may require separate committees or they may be assigned to one of the typical committees described above. Some common issues include environment; risk management; physical facilities, electronic surveillance, and safety; legal compliance; community relations; and quality control (especially important for medical organizations).

These are only the most representative committees of an organization. Committees should be formed and used as the need arises. Committees should also be reviewed and dissolved as they fulfill their function and are no longer needed. The committees that an organization uses should be particular to that organization's needs.

Bibliography

Hirzy, Ellen Cochran. *The Nominating Committee: Laying a Foundation for Your Organization's Future.* Washington, D.C.: National Center for Nonprofit Boards, 1994.

Purpose and Functions of the Audit Committee

Sally P. Trabulsi and Victor Futter

> *This chapter provides an overview of the functions of the audit committee, describes its composition and qualifications for membership, discusses continuity of membership, recommends procedures to ensure that it discharges its responsibilities, points up questions to be asked at audit committee meetings, and provides a brief bibliography.*

The audit committee is an oversight committee of the board of directors with special responsibilities in the areas of fiduciary responsibility for financial operations, accounting and internal control, legal compliance, and matters involving management integrity.

Expectations of the public and regulatory authorities have risen significantly in the last decade with respect to the performance of nonprofit organizations. The audit committee, as the communications link between the board of directors, the independent auditors, the internal auditor, and the organization's management, can help the board insure that the organization's work is being accomplished in an effective and acceptable way. Nonprofits which seek funding from outside agencies, public or private, will of course need financial statements reviewed by an independent auditor.

To insure the independence of the committee's work and to assure the objectivity of financial statements, it is important that the audit committee be composed of directors who are not current or former employees of the organization and who have no significant financial or other relationship with management.

The audit committee's responsibilities should include the following functions.

(1) Review the organization's annual financial statements and any certification, report, opinion, or review rendered by the independent auditor and any significant disagreement between management and the independent auditor in connection with the preparation of the financial statements. Particular attention must be given to the latter so that the independence of judgment of the independent auditor can be evaluated.

(2) Review the performance of the independent auditor.

(3) Review the adequacy of the organization's system of internal controls as they relate to safeguarding the assets of the organization and the integrity of the organization's financial reporting processes, both internal and external. This should be done in consultation with the independent auditor and the internal auditor, if any.

(4) Recommend to the board of directors the particular persons or firm to be appointed as an independent auditor, and review any proposed discharge of such person or firm.

(5) Review the terms of engagement of the independent auditor, scope and plan of the external audit, compensation arrangements, and independence of the independent auditor.

(6) Review the results of each audit, the report of the independent auditor including any significant suggestions for improvements provided to management by the independent auditor (the "management letter"), and management's response.

(7) Review the reports of the internal auditing function (if any) that are material to the organization as a whole and management's response.

(8) Review the appointment and/or replacement of the senior internal auditing executive.

(9) Consider major changes and questions of choice respecting the appropriate auditing and accounting principles and practices to be used in preparation of the organization's financial statements when presented by the independent auditor, management, or other party.

In essence, it is the duty of the audit committee to "oversee" and review the audit process. It is not the function of the audit committee to "audit the auditors," but rather to perform whatever inquiry is necessary to determine that the reliance of the committee on the work of the outside auditors is justified.

To implement the foregoing functions, the audit committee should carry out the following activities.

(1) Review and monitor activities, organization structure, and qualifications of the internal audit function.

(2) Review management's monitoring of compliance with the organization's code of conduct, accounting standards, and government regulations (e.g., financial and environmental reporting). The committee should establish that the organization has a Code of Ethical Conduct and that there is a system in place to provide that the organization will comply with applicable laws. There should be a regular system for reporting to the audit committee deviations which have or may have a significant financial impact or that may reflect an adverse public image. In addition, the committee should be particularly alert to matters that raise possible conflicts of interest or that might reflect adversely upon the organization or otherwise impair its ability to raise funds. In some organizations, some of the foregoing may be handled by other committees of the board or jointly by such committees and the audit committee.

(3) Review policy and procedures in effect for the review of officers' expenses and benefits. In some organizations, the audit committee reviews the expense accounts of all senior staff members and approves those of the executive director. In other organizations, the latter function may be handled by the chair of the audit committee or the executive director.

(4) Review, with the organization's counsel, any legal matter that could have a significant impact on the organization's financial statements.

(5) Review with the independent auditor and with management the extent to which changes or improvements in financial or accounting practices, as recommended by the independent auditor or management personnel, have been implemented.

(6) Review the effect of any important new pronouncements in the accounting profession and other regulatory bodies that could affect the organization's accounting policies.

(7) Consult with the independent auditor and internal auditor, if any, periodically, as appropriate, and out of the presence of management concerning the adequacy of internal controls and the fullness and accuracy of the organization's financial statements.

(8) Perform other oversight functions as requested by the board.

(9) Report any recommendations to the board through minutes or reports of committee meetings, and special presentations as necessary.

Because virtually everything the audit committee learns about internal accounting controls will be learned secondhand from the person or persons who bear organizational responsibility for the system of controls, audit committee members should ask themselves in reviewing the work of the internal auditors: who is in charge and how much confidence do I have in that person's ability to do the right thing? Similar questions might be asked about the independent auditor.

A schedule of regular meetings should be prepared for the audit committee, together with a schedule showing which item of business should be undertaken at each meeting. The schedule should be reviewed by the organization's executive director and the chair of the audit committee. This schedule will serve as a reminder and will also ensure that the required duties of the audit committee are taken up in a timely and organized way. As other items of business come up during the course of the year, they should be added to the schedule. The schedule for the audit committee should be tied into the overall matrix for the work of the board. Such a schedule will, of course, be of considerable assistance is preparing the agenda and materials for each audit committee meeting.

In small organizations, audit committee functions may be performed by the executive or some other committee. In situations where there are few or no nonmanagement directors, the board can act as an "audit committee." Because the independence of directors, both in fact and in appearance, should be apparent in the audit committee, it would be wise for boards of any size to give serious consideration to appointing two, or preferably three, directors who are neither current nor former employees of the organization and who have no significant relationship with it, and to have them serve on the audit committee. The board and management should recognize the importance of the audit committee in protecting the organization's reputation and integrity.

Continuity of membership on an audit committee is desirable to provide its members with enough time to understand technical issues and the organization's finances. On the other hand, freshness of viewpoint is also desirable. Hence, after the first three to five years, every year one or more members (depending upon the size of the committee) should be changed.

With respect to the depth of sophistication in financial and accounting matters required for membership on the audit committee, at least one or two members should have experience or training that provides a working familiarity with accounting practices and concepts. All members of the committee, however, need not possess similar qualifications. Common sense, general intelligence, and an independent and inquiring cast of mind might well be the most important qualifications.

The audit committee should exercise great caution in undertaking any additional responsibility. If the committee, for instance, becomes involved too deeply in operational or other matters, it may jeopardize the independence from management that is essential to the committee's credibility; if it becomes immersed in matters not germane to its principal function, this additional work may be detrimental to the performance of its principal responsibilities.

In order to insulate board members from potential liability and to limit the scope of the audit committee's potential liability, the board should clearly define—and set down in writing—the committee's objective and the range of its duties and responsibilities. Often, this is done through a bylaw or resolution and adopted by the board and provides the board, committee members, management, internal auditors, and independent auditors with a clear understanding of the committee's role. Such a bylaw or resolution might well list items one through nine as noted at the beginning of this chapter.

The bylaw or resolution might also deal with operational matters, such as the frequency of meetings, the composition of committee membership, and the independence of its members.

The audit committee should follow procedures that ensure the accomplishments of its functions, including the following.

(1) Minutes of all meetings of the audit committee should be kept and either the minutes or a report of the audit committee meeting should be shared with the board.

(2) It is expected that members will attend audit committee meetings and accordingly, absences should be limited. A director who finds that he or she cannot attend most of the meetings should not continue to serve.

(3) The audit committee should confer separately with the independent auditors, and internal auditors, if any, outside the presence of any member of management at its meetings. The minutes of each meeting should record these separate meetings. At such sessions, inquiry should be made to ascertain:

(a) whether any disagreement has arisen between the independent auditor and management on auditing or accounting questions;

(b) whether the independent auditor believes that there has been full cooperation of management in the performance of the audit;

(c) whether there are any matters the audit committee should know about; and

(d) whether the independent auditor is fully comfortable with the completeness and accuracy of the organization's financial statements.

A similar procedure should be followed with respect to the internal auditor, if any.[1]

The audit committee serves an important function in providing ongoing oversight on behalf of the board, but in no way does it alter the traditional role and responsibility of the organization's management, the internal auditor, and the independent auditor for the adequacy of the accounting and control functions and the accuracy and completeness of the organization's financial statements. On the other hand, the committee should recognize that the board will rely on its reports and recommendations, and is entitled to do so, and therefore the committee should pursue its tasks with diligence and care.

There are many resources available for organizations planning to institute an audit committee, as well as for members of existing committees. The nationally known accounting firms prepare guides for audit committees. Consideration should be given to providing each member of such a committee with one of these guides.

The audit committee is vital and integral to the working of a nonprofit board, to the soundness of its financial controls and financial statements, and to the organization's reputation for financial integrity. It behooves the secretary of such organizations to stay abreast of current policies and practices and to ensure that board members are well-informed.

Notes

1. American Law Institute, *Principles of Corporate Governance and Structure* (Philadelphia, 1994), 115–21.

Bibliography

American Bar Association. *Corporate Director's Guidebook*. 2d ed. Chicago: American Bar Association, 1994.

————. *The Overview Committees of the Board of Directors*. Chicago: American Bar Association, 1979.

American Law Institute. *Principles of Corporate Governance and Structure*. Philadelphia, 1994.

Alexander Grant & Company. *Audit Committee Guide*. 1982.

Coopers & Lybrand. *Audit Committee Guide*. 1988.

Johnson, Sandra L. *The Audit Committee: A Key to Financial Accountability in Nonprofit Organizations*. Washington, D.C.: National Center for Nonprofit Boards, 1993.

Overton, George, editor. *Guidebook for Directors of Nonprofit Corporations*. Chicago: American Bar Association, 1993.

Compensation

George W. Overton

Compensation and related personnel issues are an important part of a non-profit board's agenda. Despite the staff's direct interest in these problems, their resolution requires staff support, as outlined in this chapter.

As part of a guidebook for the executive director or corporate secretary of a nonprofit corporation, a chapter on compensation is necessarily addressed to one of the parties personally involved in that subject. On the one hand, analysis of issues and factual material concerning this subject and the respective roles of the board and staff in determining compensation are a necessary part of any overall review of nonprofit issues. On the other hand, a senior staff member is inevitably affected by compensation policies and, simultaneously, she or he will be the person generally relied upon by the board of directors to assemble much of the relevant data on those issues. The possibilities of a conflict emphasize and enlarge the obligations of an executive director to his or her board, rather than lessening those responsibilities.

This discussion will be an outline of issues which should be evaluated. In effect, this is a kind of agenda for a board or committee meeting to be held on this subject. The foregoing sentence implies an absolute requirement: as a matter of corporate governance, the subject must be determined by the board or a committee thereof; and with regard to the chief executive's compensation it should be discussed, determined, and known by a specific compensation committee, the executive committee, or, possibly, the entire board.

In this discussion, we are addressing the specific problems of 501(c)(3) charities or private foundations; nonprofit organizations such as trade associations and 501(c)(4) health care entities will face many of the same problems, but are free of some of the restraints that guide the discussion which follows.

The Markets for Executive and Professional Personnel Differ from Those of Subordinate Employees

This chapter emphasizes the criteria for compensation of professional and executive personnel; it is assumed that the compensation of clerical, secretarial, and subordinate personnel will be determined by the marketplace for nonprofits in the particular area where the nonprofit must compete for those skills. For example, it is assumed that clerical employees, such as typists and secretaries, will rightly demand the level of compensation which alternative employment would offer them and that their duties are basically comparable to what those alternatives require. We assume that neither the executive director nor the board of directors face any difficulties in determining the market price of subordinate personnel just as they would with any other element of expense such as rent, insurance, or other routine costs. We shall return to the subject of subordinate personnel when we discuss periodic reviews; but we postulate a difference in kind between the issues involving such personnel and those relating to executive employees.

We also exclude discussion of the volunteer employee, except where such a person occupies an executive position, because they are infinite in variety. In some instances, a public benefit corporation may obtain the services of some interested person who offers to work, not for free, but at a compensation well below his or her market rate for other employment.

Compensating the Executive Director

We will first discuss the compensation of the executive director of the organization. To sharpen the issue, let us treat the problem of compensation as it would exist at the point of initial engagement: our executive directorship is vacant; it must be filled; how much should we offer to qualified candidates? Here, of course, as throughout all discussion of compensation, we will be influenced by, or possibly controlled by, a market. But the board, or its relevant committee, must realize that the determination of *which* market is not an easy task. Even within the world of a business for profit there is no obvious assumption that a man or woman competent to run a financial institution, such as a bank, is automatically capable of executive leadership in the production of motion pictures or automobiles. In the world of commerce and industry, however, performance of staff and performance of the corporation itself are measured rather largely by numerical data; hence, some part of the relevant data eases comparisons. In the nonprofit world, the measure of success—individual or organizational—will often, perhaps usually, defy precise quantification.

The persons desired for the position of executive director are those who can command substantial compensation—often in the for-profit field. While compensation of the latter cannot be matched, substantial six-figure salaries in the nonprofit field are often appropriate and necessary. It should be recognized, however, that the media often delights in playing up such matters, misleading the public, and having a field day at the organization's expense. For the long-term good of the organizations, boards and executive directors must be able to stand up to and bear this quickly passing discomfort, even though it may have some temporary effect upon fund-raising.

Compensation Should Be Analyzed with Respect to All Benefits, Direct or Indirect, Taxable or Nontaxable

Compensation, for the purpose of this chapter, should be thought of as including all perquisites, fringe benefits, expense accounts, and the like. This is true, not only of the negotiation of appropriate reward for an executive, but also in terms of reporting to the board or its committees or, when it is appropriate, to the general public. Where scandals have emerged in the nonprofit field, they have often come from the abuses in the treatment of expenses and boards should make certain that the structure of compensation decisions assures that all such issues have been properly resolved and recorded.

The board, or an appropriate committee, should also establish the nonprofit's policy on outside remuneration. Often, probably far more often than in the business world, a nonprofit executive may receive offers of consulting fees, remuneration for speaking engagements, and the like. Potential conflicts can arise here, and at best, this is an area where there may be serious misunderstanding.

Executive and Professional Compensation Is Inevitably Related to Overall Personnel Policies and Administration

The reader will note that it is impossible to separate the analysis of executive compensation from overall job descriptions, executive search, and personnel administration generally. Many of the same questions arise in all these areas: What kind of an organization are we? What kind of leadership do we need? What parallel, comparable entity exists in our neighborhood or elsewhere that we can study? What are the qualifications of our ideal candidate? What man or woman on another organization's staff would we hire instantly if that person were available? What is the salary of that man or woman? In answering these questions, a large nonprofit will want to employ accounting firms or personnel consultants who are specialists in the nonprofit field. Publications serving the nonprofit field also offer such information from time to time (see Exhibit 1).

A Listing of Priorities Should Be Made to Assist in Resolving Compensation Issues

In defining the executive director's function so as to evaluate compensation, the board must rank a number of competing goals toward which its executive director will work. One, or some, of these goals may call for innovative adaptability as a regular function. As an example, the board of a health clinic may feel that its mission to provide services to a defined community is relatively stable and that efficiency in administration outweighs innovation and creation in the job. The administration of a community theater group, on the other hand, calls for a different set of priorities. Efficiency is never totally irrelevant to any function that involves the interaction of groups of individuals; but one would certainly state, when looking for an executive director of a theatrical company, that sensitivity to nuances of creativity—which might be irrelevant in a health care facility—becomes one of the more important criteria. We suggest a method of resolving these competing objectives.

We should, in this determination of a market, assign priorities: we will never find the complete answers to all problems, but what are the most important characteristics needed? Second, which characteristics or problems are of priority but for which some weaknesses are tolerable? Lastly, what abilities are perhaps neither essential nor critically important but add to the value of the person involved; these may help to make a difficult choice between one man or woman and another.

The following priorities or issues are the partial beginnings of a suggested list. We believe the board, aided by its executive staff, should prepare a more extensive list. We further suggest that the board assign a number to each issue included in the list: number one should be assigned to the one most important priority; number two should be assigned to the next two most important priorities; and number three for the next in rank, and so on.

Here are eight examples.

Administrative Capacity

This characteristic is always important, yes; but how important is it? How large is the subordinate staff? Is the organization so large that the board cannot directly observe administrative failings and may be able to discuss them well only after the fact?

If the employer is a hospital, this quality is obviously important; in running a neighborhood improvement association, it may be close to irrelevant. In looking at administrative capacity, we must remember that entities outside the organization may demand efficiency as part of the entity's mission, even if the board and staff would place a higher value on some other criteria; nowhere is this tension greater than in the field of health care. To what degree must the board and staff yield to this pressure?

Creativity and Imagination

Do we need a regular flow of new ideas? Do we suspect our present mission may be confused or obsolescent? Does the public we serve need new ways of solving problems?

In a field in which change seems inevitable,—e.g., today's child welfare—imagination may be imperative. But in the continuation of an established function—e.g., an alumni body financing scholarships—this may be a secondary requirement. In areas of predictably rapid change, the mission of the nonprofit and its maximum fulfillment will depend on its ability to contribute new ideas and solutions to a hungry market; do we need an executive who can supply this need? Are we willing to pay the price? Often the price of such talent is an indifference to administrative problems.

Charisma

Do we need someone who can personally convey our corporate message, perhaps becoming the personification of the organization? How important are the executive's communication skills? And among those skills, do we need that intangible quality, that ability to bring others to identify emotionally with the executive?

In any entity engaged in advocacy, such as a women's rights organization, the foregoing qualities are obviously important. In many others, the executive director can be, for all practical purposes, unknown and invisible to the outside public.

For example, a church affiliate running a homeless shelter will generally not need any public activity from its executive, who may prefer a role of relative anonymity. If, however, the church is a party to community-wide debate on the treatment of the homeless, the personality of the executive almost becomes part of the job description.

Here again, the problems of compensation and overall personnel selection and policy overlap. An organization which needs, and hence must seek, a visible and charismatic spokesperson will find that the latter will have a strong bargaining power when it comes to the issues of alternative employment or stability of public image which we will discuss below.

Fund-raising Skills

Do we rely on our executive director to devote a substantial amount of time to fund raising? Does this involve personal participation, or simply administrative or public relations skills?

If fund raising is one of the principal activities of the executive director, her or his employer will come to a market in which numerical data—the record of success in prior employment—is usually available. The nonprofit employer must recognize that a successful record with fund raising creates an immediately recognizable qualification for alternative employment.

Political Sophistication

Does the executive need experience dealing with the political environment surrounding the corporate mission? In some organizations, a "city hall savvy" is essential; in others, it would be so low on the list of criteria as to be invisible.

Organizations dealing with land-use problems, such as natural areas preservation, or needing public funds, as in almost all areas of child welfare, must place a fairly high priority on knowledge and experiences in dealing with legislatures, zoning boards, and elected officials.

Technical Knowledge

Does our executive have to be someone with substantial technical experience or training in order to perform adequately?

In health care, one would generally say such skills are necessary, however, in many fields, substantive knowledge may be of marginal importance.

Stability of Employment

Do we need an executive who can be expected to remain with the organization for a substantial period of time? Or can we deal with relatively frequent changes in leadership?

If the corporate mission calls for staff stability, the bargaining strength of the executive director is further enhanced. No easy answers are available to this problem, but all must be conscious of it.

Alternative Employment

Does the work of our nonprofit create opportunities for our executive outside the nonprofit field? How much should we yield to these pressures in determining compensation?

In certain areas of the nonprofit world, work for an entity draws attention to the executive. This attention leads to commercial or governmental organizations often able to compete for an executive's services at high figures. Organizations in the field of environmental protection, for example, have often found that their work qualifies a person as an expert in some commercial remediation process. Again, we offer no solutions to this tension, but urge a consciousness of it.

Collateral Activities

Will we tolerate and assume the employee will earn income in some spare-time activities, such as consulting work or lecturing?

In some fields, collateral work is comparable with an executive's principal function and may even enhance it; in other situations, such part-time engagements may present serious conflicts of interest.

The foregoing are suggested as a small part of a listing of skills or criteria in order to establish a market for the desired executive. The reader will note that the list resembles that of a job description, but the intent differs slightly: here we are searching for a market, as if in every community there were separate employment agencies specializing in each of these qualities.

The Identification of the Market

Having established these criteria, the board should then examine what data is available concerning the market for such personnel. Inquiries could be made about comparable institutions and even the daily newspaper may, on occasion, provide data that will aid in this point. In cities with some centralized funding, such as a United Way or a Community Trust, there may be a central source of data. Increasingly, in any large city, there are support organizations serving the nonprofit community which can advise on these matters. A list of some of the national organizations which may have local representatives can be found in Exhibit 1. If the subject nonprofit's budget permits, a management consultant's skills and database may be called for as part of an overall compensation review.

The Environment of Compensation

It should be noted, of course, that there are nonmaterial advantages to most nonprofit work. Furthermore, there is the nonprofit's ability to satisfy the executive's personal agenda and work satisfaction. A market scale of compensation based on the salaries offered by employers who do not offer these satisfactions should be treated with some caution. For many men and women, the conditions of work in a typical nonprofit corporation are preferable as a matter of choice to a business employment, even though the cash remuneration may be significantly lower and formal employment contracts may not exist.

The nonprofit, on the other hand, must examine its ability to offer security in employment. Some 501(c)(3) nonprofits lurch from one financial crisis to another and the experience of sudden financial collapses is not unknown, while other nonprofits have outlasted well-financed business corporations. The board should, however, use caution in the employment of personnel willing to take the financial risks of the nonprofit—which a prudent man or woman would avoid—if such a choice is made solely because such risk-takers are available at a lower price or without termination or severance benefits.

The Need for Equality

In this hypothetical determination of the executive's qualifications and appropriate compensation, all parties—on both sides of the table—should search for equality: that is to say, the board must make sure the staff executive is doing the organization no special favor by accepting employment at a lower compensation than she or he might elsewhere command, if, in exchange, the reward is a broader discretion given to the executive and abandonment of the board's authority. In an employment equilibrium, the board is grateful for and proud of a competent staff, but must be prepared to seek and find a replacement at any time without major budgetary dislocations; and the executive is grateful for and proud of the opportunity to display appropriate skills, but must be prepared to consider career alternatives as they may arise. Fundamental fairness as well as equality is essential.

It is impossible for the board to separate completely the economic issue of compensation from the political one of corporate governance. Frequently, an organization will depend on an executive who is underpaid (by market measurements), but who demands a freedom of action in which the board is relegated to a minor custodial role. Even if such a leader brings unusual qualities to the organization—as is often the case—the board should bear in mind that when the inevitable moment of death, resignation, or other crisis occurs, the organization will face a management crisis that may be simultaneous with a fiscal one. A board should always recognize that it must give some attention to succession in its executive staff, and the economics of compensation will affect its freedom in that task.

The second factor that should be considered in dealing with the compensation issue is the degree of job security offered to the executive. Employment contracts providing for fixed terms of employment or termination pay are known in the nonprofit field as well as in business, but the board of a nonprofit should examine, with caution, any proposal to create a financial obligation where the cost obligation would substantially impair the organization's freedom to find a new employee. Unlike a business corporation, which may contract to pay an executive extravagantly if she or he produces the gross income to cover the salary and benefits, a nonprofit has no built-in solution to funding a termination payment. All issues of executive compensation have political overtones: the board should not incur obligations to an executive so large that termination becomes fiscally impractical. On the other hand, tenure provisions should not be so generous as to induce the executive to remain in office when the corporation's board fails to give support to policies and programs that the executive feels are central to the mission. Again, tenure and termination are matters of both economics and politics.

Organizations which are basically dependent upon either earned income (e.g., tuition fees in an unendowed educational organization) or annual giving should be careful not to enter into a compensation arrangement which promises (either legally or morally) a continued flow of payments into fringe benefits.

A Nonprofit Should Avoid Compensation Based on Fractions or Percentages of Funds Raised

A 501(c)(3) organization should not offer, without careful evaluation, a compensation scheme dependent upon a percentage of gross or of gifts to the organization, although specific bonuses related to funding targets may be appropriate. Such percentages may raise serious questions of trust law and of self-dealing under the Internal Revenue Code.[1] It may be, or appear to be, inconsistent with the basic mission of the organization. For a public benefit corporation, the production of gross is never the primary corporate purpose in the first place. Nonprofit organizations should always recognize that one of the essential challenges of management is that the success or failure of the organization is going to be measured, in large part, by factors that do not lend themselves to quantification. There is no single, precise bottom line to the mission of a nonprofit organization. The financial success in meeting expenses is something that cannot possibly be ignored, but it is not the basic driving force of the corporate mission and should not become the primary issue in compensation.

All Compensation of Personnel Should Be Reviewed Periodically, and in Most Nonprofits, Annually

The foregoing discussion has centered on compensation aspects of the initial choice of an executive director. Obviously, in most nonprofit entities this should be an infrequent event. Compensation for all employees, however, both executive and subordinate, should be the subject of periodic review, and preferably annual review, as part of a general review of expenses.

For such a review, the board should create a committee that will work with the executive staff. This committee, together with the executive and staff, normally will be the structure that reviews personnel competence and functional needs as well as compensation. The reviewers should inform themselves about the market price of the skills required of each employee, as well as identifying the relevant markets involved. The executive staff should note that the skills required by the organization may shift. Even on the level of clerical personnel, job descriptions—and markets—have been changing rapidly through the almost constant introduction of new computer and communication technologies.

The unit in the corporate structure that should conduct this review will differ according to the size of the organization and its particular mission. All parties, however, will be best served if there is a specific committee that works with the executive staff to develop the payroll assumptions built into the corporation's budget and is prepared to ratify or criticize the recommendations of the staff until consensus is reached.

Preparation of a personnel budget is normally a staff and management function, but review is meaningless without input from an informed committee or subcommittee of the board.

Annual Review of the Compensation of the Executive Director

It is desirable to have a committee—either a compensation committee, an executive committee, or an ad hoc committee—make an annual review of the executive director's compensation. In some circumstances, it may not be necessary or desirable for the entire board to vote on compensation specifically, although it would never be out of order and may be desirable for a board to do so.

In a review of the executive director's compensation, all of the factors discussed above should be considered. In addition, an organization should consider adopting an annual action plan for its executive director outlining the organization's goals for the coming year. These goals should be worked out with the executive by the appropriate board committee. Goals might include:

(1) increasing the organization's use of a specific facility by 10%;
(2) increasing the amount raised in the Annual Fund Drive by 10%;

(3) establishing a new unit of the organization in some specified field; and/or
(4) filling a problematic leadership position with an outstanding candidate.

In such a program, any increase in compensation would be dependent upon the executive's success in achieving these goals. The executive should, in turn, allocate responsibility for achieving these goals to the senior officers, and their increases in compensation might be measured against their success in meeting their assigned goals.

Succession Planning

In reviewing compensation, succession planning for all senior-level executives should not be overlooked. Building the organization and its future is an essential part of the executive director's job and should be reviewed when evaluating his or her performance. It is worth noting that some executive directors, desirous of protecting their jobs, have sought weak assistants so there is no successor in sight.

Compensation of Executive Staff Should Be Related to the Possible Changes in the Status of the Corporation

A review of compensation of executive staff must be based upon an analysis of the possible changes to the nonprofit's status. In short, a compensatory scheme based on the status of the organization one year may not be relevant to the organization's position three years later. Changes involved may not be solely monetary; they may relate to changes in the mission or the importance of the organization or in one of its principal activities in its constituency of need. Here, again, in the nonprofit world, those changes may not be immediately reflected in numerical data.

On the other hand, a board or a compensation committee in the nonprofit world should not automatically assume that executive compensation must constantly rise as the organization expands. The board should be aware that the market for replacement of executive personnel will broaden greatly as the organization becomes bigger and there is, as has been noted above, no need for an automatic connection between numerical gross income and appropriate compensation. This point should be kept in mind when the board is examining, not the initial employment of an executive, but his or her renewal of a relationship.

Compensation is only part of the agenda of such a review. But as part of the compensation review, all involved should remember:

(1) sooner or later, all relevant personnel will measure their compensation against a market alternative;
(2) at least at the executive level, determining a relevant market by which to judge compensation is a difficult and challenging task; and
(3) all compensation at the executive level should be evaluated as a matter of corporate governance as well as economics.

Editor's Note

As this book goes to press, we note recent amendments to the Internal Revenue Code (Code) affecting compensation of nonprofit executives.[2] These provisions impose penalties on executives and directors involved in the payment of excessive compensation to executives described in the amendments. They apply to all organizations exempt under sections 501(c)(3)[3] and 501(c)(4)[4] of the Code. The Committee Report[5] accompanying the statute[6] states in its third paragraph:

> Existing tax-law standards[7] apply in determining reasonableness of compensation and fair market value.[8] In applying such standards, the Committee intends that the parties to a transaction are entitled to rely on a rebuttable presumption of reasonableness with respect to a compensation arrangement with a disqualified person if such arrangement was approved by a board of directors or trustees (or committee thereof) that:
>
> (1) was composed entirely of individuals unrelated to and not subject to the control of the disqualified person(s) involved in the arrangement.[9]
>
> (2) obtained and relied upon appropriate data as to comparability (e.g., compensation levels paid by similarly situated organizations, both taxable and tax-exempt, for functionally comparable positions; the location of the organization, including the availability of similar specialties in the geographic area; independent compensation surveys by nationally recognized independent firms; or actual written offers from similar institutions competing for the services of the disqualified person); and
>
> (3) adequately documented the basis for its determination (e.g., the record includes an evaluation of the individual whose compensation was being established and the basis for determining that the individual's compensation was reasonable in light of that evaluation and data).[10]
>
> If these three criteria are satisfied, penalty excise taxes could be imposed under the proposal only if the probative value of the evidence put forth by the parties to the transaction (e.g., the Internal Revenue Service could establish that the compensation data relied upon by the parties was not for functionally comparable positions or that the disqualified person, in fact, did not substantially perform the responsibilities of such position.) A similar rebuttable presumption would arise with respect to the reasonableness of the valuation of property sold, transferred or purchased by an organization to or from a disqualified person if the sale, transfer or purchase is approved by an independent board that uses appropriate comparability data and adequately documents its determination. The Secretary of the Treasury and the Internal Revenue Service are instructed to issue guidance in connection with the reasonableness standard that incorporates this presumption.[11]

Both our schedule of publication and the lack of any regulations applicable to section 4958 prevent any more detailed treatment of this problem at this time.

Notes

1. 26 I.R.C. § 503(c)(3) (1994).
2. 26 I.R.C. § 4958 (West Supp. 1996).
3. *Id.* § 503(c)(3) (1994).
4. *Id.* § 503(c)(4).
5. H.R. Rep. No. 105-106, 104th Cong. (1996), *reprinted in* 1996 U.S.C.C.A.N. 1143.
6. Pub. L. No. 104-168, 110 Stat. 1452 (1996).
7. *See* 26 I.R.C. § 162 (1994).
8. In this regard, the Committee intends that an individual need not necessarily accept reduced compensation merely because he or she renders services to a tax-exempt, as opposed to a taxable, organization. *See* Treasury Reg. § 53.4941(d)-3(c)(1) (1996).
9. A reciprocal approval arrangement whereby an individual approves compensation of the disqualified person, and the disqualified person, in turn, approved the individual's compensation does not satisfy the independence requirement.
10. The fact that a state or local legislative or agency body may have authorized or approved of a particular compensation package paid to a disqualified person is not determinative of the reasonableness of compensation paid for purposes of the excise tax penalties provided for by the proposal. Similarly, such authorization or approval is not determinative of whether a revenue sharing arrangement violates the private inurement proscription.
11. 26 I.R.C. § 4958 (West Supp. 1996).

Bibliography

Casteable. "Non-Profit Organization Ethics." *Association Management*. (April, 1995).

Hiring Handbook. Aspen Publishers, Inc., 1994.

Hopkins, Bruce. *A Legal Guide to Starting and Managing a Nonprofit Organization*. 2d ed. New York: John Wiley & Sons, 1993. (has a brief treatment of the subject in this generally excellent work)

The Nonprofit Board's Guide to Chief Executive Compensation. Washington, DC: National Center for Nonprofit Boards, 1995.

United Way of Pennsylvania. *The Pennsylvania Non-Profit Handbook*. Harrisburg, PA: Non-Profit Advocacy Network, 1992. (contains some useful guidelines)

Wolf, Thomas. *Managing a Nonprofit Organization*. New York: Prentice-Hall, 1990. (gives 4 pages out of 305 to the topic)

Readers seeking further guidance or suggestions should search the mailing lists of all the organizations listed above, but also the principal commercial publisher serving the nonprofit field:

Jossey-Bass Publishers
350 Sansome Street
San Francisco, CA 94104

Exhibit 1
National Organizations That May Be of
Assistance in Dealing with Compensation Issues

The American Society of Corporate Secretaries

521 Fifth Avenue
New York, NY 10175
212-681-2000
Fax 212-681-2005

This organization has a number of useful materials which should be examined.

The American Bar Association
Section of Business Law

750 North Lake Shore Drive
Chicago, Illinois 60611
312-988-6244

The American Bar Association has published two works which may be of assistance: *Guidebook for Directors of Nonprofit Corporations* (1993); and *Corporate Director's Guidebook* (2nd ed., 1994). The latter work is addressed to directors of business corporations, but its treatment of compensation will, to a large extent, be relevant. Copies of these publications may be obtained by writing to the address above.

The National Center for Nonprofit Boards (NCNB)

Suite 510
2000 L Street, NW
Washington, DC 20036-4907
202-452-6262
Fax: 202-452-6299

The NCNB publishes a wide variety of pamphlets and books, including one on executive compensation. See also their August 1995 issue of BOARD MEMBER, "The Nonprofit Board's Guide to Chief Executive Compensation."

The Support Centers of America

70 10th Street, Suite 201
San Francisco, CA 94103-1302
415-552-7660

The Support Centers of America have a number of local offices, and provide management assistance to nonprofits.

The Independent Sector

1828 L Street, NW
Washington, DC 20036
202-223-8100

This organization, backed by substantial foundation resources, addresses a broad spectrum of nonprofit problems. It has published *Financial Compensation in Nonprofit Organizations* by Brian O'Connell and E.B. Krauft.

The Conference Board

845 Third Avenue
New York, NY 10022-6607
212-759-0900

The Conference Board publishes a number of materials on corporate problems, including compensation. Most of these are fairly high in price.

The Role of the Nominating Committee of a Nonprofit

Robert L. Seaman

This chapter of the Guidebook *describes briefly the principal functions that may be expected to be performed by the nominating committee of a nonprofit.*

Introduction

The present concept of the nominating committee appears to have arisen out of the reaction by public corporations to claims by shareholder activists during the 1970s. It was asserted that many boards of directors of public corporations were self-perpetuating and were not sufficiently pro-active with respect to the interests of shareholders. It has been recommended, and is indeed the case today, that in most major business corporations the nominating committee is composed largely if not entirely of "outside" directors and is responsible for seeking out and recommending persons for election to the board of directors of the corporation.

The nominating committee, however, is not a new concept in the nonprofit world. There, the nominating committee was long associated with the need to persuade prominent persons to serve on the boards of nonprofits and, in that respect, it had a quasi-development function.

The Philosophy behind a Nominating Committee

The philosophy or rationale behind the nominating committee by a business corporation was that shareholders needed a greater voice in corporate governance. In the case of a nonprofit, which does not have "shareholders," the nominating committee has a much broader potential range of functions. As mentioned above, it has always had a quasi-development function. In the case of a nonprofit nominating committee, however, the principal aim is building and maintaining the most effective board of directors, which will then work in partnership with the executive director of the organization. In this regard, it would appear that the nominating committee of a nonprofit could have a different name, which describes its broader function more adequately, such as the "Nominating and Board Development Committee." As we detail the various functions of the nominating committee below, one will see more clearly how the proper operation of such a committee will dramatically enhance the potential for an effective board of directors and a dynamic partnership of goal setting, accomplishment, and review between the board and the executive director. The following are the general areas in which the nominating committee may function: (1) recommendations as to the overall size and structure of the board, including its committee structure; (2) identification and selection of potential candidates for board and committee membership; (3) oversight of the orientation of new directors once they are elected; (4) ongoing evaluation of the performance of all directors; (5) review of the mission of the organization; (6) establishment and effective functioning of procedures governing board activities; and, finally, (7) the selection process for and evaluation of the executive director.

In some organizations, some of the foregoing may be carried out by other committees. It is not essential that these functions be located with the nominating committee. It is essential that some board committee, or group of directors, have responsibility for each of the functions listed above. In carrying out its functions in all of the above areas, the nominating committee will work very closely with the executive director and the secretary of the organization. The judgment and participation of these two officers, working together with an involved board chair, is crucial to the creation and nurturing of a real partnership between the nonprofit and its board of directors.

Functions of the Nominating Committee

The Size and Composition of the Board of Directors

The size and composition of a board of directors varies not only with the type of nonprofit but may also vary, from time to time, depending upon the phase of the nonprofit's development. For example, a nonprofit with many different constituent groups may desire to have a large board of directors with members representing or having some background with respect to most of its major constituencies. On the other hand, a limited focus nonprofit may decide that it can function most effectively with a board of directors of limited size.

Fund-raising or development is often vital to the life of a nonprofit. The nominating committee can play a major role in positioning the nonprofit to meet its fund-raising needs as they vary from time to time by dealing with the often-conflicting desire for a large board versus the need for efficiency. For example, to accommodate a large number of potential supporters, should the nonprofit have a small working board and a large advisory board? Or, on the other hand, should the nonprofit have a large number of directors on its board and transact most of its business through the assistance of a small working group of directors such as an executive committee? Board membership and development go hand in hand. One result is that at the time of a fund-raising campaign most nonprofits tend to enlarge their boards of directors in order to accommodate individuals who are or may become significant donors. This, however, may lead to an unwieldy board, an unsatisfactory situation with longer-term complications.

Another issue often addressed by the nominating committee with respect to board function is that of recommending the structure of the board of directors most appropriate for the particular nonprofit. In this regard, the nominating committee may be called upon to craft an appropriate committee structure for the board. The nominating committee is also thought to be the appropriate place to review the types of skills and talents needed by persons invited to become members of the board of directors. This last comment leads into the next function of the nominating committee, which is the screening of potential members of the board.

Selection of Persons as Directors and as Members of Various Committees

The nominating committee usually maintains and should maintain a sizable "inventory" of individuals who might be desirable to serve as directors of the organization, from which it will periodically propose persons for election to the board. The committee compiles this list of individuals primarily through the contacts of board members in the community, persons of stature known to have interests compatible with those of the nonprofit, and through the assistance of a knowledgeable executive director. It is the function of the committee continually to review its list of potential candidates, to add new ones to the list, and to identify those currently on the list who, for one reason or another (including possible conflicts of interest) are no longer likely candidates for board membership. The secretary of the nonprofit usually performs a vital role in facilitating this process by updating the database on prospective board members and developing information on additional candidates.

To aid in this process, the nominating committee, often in conjunction with the entire board of directors, establishes guidelines or criteria for board membership. Integrity, candor, and independence are essential characteristics for board members. In addition, the committee may include such items as stature in the community, experience, availability to work for the organization, ability to contribute monetarily to the organization, business or legal skills, technical skills, and other talents which would be useful to the organization. All of this will be done against the background of each nonprofit's unique situation and needs, and reflected in an evolving board "profile." The continuous re-examination of the needs of the organization leads into the next function of the nominating committee, which is that of determining the appropriate committee structure for the board and the staffing of those committees.

Structure of Board Committees and the Staffing of Such Committees

The unique needs of the organization usually have a strong impact on the types of committees that are necessary. Committees common to all organizations would probably include an executive committee, a finance committee, an audit committee, a fund-raising or development committee, and perhaps a compensation committee, in addition to the nominating committee itself. After that, committees tend to diverge in function depending on the nature of the organization. For example, a school is likely to have an admissions committee and a financial aid committee. It will also have a plant and property or buildings and grounds committee. On the other hand, a nonprofit which holds no real property, but which is in the business of making grants and donations, would undoubtedly have an investment committee and a grant committee, and as needed, a capital campaign committee.

Once the committees have been established and periodically reviewed, it becomes necessary to staff them and to maintain the quality of that staffing. Staffing is often done when new directors are selected, to the extent that the skills and talents of the directors are known and desired at the time of their selection. In the case of most nonprofits, directors are usually selected because of their ability to make contributions in one or more areas. Ideally the perceived need of a particular board committee or the desire to enhance a discrete segment of the organization's function precedes the selection of the new director and the director is selected in accordance with that need. A question every potential director should ask is "what do you expect of me?" If an analysis like the one just suggested has been made, the organization will be able to answer the question. It should be able to answer the question before seeking new directors. This, then, leads us to the next function of the committee, which is the continuing evaluation of the performance of the board.

Evaluation of the Effective Functioning and Needs of the Board and its Various Committees

The nominating committee should not only continue to examine the appropriateness of the committee structure of the board as it relates to the mission of the organization, but it should also conduct periodic, probably annual, evaluations of the capabilities of directors, including their participation on board committees. In this regard the committee would wish to consider criteria such as attendance at board and committee meetings, participation in the work of the board and committees, financial contributions to the organization, the health of the board member, or the assumption of responsibilities or other changes in position outside of the board, which may make it difficult for the director to continue his or her board membership in an effective manner.

Nonprofit boards are particularly subject to circumstances requiring evaluation. Almost all members of boards of directors experience a type of institutional burnout over time, and this can be viewed as almost natural in the life of an organization. What is important is that a committee of the board be in a position to identify the decline in a director's commitment and recommend to the person that he or she make way for someone else. What may make this process more difficult is that a director's financial contribution may continue long after his or her energy has diminished; this situation will require tough decisions and delicate handling. In this regard an advisory board or other emeritus body may prove a useful expedient.

In the case of many boards, the burnout phenomenon is manifested in the board that ceases to exercise effective management oversight of the organization and, instead, becomes or develops a collegial "country club" atmosphere. It is, however, more likely that tired directors will merely run out of energy and will try to "hang on" to their positions mainly because it pleases them to have their name associated with an organization with stature in the community. To guard against either of these eventualities, the nominating committee must conduct periodic evaluations of director effectiveness.

The process of weeding out ineffective directors can be done more easily if the board has established term limits on membership and if the board has followed faithfully those criteria for continued membership enumerated above. Term limits on board membership are often easier to conceptualize in theory than to implement in practice—first because almost all directors need a warm-up period before becoming truly effective and secondly, because everybody hates to lose good directors—and you may lose them forever once they leave. Usually a one-year period of ineligibility after six to nine years is an acceptable arrangement. Both membership criteria and term limits should be carefully explained to current and prospective directors of new board members. This leads us to the next function of the nominating committee, which is orientation.

Orientation and Continuing Education of Board and Committee Members

After having gone through the process of identifying the needs of the organization, searching the developed inventory of potential board candidates, inviting the potential candidate to serve, and having the candidate accept, one might think that the work of the nominating committee would be complete. As we have seen above, however, this is far from the case. A most important task of the nominating committee—the orientation of new directors—must not be overlooked. Even though most prospective directors will not accept a board position without having a fairly clear idea of what the organization does and what is expected of them, there is a different level of understanding necessary to function effectively as a director which comes only with increased exposure to the nonprofit and its organizational culture. It is the obligation of the nominating committee to take the lead in imparting this "culture" to the new director.

It would be unusual for a prospective director not to have met other board members and senior personnel in the organization before having agreed to serve. Once elected, the new director must be introduced to all board members and to other important persons within the organization. In the case of a museum or library, for example, this should entail a detailed and lengthy visit, one-half to a full day, to see the "behind the scenes" portion of the organization in operation, during which the new director is given a working overview of how the organization delivers its product or service. Fundamental materials such as the articles of incorporation of the organization and its bylaws, and perhaps minutes of recent meetings of the board, preferably incorporated into a director's manual (see p. 37), should also be provided to the new director. Publications and other material produced by the nonprofit describing what it does are also a critical part of this package. All of the above, plus whatever additional "study sessions" are deemed appropriate, are often organized or arranged by the secretary on behalf of the nominating committee as part of a continuing education process. Perhaps most important in the continuing education of directors is one left to last, the mission statement for the organization.

The Mission Statement of the Organization

Probably the most significant procedural task of the board of directors of any nonprofit is periodically to review the organization's mission (see p. 157). The nominating committee is one of the bodies which may be asked to assume the lead in the development of an appropriate mission statement and the continuous review of the mission statement once it has been formulated. Just as the effectively functioning nonprofit is itself a living and growing entity, so also must be the mission of the organization. As the primary oversight committee of the institutional health of the board of directors, it is quite appropriate for the nominating committee to be asked to initiate mission formulation and reevaluation. Depending on the organization's preference, this function may instead be performed by a planning, executive, or special ad hoc committee. What may then flow logically from crafting the mission, which is like the constitution of the organization, is the formulation of rules of procedure by which the board or other governing body of the organization will work toward the implementation of the mission.

Establishing Rules of Procedure for the Board

Usually the committees of the board determine their own rules of procedure. Who, however, determines the rules of procedure for the board of directors itself? Absent the convening of an ad hoc committee, it is very likely that the nominating committee, which is so near to the heart of the organization, will be the one to formulate and propose the board's rules of procedure. Most importantly, these rules, which will vary with the organization, must be designed to enhance effective communication within the board itself and with the executive director of the organization. Without effective communication, there can be no effective decision making. Without effective communication, the commitment of good directors will rapidly wane. Without good communication, board meetings will be a disaster. Therefore, determining the type of information that flows to directors, when it arrives and what directors are expected to do with it; establishing the order of presentation of items at board meetings and the procedure by which decisions are reached with respect to issues at those meetings; determining how the minutes of the board are maintained and what kind of follow-up or action memoranda are needed to translate board decisions into executive actions, and who should be responsible for such tasks are all issues which the nominating committee may be requested to oversee as items of board procedure. They all contribute to building the effective, dynamic partnership which the nonprofit needs to have in order to serve its constituencies effectively. In most organizations, this is generally done by the executive director, the chair, and the secretary, and the nominating committee performs an oversight function in this area with a review at least once a year. In carrying out such oversight, the nominating committee will of necessity work very closely with the executive director and the secretary, and the actual implementation will, in all likelihood, become the responsibility of the secretary.

Composition of the Nominating Committee

It is generally agreed that the nonprofit nominating committee, like a corporate nominating committee, should consist entirely of outside directors. In order to foster the dynamic partnership between the board and the executive director, however, the executive director will be an important presence at most meetings of the committee.

Indeed, with respect to all of the matters set forth above and just about all of the committee's significant functions, the voice of the executive director and his or her judgment will be critical constituents in an effective outcome. The executive director and other "inside" directors, however, should not be members of the committee and must be excluded from those meetings of the committee at which their presence would be detrimental to full and open discussion of issues. For example, it is recommended by many commentators that the nominating committee be engaged to conduct annual evaluations of the executive director on behalf, and for the benefit, of the board. Clearly, this would not be possible if the executive director and other staff were members of the committee.

Role of the Committee in the Selection of an Executive Director for the Organization

Given the committee's knowledge of the organization and its strong background in evaluating board and management performance, it would seem natural that the nominating committee might be the logical choice to lead the way when there is the need to select a new executive director for the organization. In most nonprofits, however, this activity has traditionally been undertaken by an ad hoc "search" committee. The traditional practice is probably the more desirable practice. As an ad hoc committee, the search committee can be specially constituted and separately charged with respect to its specific mission. The nominating committee, and the compensation committee, if any, may well be able to provide advice and guidance to the search committee because of its knowledge of, and continuing attention to, the needs of the organization. A specially constituted search committee, however, may draw on constituencies other than the board for its membership and is often the embodiment of a need to take a "new look" at the leadership. Consequently, it is recommended that the nominating committee, which is likely to be closely identified with the existing culture of the organization, not be the one to conduct or oversee the selection process for a new executive director.

Conclusion

With all the functions identified as being desirable or possible for a nominating committee to undertake, it may appear to be a "supercommittee." Indeed, the work of the committee will touch on many areas of board or institutional function, but the committee's mission within all the areas will be directed toward enhancing institutional process; it must not be allowed to usurp board decision making. Its aim is really that of assuring the most effective operation of the organization and the utilization of one of its most important resources, its board of directors. With this in mind, the nominating committee will function primarily as a facilitating committee whose role is to build, balance, and coordinate the dynamic partnership between the board of directors and the executive director, which in turn will lead to more effective organizational results. The nominating committee deals primarily with the heart or soul of the nonprofit and is less concerned with the organization's substantive operations and programs. Those functions—finance, fund-raising, property, investments, grant-making, audit, admissions, collections, exhibitions, etc.—are the province of the board and its other committees of the board.

Duties and Potential Liabilities of Officers and Directors of Nonprofit Institutions and Organizations

David B. Rigney

This chapter summarizes the standards of performance and duties of directors and officers of nonprofit organizations, analyzes the application of such standards in practice, discusses the sources of advice on which directors and officers may properly rely in fulfilling their duties, and also analyzes the potential liabilities of such officers and directors.

Introduction: Standards of Performance

Nonprofit directors and officers should adhere to several important responsibilities to the organizations they serve; in the particular context of nonprofit organizations, these responsibilities may be described as the duties of care, loyalty and obedience (adherence to the organization's mission). As a leading commentator has described these duties:

> The duty of care concerns the director's competence in performing directorial functions and typically requires him to use the care that an ordinarily prudent person would exercise in a like position and under similar circumstances. The duty of loyalty requires the director's faithful pursuit of the interests of the organization he serves rather than the financial or other interests of the director or of another person or organization. And the duty of obedience requires that a director act with fidelity, within the bounds of the law generally, to the organization's 'mission', as expressed in its charter and bylaws.[1]

These duties are discussed in separate sections of this chapter, but it should be emphasized that they are, in principle and in practice, overlapping, reenforcing, and cumulative, representing an *integrated* set of responsibilities to the well-being and success of the nonprofit organization.

Duty of Care

The duties of directors and officers, vìs-a-vìs the corporation, are provided by state law, and to the extent not so provided, by the articles of incorporation and bylaws. The duty of care is defined by statute in a majority of the states. For example, New York's *Not-for-Profit Corporation Law* provides, concerning the duty of care, that directors and officers shall exercise the "degree of diligence, care and skill which ordinarily prudent men would exercise under similar circumstances in like positions."[2] A comprehensive definition of the duty of care, incorporating elements found in many separate state statutes and in the common law, is set forth in the *Revised Model Nonprofit Corporation Act.*

Section 8.30: GENERAL STANDARDS FOR DIRECTORS

(a) A director shall discharge his or her duties as a director, including his or her duties as a member of a committee:
    (1) in good faith;
    (2) with the care an ordinarily prudent person in a like position would exercise under similar circumstances; and
    (3) in a manner the director reasonably believes to be in the best interests of the corporation.

(b) In discharging his or her duties a director is entitled to rely on information, opinions, reports, or statements, including financial statements and other financial data, if prepared or presented by:
    (1) one or more officers or employees of the corporation whom the director reasonably believes to be reliable and competent in the matters presented;
    (2) legal counsel, public accountants or other persons as to matters the director reasonably believes are within the person's professional or expert competence; or
    (3) a committee of the board of which the director is not a member, as to matters within its jurisdiction, if the director reasonably believes the committee merits confidence.

(c) A director is not acting in good faith if the director has knowledge concerning the matter in question that makes reliance otherwise permitted by subsection (b) unwarranted.

(d) A director is not liable for the performance of the duties of his or her office if the director acted in compliance with this section.[3]

Although the foregoing language is addressed to the duties of directors, the applicable law would be substantially the same for officers.

The foregoing standard is applied on a *circumstantial* basis; thus, a volunteer director who is also president of a nonprofit dance company would be subject to the same standard of care as a director who is a university president. The standard, however, would be applied more rigorously to the full-time, compensated university president. The duties of one director are a duty of all directors; however, the circumstantial application of that standard may be higher or lower depending on an individual's skills and experience. Thus, a corporate lawyer could be expected to be sensitive immediately to a problem of antitrust exposure, whereas a lay director, and perhaps even a criminal lawyer, might not be expected to have that immediate perception.

All directors share in the duty of care; the responsibility of the board in this regard cannot be divided between one director and another. For example, pursuant to the obligations hereinafter described, all directors are responsible for seeing that the corporation acts in a manner that complies with the requirements of the applicable law. It may be that one member of the board will be particularly informed and sensitive to legal compliance. If so, he or she should draw these issues to the board's attention and the board should determine whether or not to rely upon that person's judgment in the resolution of the problem. The members of the board cannot say "legal issues will be handled by Jones and financial issues by Smith," and then go on to other business. The *responsibility* remains the same for all directors on an individual and collective basis. If the board determines to follow Jones's or Smith's advice, it must be because the board has reasonable confidence that he or she has examined the problem and merits confidence in its resolution.

In a nonprofit corporation there may be, with respect to legal problems, a particular difficulty because many have lawyer-directors who, understandably and quite properly, were not chosen for the specific *legal* knowledge that the organization may require. Rather, these lawyer-directors may serve on the board because of a deep interest in the nonprofit's program, for their fund-raising abilities, for governmental and political experience, or for other reasons. This suggests the importance of the board relying, to the greatest extent possible, on independent professional (including legal) advice provided, with or without fee, by professionals knowledgeable about nonprofit organizations who are *not* themselves members of the board.

When acting in good faith, officers and directors are entitled to rely on financial and other records of the organization certified as accurate by the executive director or other responsible officer, or by a certified public accountant; officers are also entitled to rely in good faith on the advice and reports of officers, counsel, and appropriately chosen consultants and committees even if such advice is later found to be mistaken. Usually the board relies on advice of a lawyer not a member of the board who has the specific responsibility of analyzing or dealing with the legal problem identified by the board. Nonprofit corporations themselves, and particularly directors who are lawyers, should avoid the risks of giving or receiving casual advice or suggestions on legal issues and the board should avoid relying upon such casual advice.

The Duty of Loyalty

The second principal duty of a director and officer is that of undivided loyalty to the interests of the nonprofit organization's mission and basic well being. The duty of loyalty requires that the director not use his or her position to further other conflicting interests—individual, family, or corporate—including the interests of other nonprofit organizations that he or she may be affiliated with, and which may have an interest in doing business with, or otherwise receiving a benefit from, the nonprofit organization.

To provide for effective enforcement of the duty of loyalty, nonprofit organizations should adopt conflict of interest policies and procedures for their directors and officers, involving regular dissemination of the conflict of interest policy, collecting of relevant information, and careful and periodic assessment of this information by a committee of the board, if not the full board. Under a typical conflict of interest policy, a director may be a party to a transaction in which he or she or an affiliated entity or person has a substantial interest, if his or her interest is disclosed or known to the board of directors, and his or her vote is not counted in approving the transaction. Officers may be held to similar standards; however, abstention from participating in discussions and from voting on any such matter is recommended, and greater restrictions may be adopted by the board of directors, in a specific policy and/or by modification of the bylaws (see p. 111).

Adherence to the Organization's Mission (Duty of Obedience)

It is a significant and distinctive responsibility of nonprofit directors to insure that nonprofit organizations operate to further their stated objectives. "Unless allowed by law, nonprofit directors may not deviate in any substantial way from the duty to fulfill the particular purposes for which the organization was created."[4] Thus, while enjoying considerable latitude and protection from liability in deciding the best means and overall strategy to fulfill the organization's purposes, the directors are held ultimately responsible to insure that the organization substantially adheres to its particular purposes.

Liability of Directors and Officers

Liability of directors and officers to third parties may be limited by state law; again, by way of example, New York's *Not-For-Profit Corporation Law* provides that no person serving without compensation as an officer, director, or trustee of a nonprofit organization described in section 501(c)(3) of the Internal Revenue Code "shall be liable to any person" other than the not-for-profit organization itself "based solely on his or her conduct in the execution of such office unless the conduct of such director, officer or trustee . . . constituted gross negligence or was intended to cause the resulting harm to the person asserting such liability."[5] It should be noted, however, that reimbursement for the expense of attending meetings usually *does not* constitute compensation. It is strongly recommended that officers and directors not rely on such provisions to provide full protection, but rather fully inform themselves of the scope of indemnification and any related insurance made available to them by the statute itself (see p. 131). The director should note that exoneration statutes also do not prohibit suits such as those described above and may not apply to causes of action arising under federal law—for example, the Internal Revenue Code creates presumptive liability of a director or officer for unpaid withholding taxes of employees. The affected director or officer may relieve him or herself from this liability by a showing that he or she held no responsibility for financial transactions but to establish this defense the director would have the burden of proof.

State law may authorize indemnification provisions in the bylaws, as well as the purchase of directors' and officers' liability insurance; for example New York *Not-For-Profit Corporation Law* sections 721, 722, and 723, provide that the basic standard for coverage is a finding that the officer acted in "good faith" in the discharge of his or her duties, and for purposes reasonably believed to be in the best interest of the organization.[6]

The exact status of such indemnification provisions under state law, bylaws, and insurance policies to implement such protection will be of significant interest and importance to all officers and directors entering into service for a nonprofit organization. The secretary and counsel should at all times be aware of such coverages and be able to advise officers and directors accordingly. In organizations active in more than one state, the diversity of these provisions may be troublesome.

Notes

1. Daniel L. Kurtz, *Board Liability: A Guide for Nonprofit Directors* (Mt. Kisco, NY: Moyer Bell Limited, 1988), 21.

2. N.Y. Not-For-Profit Corp. Law § 717 (McKinney 1996).
3. Model Nonprofit Corp. Act (1987).
4. Daniel L. Kurtz, *Board Liability*, 85.
5. N.Y. Not-For-Profit Corp. Law § 720-a (McKinney 1996).
6. N.Y. Not-For-Profit Corp. Law §§ 721-23 (McKinney 1986).

Bibliography

Overton, George W., ed. *Guidebook for Directors of Nonprofit Corporations.* Chicago: American Bar Association, 1993.

Kurtz, Daniel L. *Board Liability: Guide for Nonprofit Directors.* Mt. Kisco, NY: Moyer Bell Limited, 1988.

Runquist, Lisa A. *Responsibilities and Duties of a Director of a Nonprofit Organization.* [Englewood Cliffs, NJ]: Maxwell-MacMillan Charitable Giving and Solicitations Service, 1995.

———. "A Job Description for Directors." *Business Law Today* 4, no. 2 (1994): 10–15.

Exhibit 1
The Attorney General's Guide for Board Members
of Charitable Organizations

The Commonwealth of Massachusetts
Office of the Attorney General
One Ashburton Place
Boston, USA 02108-1698

SCOTT HARSHBARGER
ATTORNEY GENERAL

Dear Board Member:

The Office of the Attorney General offers this guidance to the members of governing boards of charitable organizations, with an appreciation of your willingness to volunteer for service as a charity board member.

You are performing a public service of the highest order—standing up to the challenge when it would be easier to sit back and let others handle it. On behalf of the public, this office thanks you for your hard work and dedication.

Sincerely,

Scott Harshbarger

Exhibit 1 is reprinted with the permission of the Office of the Attorney General, The Commonwealth of Massachusetts.

Introduction

This Guide is provided by the Attorney General's Office to help board members of charitable organizations, and is particularly meant to assist the board members of charitable corporations and associations in the exercise of your important responsibilities.

Often we are asked what we think the most important things are that a board member should do in order to do a good job. Here are our recommendations in key areas of charity stewardship. While this is not intended to prescribe the exact manner in which a Massachusetts charitable board must function, and while we recognize that charities vary greatly in the size, form and structure of their boards, we believe that this Guide will help all board members do their jobs well.

The Buck Stops with You

If you are a member of the board of a charitable organization, you and your fellow board members are responsible for governing the charity as it carries out its charitable mission. The law imposes upon you two primary duties. The duty of care means that you must act with such care as an ordinarily prudent person would employ in your position. The duty of loyalty means that you must act in good faith and in a manner that you reasonably believe is in the best interest of your charitable organization. As discussed throughout this Guide, it is your job to oversee your chief executive officer and to see that the charity is faithfully carrying out its purpose without extravagance or waste.

This means:

> You should attend board meetings and meetings of committees on which you serve. You should make sure that you receive detailed information beforehand about matters which are going to be voted on at a meeting.

> You should carefully read all the material which you receive, and prepare yourself to ask questions.

> You should use your own judgment, and not simply take the word of your CEO or fellow board members.

In short:

> You should be aware of and informed about every major action the charity takes.

Know Your Rights

In order to carry out your legal responsibilities as a board member, you must be able to make informed judgments about important matters affecting the provision of charitable services to the community served by the charity. The law permits you to reasonably rely on information from the charity's staff, its lawyer, its accountant, outside advisors, and board committees in making those judgments. If you don't have adequate information, you have the right to get it.

This means:

You have the right to have reasonable access to management.

You have the right to have reasonable access to internal information of the organization.

You have the right to have reasonable access to the organization's principal advisors, such as its auditors and consultants on executive compensation.

Senior management must be willing to facilitate board access to books and records of the charity.

Senior management must be willing to facilitate communications between the board and the principal advisors of the charity.

The board has the right, if necessary, to engage the services of outside advisors at the charity's expense to assist it with a particular matter.

In short:

You have the right to obtain the information you need to carry out your responsibilities as a board member.

Make Sure Your Board Is Vital and Diverse

A charity's board should be vigorous and responsive to the mission of the charity. You should make sure that your board's process of selecting new members assures diversity of viewpoints and rotation of board members and officers. As a board member, you have the responsibility for ensuring that the public and charitable role of the charity will be carried out in a way that is most beneficial to the charity. A nominating process which invites openness, variety, and change is important to achieving this goal.

This means:

> Your nominating process should reach out for candidates, and actively recruit individuals whose commitment, skills, life experience, background, perspective or other characteristics will serve the charity and its needs.

> A larger candidate pool may result if you include non-board members as well as board members on your nominating committee.

> Term limits for board members can be an effective way to ensure board vitality. If your board does not have term limits, board members should be reviewed periodically to confirm that they remain interested in and suitable for the board. Rotation off the board, assignments to off-board committees, and designation as emeritus members are other ways to achieve a vigorous board.

In short:

> To avoid becoming labeled as a closed club for "insiders only," choose board members who have an interest in the charity's mission, represent diverse viewpoints, and have a willingness to learn—and then be sure there are opportunities for board renewal.

Know Your Chief Executive Officer

Hiring the charity's CEO is one of the most important tasks you have. It is the job of the board to engage in a selection process which will allow the board to find the right person to carry out the charity's purpose efficiently and effectively. The charity for which you are responsible can only benefit when the entire board participates in hiring and evaluating its chief executive employee.

This means:

> The board should form a search committee at the beginning of the hiring process.

> A majority of the search committee members should be board members, but it may be beneficial to include staff members and other able people.

> The board should develop a profile of the person most likely to succeed as CEO of the charity it oversees, and look for someone who matches the profile.

If the size of the board permits, the entire board should interview the final candidates and participate in contacting their references.

The entire board should make the final decision to hire the CEO.

After the CEO is hired, the board should periodically review and assess the chief executive's performance, keeping in mind that the board has the authority to discharge as well as hire the CEO.

In short:

Board members should actively participate in selecting and evaluating the charity's CEO.

Get Involved in Setting Executive Compensation

The board is responsible for setting the compensation of the charity's chief executive employee. When setting CEO compensation, you should be mindful that the public, which supports the charity and uses its services, is interested in knowing the amount. This information is public in Massachusetts and is on file at the Division of Public Charities, Office of the Attorney General, One Ashburton Place, Boston, MA 02108.

This means:

Every board member should know what the CEO is paid. If the CEO is receiving a compensation package, you should know what it includes and its monetary value.

Even if a compensation committee is used, it should not make the final decision.

In setting compensation, the performance of your CEO and salary scales and fringe benefits of other similarly situated executives in the field are factors to consider.

You should remember that CEO compensation is important to the donors of funds, the beneficiaries of the charity, and the community at large.

In short:

Your process for setting CEO compensation, the amount of such compensation, and the terms of such compensation should all be approved by the full board and be sensitive to public concerns.

Beware of Conflicts of Interest

You, or a business you control or benefit from financially, may be considering whether or not to engage in a transaction with the charity on whose board you are sitting. A situation of this type presents a potential conflict between your own financial interests and your duty as a board member to be absolutely loyal to the charity. It also may look questionable to the public.

Because of these problems, a board member or related entity should be cautious about entering into a business relationship with the charity the board member is overseeing, and the board should be very cautious about allowing the charity to enter into such a relationship. Such a transaction should not occur unless the board determines it is clearly in the best interest of the charity. Prior to the board vote, the board member should fully disclose his or her financial interest to the entire board, and the board member should not vote on any aspect of the arrangement or be present when it is being discussed or voted upon.

This means:

> You should ensure that your board has a policy for dealing with conflicts of interest.

> The policy should include a procedure for the annual written disclosure by all board members of their business involvements with the charity and their other board memberships, both for-profit and charitable. The information disclosed should be circulated to all board members and be updated throughout the year as necessary.

> Your conflict-of-interest policy should address the issues raised if board members have or might acquire investments that may affect or be affected by the charity's investment decisions.

> The policy should also include a procedure for the following: disclosure of financial interest, and withdrawal from discussion and voting by the involved board member. This policy should be followed whenever the charity enters into a business transaction with a board member or with an entity in which a board member has an interest.

> It may be advisable to obtain an outside evaluation of any major business transaction which is being proposed between the charity and a board member or an entity in which a board member has an interest. This evaluation is to assure that the proposal is feasible, the terms are favorable to the charity, and the potential pitfalls of such a transaction have been considered.

Because of the sensitivity of conflict-of-interest issues, you may want to require that transactions involving these issues receive a greater-than-majority vote.

The Attorney General recommends that conflict-of-interest policies require that each board member make an annual disclosure to the entire board of the total amount the board member received from the charity during the previous year as a vendor of goods to the charity or on account of services rendered to the charity. Massachusetts law already requires this disclosure to be made on the annual reporting form filed by the charity.

In short:

Any conflict transaction should be scrutinized very closely by the board, both because of the dynamic it creates within the board and because of the predictable skepticism with which the public will view the transaction, no matter how scrupulously a careful policy is followed.

Follow the Money

As a board member you have primary responsibility for making sure that the charity is financially accountable, has mechanisms in place to keep it fiscally sound, operates in a fiscally sound manner, and is properly using any restricted funds it may have.

This means:

The board should make sure that a realistic annual budget is developed.

The budget should be developed early enough so that the entire board can be involved in its review and approval before the beginning of the fiscal year.

The board should be sure that the charity has adequate internal accounting systems.

Board members should expect management to produce timely and accurate income and expense statements, balance sheets and budget status reports and should expect to receive these in advance of board meetings.

The board should require periodic confirmation from management that all required filings (such as tax returns and the Massachusetts Form PC) are up-to-date and that employee withholding taxes and insurance premiums are being paid when due.

The board should consider the value of maintaining standing audit and finance committees.

The board should make sure that fund-raising is done honestly and with integrity. The board also should make sure that any contract with an outside professional fund-raiser is fair and reasonable, and that the fund-raiser's performance is monitored.

The board should confirm that any restricted gift to the charity is separately accounted for, and that the funds are being used in accordance with the terms of the restriction.

In short:

The board should be involved and informed in all aspects of the finances of the charity.

Educate Yourself

A member of the board of a charity should be knowledgeable about his or her role in the governing process, the mission of the charity, and the unique operational and financial issues which face the charity.

This means:

You should have a copy of and be familiar with the articles of organization of your charity and the by-laws of your board.

You should make sure that board education programs are offered regularly.

Particular attention should be given to providing educational opportunities for new board members.

Programs should draw on the expertise of specialists in the fields related to your board responsibilities.

If your board does not have a board manual containing governing documents and other orientation material, it may want to consider developing one.

In short:

As a board member, you must take the initiative to educate yourself on an ongoing basis about your role and responsibilities.

Where This Gets You

If you follow the advice provided here, you will be a productive and effective member of your board. You will have taken the right steps to guard against the possibility of a lawsuit because of disregard or neglect of your duty of loyalty or your duty of care. And you will experience the rewards and personal satisfaction that come with a job well done.

Resources to Assist You in Your Responsibilities

For a detailed list of books, pamphlets and articles on the responsibilities of charity board members, and a collection of other relevant materials, call the Division of Public Charities in the Office of the Attorney General (617-727-2200 x2101) and ask for the Board Members' Packet.

For training programs, technical assistance, and access to a resource library, call the New England Institute for Non-Profits at Tufts University (617-627-3549).

For help in finding legal and accounting assistance, and management training workshops, call the Support Center of Massachusetts (617-338-1331).

This Guide was developed with the assistance of the Attorney General's Advisory Committee on Public Charities, whose valuable help is gratefully acknowledged. Because this Guide is not a summary of the law and is not intended as a substitute for legal advice, we suggest you consult qualified legal counsel if specific questions arise concerning matters addressed by the Guide.

Exhibit 2
GM Board Guidelines on Significant
Corporate Governance Issues

Index

Selection and Composition of the Board

1) Board membership criteria
2) Selection and orientation of new Directors
3) Extending the invitation to a potential Director to join the Board

Board Leadership

4) Selection of Chairman and CEO
5) Lead Director Concept

Board Composition and Performance

6) Size of the Board
7) Mix of inside and outside Directors
8) Board definition of what constitutes independence for outside Directors
9) Former Chief Executive Officer's Board membership
10) Directors who change their present job responsibility
11) Term limits
12) Retirement age
13) Board compensation review
14) Executive sessions of outside Directors
15) Assessing the Board's performance
16) Board's interaction with institutional investors, press, customers, etc.

Board Relationship to Senior Management

17) Regular attendance of non-Directors at Board meetings
18) Board access to senior management

Meeting Procedures

19) Selection of agenda items for Board meetings
20) Board materials distributed in advance
21) Board presentations

Committee Matters

22) Number, structure and independence of Committees
23) Assignment and rotation of Committee members
24) Frequency and length of Committee meetings
25) Committee agenda

Leadership Development

26) Formal evaluation of the Chief Executive Officer
27) Succession planning
28) Management development

Exhibit 2 is reprinted with the permission of General Motors Corporation.

The Mission of the General Motors Board of Directors

The General Motors Board of Directors represents the owners' interest in perpetuating a successful business, including optimizing long term financial returns. The Board is responsible for determining that the Corporation is managed in such a way to ensure this result. This is an active, not a passive, responsibility. The Board has the responsibility to ensure that in good times, as well as difficult ones, Management is capably executing its responsibilities. The Board's responsibility is to regularly monitor the effectiveness of Management policies and decisions including the execution of its strategies.

In addition to fulfilling its obligations for increased stockholder value, the Board has responsibility to GM's customers, employees, suppliers and to the communities where it operates—all of whom are essential to a successful business. All of these responsibilities, however, are founded upon the successful perpetuation of the business.

Guidelines on Significant Corporate Governance Issues

Selection and Composition of the Board

1) Board Membership Criteria

The Committee on Director Affairs is responsible for reviewing with the Board, on an annual basis, the appropriate skills and characteristics required of Board members in the context of the current make-up of the Board. This assessment should include issues of diversity, age, skills such as understanding of manufacturing technologies, international background, etc.—all in the context of an assessment of the perceived needs of the Board at that point in time.

2) Selection and Orientation of New Directors

The Board itself should be responsible, in fact as well as procedure, for selecting its own members and in recommending them for election by the stockholders. The Board delegates the screening process involved to the Committee on Director Affairs with the direct input from the Chairman of the Board, as well as the Chief Executive Officer. The Board and the Company have a complete orientation process for new Directors that includes background materials, meeting with senior management and visits to Company facilities.

3) Extending the Invitation to a Potential Director to Join the Board

The invitation to join the Board should be extended by the Board itself, by the Chairman of the Committee on Director Affairs (if the Chairman and CEO hold the same position), the Chairman of the Board, and the Chief Executive Officer of the Company.

Board Leadership

4) Selection of Chairman and CEO

The Board should be free to make this choice any way that seems best for the Company at a given point in time.

Therefore, the Board does not have a policy, one way or the other, on whether or not the role of the Chief Executive and Chairman should be separate and, if it is to be separate, whether the Chairman should be selected from the non-employee Directors or be an employee.

5) Lead Director Concept

The Board adopted a policy that it have a Director selected by the outside Directors who will assume the responsibility of chairing the regularly scheduled meetings of outside Directors or other responsibilities which the outside Directors as a whole might designate from time to time.

Currently, this role is filled by the non-executive Chairman of the Board. Should the Company be organized in such a way that the Chairman is an employee of the Company, another Director would be selected for this responsibility.

Board Composition and Performance

6) Size of the Board

The Board presently has thirteen members. It is the sense of the Board that a size of fifteen is about right. However, the Board would be willing to go to a somewhat larger size in order to accommodate the availability of an outstanding candidate(s).

7) Mix of Inside and Outside Directors

The Board believes that as a matter of policy, there should be a majority of independent Directors on the GM Board (as stipulated in By-law 2.12). The Board is willing to have members of Management, in addition to the Chief Executive Officer, as Directors. But, the Board believes that Management should encourage senior managers to understand that Board membership is not necessary or a prerequisite to any higher Management position in the Company. Managers other than the Chief Executive Officer currently attend Board Meetings on a regular basis even though they are not members of the Board.

On matters of corporate governance, the Board assumes decisions will be made by the outside Directors.

8) Board Definition of What Constitutes Independence for Outside Directors

GM's By-law defining independent Directors was approved by the Board in January 1991. The Board believes there is no current relationship between any outside Director and GM that would be construed in any way to compromise any Board member being designated independent. Compliance with the By-law is reviewed annually by the Committee on Director Affairs.

9) Former Chief Executive Officer's Board Membership

The Board believes this is a matter to be decided in each individual instance. It is assumed that when the Chief Executive officer resigns from that position, he/she should submit his/her resignation from the Board at the same time. Whether the individual continues to serve on the Board is a matter for discussion at that time with the new Chief Executive Officer and the Board.

A former Chief Executive Officer serving on the Board will be considered an inside Director for purposes of voting on matters of corporate governance.

10) Directors Who Change Their Present Job Responsibility

It is the sense of the Board that individual Directors who change the responsibility they held when they were elected to the Board should submit a letter of resignation to the Board.

It is not the sense of the Board that the Directors who retire or change from the position they held when they came on the Board should necessarily leave the Board. There should, however, be an opportunity for the Board, via the Committee on Director Affairs, to review the continued appropriateness of Board membership under these circumstances.

11) Term Limits

The Board does not believe it should establish term limits. While term limits could help insure that there are fresh ideas and viewpoints available to the Board, they hold the disadvantage of losing the contribution of Directors who have been able to develop, over a period of time, increasing insight into the Company and its operations and, therefore, provide an increasing contribution to the Board as a whole.

As an alternative to term limits, the Committee on Director Affairs, in conjunction with the Chief Executive Officer and the Chairman of the Board, will formally review each Director's continuation on the Board every five years. This will also allow each Director the opportunity to conveniently confirm his/her desire to continue as a member of the Board.

12) Retirement Age

It is the sense of the Board that the current retirement age of 70 is appropriate.

13) Board Compensation Review

It is appropriate for the staff of the Company to report once a year to the Committee on Director Affairs the status of GM Board compensation in relation to other large U.S. companies. As part of a Director's total compensation and to create a direct linkage with corporate performance, the Board believes that a meaningful portion of a Director's compensation should be provided in common stock units.

Changes in Board compensation, if any, should come at the suggestion of the Committee on Director Affairs, but with full discussion and concurrence by the Board.

14) Executive Sessions of Outside Directors

The outside Directors of the Board will meet in Executive Session three times each year. The format of these meetings will include a discussion with the Chief Executive Officer on each occasion.

15) Assessing the Board's Performance

The Committee on Director Affairs is responsible to report annually to the Board an assessment of the Board's performance. This will be discussed with the full Board. This should be done following the end of each fiscal year and at the same time as the report on Board membership criteria.

This assessment should be of the Board's contribution as a whole and specifically review areas in which the Board and/or the Management believes a better contribution could be made. Its purpose is to increase the effectiveness of the Board, not to target individual Board members.

16) Board's Interaction with Institutional Investors, the Press, Customers, etc.

The Board believes that the Management speaks for General Motors. Individual Board members may, from time to time at the request of the Management, meet or otherwise communicate with various constituencies that are involved with General

Motors. If comments from the Board are appropriate, they should, in most circumstances, come from the Chairman.

Board Relationship to Senior Management

17) Regular Attendance of Non-Directors at Board Meetings

The Board welcomes the regular attendance at each Board meeting of non-Board members who are members of the President's Council.

Should the Chief Executive Officer want to add additional people as attendees on a regular basis, it is expected that this suggestion would be made to the Board for its concurrence.

18) Board Access to Senior Management

Board members have complete access to GM's Management.

It is assumed that Board members will use judgment to be sure that this contact is not distracting to the business operation of the Company and that such contact, if in writing, be copied to the Chief Executive and the Chairman.

Furthermore, the Board encourages the Management to, from time to time, bring managers into Board Meetings who: (a) can provide additional insight into the items being discussed because of personal involvement in these areas, and/or (b) represent managers with future potential that the senior management believes should be given exposure to the Board.

Meeting Procedures

19) Selection of Agenda Items for Board Meetings

The Chairman of the Board and the Chief Executive Officer (if the Chairman is not the Chief Executive Officer) will establish the agenda for each Board meeting.

Each Board member is free to suggest the inclusion of item(s) on the agenda.

20) Board Materials Distributed in Advance

It is the sense of the Board that information and data that is important to the Board's understanding of the business be distributed in writing to the Board before the Board meets. The Management will make every attempt to see that this material is as brief as possible while still providing the desired information.

21) Board Presentations

As a general rule, presentations on specific subjects should be sent to the Board members in advance so that Board meeting time may be conserved and discussion time focused on questions that the Board has about the material. On those occasions in which the subject matter is too sensitive to put on paper, the presentation will be discussed at the meeting.

Committee Matters

22) Number, Structure, and Independence of Committees

The current Committee structure of the Company seems appropriate. There will, from time to time, be occasions in which the Board may want to form a new Committee or disband a current Committee depending upon the circumstances. The current six Committees are Audit, Capital Stock, Director Affairs, Finance, Executive Compensation and Public Policy. The Committee membership, with the exception of the Finance Committee, will consist only of independent Directors as stipulated in By-law 2.12.

23) Assignment and Rotation of Committee Members

The Committee on Director Affairs is responsible, after consultation with the Chief Executive Officer and with consideration of the desires of individual Board members, for the assignment of Board members to various Committees.

It is the sense of the Board that consideration should be given to rotating Committee members periodically at about a five year interval, but the Board does not feel that such a rotation should be mandated as a policy since there may be reasons at a given point in time to maintain an individual Director's Committee membership for a longer period.

24) Frequency and Length of Committee Meetings

The Committee Chairman, in consultation with Committee members, will determine the frequency and length of the meetings of the Committee.

25) Committee Agenda

The Chairman of the Committee, in consultation with the appropriate members of the Management and staff, will develop the Committee's agenda.

Each Committee will issue a schedule of agenda subjects to be discussed for the ensuing year at the beginning of each year (to the degree these can be foreseen). This forward agenda will also be shared with the Board.

Leadership Development

26) Formal Evaluation of the Chief Executive Officer

The full Board (outside Directors) should make this evaluation annually, and it should be communicated to the Chief Executive Officer by the (non-executive) Chairman of the Board or the Lead Director.

The evaluation should be based on objective criteria including performance of the business, accomplishment of long-term strategic objectives, development of Management, etc.

The evaluation will be used by the Incentive and Compensation Committee in the course of its deliberations when considering the compensation of the Chief Executive Officer.

27) Succession Planning

There should be an annual report by the Chief Executive Officer to the Board on succession planning.

There should also be available, on a continuing basis, the Chief Executive Officer's recommendation as a successor should he/she be unexpectedly disabled.

28) Management Development

There should be an annual report to the Board by the Chief Executive Officer on the Company's program for Management development.

This report should be given to the Board at the same time as the succession planning report noted previously.

Conflict of Interest Policies and Procedures for Nonprofit Organizations

David B. Rigney

This chapter reviews the purpose and scope of conflict of interest policies for nonprofit organizations, describes the implementation of such policies, and evaluates the significance of such policies for the fiscal integrity, credibility, and well-being of nonprofit organizations.

Introduction

The importance of conflict of interest issues for nonprofit organizations has been increasingly recognized for a variety of reasons. First, conflict of interest policies and codes of ethical conduct have been extensively adopted in the for-profit corporate sector, providing examples and precedents for nonprofit organizations (see Exhibit 1). Second, there is an emerging trend to hold nonprofit organizations, and their directors and officers, to more demanding standards of responsibility, accountability, and public scrutiny. Third, well-publicized examples of conflict of interest and self-dealing among officers of nonprofit organizations have demonstrated the serious harm to the reputation and programs of nonprofit organizations that can be caused when conflict of interest and ethical standards are not sufficiently defined and monitored by nonprofit organizations. Conflict of interest policies deal with disclosure of such conflicts, the duty to disclose, and the actions taken after disclosure.

In light of these important trends, this chapter will have several objectives: (1) to define the principal issues that are typically covered in conflict of interest policies; (2) to evaluate the importance of nonprofit organizations having conflict of interest and ethical policies appropriate to the organization's mission and structure; (3) to comment on the process by which such policies should be evaluated, adopted, and thereafter monitored; and (4) the role of the secretary/counsel in facilitating this process.

Conflict of Interest Policies—Scope and Purpose

Conflict of interest principles and policies to implement such principles seek to prevent persons with decision-making authority in the organization, and who govern the exercise of such authority, from taking actions which benefit themselves, members of their immediate families, or their business and corporate affiliates. The traditional remedy for such situations is disclosure and nonparticipation by the officer or director in any formal decision concerning a transaction in which he or she may have a conflicting interest. If trustee Jones, for example, is also a director of a bank, Jones will not participate as a director of the nonprofit in any preliminary discussion or decision to select that bank to provide services to the nonprofit, or to evaluate the renewal of the engagement at the bank by the nonprofit. Further, when the decision involving the services of Jones's bank comes before any committee or the full board of the nonprofit, Jones should either be absent or not participate during the discussions, and the minutes should reflect the fact that Jones abstained from voting on the matter in question.[1] Other typical examples of transactions that would involve conflict of interest scrutiny would be the lease of office space, sale of real estate or personal property to or from the organization, and contracts for professional services.

Conflict of interest principles also apply to nonprofit organizations in ways that arguably transcend the traditional notion of conflict of interest (individual financial gain in conflict with other duties). For many nonprofit directors and officers, their relationship may involve a "duality" or "diversity" of interests, not involving personal or pecuniary advantage to the individual director or officer but rather to the interests of another nonprofit organization which has, or may seek to have, dealings with the nonprofit organization. A representative example would be the director of a grant-making organization who also sits on the board of a university, hospital, museum, or other nonprofit organization, which seeks assistance from the grant-making organization. It is important for the nonprofit organization to have appropriate conflict of interest guidelines that encompass such "duality" or "diversity" of interests. Such guidelines would seek to avoid participation by the director in any review, discussion, or final action on a proposal to benefit another organization or program in which he or she is otherwise interested.

A particular "twist" on the principle of duality of interest is sometimes found, for example, in the various potential roles of museum trustees, who, in addition, may also be collectors of art or dealers in fields in which the museum has a known, or even potential, interest. Under traditional notions of "corporate opportunity" as applied in this context, the museum trustee would owe the museum the first opportunity to acquire any work of art within the purview of the museum's current or intended collection, which the trustee identifies either through his or her private activities or through his or her activities as a trustee. This means that the trustee might have to abstain from direct bidding for a work in which the museum is also known to be bidding (see Exhibit 2).

In summary, policies for addressing conflicts and dualities of interests among the directors and officers of nonprofit organizations should include the following principal aspects.

(1) **Scope of individuals covered.** At the minimum, all directors, trustees, and officers should be included; depending on the size of the organization, other senior managers and purchasing agents should also be included. The standard for inclusion should be decision-making authority and responsibility of a significant nature; the policy should err, if at all, on the side of inclusion.

(2) **Scope of activities and relationships covered.** All transactions with the organization above a minimum annual value ($5,000, for example) should come under the conflict of interests policies. The term "transaction" should be broadly defined, both in the traditional sense of conflict of interest and in the sense of duality of interest, to include payments for goods and services, as well as grants and other assistance to other nonprofit organizations. Covered relationships should include those of the individual director; a member of his or her immediate family; a partnership, or business in which the director has a minimum percentage (5%, for example) of ownership; or any other institution in which the director is also a director or officer. In some recently publicized cases, nonprofit boards have been criticized for awarding lucrative contracts to past directors of the organization. The organization's

policies might also denote a transitional period in which transactions with former board members would be subject to the same scrutiny as transactions involving current board members or officers.

(3) **Standards and Procedures.** To properly implement conflict of interest/duality of interest principles as outlined above, it is suggested that the following procedures be followed by the nonprofit organization.

(a) There should be annual disclosure, *in writing*, by all covered individuals such as directors, officers, and senior managers of any transactions or relationships involving a possible conflict or duality of interest involving the nonprofit organization. Either the counsel or the secretary should be responsible for preparing, distributing, collecting, and initially analyzing all such disclosure forms. A typical form would ask, for example, "In the past calendar year did you, a member of your immediate family, a partnership, or a business of which you own at least 5 percent of the equity, or any other organization of which you are a director or officer, provide goods or services to us, or receive a grant or other assistance of a value above $5,000 from us? If answered yes, details should be given" (see Exhibit 3).

(b) When any matter involving a conflict of interest is under consideration by the nonprofit organization, the interested director or officer should abstain from any preliminary or final involvement with the matter, including preliminary review and discussion, as well as any vote at the committee or full board level. This restriction should be understood to extend to "lobbying" members of the staff, or other directors or officers "informally," concerning the matter in question. On the other hand, this constraint should not be understood to prohibit a director or officer from answering questions about or explaining the proposed transaction, or speaking directly on an issue of broad policy that may have relevance to actions taken by the board affecting the interest of the director. The director may discuss the need for more funding for primary health care, for example, but should not actively support a particular funding request submitted by a health-care organization in which he or she has an interest.

Whenever a director or officer abstains from participation in a committee or board vote, the abstention should be formally recorded in the minutes of the organization.

Further, there should be an annual summary and analysis of the disclosure forms, and a record of related abstentions from discussion and voting, prepared by the secretary or counsel, and made available, at least initially, to the chairman and executive director, and a committee of the board specifically identified to review such matters. It is further recommended that a summary of the conflict of interest disclosures and abstentions during the past calendar year be recorded in the minutes of the organization; in the climate of increased scrutiny and accountability, the organization may wish to consider disclosing in its annual report at least the fact of the conflict/duality of interest policy.

Importance of Conflict of Interest Policies to Nonprofit Organizations

If properly adopted and administered, conflict of interest policies can serve several valuable functions for the organization, its directors, officers, and staff, and ultimately its constituents. First, in their most traditional purpose, conflict of interest policies, through disclosure and abstention, can help to insure both that the organization receives fair value for the goods and services it obtains and that no one affiliated with the organization receives an unfair benefit from such affiliation. This might be viewed as protecting the economic or fiscal interests of the organization. Important as this purpose is, both in principle and in practice, there is a potentially more substantial interest protected by such policies (especially for nonprofit organizations): the confidence of the donor/constituency/public community in the integrity, honesty, and mission of the organization. This is also important for Internal Revenue Service (IRS) reasons—to insure that no unwarranted benefits are conferred on officers and directors. From a complementary perspective, the adoption and thorough implementation of conflict of interest policies and procedures is a primary means by which the board and officers of a nonprofit can assure themselves that their duties of loyalty and care to the organization are being fulfilled. It is therefore, arguably, even more important for a nonprofit organization than a publicly traded corporation to have clear conflict of interest policies in place. The capital and strength of a nonprofit is its reputation, integrity, and quality of programs. A conflict of interest policy, however, can only be effective to the extent it is viewed as serving and protecting the basic interests of the organization in seeing that the directors fulfill their fundamental duties and responsibilities. If it is not viewed in this fundamental context but rather is regarded as little more than a form to be filled out annually and filed in the secretary's drawer, it is of limited value at best. This process ultimately must have the full and active support of the chief executive officer and the board as it is critical to the fulfillment of the mission of the organization and the duties of its directors.

Role of the Secretary or Counsel in Adopting and Implementing Conflict of Interest Policies

The secretary or counsel can, and should, play a basic role in assisting the organization to focus on the policy issues involved in the adoption and implementation of a conflict of interest policy.

(1) The secretary or counsel should examine existing policies and procedures, and to the extent practical, consult with the chair and/or executive director concerning the policy issues involved in conflict of interest matters. The threshold point is to insure that conflict of interest matters are addressed directly and substantially by the organization.

(2) Assuming this initial leadership consensus is established, it is suggested that a special or standing committee be designated to evaluate these issues and make recommendations for ultimate review by the board; the secretary or counsel should play a leading role as staff to the committee for this purpose, in assembling relevant policies (see Exhibit 4).

(3) Upon adoption of a conflict/duality of interest policy, the secretary or counsel should be responsible for managing the process of distributing, collecting, and analyzing the disclosure forms, for recording abstentions from discussion, and voting at the committee and board level.

Other Policy Issues

In adopting and implementing conflict of interest policies, nonprofit organizations should also consider whether there are any inherent, or practical, limits to the objectives that can be achieved by such policies. Thus, even assuming the full procedural implementation of a conflict of interest policy through disclosure and abstention of the interested director, should a director or officer be in the position where his or her firm or business gains material financial benefit from goods and services provided to the nonprofit organization? This relationship may become particularly awkward—and counter-productive—when the organization may have reason to question the quality of the advice or service provided by the director's firm. In these circumstances, other directors may find it difficult to separate their views of the fellow director from a more dispassionate review of the quality of the service provided by the director or her or his firm. As noted above, there are also the IRS implications of issues of inurement to directors.[2]

Conclusion

A variety of legal and policy trends place increasing responsibilities on the directors, officers, and staff of nonprofit organizations to assure the integrity and accountability of their organizations. By a thorough review of issues involving conflict of interest and the adoption of policies to monitor and avoid such conflicts, directors of nonprofit organizations will have acted to further their fundamental duties and responsibilities in the management of the nonprofit organization, and by doing so, will strengthen the quality and integrity of their organizations.

Notes

1. Note, however, that there is no conflict of interest *vis-a-vis* the nonprofit where Jones uses his or her position with the bank to monitor its services to the nonprofit.
2. Allan D. Ullberg, *Museum Trusteeship* (Washington, D.C.: American Association of Museums, 1981).

Bibliography

Kurtz, Daniel L. *How to Manage Conflicts of Interest: A Guide for Nonprofit Boards.* Washington, D.C.: National Center for Nonprofit Boards, 1995.

Kurtz, Daniel L. *Managing Conflicts of Interest.* New York: Practicing Law Institute, 1995.

Ullberg, Alan D. *Museum Trusteeship.* Washington, D.C.: American Association of Museums, 1981.

Exhibit 1
American Society of Corporate Secretaries
Sample Corporate Conflict of Interest Policy

Subject: CONFLICT OF INTEREST POLICY

The Board of Directors of _____ has adopted the following policy to assure that the affairs of the Company and its employees are managed in an ethical manner, free from the temptations for personal gain which conflicting desires may provide. There are no exceptions to this policy.

The Company expects all employees and directors to exercise good judgment and the highest ethical standards in their private activities outside the Company which in any way can affect the Company. In particular, every employee and director has an obligation to avoid any activity, agreement, business investment or interest, or other situation which is in conflict with the Company's interests or interferes with the duty to serve the Company at all times to the best of the person's ability. To implement this principle and to establish clear guidelines, the following policy has been adopted:

1. No employee or director shall furnish Services to or seek or receive, for personal or any other person's gain, any payment, whether for services or otherwise, loan (except from a bank), gift or discount of more than nominal value, or entertainment which goes beyond common courtesies usually associated with accepted business practice, from any business enterprise which is a competitor of the Company or has current or known prospective dealings with the Company as a supplier, customer, lessor or lessee, except with the prior written approval of the Chief Executive Officer upon complete disclosure of the facts.

2. No employee or director shall for personal or any other person's gain deprive the Company of any opportunity for benefit which could be construed as related to any existing or reasonably anticipated future activity of the Company.

3. No employee or director shall for personal or any other person's gain make use of or disclose confidential information learned as a result of employment by the Company.

4. No employee shall have any outside interest which materially interferes with the time or attention the employee should devote to the Company.

Exhibit 1 is reprinted with the permission of the American Society of Corporate Secretaries.

5. No employee or director shall have a direct or indirect financial interest in, or receive any compensation or other benefits as a result of, transactions between any individual or business firm:

(a) From which the Company purchases supplies, materials or property;

(b) Which renders any service to the Company;

(c) Which enter into leases or assignments to or from the Company;

(d) To which the Company sells any of its products, materials, facilities or properties;

(e) Which has any other contractual relations or business dealings with the Company;

except with the prior written approval of the Chief Executive Officer upon complete disclosure of the facts.

The financial interests mentioned above do not include interests in corporations listed on a national stock exchange or traded over the counter, providing the financial interest is one percent or less of said corporation's outstanding shares.

6. If any employee or director or member of his or her family has or is about to assume an interest or other outside relationship which might result in a conflict of interest, it is the employee's responsibility immediately to give all the pertinent information to the Chief Executive Officer, who shall report all information to the Audit Committee of the Board of Directors.

Exhibit 2
The Art Institute of Chicago
Policy Statement Concerning Possible Conflicts of Interest

FULL NAME
ADDRESS1
ADDRESS2
ADDRESS3
ADDRESS4

Dear *SALUTATION*:

Article 8 of the Bylaws of The Art Institute of Chicago provides that a conflict of interest on the part of any Trustee must be disclosed to the Board of Trustees annually. Conflicts of interest arise when a Trustee *or a member of a Trustee's immediate family* personally benefits from their association with the Art Institute either directly or through a business relationship.

In some cases, the business firm with which the Trustee is affiliated is performing important services for the Art Institute on an arm's-length basis. The Board feels that these relationships may be continued as long as there is public disclosure thereof. Several years ago the Board of Trustees developed a Policy Statement for the guidance of Trustees and members of the Standing and Advisory Committees of the Board of Trustees. Subsequently, we extended the applicability of this Policy Statement to the members of the Woman's Board and the Auxiliary Board as well. As we approach the end of our fiscal year, we must again consider this matter. Enclosed is a copy of our Policy Statement concerning possible conflicts of interest for your review. Will you please complete the enclosed questionnaire (a sample response is enclosed for your reference) and return it to the Office of Administrative Affairs no later than July 1, 1995.

Once we have received the questionnaires, the information will be summarized, and the entire Board will have the opportunity to review the data and make recommendations on the manner in which it should be disclosed in this year's annual report. A copy of the disclosure footnote to last year's financial statements also is enclosed for your information.

Thank you very much for your support.

Very truly yours,

Exhibit 2 is reprinted with the permission of The Art Institute of Chicago.

The Art Institute of Chicago
Policy Statement Concerning Possible Conflicts of Interest

Members of the Board of Trustees
and Standing and Advisory Committees

GENERAL POLICY

Members of the Board of Trustees, members of Standing and Advisory Committees and members of the Woman's Board and Auxiliary Board of The Art Institute of Chicago (the "Institute") must conduct their personal affairs in such a manner as to avoid any possible conflict of interest with their duties and responsibilities as members of The Art Institute of Chicago organization.

As to the Trustees, the Bylaws were amended in 1977 to provide as follows:

ARTICLE VIII

Any duality of interest on the part of any Trustee shall be disclosed to the Board of Trustees, and made a matter of record through an annual procedure and also when the interest becomes a matter of Trustee action.

Any Trustee having a duality of interest shall not vote or use his personal influence on the matter, and he shall not be counted in determining the quorum for the meeting. The minutes of the meeting shall reflect that a disclosure was made, the abstention from voting and the quorum situation.

Any new Trustee will be advised of this policy upon entering the duties of his office.

A like standard shall apply to members of all Standing and Advisory Committees and members of the Woman's Board and the Auxiliary Board. *All such policies shall also be applicable to any member of one's immediate family or any person acting on his or her behalf.*

Trustees, Committee members, Woman's Board and Auxiliary Board members will be required to attest annually to their familiarity with Institute policies in this regard and to provide information concerning any possible conflict of interest so that disclosure may, if necessary, be made.

Whenever there exists a conflict the matter in question shall be made public by disclosure in the Annual Report unless otherwise directed by the Trustees.

SPECIFIC APPLICATION OF GENERAL POLICY

1. *Financial Interests:*

"Financial interest" for this purpose shall mean any position as owner, officer, board member, partner, employee or other beneficiary. A possible conflict of interest arises when a Trustee, Committee member, or member of the Woman's Board or Auxiliary Board holds a financial interest in or will receive any personal benefit from a business firm furnishing services, materials or supplies to the Institute. Assuming that the amount of business done by the Institute with any publicly held company has virtually no effect on the total results of such a company, "financial interest" shall not include the ownership of shares in a publicly held corporation.

2. *Collecting:*

A potential area of conflict of interest arises when a Trustee, Committee member, or member of the Woman's Board or Auxiliary Board collects objects of a type collected by the Art Institute. Therefore, no Trustee, Committee member, or member of the Woman's Board or Auxiliary Board shall knowingly compete with the Institute in the acquisition of objects. In the matter of collecting, any time that a conflict arises between the needs of the Institute and a person identified above, those of the Institute must prevail. No Trustee, Committee member, or member of the Woman's Board or Auxiliary Board shall bid at auction on an object which is being offered for sale by the Art Institute.

3. *Use of Institute Services, Property or Facilities:*

Another area of potential conflict involves the use of Institute services or facilities. When a Trustee, Committee member, or member of the Woman's Board or Auxiliary Board seek staff assistance or the use of Institute property or facilities they should not expect that such assistance will be rendered to an extent greater than that available to a member of the general public in similar circumstances or with similar needs. To the extent that extraordinary assistance is provided, there should be a clear understanding of how this assistance will benefit the Institute.

4. *Privileged Information:*

A Trustee, Committee member, or member of the Woman's Board or Auxiliary Board must never use information received while serving the Institute if the personal use of such information would be detrimental in any way to the Institute. Any actions that might impair the reputation of the Institute must also be avoided.

5. *Dealing:*

Trustees and members of curatorial committees shall not deal in fine art, *i.e.*, they shall not buy and sell for profit on a regular basis, maintain a financial interest in any dealership or gallery other than a passive interest of 5% or less or receive a commission or other compensation for facilitating purchases or sales of fine art. This policy shall apply to all new members elected after August 13, 1990, the date of adoption of this policy.

SAMPLE **RESPONSE**
THE ART INSTITUTE OF CHICAGO
CONFLICT OF INTEREST QUESTIONNAIRE

NAME   *Mrs. John Jones*

HOME ADDRESS   *123 Lake Avenue, Wilmette, IL 60091*

ASSOCIATION WITH ART INSTITUTE OF CHICAGO   *member of Asian Art Committee and Women's Board*

BUSINESS AND PROFESSIONAL ACTIVITIES IN WHICH YOU OR AN IMMEDIATE FAMILY MEMBER HOLD AN OWNER, OFFICER, BOARD MEMBER, PARTNER, EMPLOYEE OR OTHER BENEFICIARY POSITION AS OF JUNE 30, 1995.

NAME OF BUSINESS/PROFESSIONAL ORGANIZATIONS WITH WHICH YOU ARE ASSOCIATED	**POSITION HELD/BY WHOM**
XYZ Bank of Chicago	*Vice President - Husband*
Midwest Graphics Service	*Owner - Self*

BEFORE COMPLETING THIS QUESTIONNAIRE: This Questionnaire should be completed only after a careful reading of the Policy Statement concerning Possible Conflicts of Interest. Your response should cover the period July 1, 1994 (or the day you became associated with the Institute if subsequent to this date) through June 30, 1995.

MAIL TO: Office of the Executive Vice President of Administrative Affairs
The Art Institute of Chicago
111 S. Michigan Avenue
Chicago, Illinois 60603-6110

AFFIRMATION: I have read The Art Institute of Chicago Statement of Policy as amended August 13, 1990 and September 13, 1993. I understand its provisions and I hereby affirm that, during the period indicated above, I have not, to the best of my knowledge and belief, been in a position of possible conflict of interest, except as indicated below:

POLICY   **IF NO EXCEPTIONS, PLEASE CHECK**

1. FINANCIAL INTERESTS   No Exceptions ( )
Describe exceptions, if any: *XYZ Bank of which my husband is a Vice President provides banking services to the Institute; Midwest Graphic Services of which I am owner provides occasional graphic design services to the Institute.*

2. COLLECTING   No Exceptions ( )
Describe exceptions, if any: *I collect contemporary Japanese prints*
_____

3. USE OF INSTITUTE SERVICES, PROPERTY   No Exceptions (X)
   OR FACILITIES
Describe exceptions, if any: _____

4. PRIVILEGED INFORMATION   No Exceptions (X)
Describe exceptions, if any: _____

5. DEALING   No Exceptions (X)
Describe exceptions, if any: _____

DATE: *May 6, 1995*   SIGNATURE: */s/ Mrs. John Jones*

Exhibit 3
Mount Holyoke College
South Hadley, Massachusetts
Policy on Conflicts of Interest for Trustees and Officers

The policy set forth in this statement is applicable to all members of the Board of Trustees and to all Executive Officers of Mount Holyoke College as defined in the Bylaws of the Trustees of Mount Holyoke College.

A conflict of interest can arise whenever a Trustee or Officer or a member of his or her family: (1) has an existing or potential interest which impairs or might appear to impair his or her independent judgment in the discharge of responsibilities to the College or (2) may receive a material benefit from knowledge of information which is confidential to the College. The family of an individual includes his or her spouse, parents, siblings, children and any others living in the same household.

It is difficult to define what might be considered a potential conflict, but at least the following should be so considered:

1. Official relationship* with banks with which the College regularly does business.
2. Official relationship* with investment brokers with which the College does business.
3. Official relationship* with suppliers of goods or service to the College.
4. Official relationship* with insurance agents or carriers doing business with the College.
5. Family relationships with employees of the College.

Duty to Mount Holyoke College. Members of the Board of Trustees and Executive Officers have a clear fiduciary obligation to the College in connection with their service in such capacities. At all times they shall act in a manner consistent with this fiduciary obligation and shall exercise particular care that no detriment to the interests of the College (or appearance of such detriment) may result from a conflict between those interests and any personal interests which the individual Trustee or Executive Officer may have.

---

* In this context, "official relationship" means serving as an officer, director, employee, partner, proprietor, or owner of 10% or more of the stock of an entity which does business with the College.

Exhibit 3 is reprinted with the permission of Mount Holyoke College.

I. Conflicts of Interest with Respect to Particular Transactions:

If a Trustee or Executive officer believes that he or she may have a conflict of interest with respect to any *particular* transaction, he or she shall promptly and fully disclose the potential conflict to the President and the Chairman of the Board of Trustees, through the Secretary of the Board of Trustees.

A. If the President and the Chairman of the Board determine that there is in fact a conflict with respect to a Trustee, the conflict shall be reported to the full Board, and the affected Trustee shall agree to answer any questions about the matter that other Board members may have. If the particular transaction requires a vote of the Board, or of one of its committees, the affected Trustee shall not be counted for purposes of a quorum nor shall he or she vote on the matter. The minutes shall reflect the fact that the Trustee did not vote on the issue.

B. If the President and the Chairman of the Board determine that there is in fact a conflict concerning a *particular* transaction with respect to an officer of the College, they shall exercise their best judgment about the appropriate course to follow, which may include:

1) approval of the transaction despite the conflict if they are reasonably certain that the best interests of the College will be served thereby, or

2) referral of the issue to legal counsel for advice, or

3) referral of the issue to the appropriate committee of the Board of Trustees or to the full Board, for decision,

except that in all cases wherein the President and the Chairman of the Board determine that there is in fact a conflict of interest concerning a particular transaction involving an officer of the College, the full Board shall be notified of the resolution of the issue and the affected Officer shall agree to answer any questions about the matter that Board members may have.

C. If the President and the Chairman of the Board of Trustees determine that there is no conflict of interest with respect to a *particular* transaction involving a Trustee or Officer of the College, they need not notify the Board of Trustees, but the Secretary of the Board shall keep a record of the decision which shall be available to Board members upon request.

D. In any case in which the potential conflict with respect to a *particular* transaction involves either the President or the Chairman of the Board of Trustees, the affected party shall notify the other through the Secretary of the Board of Trustees, and the conflict shall then be reported to the full Board, and the President or Chairman of the Board shall agree to answer any questions about the matter that other Board members may have. If the particular transaction requires a vote of the Board, or one of its committees, the President or Chairman shall not be counted for purposes of a quorum nor shall he or she vote on the matter. The minutes shall reflect the fact that the President or Chairman did not vote on the issue.

II. Potential Conflicts of Interest:

Each member of the Board of Trustees and each Officer of the College shall file a statement in January of each year with the Secretary of the Board of Trustees setting forth any conflicts of interest which might be expected to occur within the following year. The statement shall disclose as fully as possible the nature of potential conflicts and the nature of the Trustee's or Officer's interest in the potential transactions, and all statements which anticipate conflicts of interest shall be circulated to members of the Board of Trustees. Each Trustee and each Officer shall agree to answer any questions about potential conflicts that Board members may have.

III. Confidentiality Policy:

All information concerning actual or potential conflicts of interest on the part of members of the Board of Trustees or Officers of the College shall be held in confidence unless the best interests of the College dictate otherwise. Any disclosure beyond the members of the Board of Trustees and the President shall take place only upon majority vote of the Board of Trustees.

Mount Holyoke College
South Hadley, Massachusetts

Annual Conflict of Interest Statement for Members of the Board of Trustees and Officers of the College

I, the undersigned, being a Trustee or Officer of the College, hereby state that to the best of my knowledge except as noted below:

1. I do not have an official relationship as defined on page one of the Policy on Conflicts of Interest with any corporation, partnership, or association that transacts business with Mount Holyoke College;

2. I, as an individual, do not transact any business, directly or indirectly, with Mount Holyoke College;

3. No member of my family, as defined on page one of the Policy on Conflicts of Interest, is in the employ of Mount Holyoke College or would come within the meaning of No. 1 or No. 2 above.

List below any exceptions to the above statements:

_____

_____

_____

I agree that if any situations arise, of which I am aware, that in any way contradict the above statement, I will immediately notify the Secretary of the Board of Trustees of any conflict, real or potential, and make full disclosure thereof. I have read the document entitled Mount Holyoke College Policy on Conflicts of Interest for Trustees and Officers adopted by the Board of Trustees on November 4, 1978. I agree to answer any questions the Board may have with respect to any actual or potential conflict of interest, but I understand that all such information will be held in confidence by the members of the Board, unless the best interests of the College dictate otherwise and a majority of the members of the Board of Trustees votes in favor of further disclosure.

| _____ | _____ |
| Date | Signature |

Exhibit 4
Harvard University
Policies Relating to Research and Other Professional
Activities within and outside the University*

1. With the acceptance of a full-time appointment in the Faculty of Arts and Sciences, an individual makes a commitment to the University that is understood to be full-time in the most inclusive sense. Every member is expected to accord the University his or her primary professional loyalty, and to arrange outside obligations, financial interests, and activities so as not to conflict or interfere with this overriding commitment to the University.

2. At the same time, no one benefits from undue interference with the legitimate external activities of officers of instruction who fulfill their primary full-time duties—teaching at the University, conducting scholarly research under its sponsorship, and meeting the other obligations to students and colleagues that faculty must share. Indeed, the involvement of faculty members in outside professional activities, both public and private, often serves not only the participants but the University as a whole. Instead of detailed rules or elaborate codes of ethics, the University has therefore provided its members with guidelines on conflicts of interest and commitment that leave as much as possible to individual discretion. It has been, and continues to be, assumed that all faculty members will be alert to the possible effects of outside activities on the objectivity of their decisions, their obligations to the University, and the University's responsibilities to others.

3. The areas of potential conflict may be divided into two broad categories. The first relates to conventional *conflicts of interest*—situations in which members may have the opportunity to influence the University's business decisions in ways that could lead to personal gain or give improper advantage to their associates. The second is concerned with *conflicts of commitment*—situations in which members' external activities, often valuable in themselves, interfere or appear to interfere with their paramount obligations to students, colleagues, and the University. Teachers and scholars are given great freedom in scheduling their activities with the understanding that their external activities will enhance the quality of their direct contributions to the University.

---

* As voted by the President and Fellows of Harvard College March 1, 1982, amended on July 25, 1987, and as subsequently amended by Vote of the Faculty of Arts and Sciences on October 29, 1987.
Exhibit 4 is reprinted with the permission of Harvard University.

4. A Standing Committee on Professional Conduct, with broad representation from the different disciplines, shall advise the Dean and individual faculty members on problems involving conflicts of interest and commitment.

5. It is assumed that minor conflicts will still be resolved primarily through individual discretion or informal administrative adjustment. It is also recognized that adequate protection for the University will frequently be derived through the traditional academic practices of scholarly publication and public disclosure of author and sponsor. However, if a member is engaged in an outside activity that could lead to serious conflict, it is mandatory that he or she inform the University of this possibility by consulting with the Dean of the Faculty or with the Chairman of the Committee on Professional Conduct. Whenever members have any doubts about whether an activity may involve a conflict of interest or commitment they are expected to seek such consultation. Guidance on what constitutes serious conflict is offered in the Appendix to this statement.

6. This statement will be distributed annually to all faculty members and published in the *Gazette* for the information of other officers.

Appendix

In the absence of specific rules (beyond the requirement of consultation), and in light of the difficulty of applying general statements of principle to specific cases, there follows a sampling of activities and situations that may present conflicts of interest or commitment. They are divided into three categories:

A. Activities that are ordinarily permissible and usually do not require consultation;

B. Activities that should be discussed with the Dean of the Faculty or with the Committee Chairman even though the problems they present can probably be resolved, often simply by ensuring that the appropriate authorities know all pertinent facts;

C. Activities that should be brought to the attention of the Dean of the Faculty or the Committee Chairman and that appear to present such serious problems that the burden of demonstrating their compatibility with University policy rests with the faculty member.

Obviously, this list of examples does not include all potential problems and the separation into categories is somewhat arbitrary.

A. Activities That Are Clearly Permissible and That May Be Pursued without Consultation:

1. Acceptance of royalties for published scholarly works and other writings, or of honoraria for commissioned papers and occasional lectures.

2. Service as a consultant to outside organizations, provided that the time and energy devoted to the task is not excessive and the arrangement in no way inhibits publication of research results obtained within the University.

3. Service on boards and committees of organizations, public or private, that does not distract unduly from University obligations.

B. Activities That Should Be Discussed with the Dean of the Faculty or with the Chairman of the Committee Even Though No Irreconcilable Conflict of Interest or Commitment Is Likely to Be Involved:

1. Relationships that might enable a member to influence Harvard's dealings with an outside organization in ways leading to personal gain or to improper advantage for anyone. For example, a member could have a financial interest in an enterprise with which the University does business and be in a position to influence relevant business decisions. Ordinarily, such problems can be resolved by full disclosure and by making arrangements that clearly exclude that member from participating in the decision.

2. Situations in which the time or creative energy a member devotes to extramural activities appears large enough to compromise the amount or quality of his or her participation in the instructional, scholarly, and administrative work of the University itself. The guideline applicable to faculty members, as defined in the Fifth Statute is that during the academic year (which extends through the summer for those who received extra summer salary) no more than 20% of one's total professional effort may be directed to outside work.

3. Activities (research projects, conferences, teaching programs, consulting agreements, etc.) that faculty members wish to undertake on an individual basis: (a) that involve or might reasonably be perceived to involve the institution, however slightly, and (b) that violate or might reasonably be perceived to violate any of the principles governing research supported by funds administered through the University (see *Principles Governing Research Conducted Within the Faculty of Arts and Sciences and Guidelines for Research Projects Undertaken in Cooperation with Industry*) insofar as these principles are relevant to individual behavior.

4. Situations in which a member directs students into a research area from which the member hopes to realize financial gain. The difficulty, in such circumstances, of making an objective independent judgment about the student's scholarly best interest is obvious.

C. Activities That Seem Likely to Present an Unacceptable Conflict of Interest or Commitment, and That Must Be Discussed with the Dean of the Faculty or with the Chairman of the Committee:

1. Situations in which the individual assumes executive responsibilities for an outside organization that might seriously divert his or her attention from University duties, or create other conflicts of loyalty. (Individuals should consult the Dean of the faculty or the Chairman of the Committee before accepting *any* outside management position.)

2. Use for personal profit of unpublished information emanating from University research or other confidential University sources, or assisting an outside organization by giving it exclusive access to such information; or consulting under arrangements that impose obligations that conflict with University patent policy or with the institution's obligations to research sponsors.

3. Circumstances in which a substantial body of research that could and ordinarily would be carried on within the University is conducted elsewhere to the disadvantage of the University and its legitimate interests.

4. Any activity (research project, conference, teaching program, consulting agreement, etc.) that a faculty member may wish to undertake on an individual basis: (a) that involves or appears to involve the institution significantly (for example, through the use of its resources or facilities, or the participation of colleagues, students, and staff, etc.), and (b) that violates any of the principles governing research supported by funds administered through the University (see *Principles Governing Research Conducted Within the Faculty of Arts and Sciences and Guidelines for Research Projects Undertaken in Cooperation with Industry*) insofar as these principles are relevant to individual behavior. (In particular, members may not give other organizations the right to censor research any part of which is performed under Harvard auspices.)

Indemnification of Directors of Nonprofit Organizations, Shield Statutes, and Director and Officer Liability Insurance

Leonard M. Polisar and William H. Cox

This chapter discusses the critically important issues of indemnification and insurance for directors and officers. The discussion is based on the Model Act,[1] and the New York[2] and Delaware[3] statutory provisions. While some states (e.g., California) may have differing precepts and standards,[4] the issues herein discussed must be addressed by any nonprofit.

Introduction

The issue of indemnification is of paramount importance to most directors of nonprofit organizations. In most cases involving charitable nonprofit organizations, directors serve without any remuneration other than reimbursement of expenses. If there is any compensation, it generally is meager, especially when compared to the risk assumed. The possibility of personal liability for actions taken as a director of a nonprofit organization therefore seems particularly burdensome. Consequently, the organization and its executive director should be aware that directors will often want assurance that the organization has the best possible provisions for indemnification in its articles of incorporation (or other relevant formation document) and bylaws. The advantage to directors of a provision in the certificate of incorporation is that it is usually much more difficult to amend than a bylaw provision. Similarly, directors may also want individual contractual provisions covering indemnification because, as contrasted to bylaw provisions, the director has much greater control over possible amendments to his or her individual contract. Furthermore, if at all possible, the nonprofit organization should carry directors' and officers' liability insurance (D&O insurance), in order to permit it to meet its obligations to indemnify an eligible director, especially because indemnification is only good if the corporation has adequate assets. Because directors often have many questions regarding the organization's indemnification policies and procedure and its D&O insurance, it is necessary for the executive director and corporate secretary to be fully knowledgeable with respect to such matters.

It is not the purpose of this handbook to summarize the history of director indemnification generally and the arguments for and against indemnification. It should be noted, however, that there are serious questions concerning the availability of indemnification for directors in the absence of specific statutory authorization. Consequently, for purposes of informing a director of her or his potential liability and rights to indemnification, it is necessary for the executive director and corporate secretary to have at least some rudimentary knowledge of the types of statutory provisions concerning liability and indemnification which exist in the state of incorporation and in the various states in which the director's activities on behalf of the nonprofit organization take place.[5] Furthermore, the issue of D&O insurance and its availability, types of coverage, and the application process need to be examined. We have attempted to review statutory indemnification provisions and the certificate of incorporation, bylaw, and contractual provisions which follow therefrom. We have also tried, in summary fashion, to review the issue of D&O insurance and limitations of liability under state laws which purport to shield directors from liability. In reviewing statutory provisions, we will focus on the Revised Model Nonprofit Corporation Act (Model Act),[6] the Delaware General Corporation Law (Delaware Law)[7] and the New York Not-For-Profit Corporation Law (New York Law).[8]

Exhibits 1 through 3 set forth sample indemnification provisions for (1) a certificate of incorporation, (2) bylaws and (3) a contract between the nonprofit organization and the director. While these New York law examples are readily adaptable for other states, before such adaptations are used in any particular state they should be reviewed by a qualified attorney in that state.

Statutory Limitation of Liability

Some states have enacted laws seeking to protect nonprofit directors by limiting their liability to situations in which gross negligence or willful misfeasance is established (so-called "shield laws"). Unlike statutory provisions which permit some limitation of the liability of directors of business corporations, shield laws do not usually require any specific provisions in the nonprofit organization's certificate of incorporation or other formation document. Of the three statutes we have reviewed, only the New York Law has a significant shield provision. Under section 720-a of the New York Law, except for specific types of actions described in the statute, a nonprofit director serving without compensation as a director, officer or trustee of a charitable organization or trust described in section 501(c)(3) of the Internal Revenue Code is liable to persons other than the organization only if his or her conduct "constituted *gross* negligence or was *intended* to cause the resulting harm to the person asserting such liability".[9] It should also be noted that for purposes of determining whether the director has been compensated for his or her board service, section 720-a of the New York Law provides an exemption for payment of the director's "actual expenses incurred in attending meetings or otherwise in the execution of" his or her office as a director.[10]

As noted, New York's shield law is applicable only to directors serving "without compensation."[11] Hence, it would not be applicable to a paid executive director (or other paid staff) serving as a member of the board.

While shield provisions such as that of the New York Law are helpful to the director, it should also be noted that they do not prevent anyone from bringing an action alleging gross negligence or willful misconduct and they may not apply with respect to questions arising under federal law, such as discrimination or antitrust actions or actions arising under the Internal Revenue Code. Accordingly, the existence of a shield law should not lull the director into a false sense of security and the director should fully review the organization's indemnification provisions and D&O insurance coverage even in those states that have enacted a shield law.

In addition to shield laws, some states have provisions which permit a corporation's certificate of incorporation to contain a provision eliminating or limiting the personal liability of a director to the corporation or its members for monetary damages for breach of fiduciary duty as a director. These provisions, however, usually do not permit elimination or limitation of liability related to breaches of the duty of loyalty, acts or omissions in bad faith involving intentional misconduct or knowing violation of law, transactions resulting in an improper personal benefit to the director, and other types of breaches or liability specified in the particular statute. The Delaware Law contains such a provision in section 102 thereof.[12] Curiously, New York has such a provision in section 402 of its Business Corporation Law,[13] but no corresponding provision in its Not-For-Profit Corporation Law.

Statutory Indemnification Provisions

As a general matter, before reviewing the specific indemnification provisions[14] set forth in the Model Act, the Delaware Law, and the New York Law, it should be noted that (1) unlike some shield laws, statutory indemnification provisions cover directors, officers, and employees who receive compensation, and (2) the concepts and provisions set forth in each of these laws are similar to those found in the statutory business corporation indemnification provisions of most states. In each case, however, the executive director or corporate secretary and the director or his attorney should specifically review the statutory provisions governing indemnification in the state in which the nonprofit organization is incorporated or organized and in those states in which it does business. The certificate of incorporation (or other relevant formation document) of the organization and its bylaws should also be reviewed to determine that the organization has provided for the (1) maximum indemnification permitted under the statute, in cases where the statute requires that such indemnification be consistent with the statute; or (2) in cases where the statute is not exclusive, the maximum indemnification which is not prohibited by the statute.[15] It is also recommended that the director and his or her attorney consider entering into a contract with the nonprofit organization providing for indemnification which is at least equal to that provided in the bylaws and if such bylaw protection is not the best available, such additional provisions as are necessary to protect the director fully. Most state statutes cover a variety of issues relating to indemnification.

Discretionary Indemnification

The Model Act and the Delaware and New York Laws all contain provisions specifying when a corporation *may* indemnify a director. The Model Act sets forth one provision governing both (1) those proceedings by or in the right of the corporation (often referred to as "derivative suits") and (2) all other proceedings. New York and Delaware set forth separate provisions for derivative suits and all other proceedings. In general the Model Act and the Delaware Law are more favorable to the director in that they clearly cover not only civil and criminal actions but also administrative proceedings and investigations. While indemnification for such administrative proceedings and investigations could be provided under New York Law, the statutory language, while not exclusive, does not specifically refer to those proceedings and investigations. Consequently, if the corporation's policy on indemnification is set forth in a certificate of incorporation or bylaw provision which only refers to the provisions of the New York statutes, the director may face problems obtaining indemnification for costs incurred in responding to an investigation or administrative proceedings.

Standard of Conduct

Each of the laws sets forth a standard of conduct which must be met by the director in order to be eligible for indemnification.

Civil Actions. In the case of civil actions, the Model Act distinguishes between the director's conduct in his or her official capacity and his or her conduct in all other cases. When acting in an official capacity, the director must act in a manner which he or she reasonably believes to be in the corporation's best interest. In all other cases the director must believe that his or her conduct was at least not opposed to the best interest of the corporation. Clearly, the threshold which the director is required to meet is much lower under the latter standard.

In the case of civil actions against a director under the New York Law, the standard of conduct required of the director depends on whether or not the actions under review are or were in connection with his or her service for an entity other than the corporation.[16] In the case of service for the corporation or in the case of any activity not described in the *following sentence,* the director must have acted in good faith and for a purpose he or she reasonably believed to be in the best interest of the corporation.[17] In the case of service by the director for any corporation, partnership, joint venture, trust, employee benefit plan, or other enterprise other than the nonprofit corporation, the director must have acted in good faith and for a purpose he or she reasonably believed was not opposed to the best interest of the corporation.

Delaware Law has the least stringent standard of conduct for a director in that in all instances the test is whether the director acted in good faith and in a manner he or she reasonably believed to be in or not opposed to the best interests of the corporation.[18]

Criminal Actions. With respect to criminal actions, all three laws are similar in that, in addition to the standard of conduct required for civil actions as described above, the director is required to have had no reasonable cause to believe that her or his conduct was unlawful.

Civil and Criminal Actions. All three statutes require that before any indemnification is paid in either civil or criminal cases, a determination must be made whether or not a director is entitled to indemnification by virtue of having met the applicable standard of conduct. Depending on the statute in question, this determination must be made by (1) a quorum of disinterested directors, (2) by the members, or (3) contingent upon a quorum of disinterested directors being unavailable (or, even if available, voting to retain independent counsel), by the board acting on the opinion of independent counsel or by such independent counsel.[19] All three statutes also provide that termination of a proceeding by judgment, order, settlement, conviction, or by plea of *nolo contendere* is not determinative of whether the director has met the required standard of conduct.[20] Also, as a general matter, unless ordered by a court, all three statutes prohibit indemnification (1) in derivative suits when the director is found liable to the corporation or (2) any instance in which the director is determined to have received an improper personal benefit. It should also be noted that, while New York Law allows a court to grant indemnification for settlement expenses, statutory provisions relating to indemnification in derivative suits often limit such indemnification to reasonable expenses incurred in connection with the proceeding (i.e., a director cannot be reimbursed for settlements or judgments in derivative suits). While indemnification may at times cover settlements, indemnification cannot cover the payment of judgments without court approval.

Mandatory Indemnification for Expenses

The Model Act provides that a director *is entitled to* indemnification for reasonable expenses incurred in connection with a proceeding in which he or she has been *wholly* successful on the merits or otherwise, unless the corporation's certificate of incorporation limits the availability of such indemnification.[21] The New York and Delaware Laws are both different from the Model Act in that they do not have any provision permitting the corporation to have a limitation in its certificate of incorporation on availability of indemnification for expenses when the director has been successful on the merits or otherwise. Both of these statutes are also different from the Model Act in that they do not require the director to be "wholly" successful in order to be entitled to mandatory indemnification. The Model Act's requirement that the director be wholly successful is apparently an attempt to prevent a director from settling some counts of an action or indictment in exchange for a release or plea bargain on other counts and subsequently claiming a mandatory right to indemnification with respect to the dismissed counts. It should also be noted that all three statutes would require mandatory indemnification of a director even if his or her success is due to the existence of a procedural defense, such as a statute of limitation.

Advancement of Expenses

Whether or not the corporation will advance the director's ongoing defense expenses is among the most significant questions for the director, given the extensive costs of mounting a defense in most cases. All three laws permit a corporation to advance expenses if certain requirements are met. The Model Act seems to be the most stringent in that it requires (1) a written affirmation by the director of her or his good faith belief that she or he has met the standard of conduct required for indemnification for the particular proceeding in question; (2) a written undertaking to repay the corporation if it is ultimately determined that the director did not meet the standard of conduct; and (3) a determination that the facts known at the time of the determination do not preclude indemnification.[22] The Delaware Law and the New York Law do not require either a written affirmation from the director or a determination whether the facts then known would preclude indemnification, but both require that there be a written undertaking to repay the corporation if the director is not ultimately entitled to indemnification. Section 725 of the New York Law also requires that there be no advancement of expenses or indemnification if to do so would (1) be inconsistent with the law governing a foreign corporation which prohibits or otherwise limits such indemnification, (2) be inconsistent with the corporation's bylaws, certificate of incorporation or contract or other governing document which prohibits or otherwise limits such indemnification, or (3) violate a settlement approved by a court.[23]

Notice to Members

The New York Law requires that whenever any expenses or other indemnification amounts are paid without either a court order or approval by the nonprofit corporation's members, the corporation must mail a statement to its members specifying the person paid, amounts paid, and the nature and status of the litigation or threatened litigation at the time of such payment.[24] Such statement must be mailed not later than the next annual meeting or within fifteen months from the payment date if the next annual meeting is within three months of the payment date. If the corporation has no members, the statement must be included in the records of the corporation open to public inspection. The Model Act and the Delaware Law do not contain any similar notice provisions. The Model Act, however, does require twenty days advance written notice to the state's attorney general before the payment of any indemnification to a director of a public benefit corporation.[25]

D&O Liability Insurance

All three laws permit the corporation to purchase insurance covering the liability a director may incur as a result of serving as a director of the corporation.[26] Obviously, such insurance is important to the director so that he or she will not have to rely entirely on the indemnification obligations of the organization or the organization's financial ability to meet such obligations. This is especially important in the case of those nonprofit organizations which have little, if any, assets. Such insurance also provides the certainty that, subject to any policy exclusions, the director will be reimbursed for his or her expenses, regardless of the outcome of the proceeding. Finally, the availability of D&O insurance may cause members and directors of a fiscally strained nonprofit organization to be less reluctant to adopt expansive indemnification policies or to authorize indemnification payments in any specific instance.

The Model Act and the Delaware Law provisions governing insurance are very similar. Both permit policies which would cover the director against liability arising out of her or his status as a director even in instances where the corporation would not have the power to indemnify the director because of limitations in the law. While this could be read as permitting insurance in cases which involve bad faith or dishonesty, as a general matter it should be noted that D&O liability policies exclude coverage for such misconduct. The New York Law specifically prohibits any D&O insurance policy from providing for any payment other than cost of defense to or on behalf of any director if a final adjudication adverse to the director establishes that his or her acts of active and deliberate dishonesty were material to the cause of action so adjudicated or that he or she personally gained a financial profit or other advantage to which the director was not legally entitled.[27] New York also prohibits any such policy from providing for any payment (other than costs of defense) in relation to any risk which is prohibited from being insured under New York insurance law.[28] Insurance, then, except as noted, can cover judgments which indemnification cannot.

If the nonprofit corporation purchases or renews D&O insurance, New York Law requires it to mail a statement to its members specifying the insurance carrier, date of contract, cost of the insurance, corporate positions insured, and a statement explaining all sums paid under any D&O insurance contract which have not previously been reported in a statement to members.[29] Such statement must be mailed within a time period similar to that previously described with regard to notice to members; if the corporation has no members, notice must be included with the records of the corporation open to public inspection. The Model Act and the Delaware Law do not contain any similar notice provisions.

While D&O liability insurance is important to the director of any organization, as discussed above, this is especially true in the case of a director of a nonprofit organization with minimal assets. Despite that fact, nonprofit corporations have generally lagged behind business corporations in terms of purchasing D&O liability policies, with approximately 73% of the nonprofits purchasing coverage compared to 85% of business corporations.[30] As a general rule, it should also be noted that insurance companies are often more willing to insure the directors of a nonprofit organization, as opposed to business corporation directors. This results from the fact that nonprofit organizations are sued less often and generally have less costly claims.[31] While, to the best of our knowledge, no specific information exists on this subject, insurers may be more willing to insure nonprofit directors due to the fact that shareholder (or member) issues are much less likely to arise in the case of a nonprofit director. One survey found that of the claims against directors and officers studied, 47% were filed by shareholders, 22% by employees, 19% by customers and clients, and 12% by competitors, government entities, and other third parties.[32] In the case of nonprofit directors, the most likely claims may be those relating to employment matters, including wrongful termination, discrimination and inadequate supervision of executives, or matters relating to wrongful application or wrongful use of endowment funds.

D&O Insurance Policy Review

In reviewing a D&O liability insurance policy and the coverage provided thereunder, the primary focus is obviously to obtain the maximum insurance at the least cost to the corporation. The policy form itself should be carefully reviewed to determine:

(1) the policy limits;

(2) the retention or deductible amounts;

(3) any co-insurance requirements;

(4) the covered persons;

(5) the definition of "claim" or "loss" and the types of claims or losses covered;

(6) the policy exclusions; and

(7) whether investigations, administrative proceedings, mediation, and other "non-adversarial" proceedings are covered.

Typical policy exclusions include those relating to employee benefit plans, environmental issues, bodily injury/property damage claims,[33] as well as dishonesty, fraud, or willful violation of a statute by the director seeking indemnification. One of the most important issues is whether the policy provides for advancement of defense costs as incurred (duty to defend policy) or only at the end of the proceeding (indemnity policy), with most policies falling within the indemnity category. It should be noted that most, if not all, of these policy provisions and exclusions can be negotiated and insurers are usually willing to make some modifications to their standard policy language. For the nonprofit organization, this often requires a cost-benefit analysis if the insurer is willing to make changes but requires additional premiums in order to do so.[34]

A review should also be made of the insurer's ability to pay as determined by Best's, Moody's, or other ratings agencies and its history or general reputation for claims payment and "allocation" disputes. These disputes arise in connection with the question of how much of defense costs (initially) and settlement or judgment amounts (ultimately) are attributable to the directors covered under the policy, as opposed to the corporation and other "non-covered" persons and entities or non-covered claims. While the D&O policy is usually divided into two parts covering (1) reimbursement to the corporation for indemnification provided to directors and officers, and (2) reimbursement to directors and officers for expenses and other amounts for which indemnification is not provided by the corporation, the policy does not cover claims in which the corporation, as opposed to the director or officer, is primarily liable. Many insurers make a routine opening offer to pay defense costs and settlement and judgment amounts on the basis of an allocation of 50 percent each for covered and non-covered persons.[35] The 1993 Wyatt D&O Survey[36] found, however, that "in those cases in which some allocation takes place, the D&O insurer eventually agreed to pay . . . judgments, settlements . . . [and] defense costs" on the basis of an allocation of 67 percent to the insured persons and 33 percent to the noncovered defendant corporation.[37]

Claims Made vs. Occurrence Policies

As a general matter, the organization should be aware that D&O policies are almost universally written on a "claims made" basis, as opposed to on an "occurrence" basis. Claims made policies cover the director against claims which are made against a director during the term of the policy, regardless of when the event which gave rise to the claim occurred. An "occurrence" policy, on the other hand, provides coverage for any occurrence (as defined in the policy) which arises during the policy period, even if the claim arising from that occurrence is not brought for years after the expiration of the policy period. This distinction is of the utmost importance and should be fully understood by the organization. An "occurrence" policy which was in effect during the period of the director's service to the organization will cover him or her for actions taken during that period and such coverage continues (regardless of whether or not the director has terminated his or her relationship with the nonprofit organization) even after the insurer no longer insures the nonprofit organization. On the other hand, if the organization's insurance is on a "claims made" basis, any failure to renew or other lapse of such insurance will result in a total lack of coverage for any matters that come to light or are brought after such lapse. This can result in the nonprofit organization being unable to meet its indemnification obligations and may result in substantial liability to a director for actions taken during a prior period when he or she felt a false sense of security due to the fact that the organization had purchased D&O insurance.

It should also be noted that in the case of claims made policies, insurers will often accept claims during a "tail" period after expiration of the policy for a relatively small additional premium. The availability and feasibility of this option should be explored. The nonprofit organization should also arrange for directors and officers to be included as named parties for a number of years after they have retired or have otherwise terminated their relationship with the nonprofit organization. It should also be noted that both occurrence and claims made policies will generally require some retention amount and coinsurance. Under the New York Law each contract of insurance must provide for retention amounts and coinsurance in a manner acceptable to the superintendent of insurance.

Application Process

Another matter which is of the utmost importance is that of the application process and the need for full disclosure to the insurer concerning existing issues or claims, background of directors, and other issues raised in the application. This results from the fact that the application is part of the insurance contract and can be used by the insurer for purposes of denying coverage if it is later found that the application was inaccurate or misleading. As such, it is important to review the D&O insurance policy to confirm that it limits any denial of coverage for misrepresentation only to those directors who either misrepresented or failed to disclose facts required by the application.

While each organization may handle the application process differently, depending on the number of directors and complexity of issues facing the organization, it is often advisable to prepare individual questionnaires for the directors so that each director focuses on the issues raised by the application. The final application should also be reviewed by a knowledgeable officer of the nonprofit organization or by its attorney.

Indemnification by Third Parties

One other area which should be reviewed by the nonprofit director is the possibility of supplementing any indemnification by the nonprofit organization or under its D&O policy with indemnification from third parties or with other insurance. Specifically, the director who is also employed by an entity other than the nonprofit organization should determine whether his or her employer will agree that his or her service as a nonprofit director will be covered under the employer's procedures for indemnification and, if necessary, will be deemed to be at the request of the employer.[38] The question of coverage under the employer's D&O policy should also be explored. Finally, if there are any instances where third parties engaging in transactions with the nonprofit organization agree to indemnify it from various liabilities, it should be determined whether such indemnification will also cover the individual director.

Coverage under Individual Umbrella Policies

Directors should be advised to review their individual umbrella insurance policies which often provide coverage for service as a director of a nonprofit organization. Many directors, who are unaware of such coverage, might appreciate having the executive director or secretary point out the availability of such individual coverage, particularly because the premium for an umbrella policy is relatively low.

Conclusion

It is clear that the issue of indemnification and of insurance coverage is of the utmost importance for directors of nonprofit organizations. Consequently, it is both necessary and advisable for the executive director, the corporate secretary, and the director to review the various issues and options discussed above. Furthermore, the director should obtain competent legal and insurance advice to eliminate, to the greatest extent possible, any liability resulting from her or his service on the board of a nonprofit organization. It may also be advisable for the nonprofit organization to have an annual review of the status and amount of its D&O coverage by either the board of directors or by a committee of the board. Finally, the corporate secretary should provide directors with a summary of applicable shield laws and indemnification provisions and the specific elements of the organization's D&O insurance. This summary should be updated on an annual basis and should also be provided to new directors.

Notes

1. Model Nonprofit Corp. Act (1987).
2. N.Y. Not-For-Profit Corp. Law (McKinney 1986 & West Supp. 1996).
3. Del. Code Ann. tit. 8 (1995).
4. Cal. Corp. Code § 1259 (1996).
5. The law of the state in which the organization is incorporated will clearly be applicable to the question of whether a nonprofit organization will be permitted or required to indemnify a director or will be prohibited from doing so. The law of jurisdictions in which the organization is doing business will also often be applicable. For example, the New York Law requires foreign corporations doing business in New York to comply with its indemnification provisions, unless any indemnification required by the New York Law is expressly prohibited by the law of the state of incorporation of such foreign corporation.
6. Model Nonprofit Corp. Act (1987).
7. Del. Code Ann. (1987).
8. N.Y. Not-For-Profit Corp. Law (McKinney 1986 & West Supp. 1996).
9. N.Y. Not-For-Profit Corp. Law § 720-a (McKinney 1986 & West Supp. 1996) (emphasis added).
10. *Id.*
11. *Id.*
12. Del. Code Ann.
13. N.Y. Bus. Corp. Law § 402 (McKinney 1986 & West Supp. 1996).
14. In reviewing statutory indemnification provisions we have concentrated on those provisions set forth in statutes governing corporations. While we are aware that nonprofit organizations may be organized as associations or trusts, we have not sought to describe any statutory provisions governing such organizations.
15. It should be noted that the New York Law (§ 721) permits indemnification beyond that provided in the certificate of incorporation or bylaws to be provided under (1) a resolution of members, (2) a resolution of directors or (3) an agreement, but only if the certificate of incorporation or bylaws authorizes such resolutions or agreement.
16. N.Y. Not-For-Profit Corp. Law § 720 (McKinney 1986 & West Supp. 1996).
17. *Id.* at § 723.
18. Del. Code Ann. § 145 (1995).
19. The three laws differ on whether the final determination can be made by counsel or whether it is still made by the Board. The Delaware Law and the Model Act permit the determination to be made by "independent legal counsel" and "special legal counsel," respectively, appointed in accord with the provisions in those laws. The New York Law permits the determination to be made by the Board upon the opinion of independent legal counsel.
20. N.Y. Not-For-Profit Corp. Law § 723 (McKinney 1986 & West Supp. 1996); Del. Code Ann. § 145 (1995).
21. N.Y. Not-For-Profit Corp. Law § 724 (McKinney 1986 & West Supp. 1996); Del. Code Ann. § 145 (1995).
22. Such determination should be made in the manner described under the heading "Civil and Criminal Actions" above.
23. N.Y. Not-For-Profit Corp. Law § 725 (McKinney 1986 & West Supp. 1996).
24. *Id.* at § 724.
25. The Model Act contemplates three types of nonprofit corporations: (1) public benefit corporations which are operated for public or charitable purposes; (2) mutual benefit corporations, which are operated for the benefit of their members or people they serve or represent; and (3) religious corporations.
26. N.Y. Not-For-Profit Corp. Law § 727 (McKinney 1986 & West Supp. 1996); Del. Code Ann. § 145 (1995).
27. N.Y. Not-For-Profit Corp. Law § 727 (McKinney 1986 & West Supp. 1996).
28. *Id.* at § 726.
29. *Id.* at § 727.

30. Selis, "New Liability Covers Officials of Non-Profits," *Business First Columbus* (Mar. 27, 1995): 7.
31. *Id.*
32. Dauer, "D&O Market Expected to Remain 'Flat' for 1994," *National Underwriter* (Mar. 14, 1994): 6.
33. These are generally covered by the nonprofit organization's comprehensive general liability policy.
34. The considerations and exclusions referred to above are covered in greater detail in the checklist on page 151.
35. Anderson and Paar, "What's Wrong with D&O Insurance?" *Risk Management* (Jan. 1995): 29.
36. The Annual Wyatt D&O Survey can be obtained from Watson Wyatt, 303 West Madison, Chicago, Illinois 60606.
37. Anderson and Paar, 29 n. 20.
38. This is necessary because state laws often require that in order for the corporation to provide indemnification for and to purchase D&O insurance covering the director's activities on behalf of an entity other than the indemnifying corporation, the director's activities for such other entity must be at the request of the indemnifying corporation.

Bibliography

Anderson and Paar. "What's Wrong with D&O Insurance?" *Risk Management* (January 1995): 29.

Bishop, Joseph Warren. *Law of Corporate Officers and Directors: Indemnification and Insurance.* New York: Clark Boardman Callaghan, 1991.

Black. "A Quick Overview of What You Need to Know about Your Directors' and Officers' Policy." *Association Management* (January 1995): L53.

Block and Hoff. "Business Combination and Director Protection Laws." *New York Law Journal* (March 16, 1995): 5.

Brodsky, Edward. "Directors' and Officers' Insurance." *New York Law Journal* (September 14, 1994): 3.

Chapman, Karen Leigh. "Statutory Responses to Boardroom Fears." *Columbia Business Law Review* (1987): 749.

Charron. "How to get the D&O coverage you need." *ABA Banking Journal* (February 1993): 63.

Dauer. "D&O Market Expected To Remain 'Flat' For 1994," *National Underwriter* (March 14, 1994): 6.

Johnston. "Should You Join a Nonprofit Board?" *Small Business Reports* (April 1994): 54.

Mallen, Ronald and David W. Evens. "Surviving the Directors' and Officers' Liability Crisis: Insurance and the Alternatives." *Delaware Journal of Corporate Law* 12 (Winter 1988): 439.

Monteleone, Joseph P. and Nicholas J. Conca. "Directors' and Officers' Indemnification and Liability Insurance: An Overview of Legal and Practical Issues." *The Business Lawyer* 51 (1996): 573.

Rosh, Robert. "New York's Response to the Director and Officer Liability Crisis: A Need to Reexamine the Importance of D&O Insurance." *Brooklyn Law Review* 54 (1989): 1305.

Schauer, Louis. *Indemnification and Insurance for Directors and Officers.* Washington, D.C.: Bureau of National Affairs, Inc., 1991.

Selis. "New Liability Covers Officials of Non-Profits." *Business First Columbus* (March 27, 1995): 7.

Tremper, Charles. "Understanding D&O Insurance." *Association Management* (January 1992): L58.

Webster. "Avoiding Personal Liability: Minimizing the Risks of Board Service." *Association Management* (January 1994): L57.

Exhibit 1
Provision for Certificate of Incorporation
under New York Law

SEVENTH: The corporation shall, to the fullest extent permitted by the Not-For-Profit Corporation Law of the State of New York, as the same may be amended and supplemented from time to time, indemnify any and all persons whom it shall have power to indemnify under said Law from and against any and all of the expenses, liabilities or other matters referred to in or covered by said Law. The indemnification provided for herein shall not be deemed exclusive of any other rights to which any person may be entitled under any bylaw, [resolution of members,]* resolution of directors, agreement or otherwise. The corporation is authorized to enter into agreements with any of its directors, officers or employees extending rights to indemnification and advancement of expenses to such person to the fullest extent permitted by applicable law, or to provide such indemnification and advancement of expenses pursuant to [a resolution of members or]* a resolution of directors.

---

*Omit if the nonprofit organization is not a membership organization.

Exhibit 2
Bylaw Provision under New York Law

ARTICLE VIII
Indemnification

Except to the extent expressly prohibited by the New York Not-For-Profit Corporation Law, the Corporation shall indemnify any person, made or threatened to be made a party to or called as a witness in or asked to provide information in connection with any pending or threatened action, proceeding, hearing or investigation, or any appeal therein (other than an action or proceeding by or in the right of the Corporation to procure a judgment in its favor), whether civil or criminal, including an action by or in the right of any other corporation of any type or kind, domestic or foreign, or any partnership, joint venture, trust, employee benefit plan or other enterprise, which any director or officer of the Corporation served in any capacity at the request of the Corporation, by reason of the fact that he or she is or was, or he or she is the executor, administrator, heir or successor of a person who is or was, a director or officer of the Corporation, or served such other corporation, partnership, joint venture, trust, employee benefit plan or other enterprise in any capacity, against judgments, fines, amounts paid in settlement and reasonable expenses, including attorneys' fees actually and necessarily incurred as a result of such action or proceeding, or any appeal therein, if such director or officer, acted in good faith, for a purpose which he or she reasonably believed to be in, or, in the case of service for any other corporation or any partnership, joint venture, trust, employee benefit plan or other enterprise, not opposed to, the best interests of the Corporation and, in criminal actions or proceedings, in addition, had no reasonable cause to believe that his or her conduct was unlawful.

Except to the extent expressly prohibited by the New York Not-For-Profit Corporation Law, the Corporation shall indemnify any person made, or threatened to be made, a party to an action by or in the right of the Corporation to procure a judgment in its favor by reason of the fact that he or she is or was, or he or she is the executor, administrator, heir or successor of a person who is or was, a director or officer of the Corporation, or is or was serving at the request of the Corporation as a director or officer of any corporation of any type or kind, domestic or foreign, of any partnership, joint venture, trust, employee benefit plan or other enterprise, against amounts paid in settlement and reasonable expenses, including attorneys' fees, actually and necessarily incurred by him or her in connection with the defense or settlement of such action, or in connection with an appeal therein, if such director or officer acted, in good faith, for a purpose which he or she reasonably believed to be in, or, in the case of service for any other corporation or any partnership, joint venture, trust, employee benefit plan or other enterprise, not opposed to, the best interests of the Corporation, except that no indemnification under this paragraph shall be made in respect to (1) a threatened action, or a pending action which is settled or otherwise disposed of, or (2) any claim, issue or matter as to which such person shall have been adjudged to be liable to the Corporation, unless and only to the extent that the court in which the action was brought, or, if no action was brought, any court of competent jurisdiction, determines upon application that, in view of all the circumstances of the case, the person is fairly and reasonably entitled to indemnity for such portion of the settlement amount and expenses as the court deems proper.

The termination of any civil or criminal action or proceeding by judgment, settlement, conviction or upon a plea of nolo contendere, or its equivalent, shall not in itself create a presumption that any such director or officer did not act, in good faith, for a purpose which he or she reasonably believed to be in, or, in the case of service for any other corporation or any partnership, joint venture, trust, employee benefit plan or other enterprise, not opposed to, the best interests of the Corporation or that he or she had reasonable cause to believe that his or her conduct was unlawful.

No indemnification shall be made under this bylaw if a judgment or other final adjudication adverse to such person establishes that his or her acts were committed in bad faith or were the result of active and deliberate dishonesty and were material to the cause of action so adjudicated, or that he or she personally gained in fact a financial profit or other advantage to which he or she was not legally entitled, and provided further that no such indemnification shall be required with respect to any settlement or other nonadjudicated disposition of any threatened or pending action or proceeding unless the Corporation has given its consent to such settlement or other disposition.

The Corporation shall advance or promptly reimburse, upon request of any person entitled to indemnification hereunder, all expenses, including attorneys' fees reasonably incurred in defending any action or proceeding in advance of the final disposition thereof, upon receipt of a written undertaking by or on behalf of such person to repay such amount if such person is ultimately found not to be entitled to indemnification or, where indemnification is granted, to the extent the expenses so advanced or reimbursed exceed the amount to which such person is entitled.

Nothing in this bylaw shall limit or affect any other right of any person to indemnification or expenses, including attorneys' fees, under any statute, rule, regulation, certificate of incorporation, bylaw, insurance policy, contract or otherwise.

No elimination of this bylaw, and no amendment of this bylaw adversely affecting the right of any person to indemnification or advancement of expenses hereunder shall be effective until the sixtieth day following notice to such person of such action, and no elimination of or amendment to this bylaw shall deprive any person of his rights hereunder arising out of alleged or actual occurrences, acts or failures to act prior to such sixtieth day. The provisions of this paragraph shall supersede anything to the contrary in these bylaws.

The Corporation shall not, except by elimination or amendment of this bylaw in a manner consistent with the preceding paragraph, take any corporate action or enter into any agreement which prohibits, or otherwise limits the rights of any person to, indemnification in accordance with the provisions of this bylaw. The indemnification of any person provided by this bylaw shall continue after such person has ceased to be a director or officer of the Corporation and shall inure to the benefit of such person's heirs, executors, administrators and legal representatives.

The Corporation is authorized to enter into agreements with any of its directors, officers or employees extending rights to indemnification and advancement of expenses to such person to the fullest extent permitted by applicable law, or to provide such indemnification and advancement of expenses pursuant to [a resolution of members or]* a resolution of directors, but the failure to enter into any such agreement or to adopt any such resolutions shall not affect or limit the rights of such person pursuant to this bylaw. It is hereby expressly recognized that all directors and officers of the Corporation, by serving as such after the adoption hereof, are acting in reliance on this bylaw and that the Corporation is estopped to contend otherwise. Additionally, it is hereby expressly recognized that all persons who are directors or officers of the Corporation and also serve as directors, officers or employees of corporations which are subsidiaries or affiliates of the Corporation (or other entities controlled by the Corporation) are conclusively presumed to serve or to have served as such at the request of the Corporation and, unless prohibited by law, are entitled to indemnification under this bylaw.

For purposes of this bylaw, the Corporation shall be deemed to have requested a director or officer of the Corporation to serve an employee benefit plan where the performance by such person of his or her duties to the Corporation also imposes duties on, or otherwise involves services by, such person to the plan or participants or beneficiaries of the plan, and excise taxes assessed on a person with respect to an employee benefit plan pursuant to applicable law shall be considered indemnifiable expenses.

A person who has been successful, on the merits or otherwise, in the defense of a civil or criminal action or proceeding shall be entitled to indemnification as authorized in the first and second paragraphs of this bylaw. Ex-

---

* Omit if the nonprofit organization is not a membership corporation.

cept as provided in the preceding sentence and unless ordered by a court, any indemnification under this bylaw, under any contract or otherwise, shall be made by the Corporation if, and only if, authorized in the specific case:

(1) By the Board of Directors acting by a quorum consisting of directors who are not parties to such action or proceeding upon a finding that the director or officer has met the standard of conduct set forth in the first or second paragraph of this bylaw, as applicable;

(2) If such a quorum is not obtainable or, even if obtainable, a quorum of disinterested directors so directs:

(a) By the Board of Directors upon the opinion in writing of independent legal counsel that indemnification is proper in the circumstances because the standard of conduct set forth in the first or second paragraph of this bylaw, as applicable, has been met by such director or officer; or

(b) By the members upon a finding that the director or officer has met the applicable standard of conduct set forth in such paragraph.*

If any expenses or other amounts are paid by way of indemnification, otherwise than by court order or action by the members, the Corporation shall, not later than the next annual meeting of members, unless such meeting is held within three months from the date of such payment and, in any event, within fifteen months from the date of such payment, mail to its members of record at the time entitled to vote for the election of directors a statement specifying the action taken, or if the Corporation has no members, such statement shall be included in the records of the Corporation open to public inspection.

For purposes of this bylaw, the term "Corporation" shall include any legal successor to the Corporation, including any corporation or other entity which acquires all or substantially all of the assets of the Corporation in one or more transactions.

In case any provision in this bylaw shall be determined at any time to be unenforceable in any respect, the other provisions shall not in any way be affected or impaired thereby, and the affected provision shall be given the fullest possible enforcement in the circumstances, it being the intention of the Corporation to afford indemnification and advancement of expenses to its directors and officers, acting in such capacities or in the other capacities specified in this bylaw, to the fullest extent permitted by law.

---

* Omit subparagraph (b) if the nonprofit organization is not a membership organization.

Exhibit 3
Contractual Provisions under New York Law

AGREEMENT, effective as of _____, 199_ between _____, a _____ corporation (the "Corporation"), and _____ (the "Director").

WHEREAS, it is essential that the Corporation retain and attract as directors the most capable persons available; and

WHEREAS, Director is a director of the Corporation; and

WHEREAS, both the Corporation and the Director recognize the increased risk of litigation and other claims being asserted against directors;

NOW, THEREFORE, in consideration of the premises and of Director agreeing to serve the Corporation directly or, at its request, with another enterprise, and intending to be legally bound hereby, the parties hereto agree as follows:

1. *Indemnification.*

(a) Except to the extent expressly prohibited by the New York Not-For-Profit Corporation Law, the Corporation shall indemnify the director and his or her heirs, executors, administrators and successors against judgments, fines, penalties, amounts paid in settlement and reasonable expenses, including attorneys' fees, incurred as a result of the director or such other party being made or threatened to be made a party to or called as a witness in or asked to provide information in connection with any pending or threatened action, proceeding, hearing or investigation, or any appeal therein (other than an action or proceeding by or in the right of the Corporation to procure a judgment in its favor), whether civil or criminal, including an action by or in the right of any other corporation of any type or kind, domestic or foreign, or any partnership, joint venture, trust, employee benefit plan or other enterprise, which the director served in any capacity at the request of the Corporation, by reason of the fact that the director is or was a director of the Corporation, or served such other corporation, partnership, joint venture, trust, employee benefit plan or other enterprise in any capacity, against judgments, fines, amounts paid in settlement and reasonable expenses, including attorneys' fees actually and necessarily incurred as a result of such action or proceeding, or any appeal therein, provided that the director has acted in good faith, for a purpose which he or she reasonably believed to be in, or, in the case of service for any other corporation or any partnership, joint venture, trust, employee benefit plan or other enterprise, not opposed to, the best interests of the Corporation and, in criminal actions or proceedings, in addition, had no reasonable cause to believe that his or her conduct was unlawful.

(b) Except to the extent expressly prohibited by the New York Not-For-Profit Corporation Law, the Corporation shall indemnify the director and his or her executors, administrators, heirs or successors if the director or such other party is made, or threatened to be made, a party to an action by or in the right of the Corporation to procure a judgment in its favor by reason of the fact that the director is or was a director or officer of the Corporation, or is or was serving at the request of the Corporation as a director or officer of any corporation of any type or kind, domestic or foreign, of any partnership, joint venture, trust, employee benefit plan or other enterprise, against amounts paid in settlement and reasonable expenses, including attorneys' fees, actually and necessarily incurred by the director in connection with the defense or settlement of such action, or in connection with an appeal therein, if the director acted in good faith, for a purpose which he or she reasonably believed to be in, or, in the case of service for any other corporation or any partnership, joint venture, trust, employee benefit plan or other enterprise, not opposed to, the best interests of the Corporation, except that no indemnification under this paragraph shall be made in respect to (1) a threatened action, or a pending action which is settled or otherwise disposed of, or (2) any claim, issue or matter as to which the director shall have been adjudged to be liable to the Corporation, unless and only to the extent that the court in which the action was brought, or, if no action was brought, any court of competent jurisdiction, determines upon application that, in view of all the circumstances of the case, the director is fairly and reasonably entitled to indemnity for such portion of the settlement amount and expenses as the court deems proper.

(c) The termination of any civil or criminal action or proceeding by judgment, settlement, conviction or upon a plea of nolo contendere, or its equivalent, shall not in itself create a presumption that the director did not act, in good faith, for a purpose which he or she reasonably believed to be in, or, in the case of service for any other corporation or any partnership, joint venture, trust, employee benefit plan or other enterprise, not opposed to, the best interests of the Corporation or that she or he had reasonable cause to believe that her or his conduct was unlawful.

2. *Denial of Indemnification.* No indemnification shall be made under this Agreement if a judgment or other final adjudication adverse to the director or his or her estate establishes that the director's acts were committed in bad faith or were the result of active and deliberate dishonesty and were material to the cause of action so adjudicated, or that the director gained in fact a financial profit or other advantage to which he or she was not legally entitled; and provided further that no such indemnification shall be required with respect to any settlement or other nonadjudicated disposition of any threatened or pending action or proceeding unless the Corporation has given its consent to such settlement or other disposition.

3. *Advances.* Upon request of the director, the Corporation shall advance or promptly reimburse all expenses, including attorneys' fees, reasonably incurred in defending any action or proceeding in advance of the final disposition thereof, provided that the director shall deliver to the Corporation a written undertaking by or on behalf of the director to repay such amount if the director is ultimately found not to be entitled to indemnification or, where indemnification is granted, to the extent the expenses so advanced or reimbursed exceed the amount to which the director is entitled.

4. *Nonexclusivity.* Nothing in this agreement shall limit or affect any other right of the director to indemnification or expenses, including attorneys' fees, under any statute, rule, regulation, certificate of incorporation, bylaw, insurance policy, contract or otherwise.

5. *Continued Indemnification.* The indemnification of the director provided by this agreement shall continue after the director has ceased to be a director of the Corporation and shall inure to the benefit of the director's heirs, executors, administrators and legal representatives.

6. *Reliance.* It is hereby expressly recognized that the director has agreed to serve or continue to serve as a director of the Corporation in reliance on the provisions of this agreement and that the Corporation is estopped to contend otherwise. Additionally, it is hereby expressly recognized that any service by the director as a director, officer or employee of any corporation which is a subsidiary or affiliate of the Corporation (or other entities controlled by the Corporation) is at the request of the Corporation and, to the extent permitted by law, the director is entitled to indemnification hereunder in connection with such service.

7. *Employee Benefit Plans.* For purposes of this agreement, the Corporation shall be deemed to have requested the director to serve an employee benefit plan where the performance by the director of the director's duties to the Corporation also imposes duties on, or otherwise involves services by, the director to the plan or participants or beneficiaries of the plan, and excise taxes assessed on the director with respect to an employee benefit plan pursuant to applicable law shall be considered indemnifiable expenses.

8. *Definitions.* For purposes of this agreement, the term "Corporation" shall include any legal successor to the Corporation, including any corporation or other entity which acquires all or substantially all of the assets of the Corporation in one or more transactions.

9. *Liability Insurance.* To the extent the Corporation maintains an insurance policy or policies providing directors' and officers' liability insurance, comprehensive general liability insurance, errors and omissions insurance or coverage for other risks, the Director shall be covered by such policy or policies, in accordance with its or their terms, to the maximum extent of the coverage available for any director or officer of the Corporation.

10. *Amendments.* No supplement, modification or amendment of this Agreement shall be binding unless executed in writing by both of the parties hereto. No waiver of any of the provisions of this Agreement shall be deemed or shall constitute a waiver of any other provisions hereof (whether or not similar) nor shall such waiver constitute a continuing waiver.

11. *No Duplication of Payments.* The Corporation shall not be liable under this Agreement to make any payment in connection with any claim made against the Director to the extent the Director has otherwise actually received payment (under any insurance policy, bylaw or otherwise) of the amounts otherwise indemnifiable hereunder.

12. *Specific Performance.* The parties recognize that if any provision of this Agreement is violated by either the corporation or the director, the other party may be without an adequate remedy at law. Accordingly, in the event of any such violation, the aggrieved party shall be entitled, if it so elects, to institute proceedings, either in law or at equity, to obtain damages, to enforce specific performance, to enjoin such violation, or to obtain any relief or any combination of the foregoing as the aggrieved party may elect to pursue.

13. *Severability and Interpretation.* In case any provision in this agreement shall be determined at any time to be unenforceable in any respect, the other provisions shall not in any way be affected or impaired thereby, and the affected provision shall be given the fullest possible enforcement in the circumstances, it being the intention of the corporation to afford indemnification and advancement of expenses to the directors in his or her capacity as a director or in the other capacities specified above, to the fullest extent permitted by law.

It witness whereof, the parties have signed this agreement on this _____ day of _____ in the year 199__.

_____
Director
Attest: XYZ Corporation

_____   By: _____
Secretary   President

Exhibit 4
Checklist of Provisions to Review in D&O Policies

1. Type of policy—claims made vs. occurrence
2. Insurer's rating by Best's or Moody's
3. Covered persons—D&O insurance usually covers only directors and officers
    (a) If managers of the organization such as its executive director, its general counsel and its controller are not clearly defined as officers in the organization's bylaws, coverage of these individuals should be clarified in an endorsement to the policy.
    (b) Coverage for the nonprofit organization is usually only for reimbursement of amounts paid as indemnification to officers and directors. Unless specifically included, coverage does not extend to direct liability of the nonprofit organization.
    (c) Depending upon the circumstances of the nonprofit organization and the differential in cost, the organization might want to seek to expand the definition of covered persons to include employees, committee members and volunteers.
4. Policy limits and premium amount
5. Retention or deductible amount—the amount which must be borne by the nonprofit organization or the director prior to any payment being made by the insurer. "Retention and deductible are often used interchangeably, but they differ technically in that a deductible—unlike a retention—is subtracted from the policy limit."*
6. Coinsurance percentage—that percentage of the overall claim, after the deduction of the retention amount, which must be borne by the nonprofit organization or the director
7. Exclusions—
    (a) Dishonesty, fraud, criminal acts, and/or gaining a personal profit or advantage to which the director is not entitled
    (b) Environmental matters, including general liability for release or discharge and cleanup cost
    (c) Bodily injury/property damage—should be covered under the nonprofit organization's comprehensive general liability policy
    (d) Employee benefit and pension liability—should be covered under the nonprofit organization's fiduciary liability insurance policy
    (e) Failure to maintain insurance—insurance required to be maintained should be specified

---

* Charles Tremper, "Understanding D&O Insurance," *Association Management* (January 1992): L58.

(f) Other coverage exists—if an insured has other coverage, does the D&O policy exclude coverage (e.g., malpractice coverage for the organization's general counsel)?

(g) Insured versus insured—eliminates coverage where one insured (e.g., a director who is also an employee or officer) brings an action against other insureds (e.g., an action for wrongful termination of employment brought by the employee/director against the remaining directors). This exclusion is at least partly an attempt to prevent collusive lawsuits by insured directors against each other. It should be modified, however, to provide an exception for employment-related claims and also for derivative suits.

(h) Are defense costs paid for claims which are otherwise excluded or are such defense costs also excluded?

8. Definition of "Claim," "Wrongful Acts" and "Loss"—in order for insureds under a D&O policy to be covered there must be a "claim" against the directors for "wrongful acts" and the insureds must have experienced a "loss."* Consequently, the definitions of each of these terms should be carefully reviewed.

    "Claim" should be defined in the policy and the definition should be as broad as possible. Specifically, the definition should include investigations and administrative, regulatory, or other governmental proceedings. The nonprofit organization should attempt to have the definition expanded so that coverage is included for mediation and other "non-adversarial" proceedings and so that coverage for a claim begins when an insured person receives a written demand for damages or nonmonetary relief.

9. Defense costs—

    (a) Three alternatives: (i) insurer has duty to defend, in which case the insurer retains counsel and defends the action or proceeding; (ii) indemnity provision, in which case defense costs are not paid by insurer until the end of proceeding; and (iii) provision for insurer advances of defense costs. Alternative (iii) is probably the most attractive for a director. If possible, the director should have the right to choose his or her counsel and the insurer should have a right of approval, which approval shall not be unreasonably withheld.

    (b) The nonprofit organization should attempt to have defense costs defined to include the costs of responding to informal investigations by governmental or administrative agencies.

---

* Weiss, "Getting the Best D&O Coverage," *Directors and Boards* (June 22, 1994): 5.

      (c) In D&O insurance policies defense costs are often deducted from the overall policy limits. As a result they are usually also subject to the retention amount and coinsurance percentage.

10. Representations in application for insurance—misrepresentation or failure to disclose by any insured person should not be imputed to any other insured person for purposes of the insurer's ability to deny coverage for misrepresentations in the insurance application.

11. Insurer's history with respect to allocation disputes

12. Cancellation provisions and notice requirements

PART II
Essential Tools and Mechanisms
of the Nonprofit Organization

This guidebook is written for the executive director and corporate secretary (who may, in a small organization, be the same person, or even the entire staff!), to sensitize them to certain issues arising in the life of a nonprofit organization. In some of the chapters which follow, our authors treat of matters which may directly affect the directors, the members (if any), and the outside world surrounding the nonprofit. These chapters are relevant to the staff in pointing out areas of service and support.

In this section we deal with tasks which, in large part, will be carried out by the staff or not at all, or where, as in discussions of the mission statement, staff input is essential if a complete and well-rounded product is to be achieved.

The Mission Statement

Philip A. Faix, Jr.

This chapter focuses briefly on what a mission statement is, and why a non-profit organization needs one; and provides simple guidelines to follow in creating one. The appendices to this chapter provide examples of mission statements from large and small nonprofit organizations and includes several examples drawn from publicly held for-profit corporations.

Purpose

Stated simply, a mission statement is a document that addresses itself to three fundamental questions about a nonprofit organization.

(1) What is the organization?
(2) What does the organization do?
(3) What does the organization want to be?

In substance, a mission statement reveals information about an organization's character, personality, and priorities.

If You Do Not Have a Mission Statement, Do You Need One?

Any organization currently without a mission statement must ask if there is an unfilled need or compelling reason to create and circulate one. Some contend that mission statements are valueless, nonmemorable, largely ignored, reflect only common sense, or are a waste of time, resources, and energy. Others maintain that such statements are vital, essential, and insightful, and necessary to focus discussions on core values, philosophy, deeper meanings, commitment, management style and priorities, and to aid in management's decision-making process. We suggest that it would be helpful for every tax-exempt nonprofit organization to have a well-articulated mission statement.

In his book entitled *The Seven Habits of Highly Effective People*, Stephen R. Covey strongly advocates the creation of organizational mission statements. He fully admits the creation and development of a mission statement takes time, patience, commitment, vision, and elucidation of values. He is a firm believer that every person in the organization should participate in the formulation of directions, values, guidelines, principles, and ideas. In his opinion, involvement in the drafting of a mission statement ensures commitment.[1]

Before Composing a Mission Statement

Before composing a mission statement for a new organization, the governing body of the organization (the board of directors) might pass a resolution appointing a special committee charged with drafting the statement. To the fullest extent practicable, all members of the governing body should be involved in the process, especially where there are few directors and where they can act effectively as a committee of the whole. A resolution authorizing the creation of a mission statement should emphasize its functional purpose.

For the mature nonprofit organization with or without a mission statement, the governing body should follow essentially the same procedures recommended above for the new organization. The board should consider taking into account, if applicable, its changing population and shifting ethnic groups, shrinking sources of governmental aid, and form a consensus on the shape and scope of the organization's finances, including operating expenses and endowments. These discussions should also probe the question: who are the members of the public whom we are committed to serve now and in the future, and who were they in the historical past?

Guidelines

The following guidelines are suggested for the composition of the mission statement.

(1) Establish fundamental parameters of purpose for the mission statement.

This requires reaching a consensus on the limitations of the mission statement. Will it be general and vague, or narrow and specific?

(2) State explicitly:

(a) The existence and purpose of the nonprofit organization.

Why does the organization exist? What needs in the community make it necessary? Would it be beneficial to research the expectations/needs/wants of the customer/consumer/beneficiary?

There should be a consensus on what the organization will seek to accomplish and an accurate and brief description of the service, product, or the philosophy of the organization, including whether in measurable goals, generalized aims, or broad concepts.

Fund-granting agencies will frequently want to review the organization's mission statement. Does the organization's governing board want such agencies to participate initially in the formation of the organization's mission statement?

(b) The member and constituencies served, who should be actively sought as readers.

To what audience or groups will the mission statement address itself—members, general public, employees, community, grant agencies, or constituencies served or sought?

(3) Establish and assemble all possible ideas for inclusion and acknowledge and treat all suggestions with respect, dignity, and sensitivity.

Do some brainstorming. Suggestions could be collected from major donors, persons benefitting from the organization's work, past and present officers, key staff persons, and members.

(4) Reach a consensus on the mission statement's content, format, appearance and distribution.

This step involves careful and thoughtful writing. The goal ought to be to express each idea clearly and avoid multiple interpretations or the possible implication of a negative concept. Be sure that the mission statement does not violate any Internal Revenue Service, state, or local legal requirements.

There are no right or wrong answers with respect to specificity or length. Some mission statements are quite succinct, while others run to several pages. Many published statements are general and vague, while some are very specific. Drafting, rewriting, and discussing is done to seek, define, and describe the organization's uniqueness.

The following questions should be considered. How much information should be contained in the statement? Will the organization's direction be changing in the near or long term future for foreseeable, or possibly unforeseen, reasons?

The form or appearance of the finalized mission statement should be agreed upon. Will it be a poster, a letter, or a placard? To whom should it be addressed? Details as to typeface, use of a logo, white space, colors, design, quality of paper, cost, and aesthetics should not be ignored.

(5) Gain final approval and wide support from the board of directors, the officers, principal staff members, membership, benefactors, and advisory groups.

Obtain acceptance over the widest spheres of influence. The board should formally approve the adoption of the mission statement, and, depending on the bylaws, serious consideration should be given to having the membership, if any, vote on its contents.

A mission statement can be extremely valuable to an organization. It shapes, forms, and directs the purposes or reasons for existence of the organization it serves. Time, persistence, patience, creativity, refinement, discernment, and compromise are required to finalize the mission statement.

The formulation and existence of a mission statement helps in the drafting of the organization's articles of incorporation and its bylaws, and is especially helpful in drafting purpose clauses and considering federal and state tax exemption requirements.

Review

Mission statements may be scrutinized by others, including the Internal Revenue Service and other governmental authorities. The organization's counsel and tax advisor should review all drafts of the mission statement for legal compliance with its articles of incorporation, bylaws, and tax-exempt status.

Notes

1. Stephen R. Covey, *The Seven Habits of Highly Effective People: Restoring the Character Ethic* (New York: Simon & Schuster, 1989).

Exhibit 1
American Bar Association
Mission and Goals

The Mission of the American Bar Association is to be the national representative of the legal profession, serving the public and the profession by promoting justice, professional excellence and respect for the law.

Goal I.   To promote improvements in the American system of justice.

Goal II.   To promote meaningful access to legal representation and the American system of justice for all persons regardless of their economic or social condition.

Goal III.   To provide ongoing leadership in improving the law to serve the changing needs of society.

Goal IV.   To increase public understanding of and respect for the law, the legal process, and the role of the legal profession.

Goal V.   To achieve the highest standards of professionalism, competence, and ethical conduct.

Goal VI.   To serve as the national representative of the legal profession.

Goal VII.   To provide benefits, programs and services which promote professional growth and enhance the quality of life of the members.

Goal VIII. To advance the rule of law in the world.

Goal IX.   To promote full and equal participation in the legal profession by minorities and women.

Goal X.   Preserve and enhance the ideals of the legal profession as a common calling and its dedication to public service.

Goal XI.   To preserve the independence of the legal profession and the judiciary as fundamental to a free society.

Exhibit 1 is reprinted with the permission of the American Bar Association.

Exhibit 2
American Bar Association
Senior Lawyers Division
Mission and Goals

■ **MISSION** —

The Senior Lawyers Division serves the interests and needs of the legal profession and the public by sharing the accumulated knowledge and experience of its members.

■ **GOALS** —

1. To be the voice of the senior lawyer within the American Bar Association.
2. To assist in promoting improvements in the American system of justice and to preserve and uphold the dignity and ideals of the legal profession.
3. To encourage interest in and the advancement of substantive elder law.
4. To assist the elderly and needy to obtain proper legal representation.
5. To maintain an interest in programs for the elderly.
6. To assist the legal profession to develop competent and caring lawyers through its state and local bar associations and mentor programs.
7. To provide guidance and assistance to senior lawyers in preparing for and adjusting to changes in their professional and financial activities.
8. To act as a support group to other sections and divisions of the American Bar Association (programs and activities).
9. To enhance the quality of life of the senior lawyer.
10. To provide services and publications which enhance the continued careers and quality of life of its members.
11. To continually monitor, evaluate and communicate to senior lawyers:
    (a) The changing role of lawyers
    (b) The future role of lawyers
    (c) The methods by which lawyers may deal with their environment and role in life.

Exhibit 2 is reprinted with the permission of the American Bar Association, Senior Lawyers Division.

Exhibit 3
American Society of Corporate Secretaries
Mission Statement

The American Society of Corporate Secretaries is dedicated to providing services that enhance the professional skills of its members, who are business executives involved in duties normally associated with the corporate secretarial function. The Society provides a forum for the exchange of information and networking through its chapters, national committees, educational seminars, conferences and national office.

The Society is committed to:
- Performing a leadership role in assisting its members and their organizations in implementing sound business practices in furtherance of effective corporate governance;
- Helping its members achieve and maintain the highest levels of professionalism and ethics; and
- Identifying relevant issues of interest and concern to its members and their organizations and advocating, on behalf of its members, highly informed positions on such issues to governmental and other entities.

Exhibit 3 is reprinted with the permission of the American Society of Corporate Secretaries.

Exhibit 4
Fairleigh Dickinson University
Mission Statement

Preamble:

Fairleigh Dickinson University is an independent, non-sectarian institution of higher education, dedicated to making a difference in the lives and careers of our students.

The Board of Trustees, the administration, faculty, students, staff and alumni are committed to the University's continuing achievement of its public purposes of education and scholarship. To that end, we must ensure the institution's vitality and direction in a world of rapid and challenging change.

Mission Statement

In an ever-changing global environment, Fairleigh Dickinson University is dedicated to being the region's leading institution of lifelong learning.

The University is committed to excellence in teaching and student learning. The University supports a community in which intellectual freedom, scholarship, professional development, and shared intellectual experiences flourish. The University is dedicated to being inclusive by recruiting and retaining qualified students, faculty, staff, and trustees from diverse ethnic, cultural, and national backgrounds and heritage.

The University seeks to serve diverse local, national, and international constituencies at two New Jersey campuses, an overseas campus in Wroxton, England, and at other sites. The multi-campus structure, with separate and distinctive missions for each campus, provides the benefits of small college communities within a comprehensive institution. The two major campuses draw upon and contribute to the rich cultural and economic resources of the New Jersey-New York metropolitan area.

Exhibit 4 is reprinted with the permission of Fairleigh Dickinson University.

Exhibit 5
Openlands Project
Mission Statement

Mission Statement

Openlands Project protects, expands, and enhances open space—lands and waters—to provide an improved environment and a more livable place for people of the region.

Openlands initiates and achieves change by advocating sound open space policies, educating the general public, and bringing individuals, communities, and organizations together.

Region Served

The core of Openlands Project's region is Chicago and its surrounding suburbs and rural areas. The region is not restricted by political boundaries. It encompasses natural watersheds and other corridors that are integral parts of northeastern Illinois' bioregion.

Exhibit 5 is reprinted with the permission of the Openlands Project.

Exhibit 6
Northeast Valley Health Corporation
Mission Statement

The mission of the Northeast Valley Health Corporation is to provide coordinated, comprehensive and high quality health care service to the residents of the San Fernando Valley with particular attention to the medically underserved and low income populations. These services will be accessible, acceptable and delivered in a manner that is congruent with economical, cultural and social needs of the community. The Corporation will provide leadership in health education, advocate for health services and pursue dynamic health care programs to meet the needs of the community.

Exhibit 6 is reprinted with the permission of the Northeast Valley Health Corporation.

Exhibit 7
Johnson & Johnson Mission Statement

OUR CREDO

We believe our first responsibility is to the doctors, nurses and patients, to mothers and fathers and all others who use our products and services. In meeting their needs everything we do must be of high quality. We must constantly strive to reduce our costs in order to maintain reasonable prices. Customers' orders must be serviced promptly and accurately. Our suppliers and distributors must have an opportunity to make a fair profit.

We are responsible to our employees, the men and women who work with us throughout the world. Everyone must be considered as an individual. We must respect their dignity and recognize their merit. They must have a sense of security in their jobs. Compensation must be fair and adequate, and working conditions clean, orderly and safe. We must be mindful of ways to help our employees fulfill their family responsibilities. Employees must feel free to make suggestions and complaints. There must be equal opportunity for employment, development and advancement for those qualified. We must provide competent management, and their actions must be just and ethical.

We are responsible to the communities in which we live and work and to the world community as well. We must be good citizens—support good works and charities and bear our fair share of taxes. We must encourage civic improvements and better health and education. We must maintain in good order the property we are privileged to use, protecting the environment and natural resources.

Our final responsibility is to our stockholders. Business must make a sound profit. We must experiment with new ideas. Research must be carried on, innovative programs developed and mistakes paid for. New equipment must be purchased, new facilities provided and new products launched. Reserves must be created to provide for adverse times. When we operate according to these principles, the stockholders should realize a fair return.

Exhibit 7 is reprinted with the permission of Johnson & Johnson.

Exhibit 8
New York Chapter
National Association of Corporate Directors
Mission Statement

The overall mission of the National Association of Corporate Directors, essentially, is to serve the needs of individual directors by focusing on the concerns of the boardroom and the development of professional excellence in board performance.

The primary focus of NACD—NY's mission shall be to provide its members opportunities for

- *Professional Development* as Directors
- *Networking and Idea Exchange* Among Directors
- *Information Updates* (timely and crucial) Regarding Director-Related Issues and Trends
- *Education* Regarding Corporate Governance or Conduct
- *Participation in Public Forums* Concerned with Director-Related Issues

Its *members* shall include those involved with profit or not-for-profit organizations as:

- Inside Directors and Senior Officers
- Outside Directors
- Advisory Directors
- Providers of Support Services to Directors and Others Concerned with Corporate Governance

---

Exhibit 8 is reprinted with the permission of the New York Chapter of the National Association of Corporate Directors.

Delegations of Authority in the Nonprofit Organization

Victor Futter[1]

This chapter describes the reasons why the board of a nonprofit organization should adopt written resolutions, procedures, or bylaws to specify those management actions which require board approval and those that are delegated to committees, officers, and others.

Introduction

For the effective administration of a nonprofit organization, it must be clear who has authority to act on behalf of the organization and the scope of such authority. The following are three common examples of delegation problems:

(1) Most would agree that the transactions involving significant expenditures of funds and commitments to make such expenditures should be approved by the board. But what is "significant"? Who decides?

(2) The executive director needs authority to act on matters between board meetings. How may this be done by the board without abdication of its responsibilities?

(3) The landlord who is leasing office space to the organization wants the opinion of the organization's counsel that the officer who signed the lease on behalf of the organization was "duly authorized" to do so. What may the organization's counsel rely upon for his or her opinion?

The delegation of its authority by the organization's board will vary with business needs and management style. What should not vary, however, is the ability to point to something in writing that clearly establishes who has the authority to take every kind of organizational action.

State statutes, the certificate of incorporation, or the bylaws typically provide that the business, property, and affairs of the organization shall be the responsibility of the board of directors.[2] Usually it is impractical and unwise for the board actively to administer the organization's day-to-day business or to become immersed in operating details.

It is generally recognized that the board may delegate, to appropriate officers of the organization, the authority to exercise powers that are not required by law to be exercised by the board itself. While such delegation will not serve to relieve the board of its responsibilities of oversight, it is generally held, in some states by legislation, that directors not be held personally responsible for actions or omissions of officers, employees, or agents of the organization so long as the directors, complying with the enunciated standard of care, have reasonably relied upon such officers, employees, or agents.

Suggested General Resolutions

Described below are some approaches to delegations of authority. In these suggested resolutions, the executive director's authority is limited with respect to certain important matters (capital and non-capital expenditures, borrowing and the hiring of certain employees), but the executive director is given broad authority with respect to all other matters. Needless to say, each organization will decide for itself in which areas (in addition to those mentioned above) and the extent to which the executive director's authority should be limited.

If the organization is large enough, such delegations generally will be drafted initially by the secretary. In any event, they should be reviewed carefully by the executive director before being presented to the appropriate board committee for study and approval and then to the full board for adoption. The schedules referred to should be prepared for each organization depending on its need.

Another form of resolutions is set forth as Exhibit 1. Each organization will, of course, wish to vary the dollar amounts or other limitations contained in this exhibit depending upon the size and culture of the organization.

Authority Levels

RESOLVED, the board of directors of the organization hereby delegates the levels of authority shown on the attached schedule of executive approvals to the executive director and others, subject to the resolutions which follow. The authority of any person holding a position shown in this schedule applies only to her or his area of responsibility and represents the maximum authority of that person to commit the organization.[3]

RESOLVED, that the executive director is authorized, except where otherwise noted, to delegate (with right of further delegation) to any other officer, employee or agent of the corporation all or part of the authority granted to him or her by this schedule, and any such delegation may be general or specific and subject to such limitations and restrictions as the delegating officer shall determine.

Any delegation of authority made pursuant hereto shall be made by a written instrument which shall state the authority delegated and any limitations and restrictions on such authority. One copy of such delegation shall be delivered to the person to whom authority is delegated and additional copies shall be delivered to the chief financial officer and the secretary.

RESOLVED, the executive director is authorized to adjust the approval levels within this schedule from time to time by written instrument, one copy of which shall be delivered to the person whose authority is adjusted and additional copies shall be delivered to the chief financial officer and the secretary, provided that such adjusted levels shall not exceed the authority granted to the executive director.

RESOLVED, the executive director is authorized to take (or authorize others to take) such action as he or she deems appropriate in connection with any other matters within the general business of the corporation which are not specifically described on this schedule.

Capital Expenditures

RESOLVED, that each capital expenditure by the organization (including the present value of leases of _____ years or longer) (i) of more than $_____ shall require board authorization, and (ii) of up to $_____ shall require the authorization of the executive director, or such other employee or committee of the organization as either the board or the executive director may designate in writing for this purpose.

Non-Capital Expenditures

RESOLVED, that each non-capital expenditure or commitment by the organization in excess of $_____ (including contracts and leases of more than three years) shall require board authorization, and commitments of up to $_____ (including leases up to 3 years) shall require the authorization of the executive director, or such other employee or committee of the organization as either the board or the executive director may designate in writing for this purpose.

Borrowing

RESOLVED, that each borrowing by the organization or the guarantee by the organization for money borrowed by the organization or others (i) of more than $_____ shall require board authorization, and (ii) of up to $_____ shall require authorization of the executive director, or such other employee or committee of the organization as either the board or the executive director may designate in writing for this purpose.

Hiring

RESOLVED, that the hiring of an employee of the organization or an independent contractor (i) for a term of more than _____ years or for an annual compensation of more than $_____ shall require board authorization, and (ii) of up to _____ years or up to $_____ shall require authorization of the executive director, or such other employee or committee of the organization as either the board or the executive director may designate in writing for this purpose.

Authority to Take Necessary Actions, Execute Documents and Certifications

RESOLVED, that the proper officers of the organization are authorized to take all necessary actions and to execute and deliver all such documents, agreements, instruments, legal opinions, certificates and notices as such officers, or any of them, may deem necessary or advisable to carry out the intent of the foregoing resolutions.

Banking Resolutions

Banking resolutions sometimes present particular problems. Set forth below are various forms of sample resolutions giving blanket authority with respect to establishing banking relationships. Some banks require the adoption of their standard resolutions. Other forms of banking resolutions are contained in Exhibits 2 and 3.

A board should consider whether the following resolutions (describing signatories by title only) are preferable, in view of their flexibility, over authorizations of named individuals).

Banking Accounts

RESOLVED, that the forms of banking resolutions generally used by any banks in which accounts of the organization are established are hereby approved and adopted as if set forth herein in full.

Authorization to Open Commercial Banking Accounts

RESOLVED, that the executive director, any vice president or the treasurer of the organization is hereby authorized from time to time to open one or more commercial banking accounts in the name of the organization anywhere within the United States and to deposit to the credit of the organization in such banking accounts any monies, checks, drafts, orders or other commercial paper payable to the organization.

Authorization to Withdraw from Commercial Banking Accounts

RESOLVED, that the executive director, any vice president or the treasurer of the organization is hereby authorized to withdraw (by check or otherwise) all or any part of the funds on deposit in the name of the organization in any commercial banking account upon the signature of the executive director, any vice president or the treasurer or any of them or their designees; provided, however, that any withdrawal of more than $_____ shall require the signatures of any two of said officers.

Checking Account Authorization

RESOLVED, that the executive director, any vice president, or the treasurer of the organization is hereby authorized to execute on behalf of the organization and to file with any commercial bank (and the secretary of the organization is hereby authorized to certify) such forms of banking resolutions, together with proper signature cards designating the officers of the organization who are authorized to sign checks and drafts to be paid from the organization's accounts in such banks, and copies of such resolutions are ordered to be filed in the minute book of the organization.

Bank Reliance on Signature Card

RESOLVED, that with respect to any commercial banking account, any banking institution may act in reliance on such banking resolutions and signature cards until receipt of actual notice of the modification or revocation of the same.

Conclusion

How much authority can and should be delegated depends in part upon the state law of incorporation and in part upon the particular needs and management style of each organization. But it is vitally important that written resolutions, procedures, or bylaws be adopted by the board to specify those management actions that require board approval and those that are delegated to committees, officers, and others.

Notes

1. The author acknowledges the considerable assistance received from Manuel Schultz, chairman of the Legal Center for Connecticut Nonprofit Organizations, Inc., and from Frederick G. Emerson, secretary of the Dial Corporation, in the preparation of this chapter.

2. *See* Model Nonprofit Corp. Act § 8.01 (1987), which states:

(a) Each corporation must have a board of directors.

(b) Except as provided in this Act or subsection (c), all corporate powers shall be exercised by or under the authority of, and the affairs of the corporation managed under the direction of, its board.

(c) The articles may authorize a person or persons to exercise all of the powers which would otherwise be exercised by a board. To the extent so authorized any such person or persons shall have the duties and responsibilities of the directors, and the directors shall be relieved to the extent from such duties and responsibilities.

3. The resolutions offered here (pp. 170–172) as examples are printed with the permission of Allied Signal, Inc.

Exhibit 1
General Delegations

RESOLVED, that the authority granted to any officer or officers of the Corporation by any resolution which has been adopted by the Board of Directors or the Executive Committee of this Corporation may be delegated by the officer to whom such authority is granted unless such resolution specifically forbids or restricts such delegation, provided that such officer executes a specific written authorization or power-of-attorney authorizing another person to act on his behalf in a specific transaction or clearly defined category of transactions;

FURTHER RESOLVED, that this Corporation may, acting through its officers:

(A) make a capital expenditure, investment, or advance, or execute a lease, if authorized by:

(1) a Vice President of this Corporation if the amount thereof does not exceed $60,000; or

(2) the Executive Director of this Corporation if the amount thereof does not exceed $2,000,000 for a capital expenditure, investment, or advance, and if the amount to be paid out or received in any one year does not exceed $2,000,000 and does not, during its entire term, exceed $5,000,000 for a lease;

provided that further approval shall not be required of an approved expenditure which ultimately exceeds the amount approved by not more than 10% and

further provided that no advances shall be made to an officer or employee and no corporation shall be formed unless approved by the Executive Director of this Corporation;

(B) execute a contract with a labor union if authorized by:

(1) a Vice President of this Corporation if the term is no more than six years and the additional annual cost to the Corporation over the contract in effect during the immediately preceding annual period does not exceed $50,000; or

(2) the Executive Director of this Corporation who may authorize such contracts if the term is more than six years and the additional annual cost to the Corporation over the contract in effect during the immediately preceding annual period exceeds $50,000;

Exhibit 1 is reprinted with the permission of the Viad Corporation.

(C) execute a contract which involves only the incurring of operating expenses which are usual and customary in the conduct of the business if authorized by:

    (1) a Vice President of this Corporation if the term is no more than six years and the annual cost to the Corporation does not exceed $70,000; or

    (2) the Executive Director of this Corporation who may authorize such contracts in which the term is more than six years and the annual cost to the Corporation exceeds $70,000;

(D) execute a contract which involves only the sale in the ordinary course of business of the products or services which this Corporation customarily sells to its customers if within the same authorities and limits set forth in paragraph (E) following, except that if the sale is for cash (payable within normal credit terms) or to an office, agency or other entity of government, the Executive Director of this Corporation may authorize such contracts;

(E) execute any other contract not specifically governed by the provisions of another paragraph herein if authorized by:

    (1) a Vice President of this Corporation if the total amount to be paid out or received in any one year does not exceed $70,000 and does not, during its entire term, exceed $325,000; or

    (2) the Executive Director of this Corporation if the amount to be paid out or received in any one year does not exceed $2,000,000 and does not, during its entire term, exceed $5,000,000;

(F) establish or increase the salary of an employee of this Corporation if authorized by:

    (1) a Vice President of this Corporation if the salary established or as increased does not exceed $50,000 per annum; or

    (2) the Executive Director of this Corporation if the salary established or as increased exceeds $50,000 per annum, except the salaries for Officers of the Corporation, which shall be approved by the Executive Compensation Committee;

(G) sell, transfer, or retire an asset owned by this Corporation or write off or write down an account of this Corporation, if authorized by:

    (1) a Vice President of this Corporation if neither its book value nor its current value exceeds $60,000; or

    (2) the Executive Director of this Corporation if neither its book value nor its current value exceeds $2,000,000, except that the Executive Director may approve sales or transfers of as-

sets in excess of $2,000,000 between this Corporation and its subsidiaries or among subsidiaries of this Corporation;

(H) settle a claim (including a judgment) against this Corporation, arising out of an accident, if authorized by:

(1) a Vice President of this Corporation if the amount of the settlement does not exceed $35,000; or

(2) the Executive Director of this Corporation who may authorize the settlement of such claims which exceed $35,000;

(I) settle a claim (including a judgment) against this Corporation, not arising out of an accident and not under an insurance contract, if authorized by:

(1) a Vice President of this Corporation if the amount of the settlement does not exceed $30,000; or

(2) the Executive Director of this Corporation if the amount of the settlement does not exceed $2,000,000.

Any expenditures, investments, advances, contracts, leases, salaries, claims, accounting entries, or other transactions or actions which are not authorized above must be authorized by the Board of Directors or Executive Committee of this Corporation before the same shall be made, entered into or taken, and before this Corporation shall be committed to make, enter into or take the same. Such authorization by the Board of Directors or Executive Committee of this Corporation may be given a resolution duly adopted or by a writing signed by a quorum of the members of such Board of Directors or Executive Committee.

Exhibit 2
Authority Over Financial Matters

At the _____, 1995, meeting of the Board of Directors of the [name of organization] the following resolutions were approved:

RESOLVED, that the Executive Director, any Vice President, or Treasurer of the _____, and each of them, is hereby authorized to open one or more commercial banking accounts or other accounts at other financial or brokerage institutions for and in the name of _____ anywhere within the United States, at any time and from time to time, and to deposit to the credit of _____ in such accounts any monies, checks, drafts, orders, or traded securities payable to _____ or to its order, and at any time and from time to time to withdraw or transfer to any other account all or any part of the funds on deposit in the name of _____ in any such banking accounts upon the signature or verbal authorization of the Executive Director, any Vice President, the Treasurer, or any of them or their designees, and any such officer may execute and deliver an agreement with any bank or other financial or brokerage institutions in connection therewith;

RESOLVED, that the forms of banking resolutions used by any banks or other financial or brokerage institutions in which accounts of _____ are established pursuant to the immediate preceding resolution are hereby approved and adopted as if set forth herein in full;

RESOLVED, that the Executive Director, any Vice President, or the Treasurer of _____, and each of them, is hereby authorized to execute on behalf of _____ and to file with such banks or other financial or brokerage institutions, and the Secretary of _____ is hereby authorized to certify, such forms of banking resolutions, together with proper signature cards designating the officers and agents of _____ who are authorized to sign checks and drafts to be paid from _____ accounts in such banks or other financial or brokerage institutions, as such officer(s) may deem appropriate.

RESOLVED, that with respect to any such banking accounts, any banking or other financial or brokerage institution may act in reliance on such banking resolutions and signature cards until receipt of actual notice of the modification or revocation of the same.

I hereby certify that such resolutions are in full force and effect as of the date hereby affixed.

[SEAL] _____   _____
　　　　　　　　　　　　　　　　　　　　　　　　　　　　　　　　　DATE

_____

Exhibit 2 is reprinted with the permission of the Viad Corporation.

Exhibit 3
Amended Bank Resolutions
Based on Report of the Audit Committee

The Audit Committee has reviewed the [Corporation] bank resolutions and subsequently has proposed that the Board of Directors rescind the resolution adopted on [date] and adopt the following resolution:

RESOLVED, that the Board of Directors of [Corporation] authorizes the use of the following banks in accordance with the following authorization/limitations:

[list banks and cities]

FURTHER RESOLVED, that the signatories listed below are empowered to:

1. Sign checks and other orders for the payment of money from such account(s);
2. Initiate transactions resulting in credits or debits to such account(s) in any manner authorized by the Bank(s), including by means of oral instruction, code, card or other device by or through an electronic terminal, telephone, telex, facsimile transmission, wire computer, magnetic or other tape or any other form of funds transfer facility;
3. Endorse checks and other instruments for deposits in such account(s) or for collection by the Bank or for negotiation;
4. Identify, approve, endorse and guarantee the endorsement of any payee or endorser on any checks or drafts, whether drawn by this Organization or anyone else, and to guarantee payment of such items and to delegate to others this authority; and
5. Waive presentment, demand, protest, notice of dishonor or protest of any instrument made, drawn or endorsed by this Organization.

FURTHER RESOLVED, that all checks, drafts, notes, orders or electronic funds transfers drawn against said account(s) for disbursements through Fifty Thousand Dollars ($50,000), shall require one of the authorized signatures. Disbursements over Fifty Thousand Dollars ($50,000) shall require two of the authorized signatures while electronic funds transfers shall require approval of one signatory before transmission by a second signatory. The following transactions can be authorized by the Executive Director or the Treasurer without further approval:

1. Purchase securities in the name of the Corporation up to a per-transaction limit of One Million Dollars ($1,000,000);
2. Transfer funds between bank accounts held in the name of the Corporation.

FURTHER RESOLVED, that the Corporation is allowed to use a facsimile signature of the Executive Director for the signing of checks.

FURTHER RESOLVED, that the officers of the Corporation are directed to adopt a policy which prohibits any of the authorized signatories from signing any check or other instrument drawn on any account which is payable to himself.

FURTHER RESOLVED, that the authorized signatories, or the duly appointed replacements for the positions indicated, for all banks other than [bank and city], shall be:

[list signatories]

FURTHER RESOLVED, that the authorized signatories, or the duly approved replacements for the positions indicated, for [different bank if necessary] shall be:

[list signatories]

FURTHER RESOLVED, that the resolution of the Board of Directors of [Corporation] adopted on [date], is hereby rescinded.

Information Flow

Victor Futter

This chapter describes the type of information that a board of directors should receive in advance of a board meeting and the types of information that a board should be given between meetings.

In considering the relationship between a board and the executive director or staff, one of the most important elements is the prompt and adequate flow of information from the organization to the board. The key with respect to information flow is the *timeliness* and the *quality* of the information provided.

For Board Meetings

Let's begin by looking at a typical board meeting. If information flow is being properly handled by the executive director and the secretary, then, in *advance* of each board meeting, and *preferably* by the *weekend* before the board meeting, each director should receive a packet containing:

(1) An agenda

The agenda should make clear (a) what resolutions the board of directors will be asked to act on ("Action Items"); (b) what items are presented for discussion ("Discussion Items"); and (c) what items are presented as a matter of information ("Information Items"). In other words, the agenda should make clear what the board of directors will be called upon to do.

Two suggestions for developing the agenda are worth considering.

(a) The secretary or executive director should meet with the chair prior to the board meeting to provide in-depth information with respect to the items on the agenda and to determine whether the chairman wishes to add any item to the agenda or desires the board to be supplied with any additional information.

(b) The agenda should be sent to the full board thirty days in advance of the meeting with an inquiry whether there are any other items or other suggestions board members might have. This enables the board members to have input and may serve to eliminate potential sources of friction. It enables the executive director to head off potential trouble areas by individual discussions with concerned directors.

(2) The minutes of the previous meeting
(3) Any proposed resolutions
(4) Backup material for each item on the agenda
(5) Reports (or minutes) of committee meetings

(6) Financial statements, including balance sheets and income and expense statements (with comparisons to budget), and, particularly in nonprofits, cash-flow statements

Financial statements should also have a cover page describing important changes since the last statement.

(7) A comparison of the current level of contributions to the budget and to the previous year's contributions

This item is particularly important to a nonprofit.

(8) A report highlighting important developments in the organization since the last meeting

The executive director can summarize developments in a one- to three-page report placed in the front of the packet.

(9) A membership statement

Especially important for organizations dependent on membership dues, this statement should include current membership, last year's membership, and the anticipated membership (the number used in developing the budget).

This list is meant to be illustrative, not exhaustive. The important thing is to have a regular program of information. This is vastly superior to a sporadic hit-or-miss distribution of information and will be greatly appreciated by the directors.

The board packets should go out, preferably via overnight delivery or priority mail, by Wednesday or Thursday night of the week preceding the board meeting. This gives the directors the opportunity to read the material over the weekend. Regular mail may also be used, but given the uncertainty of delivery, a longer period of time will be required. Some organizations use a longer schedule and send their materials to directors two weeks in advance of meetings.

The point is that it is grossly unfair to dump a bunch of papers on a director at a board meeting and to ask him or her to respond intelligently to them. This is so irksome that if it is continued, it may well lead your best directors to resign.

In putting board materials together, a sense of balance is required. The board needs sufficient information, but it should not be "snowed" with an avalanche of paper. Keep the materials concise and to the point. The executive director and the secretary should be asking themselves: is the material effectively presented? is it accurate? If lengthy materials are sometimes necessary, they should be accompanied by an executive summary.

It is recognized that sometimes emergencies require the last-minute preparation of an item and its presentation at the board meeting itself. To the greatest extent possible, this should be avoided. It can be somewhat alleviated by faxing the item in advance of the meeting.

Board committees should similarly be supplied with information in advance of each meeting. This should include items (1) through (4) above plus such other items as are appropriate to the particular committee meeting. To the extent possible, a tentative schedule of matters to be discussed at each board and committee meeting should be prepared at the beginning of each year. Such a schedule will, of course, require modification as events develop during the course of the year, but they do insure that basic and recurring items are not overlooked.

Between Board Meetings

In addition to information for board and committee meetings, there is other information to which a director is entitled during the course of the year and outside of meetings.

(1) All significant press or media mentions—good or bad—and we stress: including the bad press

    The directors will find out about the coverage anyway. The information they are given is a test of the executive director's credibility and honesty. One of the most important attributes for an executive director is candor and complete honesty with the board. Boards will accept failures of which they are advised; they will not tolerate deceit, excuses, or cover-up.

(2) Periodic mailings by the executive director of press releases, speeches, or memos on important topics

    Keep your directors informed. A director can only be as good as the information you provide to educate him or her.

(3) Items of general interest in areas with which your organization is concerned

(4) Information about what competing organizations are doing

(5) How your organization compares with similar organizations

Information like the foregoing is particularly important for nonprofit boards because of their size, which is generally larger than the average corporate board; the diversity of background of their members; and because nonprofit boards generally do not meet as frequently as major for-profit corporations.

As a final suggestion, you might consider having a board committee review with the secretary, at least once a year, the type and timeliness of the information supplied to the board. Ask board members specifically what types of information they would like to have and are not getting; and if there are any materials being received that board members do not find useful.

Bibliography

Berger, Robert O. and J. Garefield Donelson. "Getting Insiders the Information They Need." *Price Waterhouse & Co. Review* 21 (1976): 36.

Maurer, Richard S. "Director Information Systems: The Advance Information Package, Minutes and Corporate Reports, Records." In *Handbook for Corporate Directors*. Chicago: R.R. Donnelley & Sons, 1985.

Mountjoy, John. "Information Flow to Directors." In *The Corporate Secretary and the Board of Directors: A Comprehensive Guidebook*. New York: American Society of Corporate Secretaries, 1987.

Functions and Responsibilities of the Secretary in Nonprofit Corporations

Carol M. Barker

This chapter discusses the functions and duties of the secretary of a nonprofit. The reader is reminded that throughout the work we are using the term "secretary" to describe a member of the organization's staff or to describe the functions embraced by the secretary's office.

Introduction

The basic functions of the secretary, in nonprofit and for-profit corporations alike, are legally required, essential to good governance, and necessary to the smooth operation of the organization. All nonprofit corporations need to be attentive to these functions.

Bylaws typically list the duties of the secretary as:

(1) to take the minutes of meetings of the board and its committees and of the annual meeting;

(2) to see that all notices are duly given;

(3) to be custodian of the seal of the organization, if any, and to affix and attest the seal;

(4) in general, to perform all duties incident to the office of the secretary; and

(5) to perform all other duties as may be assigned by the executive director.

The secretary may be a member of the board or may be a staff officer appointed by the executive director and approved by the board. In organizations with any significant staff, even if the secretary is a board member, all but the most formal functions of the office—that is, signing and sealing certain documents—are likely to be assigned to one or more staff members. When the secretary is a board member, the staff member with chief responsibilities for the secretarial function may be given the title of assistant secretary.

The purpose of this brief chapter is to outline and comment on the nature of the functions of the office of the secretary, those specified above and those "incident to the office of the secretary," which in larger organizations may be quite extended and complex. These functions are described in more detail in other chapters of this manual.

The "other duties assigned" to the secretary vary depending on the nature of the organization and even among similar organizations. In small organizations, the staff member or members responsible for these functions will very likely have other responsibilities unrelated to the secretarial function. Even in larger organizations, the secretary may have varied responsibilities, reflecting the nature of the organization and the needs of the board and the executive director.

However the functions of the secretary are assigned and whatever the title of the person carrying them out, these functions support the continuity, the integrity, and the accountability of the corporation. The person carrying them out should have broad knowledge of the mission, purposes, and programs of the organization and should hold the confidence of the board, the executive director, and other officers.

Functions

Minutes and Recordkeeping

The most basic of the functions of the secretary is the preparation of minutes for the official meetings of the corporation—the annual meeting, the meetings of the board of directors, and the meetings of board committees—and the maintenance of these official corporate records.

Minutes should record the date, time, place, participants, and actions of official meetings of the organization. Minutes report in greater or lesser detail the discussions that took place, depending on organizational practice, and the needs and expectations of the board and the executive director (see p. 39). Minutes are submitted for approval by the board or the committees, and with approval, become the official record of the meeting and actions taken during it.

In preparing minutes, the secretary provides continuity and collective memory between meetings. The contrast between a mere mechanical record of a meeting, or a transcript, full of irrelevant comment and unclear communication, and minutes is dramatic. Minutes record selectively, providing information essential to governance and management of the organization. Minutes may be used to resolve controversial matters and must be precise, clear, accurate, and consistent with the understanding of the participants in the meeting. Nonessential details may confuse the record and, in the worst case, create legal difficulties. Minutes should be circulated for review by the executive director, other senior staff, and general counsel before being submitted to the members of the board or committees for their approval. Far from being a routine matter, minutes depend on and reflect the organizational knowledge and understanding of the secretary.

In extension of this recordkeeping responsibility, the secretary may be assigned responsibility for the corporate records and archives, making sure essential records are preserved and accessible to appropriate parties. The secretary may also be assigned responsibility for developing and implementing a records management program for the organization as a whole, which provides guidelines and schedules for maintaining and disposing of records in various media (including paper, film, and electronics) consistent with management, legal, and fiscal requirements (see p. 287).

Meetings

The secretary is responsible for the proper conduct of official meetings of the corporation—the annual meeting and meetings of the board of directors and board committees. Consistent with the bylaws, the secretary schedules and provides notice of the time, place, and agenda of the meeting in question to the participants in a timely fashion. In consultation with the executive director and/or the chair, the secretary prepares the agenda for the meeting and produces and distributes meeting materials in a timely fashion. The secretary is also responsible for planning and managing meeting logistics.

In carrying out the meeting function, the secretary ensures that members of the corporation and the board can fulfill their fiduciary responsibilities, exercise their rights, and fulfill their responsibilities in the governance of the corporation. Schedules, agendas, and logistics should meet the needs of both board and management. Adequate notice, timely and focused agendas, and clearly written and concise background materials distributed in advance of the meeting encourage participation, foster effective communication, contribute to understanding between board and management, and consequently, confidence in management.

Responsibility for meetings, especially the annual meeting, may be quite extensive. In a membership organization—especially one with a large, active, and dispersed membership—provision must be made for communication with and participation, in person or by proxy, of all those legally entitled to participate. The annual meeting is a formal occasion with a carefully developed script. Beyond these responsibilities "incident to the office of the secretary," the secretary may also be assigned responsibility for planning and managing the educational, informational, and social activities surrounding the annual meeting. These activities often develop a life of their own independent of corporate governance, requiring a variety of meeting planning skills—programmatic, promotional, and logistical.

Compliance

The official functions of the secretary include signing and sealing certain documents and attesting to the signatures of other officers and the validity of certain corporate actions. These official, but usually routine, matters must be carried out by the secretary, whether she or he be a board member or staff, or must be officially delegated to an assistant secretary.

In carrying out these official functions, the secretary is affirming the corporation's compliance with the laws of the state of incorporation, the charter and bylaws, and standing resolutions of the members and the board of directors. For example, the secretary may be called upon from time to time to certify formal delegations of authority. To be prepared for such occasions, the secretary should make certain the board has approved appropriate delegations (see p. 169). Like other functions of the office of the secretary, these compliance functions have also been extended, in this case to responsibility for interpreting the bylaws and standing resolutions of the corporation, and to the drafting of resolutions for consideration by the board of directors. The secretary may also be assigned responsibility for meeting the reporting requirements of regulatory bodies to which the corporation is subject. These compliance responsibilities should be carried out in consultation with legal counsel as necessary.

The secretary's responsibility for interpreting the bylaws should include support for periodic review of the bylaws by the board or by a committee of the board or membership. Such reviews may lead to revision of the bylaws to take account of changing conditions.

Supporting the Board

After the executive director, the secretary is the staff member with the most direct and continuous dealings with the board of directors. In addition to planning and preparing the minutes of board and committee meetings, the secretary supports the participation of board members in meetings and handles communications with board members between meetings.

Board members volunteer their support and attention, whether compensated or not, and the secretary should be immediately responsive to their needs and should make every effort to ensure that they are well-informed about the organization they have agreed to serve.

While much of this support and communication is either general or routine, informal and individual communication occurs that may be significant and sensitive. Board members often turn first to the secretary for information and may also provide information, raise questions, and express concerns to the secretary. The secretary has a responsibility to inform the executive director and or the chair of such communications or to encourage the board member to communicate directly. In turn, the secretary should be clear about the limits of the authority with which he or she responds to such communications and should be careful, while being attentive to the needs of the board member, not to create unrealistic expectations of action.

The secretary may be assigned responsibilities for supporting the nominating process for new board members. This responsibility may involve providing analyses of the current composition of the board, soliciting suggestions for nominations from appropriate constituencies such as the members in a membership organization, and providing information about possible new board members to the nominating committee.

The secretary may support new board members by providing a statement of board responsibilities, preparing a board member manual (see p. 37), and planning orientation activities for new board members (see p. 35) in consultation with the executive director and the chair.

Planning board retreats (see p. 51) will call on all of the secretary's knowledge of the board and its expectations, the objectives and plans of senior management, and meeting planning skills. Whatever the specific objectives, the purpose of board retreats is to promote mutual understanding and agreement between the board and management about the future of the organization. While a committee, other officers and staff, and/or outside facilitators may be involved in the planning, the secretary has a special responsibility to make sure that the retreat serves the needs of the board and the organization.

Support for the Members

The secretary of a membership organization has responsibilities particular to such organizations. In such entities, the members are a vital constituency, supporting and often using the services of the organization. All or some classes of members may be entitled to participate in corporate governance through the annual meeting, in person or by proxy, or through mail ballot. The secretary is responsible for maintaining membership records, for making sure: (1) that members receive timely notice of membership meetings; (2) that members entitled to vote have the opportunity to do so, and (3) that the results of such votes have been validated. The annual meeting in a membership organization, as mentioned above, may be a major event, requiring much advance planning. In addition, the secretary in a membership organization may be assigned responsibility for membership recruitment and member relations and communications.

Corporate Governance

In one way or another, most of the preceding responsibilities relate to corporate governance. The secretary is well positioned to monitor how well corporate governance meets the needs of the board, the members, if any, and senior management, and to recommend changes in by-laws, structure, or procedures if they are needed. In recent decades, governance of for-profit corporations has had to respond to public demands for accountability and responsibility. Nonprofit organizations have not been immune to public scrutiny and there are indications that such scrutiny will intensify. The secretary should keep informed of trends in corporate governance and recommend ways the organization can anticipate and respond to changes in public expectations.

Conclusion

The position of secretary supports the organization as a corporate entity. The position is located at the interface between the board and staff and between the organization and some of its most important external constituencies. This position creates special responsibilities and rewards. The responsibilities are complicated if, as so often happens in the nonprofit world, the secretary has multiple responsibilities, i.e., "wears more than one hat."

The objectives of the secretary must be the organization's objectives. An effective secretary understands the history and mission of the organization and is well-informed about its current policies, programs, and the environment in which it operates.

Successful nonprofit organizations have a clear understanding of the functions of the board and the members, if any, and the functions of management, and they maintain an appropriate balance between them. If management loses touch with the board and membership, or if the board and members intervene in day-to-day management, trouble is likely to result. The secretary can play an important role in maintaining a healthy balance.

The secretary serves both board and members and senior management by encouraging open and honest communications between them, by facilitating the participation of board and members in shaping policy and supporting the organization, and by keeping the executive director and other officers informed of board and member needs and expectations. To do so effectively, the secretary must be an excellent communicator, both in written and in interpersonal communications, and must use judgment and discretion.

By combining knowledge of the organization's structure, history, and mission with an awareness of its key constituencies, the secretary can contribute significantly to its responses to a changing environment and heightened public expectations of accountability.

Organizing a Nonprofit Corporation

Philip A. Faix, Jr.

*This chapter focuses on the practical steps to be taken, provides examples
and cites references to forms to organize a tax-exempt organization and obtain Internal Revenue Service (IRS) and state tax-exempt status. It emphasizes the desirability of the organization's obtaining the services and advice of
highly competent and experienced tax counsel to draft the articles of incorporation, bylaws and applications seeking tax-exempt status from the imposition of federal and state income tax, using the example of a 501(c)(3) organization under the Internal Revenue Code (Code).[1]*

Introduction

In 1987, the Model Nonprofit Corporation Law Subcommittee (Subcommittee) of the Amer-
ican Bar Association's Business Law Section (Section) completed its revision of the Model
Nonprofit Corporation Act and published the Revised Model Act. In 1993, the Section's
Committee on Nonprofit Corporations issued the *Guidebook for Directors of Nonprofit
Corporations*. The original Subcommittee's report grouped nonprofit organizations into three
basic types. These groupings were:

(1) *public benefit*—organizations holding themselves out as operating for public or
charitable purposes by doing good works that benefit society or improve the human condition;

(2) *mutual benefit*—organizations benefitting their members or a group of persons
that they serve or represent; and

(3) *religious*—organizations operating primarily or exclusively for religious purposes.

Formation and Regulation of Tax-Exempt Organizations

Before a nonprofit organization is organized, its founders and their advisors should seriously
consider the various types of organizations that are described in the Internal Revenue Code
(Code) and are exempt from the imposition of federal income tax. These organizations are
described in sections 501(c),[2] 501(d),[3] and 401(a)[4] of the Code. The basic organizational
choices are nonprofit corporation, trust (inter vivos or testamentary), or unincorporated associations.

Section 501(c) lists twenty-five different classes or types of organizations that qualify
for tax exemption provided they meet certain organizational and operational tests.[5] Section
501(d) exempts certain religious and apostolic associations,[6] and section 401(a) exempts certain qualified pension, profit-sharing and stock bonus plans.[7]

Private foundations, which are a form of 501(c)(3) organizations, are subject to special organizational rules under the federal tax laws in addition to ones required of "charitable" organizations generally.[8] Throughout this chapter, a section 501(c)(3)-type organization will be presumed as the illustration.

To organize a nonprofit corporation for any purpose under the laws of any state, territory or possession of the United States, the following steps or guidelines are recommended.

Step One—Determine whether the organization is to be a membership corporation; that is, whether there are to be persons or entities whose votes must be counted in order for various corporate actions to be valid.

Commentary—All subsequent steps in organization are dependent on this initial decision. Voting rights may be required for the election of directors or in some cases, if the directors are selected in some other manner, there may be the right to vote on certain reorganizations or alterations of the mission. The determination of membership, when it begins and when it ends, is of great importance.

Step Two—Contact the office of the secretary of state or the appropriate public official who is charged with the responsibility of handling the incorporation of nonprofit organizations. You should request information, materials, forms, instructions, and a schedule of fees.

Commentary—The organization has the option to request materials by letter or telephone. It is highly recommended that the organization telephone the appropriate office initially to ascertain what kinds of materials, information, forms, and instructions are available and what charges may apply.

The following are examples of materials the organization may request:

(1) Blank forms and accompanying instructions for a nonprofit organization's articles of incorporation or charter;
(2) Copy of the nonprofit organization statutes and any existing rules, regulations, and amendments;
(3) Forms, instructions, and procedures to check the availability and reservation of a particular corporate name;
(4) Forms, instructions, and procedures to amend existing articles of incorporation or charter; to change the corporation's registered office or agent; to register an assumed or fictitious name (a name different from the corporate name listed in its incorporation papers); and
(5) Schedule of fees and other current charges to file the original or any amendment to its articles of incorporation or charter, reserve a corporate name, or obtain certified copies from the record of any filed document and other pre-and post-incorporation documents including the name and precise mailing and street address for overnight delivery to the office of secretary of state and the exact name of the payee for any check or money order.

In addition, the organization should inquire who can be an incorporator (a signer of the original articles of incorporation or charter) and how many incorporators are minimally necessary. In general, natural persons of a certain minimum age, business corporations, and other nonprofit corporations may serve as incorporators. Normally, incorporators serve only to the time of the first meeting of the organization following incorporation when directors and officers are elected and/or appointed, and then the incorporators customarily resign.

Incorporation of a nonprofit corporation does not automatically grant an organization exemption from the imposition of federal, state or local income tax. For example, the IRS has separate and specialized application forms which must be completed, filed, and approved before the exempt status determination letter is issued (see p. 195).

Step Three—Choose a proper and appropriate corporate name.

Commentary—The organization may wish to contact a lawyer or corporate name service, such as Prentice Hall or Commerce Clearing House, that is familiar with the current statutory and legal requirements applicable to the choice, reservation, and use of a legally acceptable corporate name, especially if the organization is seeking nonprofit status under the Code.

In general, the nonprofit organization statutes provide that any proposed corporate name must not be the same as, or confusingly similar to, a name already on file with a particular secretary of state. Typically such names include:

(1) names of corporations (profit or nonprofit) already organized or incorporated in the state;

(2) names of corporations (profit or nonprofit) qualified to do business in the state, but organized or incorporated elsewhere;

(3) names reserved by individuals or others planning to incorporate or renew for a varying period (30-180 days);

(4) names reserved in the state by corporations organized or incorporated elsewhere;

(5) names registered as trade or service marks or registered as assumed or fictitious names; and

(6) names listed in the IRS compendium, in order not to duplicate an existing tax-exempt organization.

Many states mandate the use of a corporate designation in the proposed name like "Incorporated," "Corporation," "Company," or "Limited," or abbreviations of them. Others prohibit the use of specific words such as "United States." In addition, words or phrases implying or suggesting a profit-making business, motive, venture, or opportunity should be avoided.

The organization is advised to check out local directories of nonprofit corporations, the *Federal Trademark Register*, *Encyclopedia of Associations*, or similar resources dealing with existing nonprofit corporate names. Through research and taking time, a corporate name can be designed which identifies the organization and its principal purposes.

Step Four—Draft and prepare the organization's articles of incorporation or charter after reviewing the applicable provisions of any federal, state, or local law on tax exemption requirements.

Commentary—Most states will provide free of charge an approved, printed blank articles of incorporation or charter form that meets the statutory requirements. A typical format might be this chapter's Exhibit 1; even if a particular state form differs, this exhibit will identify issues that should be examined.

Step Five—File the articles of incorporation or charter, the copies to be certified and returned, and a check to cover the filing fee with the secretary of state for the state in which you seek to be incorporated.

Commentary—The filing of the organization's original articles of incorporation or charter can typically be done by mail or in person. Normally, the organization prepares a transmittal letter addressed to the secretary of state, or other designated official, enclosing the original articles of incorporation to be filed, plus the required number of copies. The letter should request that the copies be filed, date stamped, and returned in a postage-paid envelope. A check must be enclosed to cover the required filing and processing fees. Please note that some states require a cashier's check or money order. Include with the filing any pertinent documents relating to the reservation of the corporate name; these should indicate the docket number and issuance date.

Step Six—Draft and prepare the organization's bylaws, taking into consideration federal, state, and local laws with respect to tax-exempt nonprofit corporations.

Commentary—a competent lawyer or law firm specializing in nonprofit corporations and familiar with the federal, state, and local provisions with respect to such entities may be retained to draft the articles of incorporation and the bylaws. As the sample bylaws on pages 207–30 indicate, an organization's bylaws should cover the following subjects:

(1) the name of the nonprofit organization;

(2) location of principal office;

(3) statement of purposes;

(4) membership (if any): qualifications, classes, voting rights at meetings, dues and initiation fees, and expulsion and termination criteria;

(5) meetings of members: regular and special, time and place, notice and waiver, quorum, telephone meetings, telephone and fax notices, use of proxies, and voting procedures and actions by written consent;

(6) number, qualifications, terms, removal, and compensation (if any) of the directors;

(7) regular and special meetings of the board of directors and vacancies and absences;

(8) notice, waiver, and quorum and actions by written consent;

(9) designation, power and authority of committees of the board such as audit, capital, campaign, compensation, executive, fund-raising, and nominating;

(10) appointment/election of officers;

(11) number, qualifications, term, removal, duties and responsibilities and compensation of officers, and filling vacancies;

(12) duties and responsibilities of officers such as the president, executive director, chief executive officer, chief operating officer, vice president, secretary, assistant secretary, treasurer, and assistant treasurer;

(13) affiliates and affiliated organizations (if any);

(14) indemnification of directors, officers, employees, and agents including advances for litigation expenses;

(15) insurance coverage for directors, officers, employees, and agents;

(16) exoneration, if not automatically provided by statute;

(17) financial, annual audited reports if available and other reports;

(18) annual report by chief executive officer or by executive director, if not chief executive officer;

(19) right to inspect books and records;

(20) fiscal year;

(21) conflicts of interest;

(22) use of membership lists; and

(23) amendments and interpretation.

Step Seven—Review, draft, and prepare the federal income tax exemption application forms.

Commentary—The organization's tax counsel should acquire from the nearest IRS office such of the following current federal tax forms and publications or their successors, and such other forms and publications as may be relevant:

(1) Form SS-4—Application for Employer Identification Number;

(2) Form 8718—User Fee for Exempt Organization Determination Letter Request;

(3) Package 1023—Application for Recognition of Exemption with Instructions, or form 1024 if exemption other than under Section 501(c)(3) is sought;

(4) Publication 557—Tax-Exempt Status for Your Organization;

(5) Publication 578—Tax Information for Private Foundations and Foundation Managers; and

(6) IRS Form 5768—Election by an Eligible Section 501(c)(3) Organization to Make Expenditures to Influence Legislation.

If the organization cannot obtain one or more of these forms or publications, it may contact the national request number of the IRS: 1-800-829-FORM.

Because tax forms, like Form 1023, contain several schedules, a professional tax advisor and/or counsel may be retained to prepare the forms. The most common application for tax exemption is under Section 501(c)(3), which involves the completion and submission to the IRS of Form 1023 contained in Package 1023.

Step Eight—Obtain exemption from the imposition of state corporate income tax.

Commentary—Most states impose an annual corporate income or other form of taxation like a franchise tax upon the net income of the organization, or minimally require the organization to file informational corporate income tax returns. In those states, the nonprofit organizations may explore the possibility of obtaining an exemption from the payment of corporate income taxes.

The organization may contact the appropriate state agency or department administering the corporate revenue laws for the appropriate forms and procedures to obtain the exemption. In many states, obtaining an exemption from the payment and/or the requirement to file annual income tax returns is a formality. For example, an organization may be required to send a certified copy of its articles of incorporation and bylaws and a copy of the IRS determination letter of a 501(c)(3) organization. It may also be necessary to complete a detailed questionnaire, supply financial information, audited or unaudited financial statements, or an account for the historical and current use of the organization's funds.

Step Nine—Obtain and file an assumed or fictitious name statement.

Commentary—If the nonprofit organization intends to engage in activities like fund raising, applying for grants, gifts, contributions, or providing or selling goods or services, and uses a name other than the exact corporate name set forth in its articles of incorporation or charter, the organization may need to obtain and file the proper form to register an assumed or fictitious name from the applicable governmental bodies, state, county, or local.

The nonprofit organization may initially contact any state, county, municipal, or local office charged with the registration of assumed or fictitious names to obtain the proper forms, instructions, fee schedules, and any advertising, filing, or other requirements.

Typically, the secretary of state handles the registration of fictitious or assumed names, but the county or local government may impose similar regulations. As part of the registration process, it may be necessary for the organization to advertise in several newspapers—one of general circulation and the local legal paper for legal notice in that county—and submit proofs of publication to the governmental office handling the registration of its assumed or fictitious names. Some statutes are strict with respect to the use of fictitious or assumed names in nonprofit situations and do not permit the use of names similar or confusingly similar to already existing and permissible corporate names.

Step Ten—Apply for a nonprofit mailing permit from the U.S. Postal Service.

Commentary—Certain nonprofit organizations, especially ones which are considered tax-exempt under section 501(c)(3) of the Code, are eligible to obtain a third-class nonprofit organization mailing permit from the U.S. Postal Service. These permits allow immense postage savings for eligible nonprofit organizations if postal regulations and procedures are followed.

First, the organization should contact the local post office which it intends to utilize and inquire what documents are necessary to obtain a nonprofit mailing permit. Normally, the local postal officials require the following documents:

(1) a certified copy of the organization's articles of incorporation or charter;
(2) a copy of the organization's bylaws;
(3) a copy of the organization's IRS tax exemption determination letter; and
(4) copies of news bulletins or letters, membership brochures, program notices, and other materials that the organization typically mails to its constituency.

The completed application form may be forwarded from the local post office to the main office or to a regional office for a final determination.

The organization is required to pay a one-time fee and an annual fee once the permit has been granted. The organization is well-advised to familiarize itself with the imprint stamp, special mailing forms, and options for using a mailing service to handle large mailings if frequent bulk mailing is contemplated.

Step Eleven—Apply for all property, sales, use, franchise, and other tax exemptions.

Commentary—A nonprofit organization may be eligible to apply for an exemption from the imposition of a myriad of state, county, municipal, and local taxes. Examples are franchise and income taxes; excise, use, and real or personal property taxes; hotel and meal taxes; sales taxes; and business privilege taxes.

The organization may contact each taxing body to determine the procedure to obtain a letter of exemption, and obtain the proper forms, instructions, and applications. The organization may inquire what documentation, such as a certified copy of its articles of incorporation or charter, a copy of its bylaws, and a copy of IRS tax exemption determination letter, is required by each taxing authority for obtaining tax-exempt status. *The most commonly overlooked tax exemption is sales tax.* Other nonprofit organizations might be contacted for suggestions about additional exemptions which might be pursued.

The organization may also inquire about any full- or part-time fee exemptions for professional and business license fees or permits, such as construction or operating permits.

Step Twelve—File, in a timely manner, any required nonprofit organization report statements or forms.

Commentary—In addition to IRS Form 990, many states require nonprofit organizations that are incorporated or registered to do business under its laws, to file periodically or annually a form or statement with the secretary of state, attorney general, and/or other public official. The required disclosure varies from state to state, but typically includes such basic information as the name of the organization, the address of its principal or registered office and the names and addresses of its directors and officers. Some states require the disclosure of financial statements or more specific data such as compensation of directors, officers, and key employees; amounts raised from fund-raising activities; and the specific receivers of any grants, gifts, donations, awards, scholarships, or other monies. This filed information is typically made available to the public.

The failure to file such mandated reports or statements on time may require the payment of a fine, suspension of activities, or forfeiture of all corporate powers. The organization may contact other similarly situated nonprofit corporations on how they approach and how much they disclose in such filed documents.

Step Thirteen—Register the nonprofit organization with the office of the attorney general and, if applicable, with any county or local official administering a solicitation ordinance or law.

Commentary—In many states, nonprofit organizations are required to register and report their activities. These states mandate such organizations to register with them before the initiation of any solicitations or before fund raising may commence. In general, the attorney general's office is concerned that the acquired assets of nonprofit organizations are utilized properly—for valid public or charitable purposes, not for private purposes or gain.

The registration and reporting processes vary considerably, but, in general, the reporting requirements focus on whether the funds solicited from the public are in fact being utilized for the advertised or stated purposes, and whether the directors, principals and staffs are being overly compensated or benefitted by nonprofit programs or funds.

The nonprofit organization may also inquire about any registration forms or periodic reports to see if it is exempt by reason of its specific tax exemption status. On the local level, the organization should comply with any solicitation ordinances, statutes, or laws concerning public fund-raising or door-to-door drives. These local laws may require the filing or disclosure in advance or approval of specific fund-raising materials or the sources of net receipts.

More governmental bodies are taking a proactive interest in regulating nonprofit solicitations by inquiring which persons receive the proceeds from fund-raising efforts.

Step Fourteen—Comply with any local, county, or state lobbying reporting requirements.

Commentary—Subject to IRS regulations, many nonprofit organizations plan to engage in lobbying activities—favor or oppose legislation; support or oppose state, county, city, or local plans, proposals, rules, regulations, orders, directions, ordinances, or statutes; or engage a lobbyist. Such activity may necessitate that the organization register and/or report its activities with some state, county or local governmental body such as a fair political practices commission.

The organization may contact other nonprofits in its community or environment to acquire knowledge of any registration or reporting requirements imposed by any applicable governmental bodies.

Subsidiaries

The law is reasonably clear that any tax-exempt organization can have one or more tax-exempt subsidiaries and/or one or more for-profit subsidiaries. In the last situation, the tax-exempt parent organization can own some or all of the equity (usually stock) of the for-profit subsidiary unless the parent is a private foundation, in which case special rules apply.

Most parent organizations, because control over the taxable entity is crucial, favor corporations over partnerships or proprietorships, because the latter two types of organizations raise some serious questions. This subject matter must be handled carefully by competent legal and tax counsel in order that the parent organization's tax-exempt status is not jeopardized. Some states permit the use of "business trusts," which may be available to nonprofit organizations. To form a for-profit subsidiary corporation, it is necessary for the parent organization to consider the tax implications at the federal and state levels, the problems in maintaining the parent organization separate and distinct from its subsidiaries and its ability to receive tax deductible contributions. The for-profit subsidiary will be subject to federal, state, and local taxes, but the dividends payable to the parent organization are not taxable to the parent.

Annual Reports

To maintain its tax-exempt status, the organization must file an annual return with the IRS, generally on Form 990, or in the case of private foundations, on Form 990-PF. This annual return discloses specifically items of gross income, receipts and disbursements, and other financial information as well as highlighting the continuous keeping of records.

Conclusion

This chapter emphasizes the importance of having experienced counsel prepare or review the organization's articles of incorporation or charter and inferentially its bylaws; the federal and state income tax exemption process; and the many benefits that accrue from obtaining tax-exempt status at all levels—federal, state, and local; and the savings created by the use of specialized mailing permits. The chapter focuses on a step-wise approach to the many issues facing a nonprofit organization as it contemplates initial and ongoing governmental regulation.

Notes

1. 26 I.R.C. § 501(c)(3)(1994).
2. *Id.* § 501(c) (1994 & West Supp. 1996).
3. *Id.* § 501(d) (1994).
4. *Id.* § 401(a) (1994 & West Supp. 1996).
5. 26 I.R.C. § 501(c) (1994 & West Supp. 1996).
6. *Id.* § 501(d) (1994).
7. *Id.* § 401(a) (1994 & West Supp. 1996).
8. *Id.* § 508(e) (1994).

Exhibit 1
Sample Articles of Incorporation
ABC, Inc.
A Nonprofit Corporation

Pursuant to the nonprofit provisions of the Nonprofit Corporation Act of the State of _____, the undersigned incorporators adopt the following articles.

ARTICLE I

The name of this nonprofit corporation is ABC, INC.

ARTICLE II

The name and address of the registered agent and office of this nonprofit corporation is:

[*Note*: The initial registered agent may be a corporate service specializing in accepting service of legal process, or the organization can assign a director or an officer to accept service. The address is usually a street address as opposed to a post office box].

ARTICLE III

The purposes for which this nonprofit corporation is organized are:

[*Note*: Considerable care should be used in drafting this article to comply with any specific purposes required under state law. The organization's drafter also should be cognizant of federal tax law implications. For example, organizations considering Section 501(c)(3) tax exempt status might consider the following language: "This nonprofit corporation is organized exclusively for one or more of the purposes as specified in Section 501(c)(3) of the Internal Revenue Code, including, for such purposes, the making of distributions to organizations that qualify as exempt organizations under Section 501(c)(3) of the Internal Revenue Code, or the corresponding section of any future federal tax code."]

ARTICLE IV

The number of initial directors of this nonprofit corporation shall be _____ and the names and addresses of these initial directors are as follows: _____ _____. Succeeding directors are as established by the bylaws.

[*Note*: Street addresses are usually required by state law as distinguished from post office boxes.

ARTICLE V

The names and addresses of the incorporators of this nonprofit corporation are:

[*Note*: List the names and complete street address of each incorporator who is a legal or natural person who is authorized under state law to sign the articles of incorporation or charter.] See STEP TWO, *supra.* on who may be an incorporator.

ARTICLE VI

The period of the duration of this nonprofit corporation is:

[*Note*: The usual length of time is perpetual, but a shorter time frame may be specified.]

ARTICLE VII

The classes, rights, privileges, and qualifications of the members of this nonprofit corporation are as follows:

[*Note*: If "members" (see definitions in "A Warning on Words" at end of General Introduction) are to have voting rights, such rights should be defined in the Articles of Incorporation or Bylaws. If "members" refers to persons who have no voting rights or other powers, the Articles should so state.]

ARTICLE VIII

[Additional provisions such as the following should be included in light of any applicable requirements of federal tax law and state law on nonprofit corporations.] For example, the following sample provisions are illustrative:

1. *A provision dealing with dissolution:*

"Upon dissolution of this nonprofit corporation, its net assets remaining after payment, or provision for payment, of all debts and liabilities of this nonprofit corporation shall be distributed for one or more exempt purposes within the meaning of Section 501(c)(3) of the Internal Revenue Code, or shall be distributed to the federal government, or to a state or local government, for a public purpose."

2. *A provision concerning political activities:*

"No substantial part of the activities of this nonprofit corporation shall consist of promoting propaganda, or otherwise attempting to influence legislation, except as otherwise provided by Section 501(c)(3) of the Internal Revenue Code, and this nonprofit corporation shall not participate in, or intervene in, including the publishing or distribution of statements, any political campaign on behalf of, or in opposition to, any candidate for public office."

3. *A provision addressing the distribution of net earnings:*

"No part of the net earnings of this nonprofit corporation shall inure to the benefit of, or be distributable to, its directors, officers, members or other private persons, except this nonprofit corporation shall be authorized and empowered to pay reasonable compensation for services rendered and to make payments and distributions in furtherance of the purposes set forth in these Articles of Incorporation."

4. *A provision dealing with general limitations on activities mandated by certain sections of the Internal Revenue Code:*

"Notwithstanding any other provision of these Articles of Incorporation, this nonprofit corporation shall not engage in any activities that are not permitted: (1) by a nonprofit corporation exempt from federal corporate income tax under Section 501(c)(3) of the Internal Revenue Code or (2) by a nonprofit corporation whose contributions are deductible under Section 170(c)(2) of the Internal Revenue Code."

[*Note*: Existing organizations should be aware that the Internal Revenue Service has published guidelines to identify states and circumstances where an express dissolution clause for a charitable organization is not required.]

5. *Additional provisions may be required by state law:*

[It would be prudent for an organization to have the advice of counsel knowledgeable in federal and state tax laws as well as the state nonprofit corporation law.]

The undersigned incorporators declare hereby that the statements made in the foregoing articles of incorporation are true:

Signature of Incorporator(s)　　　　　　　　　*Date:* _____

_____

_____

_____

_____

_____

[*Note*: Some states require the signatures to be notarized.]

Exhibit 2
Transmittal Letter

The following is a transmittal letter that the organization might use with its filing.

Secretary of State
[Street Address]
[City, State Zip Code]

[Date]

Dear Sir/Madam:

I enclose the original and _____ copies of the Articles of Incorporation of [*Name of Corporation*].

Please file the original Articles of Incorporation [immediately, or on a date certain] and return the copies, after date- and file-stamping them, in the self-addressed stamped envelope provided.

A check/money order payable to _____ and in the amount of $_____, covering the filing fees is also enclosed.

The corporate name was reserved pursuant to #_____ and is-sued on [*date*].

Very truly yours,
[*Signature of Incorporator or Agent*]

Bylaws

Frank W. Evans

This chapter outlines the functions of bylaws, with some examples of their language.

Bylaws, once legally adopted, outline the governance structure and basic operating rules for an organization. While the articles of incorporation, or a similar organizational document, outline the general purposes of the organization, the bylaws detail the specifics of how the organization is structured and governed.

These bylaws are provided solely as a model. Your organization may wish to consider whether it should be a membership or non-membership corporation, whether there should be staggered board terms, whether there should be limits on the number of terms a director or officer may serve, and so forth. An attorney, or someone familiar with your state's nonprofit corporation laws, can advise on indemnification issues and whether time requirements and procedures provided for in your bylaws conform to your state's statutes.

If your organization currently has bylaws, you are encouraged to review them periodically to ensure that they are consistent with the way you operate and with state law. As your organization grows and develops, inconsistencies may develop between actual operations and bylaw requirements. If the bylaws are found to be inconsistent with current operating practices, it may be desirable to form a bylaws committee of your board to recommend amendments or draft new bylaws. The secretary may be the best candidate to chair such a committee.

Because reviewing and drafting new bylaws are usually not high on an executive's list of favorite things to do, the attached draft (Exhibit 1) is meant to be as user-friendly as possible. These model bylaws include prompts where language appropriate to your organization or situation needs to be added. These prompts are shown in brackets containing bold, italicized type *[such as this]*.

These draft bylaws assume an organization of significant size. Some of the suggested provisions may not be applicable to smaller organizations. The chief volunteer leader is assumed to be the board chair. The chief staff officer is assumed to have the title executive director. If your organization does not meet these assumptions, the draft bylaws will need to be modified to reflect your board and staff title structure, for example, by changing the word "executive director" throughout to "president," if your chief staff officer bears that title.

Smaller organizations may wish for a scaled-down set of bylaws. Depending on the needs of your organization, you may wish to start with the version set forth in Exhibit 1 and then eliminate elements that are inappropriate for your organization.

As part of a bylaws review/development process the organization is encouraged to engage an attorney to participate in the preparation of the final drafts to ensure that they comply with the nonprofit corporation laws of your state.

Bylaws

Outline of Content

Bylaws should be tailored to fit the purpose and mission of the organization. They should reflect, and be consistent with, the operating practices followed by the organization. As a situation or operations change, bylaws should be amended to stay current. The bylaws should also specify the process for adopting amendments.

The following outline is provided to serve as a general guide for developing nonprofit corporation bylaws.

(1) **Name,** purpose of the organization, and corporate office
(2) **Membership:** (if a membership corporation) qualification, term, listing duties and rights, quorum, voting, types of meetings, notices of meetings, proxies, annual reports to membership, and expulsion
(3) **Board of directors:** nomination and election, general powers, qualification, term, duties, quorum, notices of meetings, types of meetings, voting, vacancies, and board officers
(4) **Officers and agents:** number and qualification, election and term of office, vacancies, compensation, authority and duties of office, surety bonds, reports of officers and agents, and removal from office
(5) **Committees of the board:** designation of committees, limitation of power, committee chairs, committee meetings, and authority and powers of specific committees
(6) **Indemnification and insurance:** sufficient detail should be included to satisfy the legal requirements of the state in which the organization is incorporated and the chosen policies of the organization
(7) **Conflict of interest:** definition, disclosure, required abstention from vote and absence from discussion, notation in minutes, and annual review of policy
(8) **Account books and minutes**
(9) **Fiscal year and audit**
(10) **Loans to directors and officers**
(11) **No private inurement** (this provision should also be in the articles of incorporation)
(12) **Dissolution:** procedures and disposition of surplus assets upon dissolution
(13) **Amendments to the bylaws:** how they are to be made and approved
(14) **Bylaws certification:** stating date and circumstances of adoption or amendment

Bibliography

Zeitlin, Kim Arthur, and Susan E. Dorn. *The Nonprofit Board's Guide to Bylaws: Creating a Framework for Effective Governance.* Washington, D.C.: National Center for Nonprofit Boards, 1996.

Exhibit 1
Sample Bylaws

ARTICLE 1
Name and Offices

{COMMENTARY: This article establishes the official name of the organization, as well as its purpose and location of its principal office.}

Section 1.1 NAME. The name of this corporation shall be "*[Name of Organization]* Inc."

Section 1.2 CORPORATE OFFICES. The principal office of this corporation shall be located within *[County, State]*. The corporation may establish other offices, as the board of directors may designate or as the affairs of the corporation may require from time to time.

Section 1.3 PURPOSE. The purpose for which this corporation was formed is *[insert purpose statement or description of the activities or programs offered; check state statutes for possible form and applicable provisions of the Internal Revenue Code]*.

ARTICLE II
Members

{COMMENTARY: This article defines "members," their responsibilities, duties, meetings, etc. Many nonprofit organizations are organized as "membership" corporations, and as such confer certain obligations and authority upon members, primarily the authority to elect the directors and/or officers of the corporation. The bylaws or the articles of incorporation usually specify whether the organization is to be a "membership" corporation. The bylaws, or sometimes the articles of incorporation, usually define who the members are. (See pages 233–38 on "membership" for a more detailed discussion.) An alternative is to form a "non-membership" corporation, in which the directors have all the responsibility and authority. Check the nonprofit corporation laws for your state to see if this alternative is possible. A decision to convert to a non-membership corporation should include a discussion focusing on the desire for a democratic structure, the cost and complexity of operations associated with having members, the need for member input, and the desirability of having a body to whom the directors are ultimately accountable. Article II would not be included in the bylaws if a non-membership form of organizational structure is used.}

Section 2.1 MEMBERS. The members of the corporation shall be *[insert definition, such as dues-paying members or selected from the contributors or some other definition]*.

2.1.1 Authority of members. Members of the corporation shall have authority to vote for the election of directors, to receive the annual report of the *[board chair or president or directors]* and other reports, to vote on any proposal of merger, consolidation or dissolution, and to vote on the sale of major assets of the organization.

Section 2.2 ANNUAL MEETING. The annual meeting of members to elect directors, to receive the annual report of *[board chair or president or directors]* and any other reports, and to transact such other business as may properly come before the meeting, shall be held each year in the month of *[Month]* at such date, time and place as may be fixed by the board of directors or such other date, time and place as may be fixed by the board of directors. The record date for establishing members entitled to vote shall be the last day of the month *[or some other specific date]* preceding the month in which the meeting is to be held. *(NOTE: Bylaws should also establish whether matters may be raised from the floor during the annual meeting of Members.)*

(NOTE: The next several sections periodically refer to certain numbers of days or certain numbers of members of the corporation or directors required to call a meeting, take action, etc. When such a number is cited, it is intended only as a model. Check your state's nonprofit corporation laws to determine if local statutes require specific numbers be used in those instances.)

Section 2.3 SPECIAL MEETING. Special meetings of the members may be called by the president of the corporation, board chair or by *[specify number or percentage]* directors and shall be called by the board chair upon the written request of members having not less than *[specify number or percentage]* of the votes entitled to be cast at the meeting. The record date for establishing members entitled to vote shall be the last day of the month *[or some other specific date]* preceding the month in which the meeting is to be held.

Section 2.4 NOTICE AND WAIVER. Written notice of each meeting of members, stating the place, day and hour of the meeting and the purpose or purposes for which the meeting is called, shall be mailed at least *[seven]* (*[7]*) but not more than *[fifty]* (*[50]*) days prior to such meeting to each member of the corporation at his or her address as the same appears on the lists of members of the corporation. A written waiver of notice signed by the member or members entitled to such notice, whether before or after the time stated therein, shall be equivalent to the giving of such notice.

Section 2.5 CERTIFICATION AND VOTING LIST. As soon after the record date as is feasible, the secretary shall prepare and certify a list of members of the corporation, in accordance with the criteria for members specified in Section 2.1 of these bylaws. Members so certified shall receive notice of, and shall have the sole privilege of voting on matters submitted to them at annual and special meetings of the membership of the corporation. A complete and current list of members of the corporation shall be regularly maintained and kept on file and available for inspection by any member at the principal office of the corporation for at least *[seven]* *([7])* days *(NOTE: check your state statute for any required time period)* prior to each annual or special meeting.

Section 2.6 QUORUM. *[Number or percentage—spelled out; i.e., ten or ten percent]* *([number or percentage—numeric; i.e., 10 or 10%])* members entitled to vote, and present in person or by proxy, shall constitute a quorum for the transaction of any business.

Section 2.7 VOTING. Each member entitled to vote shall be entitled to one (1) vote, in person or by proxy, on all matters properly submitted to the membership. Except as is otherwise provided by law, by the articles of incorporation or by these bylaws, all action shall be decided by a majority vote of the members present in person or by proxy. *(NOTE: Some nonprofit organizations provide for different classes of membership with differing voting authority. If so, provision will have to be made for such matters.)*

Section 2.8 ACTION WITHOUT MEETING. Any action required or permitted to be taken at a meeting of members may be taken without a meeting if a consent in writing, setting forth the action so taken or to be taken, is signed by all of the members entitled to vote upon such action at a meeting, or by their duly authorized attorney-in-fact and shall be filed with the secretary. Such consent may be signed in counterparts and shall have the same force and effect as a unanimous vote of the members.

(NOTE: In certain instances, for any type of nonprofit with members, it may be necessary to suspend, expel or terminate a member. The following section is included to cover such actions.)

Section 2.9 TERMINATION, EXPULSION OR SUSPENSION OF MEMBERS. No member may be expelled or suspended, and no membership or memberships in the organization may be terminated or suspended except pursuant to a procedure that is fair and reasonable and is carried out in good faith. The board of directors shall, by resolution, establish a procedure to terminate, expel or suspend a member. In the event the board of directors does not adopt procedures, the following procedures shall apply.

2.9.1 Written notice. An intent to terminate, expel or suspend a member shall be preceded by *[twenty]* *([20])* days written notice of the date when a hearing will be held to determine whether the member shall be expelled, suspended, or terminated. Such notice shall set forth the reasons therefore. Said written notice must be given by first-class or certified mail sent to the last address of the member to be expelled, suspended or terminated, as shown on the organization's records.

2.9.2 Hearing. An opportunity shall be provided for the member to be heard, orally and in writing. The member shall be entitled to have counsel present at and to participate in the hearing at his or her expense, and to present and cross-examine any witnesses.

2.9.3 Liability. A member who has been expelled or suspended may be liable to the organization for dues, assessments or fees as a result of obligations incurred or commitments made prior to expulsion or suspension.

2.9.4 Challenges. Any proceeding challenging an expulsion, suspension or termination, including a proceeding in which defective notice is alleged, must be commenced within one year after the effective date of the expulsion, suspension or termination.

ARTICLE III
Board of Directors

{COMMENTARY: This article defines the responsibilities of directors, defines various types of meetings and establishes the broad framework within which the board should function. Beyond this framework the board may periodically adopt resolutions or policies which additionally govern its organization and operation.}

Section 3.1 GENERAL POWERS. The business and affairs of the corporation shall be conducted under the direction of, and the control and disposal of the corporation's properties and funds shall be vested in, its board of directors, except as otherwise provided in the **[state]** Nonprofit Corporation Act, the corporation's articles of incorporation or these bylaws.

(NOTE: Section 3.2 establishes the framework for a board which is divided into three (3) classes of equal or nearly-equal numbers of directors. Each year one-third of the directors is elected or reelected. Another option is to have all directors elected at the same time, such as at the annual meeting of members. An advantage of the structure in which the board is elected in thirds over a three-year period is to provide continuity and consistency. In other words, an external or internal force cannot easily gain control and direction of the organization if only one-third of directors are elected each year. However, it must be recognized that such a provision would make it difficult to quickly change control of the board and management should that be necessary for the benefit of the organization.)

Section 3.2 NUMBER, ELECTION, TENURE AND QUALIFICATIONS. There shall be not less than **[number—spelled out; recommend it be a number divisible by 3 so each term/class is same size]** (**[number—numeric]**) directors of the corporation and no more than **[number—spelled out]** (**[number—numeric]**) directors. *(NOTE: Check state laws for requirements concerning the number of directors.)* The number of directors shall be set from time to time by *[resolution of the directors or vote of the members]*. The directors shall be divided into three (3) groups as nearly equal in number as possible, and shall be known as Class I, Class II and Class III. Initially, the directors of Class I shall serve for a term of one (1) year, those of Class II for a term of two (2) years, and those of Class III for a term of three (3) years, commencing on the date of election and each director shall hold office until his or her successor is elected and qualified, or until his or her death, resignation or removal. At each subsequent annual meeting of members, the successors of those directors whose term then expires shall be elected to serve for a term of three (3) years and until their successors are elected and qualified, or until their death, resignation or removal. *(NOTE: A trend among nonprofit organizations is to limit the number of terms a director may serve. A common pattern is to limit service to two (2) three-year terms, after which the individual must step down and wait one year before he or she is once again eligible to be elected to the board of directors. An advantage of this approach is that it provides for regular turnover of directors, thus bringing new thought processes to the governance function. A disadvantage is the possibility that a major supporter or vitally active member of the board, unable to stand for reelection to a third term on the board, would be alienated and withdraw support. It should be recognized that if there is too great a turnover of directors, the role of staff is strengthened in relation to the board. If such a provision is desired, it should be specified in this section. See also the discussion of this subject on pages 25–34, "Building an Effective Board.")*

Section 3.3 BOARD MEMBER ATTENDANCE. If a director fails to attend a minimum of *[number—spelled out]* (*[number—numeric]*) meetings per year, his or her position shall become vacant for the remainder of the term or until the vacancy is filled pursuant to Section 3.5. At the discretion of the board chair, imposition of this rule may be waived due to extenuating circumstances. *(NOTE: An alternative approach is to replace the first sentence with:* "If a director is absent from *[number—spelled out]* (*[number—numeric]*) consecutive meetings, unless excused, his or her office shall become vacant for the remainder of the term. The minutes should note any excused absence(s)."*)*

Section 3.4 NOMINATION OF DIRECTORS. Recommendations for director nominees may be submitted by *[name sources authorized to nominate directors, such as members, affiliate units, incumbent directors, officers, staff, etc.]* to the Nominating Committee. *[If a membership organization, add the dates when such action should be taken.]*

The nominating committee shall, after giving due consideration to all such recommendations and such other persons as it may wish to consider, present its slate of director-nominees to the board *[or, if a membership organization: to the board and to the members ([insert number, numeric]) days prior to the next annual meeting of members]*. *(NOTE: There are various means to disseminate background information on new director-nominees,*

*such as by letter, electronic communications, facsimile, publication in orga-
nization's newsletter, etc. The number of days required should be consistent
with the notice requirements of Section 2.4.)*

Section 3.5 VACANCIES. Any director may resign at any time by giving written notice to the board chair, president or the secretary of the corporation. Such resignation shall take effect at the time specified therein, and
if not specified therein, it shall take effect upon receipt and the acceptance of
such resignation shall not be necessary to make it effective. Any vacancy occurring in the board of directors for any reason may be filled by the affirmative vote of a majority of the remaining directors even if less than a quorum. A director elected to fill a vacancy shall be elected for the unexpired
term of his or her predecessor and until his or her successor is elected and
qualified, or until his or her death, resignation or removal.

Section 3.6 REGULAR MEETINGS. A regular annual meeting of the
board of directors shall be held promptly *[after the annual meeting of members, if any]* at the time and place, determined by the board, for the purpose
of electing officers *(see note, below)* and for the transaction of such other
business as may come before the meeting. There shall be no less than *[num-
ber—spelled out]* (*[number—numeric]*) regular meetings, including any annual meeting, of the board of directors in each *[fiscal or calendar]* year, and
the board of directors shall provide by resolution the time and place for the
holding of such additional regular meetings. *(NOTE: In some member organizations, it is the members who elect the president; if that is the case, appropriate language needs to be inserted in Article IV.)*

Section 3.7 SPECIAL MEETINGS. The board chair may call a special
meeting of the board of directors whenever he or she deems it necessary,
and shall call a special meeting whenever requested to do so in writing by
three (3) or more directors or by the president *[or by the secretary if de-
manded by (a specified) percentage of the members, if the organization is a
membership organization]*. The board chair shall fix the place and time for
holding any special meeting of the board of directors. Notice of each special
meeting stating the purpose, place, day and hour of the meeting shall be
given to each director at his or her last known business or home address at
least *[seven]* (*[7]*) days *(NOTE: check your state statutes for a required
time period)* prior thereto by the mailing of written notice, or at least two
(2) days prior thereto by personal delivery of written notice or by telephonic
or telegraphic notice, or other electronic means of notice (and the method of
notice need not be the same to each director). If mailed, such notice shall be
deemed to be given when deposited in the United States mail, with postage
thereon prepaid. If sent by facsimile machine, or other electronic means,
such notice shall be deemed to be given when the facsimile machine or other
electronic means prints or acknowledges that the transmission was successfully executed.

Section 3.8 WAIVER OF NOTICE. Any director may waive notice of
any meeting before, at, or after such meeting. The attendance of a director

at a meeting shall constitute a waiver of notice of such meeting, except where a director attends a meeting for the express purpose of objecting to the transaction of any business because the meeting is not lawfully called or convened. Neither the business to be transacted nor the purpose of any regular meeting of the board of directors need be specified in the notice or waiver of notice of such meeting.

Section 3.9 PRESUMPTION OF ASSENT. A director of the corporation who is present at a meeting of the board of directors at which action on any corporate matter is taken shall be presumed to have assented to the action taken unless his or her dissent shall be entered in the minutes of the meeting, or unless he or she shall file his or her written dissent to such action with the person acting as the secretary of the meeting before the adjournment thereof or shall forward such dissent by registered mail to the secretary of the corporation immediately after the adjournment of the meeting or if dissent is not noted when the minutes are circulated or approved, the dissenting director(s) may direct its inclusion. Such right to dissent shall not apply to a director who voted in favor of such action.

Section 3.10 QUORUM AND VOTING. *[Portion, i.e., A majority; check state statutes to determine if there are any statutory requirements]* of the directors shall constitute a quorum for the transaction of business at any meeting of the board of directors. Each director shall be entitled to one (1) vote and the vote of a majority of the directors present in person at a meeting at which a quorum is present shall be the act of the board of directors unless a greater number is specifically required by these bylaws, by the corporation's articles of incorporation or by state law. If less than a quorum is present at a meeting, a majority of the directors present may adjourn the meeting from time to time without further notice other than announcement at the meeting, until a quorum shall be present. A director may not vote or act by proxy at any meeting of directors.

Section 3.11 COMPENSATION. Directors shall not receive compensation for their services as such, although the reasonable expenses of directors for attendance at board meetings may be paid or reimbursed by the corporation. Directors shall not be disqualified from receiving reasonable compensation for services rendered to or for the benefit of the corporation in any other capacity. *(NOTE: Some organizations do compensate their directors, in which case the wording of the first sentence should be modified to:* "*Directors may receive compensation . . ."*)

Section 3.12 MEETINGS BY TELEPHONE OR TELECONFERENCE. Members of the board of directors or any committee may participate in a meeting of the board or committee by means of conference telephone or similar communications equipment by which all persons participating in the meeting can hear each other at the same time. Such participation shall constitute presence in person at the meeting.

Section 3.13 ACTION WITHOUT A MEETING. Any action required or permitted to be taken at a meeting of the directors or any committee thereof may be taken without a meeting if a consent in writing, setting forth the action so taken or to be taken, is signed by all of the directors or committee members entitled to vote upon such action at a meeting. Such consent (which may be signed in counterparts) shall have the same force and effect as a unanimous vote of the directors or committee members.

Section 3.14 BOARD CHAIR. At its annual organizational meeting *[if a membership organization, add: "following the annual meeting of members"]*, the board of directors shall elect, from among those who are, or are to be, directors of the corporation, a board chair who shall, when present, preside at all regular and special meetings of the board of directors and of the members of the corporation, shall present at the annual meeting of the members of the corporation a report on the activities of the corporation during the preceding year, and shall generally perform all other duties incident to the office, required by the bylaws or from time to time assigned to him or her by the board of directors.

3.14.1 Vice chair of the board. If one or more shall be elected by the board of directors from among those who are, or are to be, directors of the corporation, the vice chair(s) of the board shall assist the board chair, as requested, in the performance of his or her duties and shall have such other functions as these bylaws may provide or as the board of directors or board chair may assign from time to time. In addition to the foregoing, the vice chair shall possess the powers and perform the duties incumbent upon the board chair during his or her absence or disability. In the event there is more than one vice chair, the board of directors shall designate one to possess the powers and perform the duties incumbent upon the board chair during his or her absence or disability.

ARTICLE IV
Officers and Agents

{COMMENTARY: This article defines the various officers of the organization and their duties, along with such considerations as compensation, removal from office, vacancies, etc. In larger organizations, especially those with full time employees who do the staff work associated with various board and/or committee functions, it may be necessary to provide in the bylaws for "assistant" officers. In these model bylaws, the officer (e.g., treasurer) has the full authority and responsibility to carry out the function, while the assistant officer (e.g., assistant treasurer) is responsible for doing or supervising the staff work necessary to perform that particular function.}

Section 4.1 NUMBER AND QUALIFICATIONS. The officers of the corporation shall consist of a president, one or more vice presidents, a secretary, a treasurer, and such other officers, assistant officers and agents, assistant secretaries and assistant treasurers, as may be deemed necessary or desirable by the corporation's directors or state law. One person may hold more than one office at a time, except that no person may simultaneously hold the offices of president and secretary. The president shall be *[shall not be]* a member of the board of directors. *(NOTE: Each organization will have to determine whether other officers should be, or should not be, members of the board.)*

Section 4.2 ELECTION AND TERM OF OFFICE. The officers of the corporation shall be elected, for a term commencing on election, by the corporation's directors at the annual meeting of the board of directors [held after the annual meeting of the members]. Each officer shall hold office for a term of one (1) year or until his or her successor shall have been duly elected and shall have qualified, or until his or her earlier death, resignation or removal. *(NOTE: Some organizations impose limits on the number of terms a non-staff officer can hold office, such as two (2) one-year terms. If so, provision should be made for this in this section. Also, in some "member" organizations it is the members, at their annual meeting, who elect the board chair and/or president and sometimes other officers as well. If so, provision should be made here for that procedure.)*

Section 4.3 COMPENSATION. The compensation of the president shall be fixed from time to time by the board of directors. No officer shall be prevented from receiving a salary by reason of the fact that he or she is also a director of the corporation. However, during any period in which the corporation is a private foundation as described in section 509(a) of the Internal Revenue Code, no payment of compensation (or payment or reimbursement of expenses) shall be made in any manner which might result in the imposition of any liability under section 4941 of the Internal Revenue Code.

Section 4.4 REMOVAL. Any officer or agent may be removed by the board of directors, or a committee appointed by the board for such purpose, with or without cause, whenever in its judgment the best interests of the corporation will be served thereby, but such removal shall be without prejudice to the contract rights, if any, of the person so removed. Election or appointment of an officer or agent shall not in itself create contract rights.

Section 4.5 VACANCIES. Any officer may resign at any time, subject to any rights or obligations under any existing contracts between the officer and the corporation, by giving written notice to the board chair or the president or the secretary. An officer's resignation shall take effect at the time specified in such notice, and unless otherwise specified therein, the acceptance of such resignation shall not be necessary to make it effective. A vacancy in any office, however occurring, may be filled for the unexpired portion of the term by action of the board of directors if the vacant position is one held by a director or by the president; or by the president, with the advice and counsel of the board chair, if the vacant office is a staff position.

Section 4.6 AUTHORITY AND DUTIES OF OFFICERS. The officers of the corporation shall have the authority and shall exercise the powers and perform the duties specified by the president, the board of directors or these bylaws, except that in any event each officer shall exercise such powers and perform such duties as may be required by law.

4.6.1 Executive director (president). The board of directors shall elect a executive director (president) who, as chief *[executive or operating]* officer under its supervision and direction, shall carry on the general affairs of the Corporation. The executive director shall be a member of the staff of the corporation and shall be *[or shall not be]* a voting member of all committees except the Compensation and Audit Committees. It shall be his or her duty to approve the expenditure of the monies appropriated by the board of directors in accordance with the budget approved by the board of directors. The executive director shall make an annual report and periodic reports to the board of directors concerning the programs of the corporation. He or she shall comply with all orders from the board of directors. All officers, except the board chair and vice chair, agents and employees shall report, and be responsible, to the executive director. He or she shall perform such other duties as may be determined from time to time by the board of directors. *(NOTE: These model bylaws contemplate that the executive director is the organization's chief staff officer. Some organizations permit the executive director to be a voting member of the board of directors. Standard 1.g., established by the National Charities Information Bureau [NCIB], permits one staff person to be a member of the board of directors. That person is usually the chief staff officer. NCIB standards further stipulate that a member of the board who is also staff shall not serve as board chair or treasurer.)*

4.6.2 Vice president(s). The board of directors shall elect one or more vice presidents who shall assist the president in carrying out the programs of the corporation. In the event of the prolonged absence or disability of the president, the board shall appoint one vice president as acting president, and, as such the acting president shall have all the authority and duties vested in the president. *(NOTE: Depending on the size of the organizations, it may be desirable, especially in larger nonprofit organizations, to establish several categories of vice presidents, such as corporate vice presidents, who are elected by the board of directors, and administrative vice presidents, who are appointed by the president.)*

4.6.3 Secretary. The board of directors shall elect a secretary who shall attend the meetings of the members and of the directors and of all committees of the board, and shall record the proceedings of the corporation and of the board of directors and of all committees of the board, at their respective meetings. He or she shall provide for notification of the members and directors of the corporation of their respective meetings in accordance with these bylaws of the corporation, shall be the custodian of the corporate records and seal, shall make certifications of board actions, bylaws and all organizational documents, and shall perform such other duties as may be required by these bylaws or as may be assigned by the board of directors or the president.

4.6.4 Assistant secretary. If one or more shall be elected, the assistant secretary(s), in the absence of the secretary, shall have all the authority and duties vested in the secretary. He or she shall perform such duties as may be assigned to him or her by the secretary, the board of directors or the president.

4.6.5 Treasurer. The board of directors shall elect a treasurer who shall be the financial officer of the corporation and shall receive and deposit in a bank or banks to be approved by the board of directors all the monies of the corporation and keep an accurate account thereof. He or she shall make disbursements subject to such regulations as may be determined from time to time by the board of directors, and shall make reports of the finances of the corporation annually and whenever requested by the board of directors or the executive director. He or she shall perform such other duties as may be required by these bylaws or as may be assigned by the board of directors or the president. At the end of his or her term of office, the treasurer shall deliver to his or her successor all books, monies, and other property of the corporation then in his or her possession. The board of directors may require the treasurer to give such security as it may direct for the faithful performance of his or her duties.

4.6.6 Assistant treasurer. If one or more shall be elected, the assistant treasurer, in the absence of the treasurer, shall have all the authority and duties vested in the treasurer. He or she shall perform such duties as may be assigned to him or her by the treasurer, the board of directors or the president.

(NOTE: Depending on the size of the organization, the above mentioned positions—treasurer, assistant treasurer, secretary and assistant secretary—may be either paid staff or non-paid volunteers, or a combination thereof. Such a combination might be a volunteer treasurer, who is also a member of the board of directors, but is supported in that role by an assistant treasurer, who is a paid staff member of the organization.)

ARTICLE V
Committees of the Board

{COMMENTARY: Many nonprofit organizations, by their very nature, depend upon committees of directors and/or members and/or other constituents to define and shape their work, ranging from program implementation to formation of organizational policy. This article defines the establishment of various committees. Since it defines only an executive committee and standing committees such as nominating, audit, and compensation committees, it is purposely broad. The bylaws might also include provision for a development committee, a planning committee and other committees. See pages 55–61 on committees. Since the needs of organizations change, these bylaws provide for the board of directors to determine

periodically the need for various committees. If specific ad hoc committees were included in the bylaws, then every time the programs or activities of the organization changed, it would also be necessary to amend the bylaws.}

Section 5.1 DESIGNATION OF COMMITTEES. The board of directors may designate one or more standing or special committees to direct the business of the corporation. Each such committee may exercise the authority granted to it by the board's enabling resolution.

Section 5.2 LIMITATION ON COMMITTEE POWERS. No committee shall have the authority of the board of directors to amend, alter or repeal these bylaws; to elect, appoint or remove any member of any such committee or any officer or director of the corporation (except as provided specifically below in this section 5.2); to amend the articles of incorporation of the corporation; to restate the corporation's articles of incorporation; to adopt a plan of merger or adopt a plan of consolidation with another corporation; to authorize the sale, lease, exchange or mortgage of all or substantially all of the property and assets of the corporation; to authorize the voluntary dissolution of the corporation or to revoke proceedings therefore; to adopt a plan for the distribution of the assets of the corporation; to amend, alter or repeal any resolution of the board of directors; or as otherwise may be prohibited by law. Rules governing procedures for meetings of any committee of the board shall be as established by the board of directors, or in the absence thereof, by the committee itself. If no rules are established, then the rules that govern the directors shall govern each committee. All committees are to report promptly to the board and only take such action(s) as is specifically designated in the bylaws or in the resolution chartering the committee. Each committee shall consist of two (2) or more directors and, such other persons as the board may designate, who need not be members of the board of directors. The board may designate one or more persons as alternate members of any committee, and such alternates may replace any absent or disqualified member of the committee at any meeting of the committee. In the absence or disqualification of a member of the committee, and the alternate or alternates, if any, designated for such committee member, the member or members of the committee present at any meeting and entitled to vote, whether or not they constitute a quorum, may unanimously appoint another person to act at the meeting in the place of any such absent or disqualified member of the committee. Members of a committee shall serve until the next annual meeting of the corporation or until their successors are appointed.

(NOTE: State laws vary widely on the powers of committees; some of the provisions set forth above would be contrary to law in California, for example.)

Section 5.3 COMMITTEE CHAIR. The board chair, with the approval of the board of directors, shall appoint all committee chairs for the ensuing year at or within a reasonable time after the annual meeting of the board of directors. Committee chairs shall be members of the corporation's board of directors. If the board of directors charters a new committee by resolution at a meeting other than the annual meeting of the board of directors, the board of directors shall similarly appoint its chair at the time the committee is chartered or within a reasonable time after the establishment of the committee.

Section 5.4 COMMITTEE MEETINGS. Meetings of the committees of the board of directors may be called by the respective chairs thereof or by any two (2) members of the committee. At all meetings of any committee, a majority of the members of the committee shall constitute a quorum for the transaction of business, and the act of a majority of the members of the committee present at any meeting thereof at which there is a quorum, shall be the act of the committee, except as may be otherwise specifically provided for by these bylaws.

(NOTE: Organizations with a large board of directors, which meets infrequently because of size, or other factors, may find it desirable for the bylaws to establish an executive committee. If an executive committee is desirable, the following wording may be used.)

Section 5.5 EXECUTIVE COMMITTEE. Each year, at its annual meeting, the directors shall elect from among those who are, or are to be, directors of the corporation upon election, an executive committee consisting of at least *[number—spelled out]* (*[number—numeric]*) directors.

5.5.1 Composition. The executive committee so elected shall include the board chair, all vice chairs of the board, and *[designate other categories of members, as appropriate]*. Vacancies in the executive committee shall be filled by the board of directors. The president shall, if a member of the board, serve as a member of the executive committee. *(NOTE: If the president does not serve as a member of the board, appropriate wording should be inserted to provide that the president should attend all executive committee meetings.)*

5.5.2 Powers and functions. During the intervals between meetings of the board of directors, the executive committee shall, subject to section 5.2 hereof, possess and may exercise all the powers and functions of the board of directors in the management and direction of the affairs of the organization in all cases in which specific direction shall not have been given by the board of directors. *(NOTE: In addition to the limitations contained in section 5.2, the bylaws may otherwise limit the power of the executive committee.)*

5.5.3 Reports to board required. All actions of the executive committee shall be reported to the board of directors at its meeting next succeeding such action. Regular minutes of the proceedings of the executive committee shall be kept. A majority of the members of the executive committee in office at the time shall be necessary to constitute a quorum and in every case an affirmative vote of a majority of the members of the committee present at a meeting shall be necessary for the taking of any action.

5.5.4 Rules of procedure. The executive committee shall fix and establish its own rules of procedure and shall meet as provided by such rules, and shall also meet at the call of its chair or of any other two members of the committee.

Section 5.6 NOMINATING COMMITTEE. The board of directors shall designate, at or within a reasonable time after the annual meeting of the board of directors, a nominating committee which shall be responsible for proposing persons for election as directors at the next annual meeting of the corporation, or in the event of director vacancies between annual meetings of the members of the corporation, may propose replacement directors for election by the board of directors, and shall also recommend persons for consideration as officers to be elected at the next annual meeting of the board of directors *[if a membership organization, add: "; provided however that at the relevant annual meeting of the members, any member of the corporation may present nominations thirty (30) days in advance by written notice to the secretary, in addition to those presented by the Nominating Committee].* *[The nominating committee should annually, or more frequently, if necessary, review the composition of the board with respect to such factors as gender, ethnicity, age, industry representation, geographic dispersion, the number, function and expertise needs of committees, and the needs of the board and the corporation. Based upon that review, the nominating committee shall make recommendations to the board.]*

(NOTE: Section 5.6 defines the role of the nominating committee. Some organizations have chosen to replace the nominating committee with a "governance committee" which has a role that encompasses nominating new directors and officers and oversight of board structure and operations. When and if a staff president is to be selected, this function is generally handled by an ad hoc presidential selection committee rather than by the nominating committee. Some membership organizations place further restrictions on the composition of the nominating committee.)

Section 5.7 AUDIT COMMITTEE. The board of directors shall designate, at or within a reasonable time after the annual meeting of the board of directors, an audit committee which shall:

5.7.1 Recommend independent auditor. Recommend the firm to be employed as the organization's independent auditor, and review and approve the discharge of any such firm. The committee shall also review and approve the independent auditor's compensation and the term of its engagement and the independence of such auditor.

5.7.2 Review independent audit. Review, in consultation with the independent auditor, the result of each independent audit of the organization, the report of the auditor, any related management letter, and management's responses to recommendations made by the independent auditor in connection with the audit. *(NOTE: Some smaller organizations may prefer a less* *costly and less thorough financial examination, such as an "examination of accounts and limited audit" and the smallest entities may not have an outside accountant.)*

5.7.3 Review annual financial statements. Review, in consultation with the independent auditor and management, the organization's annual financial statements; any certification, report, opinion, or review rendered by the independent auditor in connection with those financial statements; and, any dispute between management and the independent auditor that arose in connection with the preparation of those financial statements; the committee shall review and report to the board with respect to the financial portions of the organization's annual report.

5.7.4 Review financial statements. Review, before or after publication, the organization's *[state frequency at which interim financial statements are issued, such as monthly, quarterly, semi-annually, etc.]* financial statements.

5.7.5 Plan external audits. Consider, in consultation with the independent auditor, the scope and plan of forthcoming external audits.

5.7.6 Evaluate internal accounting controls. Consider, in consultation with the independent auditor and the chief internal auditor, if any, the adequacy of the organization's internal accounting controls.

5.7.7 Evaluate auditing and accounting principles and practices. Consider, when presented by the independent auditor or otherwise, material questions of choice with respect to the choice of appropriate auditing and accounting principles and practices to be used in the preparation of the organization's financial statements.

5.7.8 Compliance with conflict of interest and code of ethics. Review the expense accounts and perquisites of officers and senior staff and the corporation's compliance with its conflict of interest policy and code of ethical conduct. *(NOTE: This function could be assigned to another committee.)*

5.7.9 Consider other financial matters. Have power to inquire into any financial matters in addition to those set forth in sections 5.7.1 through 5.7.8.

5.7.10 Perform other assignments. Perform such other functions as may be assigned to it by law, the organization's bylaws, or by the board of directors.

Section 5.8 COMPENSATION COMMITTEE. The board of directors shall designate, at or within a reasonable time after the annual meeting of the board of directors, a compensation committee which shall review and evaluate the performance, and recommend to the board, or determine, the annual salary, other benefits, direct or indirect, of the senior executives of the organization. *(NOTE: In some organizations, because of the size and nature of the board, the compensation committee or the executive committee is authorized to determine and fix senior executive compensation. The executive evaluation function should be included in the role of either the compensation, nominating or executive committee.)*

(NOTE: If other committees are to be specified in the bylaws, there should be additional sections added at this point to specify the scope and roles of such committees. The role and functions of such other committees could also be covered by board resolution or board-adopted policy statements. See pages 55–61 on committees.)

ARTICLE VI
Directors-Emeritus

{COMMENTARY: It is sometimes desirable to maintain an affiliation with a well-known or long-term director for various reasons. This may be someone who was a founder, major funder, etc., but who may not be able to attend all meetings because of his or her travel schedule, age, health, etc. This article provides for a category of director called director-emeritus, an honorary position without power to make motions or vote, although that provision may be modified, depending upon the desires of the board.}

Upon recommendation by the nominating committee, the board may elect one or more director(s)-emeritus with the right to attend all regular and special meetings thereof, but with no power to make motions or to vote and who shall not be counted in determining a quorum and with no right to receive notices of meetings. *(NOTE: The presence of a director-emeritus may possibly raise a question with respect to the protection of confidential communications when counsel is making disclosures to the board.)*

ARTICLE VII
Advisory Council

{COMMENTARY: It may be desirable to establish an "advisory council" of individuals who have had a leadership role in the organization in the past, no longer wish to be involved in the functioning of the organization, or of major funders, prominent officials, etc. This group may meet infrequently to provide feedback, or may be asked to perform special or ceremonial functions on behalf of the organization. Alternatively, the advisory council may also be used to establish and build relationships with potential future members of the board.}

Section 7.1 COMPOSITION AND PURPOSE. The board chair may appoint, with the approval of the board, an advisory council to promote the objectives of the organization, further its purposes, and advise the board of directors concerning the general policies applicable to, and the progress of the work of, the organization.

Section 7.2 ADVISORY COUNCIL CHAIR. The organization's board chair shall appoint the chair of the advisory council, with the approval of the board.

ARTICLE VIII
Indemnification

{COMMENTARY: Legal counsel familiar with the indemnification require-ments in your state should be consulted in order to modify this section to comply with the laws of the applicable state. See also page 131.}

Except to the extent expressly prohibited by the New York Not-For-Profit Corporation Law, the Corporation shall indemnify any person, made or threatened to be made a party to or called as a witness in or asked to provide information in connection with any pending or threatened action, proceeding, hearing or investigation, or any appeal therein (other than an action or proceeding by or in the right of the Corporation to procure a judgment in its favor), whether civil or criminal, including an action by or in the right of any other corporation of any type or kind, domestic or foreign, or any partnership, joint venture, trust, employee benefit plan or other enterprise, which any director or officer of the Corporation served in any capacity at the request of the Corporation, by reason of the fact that he or she is or was, or he or she is the executor, administrator, heir or successor of a person who is or was, a director or officer of the Corporation, or served such other corporation, partnership, joint venture, trust, employee benefit plan or other enterprise in any capacity, against judgments, fines, amounts paid in settlement and reasonable expenses, including attorneys' fees actually and necessarily incurred as a result of such action or proceeding, or any appeal therein, if such director or officer acted in good faith, for a purpose which he reasonably believed to be in, or, in the case of service for any corporation or any partnership, joint venture, trust, employee benefit plan or other enterprise, not opposed to, the best interests of the Corporation and, in criminal actions or proceedings, in addition, had no reasonable cause to believe that his or her conduct was unlawful.

Except to the extent expressly prohibited by the Not-For-Profit Corporation Law, the Corporation shall indemnify any person made, or threatened to be made, a party to an action by or in the right of the Corporation to procure a judgment in its favor by reason of the fact that he or she is or was, or he or she is the executor, administrator, heir or successor of a person who is or was, a director or officer of the Corporation, or is or was serving at the request of the Corporation as a director or officer of any corporation of any type or kind, domestic or foreign, of any partnership, joint venture, trust, employee benefit plan or other enterprise, against amounts paid in settlement and reasonable expenses, including attorneys' fees, actually and necessarily incurred by him or her in connection with the defense or settlement of such action, or in connection with an appeal therein, if such director or officer acted, in good faith, for a purpose which he reasonably believed to be in, or, in the case of service for any corporation or any partnership, joint venture, trust, employee benefit plan or other enterprise, not opposed to, the best interests of the Corporation, except that no indemnification under this paragraph shall be made in respect to (1) a threatened action, or a pending action which is settled or otherwise disposed of, or (2) any claim, issue or matter as to which such person shall have been adjudged to be liable to the Corporation, unless and only to the extent that the court in which the action was brought, or if no action was brought, any court of competent jurisdiction, determines upon application that, in view of all the circumstances of the case, the person is fairly and reasonably entitled to indemnity for such portion of the settlement amount and expenses as the court deems proper.

The termination of any civil or criminal action or proceeding by judgment, settlement, conviction or upon a plea of nolo contendere, or its equivalent, shall not in itself create a presumption that any such director or officer did not act, in good faith, for a purpose which he or she reasonably believed to be in, or, in the case of service for any other corporation or any partnership, joint venture, trust, employee benefit plan or other enterprise, not opposed to, the best interests of the Corporation or that he or she had reasonable cause to believe that his or her conduct was unlawful.

No indemnification shall be made under this bylaw if a judgment or other final adjudication adverse to such person establishes that his or her acts were committed in bad faith or were the result of active and deliberate dishonesty and were material to the cause of action so adjudicated, or that he personally gained in fact a financial profit or other advantage to which he was not legally entitled, and provided further that no such indemnification shall be required with respect to any settlement or other nonadjudicated disposition of any threatened or pending action or proceeding unless the Corporation has given its consent to such settlement or other disposition.

The Corporation shall advance or promptly reimburse, upon request of any person entitled to indemnification hereunder, all expenses, including attorneys' fees reasonably incurred in defending any action or proceeding in advance of the final disposition thereof, upon receipt of a written undertaking by or on behalf of such person to repay such amount if such person is ultimately found not to be entitled to indemnification or, where indemnification is granted, to the extent the expenses so advanced or reimbursed exceed the amount to which such person is entitled.

Nothing in the bylaw shall limit or affect any other right of any person to indemnification or expenses, including attorneys' fees, under any statute, rule, regulation, certificate of incorporation, bylaw, insurance policy, contract or otherwise.

No elimination of this bylaw, and no amendment of this bylaw adversely affecting the right of any person to indemnification or advancement of expenses hereunder shall be effective until the sixtieth day following notice to such person of such action, and no elimination of or amendment to this bylaw shall deprive any person of his rights hereunder arising out of alleged or actual occurrences, acts or failures to act prior to such sixtieth day. The provisions of this paragraph shall supersede anything to the contrary in these bylaws.

The Corporation shall not, except by elimination or amendment of this bylaw in a manner consistent with the preceding paragraph, take any corporate action or enter into any agreement which prohibits, or otherwise limits the rights of any person to, indemnification in accordance with the provisions of this bylaw. The indemnification of any person provided by this bylaw shall continue after such person has ceased to be a director or officer of the Corporation and shall inure to the benefit of such person's heirs, executors, administrators and legal representatives.

The Corporation is authorized to enter into agreements with any of its directors, officers or employees extending rights to indemnification and advancement of expenses to such person to the fullest extent permitted by applicable law, or to provide such indemnification and advancement of expenses pursuant to **[a resolution of members or]** a resolution of directors, but the failure to enter into any such agreement or to adopt any such resolutions shall not affect or limit the rights of such person pursuant to this bylaw. It is hereby expressly recognized that all directors and officers of the Corporation, by serving as such after the adoption hereof, are acting in reliance on this bylaw and that the Corporation is estopped to contend otherwise. Additionally, it is hereby expressly recognized that all persons who are directors or officers of the Corporation and also serve as directors, officers or employees of corporations which are subsidiaries or affiliates of the Corporation (or otherwise entities controlled by the Corporation) are conclusively presumed to serve or to have served as such at the request of the Corporation and, unless prohibited by law, are entitled to indemnification under this bylaw. **(NOTE: Omit the bold, italicized words above if the nonprofit organization is not a membership organization.)**

For purposes of this bylaw, the Corporation shall be deemed to have requested a director or officer of the Corporation to serve an employee benefit plan where the performance by such person of his or her duties to the Corporation also imposes duties on, or otherwise involves services by, such person to the plan or participants or beneficiaries of the plan, and excise taxes assessed on a person with respect to an employee benefit plan pursuant to applicable law shall be considered indemnifiable expenses.

A person who has been successful, on the merits or otherwise, in the defenses of a civil or criminal action or proceeding shall be entitled to indemnification as authorized in such paragraph. Except as provided in the proceedings sentence and unless ordered by a court, any indemnification under this bylaw, under any contract or otherwise, shall be made by the Corporation if, and only if, authorized in the specific case:

(1) By the board of directors acting by quorum consisting of directors who are not parties to such action or proceeding upon a find-

ing that the director or officer has met the standard of conduct set forth in the first paragraph of this bylaw;

(2) If such a quorum is not obtainable or, even if obtainable, a quorum of disinterested directors so directs:

(a) By the board of directors upon the opinion in writing of independent legal counsel that indemnification is proper in the circumstances because the standard of conduct set forth in the first or second paragraph of this bylaw has been met by such director or officer; or

[(b) By the members upon a finding that the director or officer has met the applicable standard of conduct set forth in either of such paragraphs.] (NOTE: Omit this subparagraph (b) if the nonprofit organization is not a membership organization.)

If any expenses or other amounts are paid by way of indemnification, otherwise than by court order or action by the members, the Corporation shall, not later than the next annual meeting of members, unless such meeting is held within three months from the date of such payment and, in any event, within fifteen months from the date of such payment, mail to its members of record at the time entitled to vote for the election of directors a statement specifying the action taken, or if the Corporation has no members, such statement shall be included in the records of the Corporation open to public inspection.

For purposes of this bylaw, the term "Corporation" shall include any legal successor to the Corporation, including any corporation or other entity which acquires all or substantially all of the assets of the Corporation in one or more transactions.

In case any provision in this bylaw shall be determined at any time to be unenforceable in any respect, the other provisions shall not in any way be affected or impaired thereby, and the affected provision shall be given the fullest possible enforcement in the circumstances, it being the intention of the Corporation to afford indemnification and advancement of expenses to its directors and officers, acting in such capacities or in the other capacities specified in this bylaw, to the fullest extent permitted by law.

ARTICLE IX
Conflict of Interest

{COMMENTARY: The National Charities Information Bureau [NCIB] requires, in order to meet its giving standards, that nonprofit organizations adopt a policy on conflict of interest. The following article meets the requirements of the NCIB, and provides the framework for developing a more comprehensive and detailed policy. Some organizations prefer to treat this subject in a policy adopted by the board rather than including it in the bylaws.}

Section 9.1 CONFLICT DEFINED. A conflict of interest may exist when the interests or activities of any director, officer or staff member may be seen as competing with the interests or activities of this corporation, or the director, officer or staff member derives a financial or other material gain as a result of a direct or indirect relationship. *(NOTE: For example, landlord, attorney, auditor, etc.)*

Section 9.2 DISCLOSURE REQUIRED. Any possible conflict of interest shall be disclosed to the board of directors by the person concerned, if that person is a director or the president of the corporation, or to the president, or to such person or persons as he or she may designate, if the person is a member of the staff.

9.2.1 ABSTINENCE FROM VOTE. When any conflict of interest is relevant to a matter requiring action by the board of directors, the interested person shall call it to the attention of the board of directors or its appropriate committee and such person shall not vote on the matter; provided however, any director disclosing a possible conflict of interest may be counted in determining the presence of a quorum at a meeting of the board of directors or a committee thereof. (For smaller organizations, see note to section 5.7.2 *supra*)

Section 9.3 ABSENCE FROM DISCUSSION. Unless requested to remain present during the meeting, the person having the conflict shall retire from the room in which the board or its committee is meeting and shall not participate in the final deliberation or decision regarding the matter under consideration. However, that person shall provide the board or committee with any and all relevant information.

Section 9.4 MINUTES. The minutes of the meeting of the board or committee shall reflect that the conflict of interest was disclosed and that the interested person was not present during the final discussion or vote and did not vote. When there is doubt as to whether a conflict of interest exists, the matter shall be resolved by a vote of the board of directors or its committee, excluding the person concerning whose situation the doubt has arisen.

Section 9.5 ANNUAL REVIEW. A copy of this conflict of interest bylaw shall be furnished each director, officer and senior staff member who is presently serving the corporation, or who may hereafter become associated with the corporation. This policy shall be reviewed annually for the information and guidance of directors, officers and staff members. Any new directors, officers or staff members shall be advised of this policy upon undertaking the duties of such office.

ARTICLE X
Miscellaneous

{COMMENTARY: This article defines various other operating guidelines for the organization, such as the term of its fiscal year, no private inurement,

designation of gifts, process for amending these bylaws, etc. A number of the bylaws, by their references to the tax code, are intended primarily for 501(c)(3) organizations.}

Section 10.1 BOOKS AND MINUTES. The corporation shall keep correct and complete books and records of account and financial statements and shall also keep minutes of the proceedings of its board of directors and committees. All books and records of the corporation may be inspected by any director or his or her accredited agent or attorney, for any proper purpose at any reasonable time, and by such members who may have voting rights.

Section 10.2 FISCAL YEAR AND AUDIT. The fiscal year of the corporation shall be *[date on which fiscal year begins, such as January 1 or July 1]* through *[date on which fiscal year ends, such as December 31 or June 30]*, inclusive. After the close of each fiscal year of the corporation, financial transactions of the corporation for the preceding fiscal year shall be audited by certified public accountants, as directed by the board of directors, and a report of the audit shall be made to the board of directors within ninety (90) days after the close of the fiscal year.

Section 10.3 CONVEYANCES AND ENCUMBRANCES. Property of the corporation may be assigned, conveyed or encumbered by such officers of the corporation as may be authorized to do so by the board of directors, and such authorized persons shall have power to execute and deliver any and all instruments of assignment, conveyance and encumbrance; however, the sale, exchange, lease or other disposition of all or substantially all of the property and assets of the corporation shall be authorized only in the manner prescribed by the applicable law.

Section 10.4 DESIGNATED CONTRIBUTIONS. The officers of the corporation may accept on its behalf, in accordance with policies and procedures set by the board of directors, any designated contribution, grant, bequest or devise consistent with its general tax-exempt purposes, as set forth in the corporation's articles of incorporation. As so limited, donor designated contributions will be accepted for special funds, purposes or uses. Further, the corporation shall retain sufficient control over all donated funds (including designated contributions) to assure that such funds will be used consistent with the restrictions contained in the grant and the corporation's tax-exempt purposes. *(NOTE: The board should adopt "gift acceptance policies" to avoid the imposition of future liabilities; for example, the acceptance of a building carries liabilities for maintenance of the building.)*

Section 10.5 LOANS TO DIRECTORS AND OFFICERS PROHIBITED. No loans or advances, other than customary travel advances, shall be made by the corporation to any of its directors or officers.

Section 10.6 NO PRIVATE INUREMENT. The corporation is not organized for profit and is to be operated exclusively for one or more of the purposes as specified in Section 501(c)(3) of the Internal Revenue Code, including, for such purposes, the making of distributions to organizations that qualify as exempt organizations under Section 501(c)(3) of the Internal Revenue Code, or the corresponding section of any future federal tax code, and in the promotion of social welfare in accordance with the purposes stated in the organization's articles of incorporation. The net earnings of the organization shall be devoted exclusively to charitable and educational purposes and shall not inure to the benefit of any private individual. No director or person from whom the organization may receive any property or funds shall receive or shall be entitled to receive any pecuniary profit from the operation thereof, and in no event shall any part of the funds or assets of the organization be paid as salary or compensation to, or distributed to, or inure to the benefit of any member of the board of directors; provided, however, that (a) reasonable compensation may be paid to any director while acting as an agent, contractor, or employee of the corporation for services rendered in affecting one or more of the purposes of the organization; and (b) any director may, from time to time, be reimbursed for his or her actual and reasonable expenses incurred in connection with the administration of the affairs of the organization. *(NOTE: This section should be appropriately modified if the organization is not a Section 501(c)(3) organization.)*

   Section 10.7 REFERENCES TO INTERNAL REVENUE CODE. All references in these bylaws to provisions of the Internal Revenue Code are to the provisions of the Internal Revenue Code of 1986, as amended, and shall include the corresponding provisions of any subsequent federal tax laws.

   Section 10.8 AMENDMENTS. These bylaws may be amended, repealed or modified, and new bylaws adopted, by the affirmative vote of a *[majority or two-thirds]* of the board of directors *[if a membership organization, insert: "or the membership"]*. Any notice of a meeting at which these bylaws are to be amended, repealed or modified shall include notice of such proposed action. *(NOTE: Statutes generally provide that bylaws can be amended by either members or directors. The amending process may be specified in the articles of incorporation, so the articles should be checked to be sure that the procedure specified in the bylaws is consistent with the articles. This provision contains language permitting amendment by vote of the directors. It should be noted that to amend by vote of the members is a more cumbersome process. Check your state statutes for specific requirements concerning the bylaw amendment process.)*

   Section 10.9 PRIVATE INUREMENT. Notwithstanding any other provision of the articles of incorporation or these bylaws, the corporation shall not engage in any activities which are not permitted (1) by a nonprofit corporation exempt from federal corporate tax under Section 501(c)(3) of the Internal Revenue Code, or (2) by a nonprofit corporation's contributions to which are to be deductible under Section 170(c)(2) of the Internal Revenue Code.

(NOTE: The following section dealing with dissolution may be covered in the articles of incorporation. In such a case it may not be necessary to include a section on dissolution.)

Section 10.10 DISSOLUTION. On dissolution of the corporation, all of its net assets shall be paid over or transferred to one or more exempt organizations of the kind described in Internal Revenue Code Section 501(c)(3). The organization to receive such property shall be designated by the board of directors. Any assets not so disposed of shall be disposed of by the *[District or County]* Court in and for the County of *[name of county]* exclusively for one or more exempt purposes within the meaning of Internal Revenue Code Section 501(c)(3), or to such organization or organizations, as said court shall determine, which are organized and operated exclusively for such purposes. *(NOTE: A dissolution clause may not be necessary where the subject is adequately covered by state statute. Check your state statutes.)*

Section 10.11 SEVERABILITY. The invalidity of any provision of these bylaws shall not affect the other provisions hereof, and in such event these bylaws shall be construed in all respects as if such invalid provisions were omitted.

BYLAWS CERTIFICATE

The undersigned certifies that *[s]*he is the Secretary of *[Organization]*, a *[state]* nonprofit corporation, and that, as such, *[s]*he is authorized to execute this certificate on behalf of said corporation, and further certifies that the foregoing bylaws, consisting of *[number—spelled out]* (*[number—numeric]*) pages, including this page, constitute the bylaws of the corporation as of this date, duly adopted by the *[members or directors, depending on whether articles of incorporation specifies members or directors are entitled to adopt bylaws]*, of the corporation at their *[date]* *[annual, special, or regular]* meeting, as amended from time to time prior to the date hereof.

Dated: *[date]*

/s/ *Secretary*

[NAME], Secretary

PART III
Specific Problem Areas in the Nonprofit World

In this part of the guidebook we examine a number of areas which affect nonprofit management, areas where the board of directors may often delegate responsibility without clear standards and direction, or where a board may count on staff initiative to define the issues and suggest the appropriate decisions. Thus records management is both a practical problem—how big is the task? what are our choices? what will each choice cost?—and it is also an area of corporate risk-bearing decisions. A board is helpless in addressing such an issue without staff support and analysis. In a similar way, a board will count on its staff to catalogue its risks and point out the appropriate solutions to these exposures.

Membership

George W. Overton and Joan Elise Dubinsky

This chapter discusses membership rights and functions from two standpoints: first, the problems created by a membership, from the standpoint of the organization's efficiency; and secondly, the rights of members in a nonprofit. The reader is reminded that throughout this volume, the word "member" refers solely to persons or entities having voting or other rights in organizational governance.

The Problems of Membership

As noted in the introduction (see p. xviii), we use the word "member" to mean only a person or entity with voting rights in the nonprofit organization. As we noted, the word is otherwise frequently used for a wide variety of relationships. Often it means little more than that an individual has made a minimal annual contribution to an art museum or a library, for example.

Our definition serves an important purpose. If there are members who have voting rights, it is critically important to define these people or entities quite precisely. It is the frequent experience of nonprofit organizations with such members that, when a dispute arises which requires an action of the membership for resolution, the question of who is entitled to vote becomes quite difficult. In general, if the mission and function of the corporation can otherwise be satisfied, it is prudent to confine the voting membership to persons making substantial contributions of a defined minimum or having some other precise qualification.

One should search for criteria that will assure records concerning such persons are going to be cared for and maintained adequately. To define a voting membership by a small annual contribution, particularly if such contributions are sought and received at varying times throughout the year, is to invite chaos if a serious contested vote has to be taken. Few organizations are going to keep precise records when a $25.00 contribution has been received.

In the operation of a charitable organization, as that term is traditionally used in both corporate law and tax law, the existence of a membership can create additional complexities where conflicting loyalties and obligations of the directors are already complex enough. Directors of a child welfare agency, for example, face the following duties:

(1) a duty to the children of the particular constituency who are to be served;
(2) duties to such regulatory agencies as may supervise child care entities;
(3) a duty to the attorney general as the voice of the public interest in the maintenance of the agency's mission; and
(4) possible duties to donors under various theories of trust law, although in general the obligation of the charitable trustee to a donor is limited.

A nonprofit should examine whether it can, without impairment of its public relations or corporate mission, dispense with the voting membership as a needless complexity in managing its affairs. If such a question must be answered in the negative, organizations should be prepared to devote significant attention to accurate membership records, including the dates (if membership is conditioned upon annual dues) of payment of such dues. At any membership meeting a secretary should be able to certify the number of members present and the number present by proxy, the number of members entitled to vote, and the number necessary to establish a quorum.

The secretary should establish or insist that the board establish the conditions for a proxy for any meeting of the members and be able to report to the board on the presence of proxies and those that have been revoked by attendance. The secretary should be able to verify the standing of those present at any meeting and attend to all details concerning notices and call for such meetings in conformity with the bylaws.

Membership Rights in Nonprofit Organizations

This section[1] summarizes the basic duties and obligations of members of a nonprofit organization. The analysis is based upon the American Bar Association's Revised Model Nonprofit Corporation Act (1987).[2] Again, as stated in the introduction, the word "member" refers to a person having voting or other specific legal rights.

Members and Shareholders

A member of a nonprofit organization and a shareholder in a for-profit corporation share some common characteristics. Members and shareholders alike have definable "stakes" or interest in the underlying corporate entity. Yet each has a markedly different perspective about what makes that corporate collective a cohesive unit.

Shareholders in a publicly-held corporation have clearly defined ownership and voting rights in the corporate entity. These owners have invested in the corporation, expect a return on that investment, and hold at least a small amount of control over the running of the corporation.

Members of a nonprofit organization share a similar relationship to their corporate entity. Members generally are financial contributors to the corporation. They may attend meetings and participate in the decision-making process of their nonprofit organization. They may increase or decrease their commitment and emotional investment in the nonprofit by their active involvement. Yet they do not own the nonprofit in the same sense that shareholders own discrete, marketable shares of stock.

A member of a nonprofit cannot easily measure his or her contribution relative to another member's by comparing the number of shares owned. The value of shares held also has no meaning whatsoever in the nonprofit world. Without the profit motive undergirding the relationship of investor/owner to corporate entity, other means of analyzing a contribution must be identified. It is these "other means" which can be called the rights, duties and obligations of members of a nonprofit organization.

A nonprofit organization may have members or may not have members, depending on how it is established. The entire operation of the nonprofit could be conducted by the board of directors and its staff. In a membership organization, the members are the readily definable group of individuals responsible for selecting the nonprofit's board of directors. In non-membership organizations, the board of directors is usually self-perpetuating.

The Optimum Use and Function of Members

At the most fundamental of levels, members of a nonprofit organization usually provide the pool from which its future leaders are drawn. That group of individuals, defined as members by the nonprofit's bylaws or articles of incorporation, generally serves as both the proving ground for future leaders on the nonprofit's board of directors as well as being the voters who elect the board.

There can be a democratic flavor to this process. If we assume that the membership of the nonprofit represents that group of individuals who are most keenly interested in the mission of the organization, then they should be extremely knowledgeable as voters. The annual meeting can provide a forum for its committed members. In a well-run nonprofit, this process can add great strength to the organization.

The annual meeting of the nonprofit is generally reserved for two or three essential agenda items: election of directors for the coming term, receipt of reports of general interest to the members, and presentation of a formal address by the chair of the organization. Generally, the nominating committee presents its slate, the nominees agree to serve if elected, the members vote and the official business of the meeting concludes. Many nonprofits, however, use the opportunity of having a large assemblage of members present at the annual meeting to recognize the valuable ways in which members participate.

For example, the board of directors may provide public recognition of those members whose contributions during the year have been extraordinary. The recognition or award program notes, explicitly or implicitly, that such contributions exemplify the type of member commitment desired by the organization. Public recognition of such members' contributions may spur other members to increase their giving or to become more actively involved in the daily operations and activities of the organization.

Defining Membership

It is of critical importance in a nonprofit that the articles of incorporation and bylaws enable all interested persons to know who is and who is not a member.

Membership need not be defined by financial contributions. Depending on the size, complexity and mission of the organization, members may be distinguished from other types of supporters. For instance, each individual who donates clothing to a charity may not claim membership rights in the nonprofit corporations affiliated with that charity. Yet, another nonprofit organization may wish to count as members each and every financial contributor solicited during a door-to-door campaign. The bylaws or articles of incorporation of the corporation are the final arbiters of membership definition and membership rights.

There is no one standard method to distinguish members (who—by this volume's definition—have certain rights and obligations as defined by the bylaws) from supporters (who do not have such rights). A nonprofit could provide that membership will be dependent upon the payment of specified minimum dues. All other financial contributors could be defined as supporters. Alternatively, members could be defined by the donation of a specified number of hours of voluntary service to the organization. A nonprofit should note that defining membership by criteria other than the payment of money may be difficult and precision is always to be given a high priority. If financial contributions are not used, other specific criteria should be defined.

Many nonprofit corporations succeed in direct proportion to the dedication of their supporters and volunteers. These volunteers—individuals who provide non-compensated labor, service, time, and skills to further the mission of the nonprofit—often are the lifeblood of the organization. Volunteers may operate the telephone banks, serve as museum docents, conduct door-to-door canvassing, provide direct counseling services to disadvantaged client groups, rebuild communities devastated by disaster, or serve as advocates for the elderly and disabled. Whatever the mission of the nonprofit, it is often through the activities of such volunteers that the mission becomes reality. Those individuals who serve as volunteers in the daily operations of the nonprofit may be supporters, members, or both. By including active supporters within the definition of members, the nonprofit may expand its basic level of community support.

Statutory Provisions

The Revised Model Nonprofit Corporation Act, section 6, as promulgated by the American Bar Association in 1987, defines members as those persons who consent to be members and who are entitled to vote for directors of the nonprofit corporation.[3]

State laws may provide further insight into the expected role of members. Many state statutes recognize the great need for flexibility in defining membership rights. In recognition of the social contract between member and nonprofit, some state statutes explicitly direct that the definition of members and the delineation of membership rights must be found in the corporation's bylaws.[4] Whether required by statute or not, however, an organization's bylaws and articles of incorporation must define membership.

It should be an easy task to define a nonprofit's membership. Any corporate secretary recognizes the recurrent nightmare of arriving at an annual meeting without any way to verify the voting privileges of those in attendance. The nonprofit must establish a clear definition of membership because this definition ultimately determines eligibility to vote at an annual meeting and answers credential challenges at an annual meeting gone awry.

For this reason, the corporate secretary should maintain a current list of all members entitled to vote, and the list should be available for consultation at any meeting of members. The secretary should remember also that proxies, if permitted, should be checked, and, if signatures of members are available, they should also be brought to the meeting to check signatures on proxies which may be presented at the meeting.

However membership is defined, the bylaws or articles of incorporation of the nonprofit must memorialize the definition. This definition may only rarely be scrutinized. Battles do erupt, however, at membership meetings. If voting rights are challenged, the definition of membership will be carefully analyzed. In the event of controversy at the annual meeting, a clear definition of members' voting rights and an accurate list of all current members eligible to vote could forestall procedural challenges to the conduct of the meeting.

Bylaws

The bylaws of a nonprofit organization should set forth the essential rights and obligations of members, voting and otherwise, and must meet state statutory requirements. Generally, a specified percentage of the membership can call for a special meeting of the members and the bylaws should outline the process for calling such a meeting. A typical process includes either a published meeting notice or a petition from a substantial number of members requiring the chair of the board of directors to hold and conduct a special membership meeting. Special meetings of members will probably occur infrequently, although they may become the locus for controversy and discussion about fundamental survival questions for the nonprofit (see p. 208).

Finally, the bylaws may vest in the members all or partial control over the adoption of amendments to the nonprofit's bylaws. The bylaws may have been initially adopted by the members at the conception of the organization. Generally, that first vote for the bylaws occurred when membership was limited and the board of directors was full of enthusiasm. A nonprofit considering bylaw amendments may have matured by dint of the number of years of operation or the number of difficulties conquered. The bylaws themselves should provide the avenue for consideration of amendments, with a specific article usually addressing the procedure for lawful adoption of amendments (see p. 229).

The bylaws should not be amended without considerable thought and agreement as to why change is needed.

Removal from Membership

There comes a time in the life of some nonprofits that demands considerable soul searching. Infrequently, the activity and conduct of a single member jeopardizes the nonprofit organization's standing in its community. If dissent is broadcast beyond the confines of the nonprofit, then corporate goodwill may diminish and public support erode.

Nonprofit organizations may wish to adopt self-policing rules which allow for the removal of membership rights in the event that a member acts in a way that is deleterious to the organization. The nonprofit could classify this type of self-policing as suspending or terminating a member, or withdrawing or limiting membership privileges.

Any such removal provision codified in the bylaws must include a description of the process to be followed and the vote required to accomplish the removal. Removal of membership rights could be a question for the general membership to consider, or removal procedures could be addressed by the board of directors or its designated subcommittee. When weighing the interests of the nonprofit, the individual member, and the elected officers of the nonprofit, it is thought best to leave decisions concerning removal of membership privileges to the board as the simplest procedure.

The removal of membership rights is generally preceded by some type of process that we have labelled "fair." A fair process includes some notice of the problem or issues causing concern and a hearing process which allows the major players in the drama to be heard. If membership in the nonprofit is voluntary, then the removal of membership privileges should be taken with great care and respect.

The Revised Model Nonprofit Corporation Act sets forth several fundamental principles which codify a fair and reasonable procedure for terminating membership privileges.[5]

The entire process should be carried out in good faith by the board of directors, or by those leaders to whom the responsibility has been delegated. The member in question should receive at least 15 days' written notice of the pending action and be provided with an opportunity to be heard by the final decision makers, either orally or in writing, at least five days before the action becomes final (see p. 209).

Litigation and Indemnification

In our society, nonprofit organizations and their boards of directors have become sensitized to the reality of litigation. In theory, a former member whose privileges have been revoked could bring some type of civil claim against the organization to seek reinstatement of membership rights, other equitable relief, or some type of monetary compensation. A fair process, as detailed above, should serve as the nonprofit's primary defense in the event that litigation ensues.

The organization may also be liable for the actions of its members, should the members make commitments on behalf of the organization which cannot be fulfilled by the nonprofit, or which appear to be inconsistent with the corporate mission. In such a situation, questions of the member's real or apparent agency would be primary in determining legal culpability. For example, a knowledgeable business person should not agree to contract for the delivery of goods to the nonprofit's headquarters upon the oral promise of a mere member.

Several states have adopted statutes that provide some measure of immunity to volunteers, members, and other supporters of nonprofit organizations. These statutes generally identify the categories of individuals who, because of their nonprofit affiliation or involvement, are immune to certain types of tort liability. Even though the individual volunteer may be immune from liability, the nonprofit organization would not similarly be immune from liability caused by the actions of its individual members or supporters, and therefore should consider insurance to cover such matters.

Conclusion

A nonprofit corporation's bylaws and articles of incorporation establish the minimal rights and duties of members. The members may serve as the voting public for the nonprofit. Members may choose to become more involved in the daily operations and activities of their nonprofit. By fully involving members, the nonprofit will find itself strengthened, will have a more informed electorate, and will develop future leaders. The nonprofit will also fulfill its mission and purpose through reliance on the active volunteer involvement of members.

Notes

1. This section was prepared by Joan Elise Dubinsky.
2. Model Nonprofit Corp. Act (1987).
3. *Id.*
4. *See* Fla. Stat. Ann. § 617.1806 (West Supp. 1996); Ga. Code Ann. § 14-3-101 (1994). In all cases, the bylaws and articles must define their status.
5. Model Nonprofit Corp. Act (1987).

Lobbying Conducted by Nonprofit Organizations

Robert W. Bishop

Nonprofit organizations have the legal right to communicate their views on matters of importance to the organization to elected representatives and their staffs and, if appropriate, to members of the federal executive branch. Congress has established significant constraints that must be evaluated carefully before a nonprofit organization commences any lobbying activities. During the course of those activities, the organization must ensure that both the statutory requirements and the implementing regulations of the Internal Revenue Service have been satisfied. As a consequence of being a section 501(c)(3) nonprofit organization, only limited lobbying is permitted, and no political activity, such as supporting a candidate for public office, is permitted. This chapter will explore the requirements pertinent to lobbying conducted by nonprofit organizations.

Introduction

Nonprofit organizations, like individual members of the public or business corporations, are allowed to seek to influence the conduct of government operations (i.e., to "lobby"). This right flows from the First Amendment to the U.S. Constitution, which guarantees "the right of the people . . . to petition the government for a redress of grievances."[1] Federal tax-exempt nonprofit organizations, however, are not allowed to participate in any partisan political activities, including supporting individual candidates, making financial contributions to candidates, or supporting a political party. Nor can a nonprofit organization attempt to justify being bipartisan; it must be nonpartisan—it cannot participate in partisan politics. In fact, a tax-exempt organization risks losing its tax-exempt status if it participates in a political campaign on behalf of or in opposition to a candidate for public office. Further, many states and even some localities have enacted restrictions and/or reporting requirements that also must be followed by a tax-exempt organization that desires to participate in state or local lobbying activities in those jurisdictions.

Conducting Lobbying Activities

Some think of lobbying as a distasteful or even corrupt activity. It is or perhaps should be, however, part of the legitimate functions of many, perhaps most, nonprofit organizations. Our legislative system, in a country as large and as diverse as the United States, must rely on sources outside Congress or the White House for the information needed for intelligent decisions to be made. A nonprofit organization whose activities may be materially advanced or curtailed by proposed legislation should give serious consideration whether it has, not a right or a privilege, but a duty to shape that legislation as best it can as part of its overall corporate mission.

Of course, there are improper or even corrupt methods of altering the legislative agenda. The standards and prohibitions outlined in this chapter largely came into being to address those abuses.

Many tax-exempt organizations have concluded that it is very important for them to conduct lobbying activities to accomplish their organization's goals. They have found that to lobby effectively they must:

(1) provide factual, reliable information;
(2) make it easy for the individuals being contacted to come to the right conclusion—provide them with information they will need to make a decision;
(3) be prepared to respond to the arguments of those opposed to their position;
(4) encourage direct letters from the constituency to their elected representatives; and
(5) ensure that they maintain personal and professional integrity as they conduct these activities.

There are two principles with which most legislators of every political persuasion will agree:

(1) any individual organization which builds confidence in the factual accuracy of its communications will find itself not only heard, but often sought out, even by legislators generally opposed to the organization's program; and
(2) any organization anticipating the need for legislative activity in the future would be wise to contact and establish regular communications with its elected representatives. It will be most productive to establish a good relationship *before* a specific issue arises, lest your elected representatives presume that you are only interested in them when you need help.

Statutory Requirements

This chapter will address solely the three federal statutes that control the conduct of lobbying activities by nonprofit organizations. Some of these statutes apply to all nonprofits, while others impose conditions on section 501(c)(3) organizations (charities) that must be satisfied for them to retain their tax-exempt status and to enable gifts to them to be deductible by the donor. In all of these areas there may be state and local laws or regulations that establish registration or other requirements that relate to state or local lobbying activities.

Lobbying Disclosure Act of 1995
The Lobbying Disclosure Act of 1995 ("Lobbying Disclosure Act")[2] repealed the Federal Regulation of Lobbying Act of 1946, as amended. All lobbyists (and, as noted below, the new definition of lobbyist is very broad) and organizations employing lobbyists must register under the Lobbying Disclosure Act within forty-five days of making a lobbying contact or being employed to lobby, whichever is earlier. Registration forms and associated instructions are available at the House Legislative Resource Center and the Senate Office of Public Records. Once registered, lobbyists and organizations employing lobbyists must file reports with the

House and Senate on a semi-annual basis. Reports are due August 14 for the period January 1 through June 30, and February 14 for the period July 1 through December 31 of each year.[3]

A "lobbyist" is an individual employed or retained, even though not compensated, to make more than one lobbying contact *and* whose lobbying activities constitute at least twenty percent of the services performed for their employer or a client during a six-month period. This includes time spent in research, preparation, and planning activities supporting or otherwise associated with lobbying activities. Individuals involved solely in research and preparation activities, but who do not make any lobbying contacts themselves, however, are not included.

A "lobbying contact" means *any* oral or written communication to a "covered legislative branch official" or a "covered executive branch official" as those terms are defined. "Covered legislative branch officials" include members of the House of Representatives and Senate and their staffs, committee and joint committee staff, working groups or caucuses organized to provide legislative services or other assistance to members of Congress, and all legislative employees required to file financial disclosure reports under the Ethics in Government Act ("Act").[4] "Covered executive branch officials" include the president and vice president, levels I-V of the executive schedule,[5] or *any* officer or employee in a position of a confidential policy-determining, policy-making, or policy-advocating character as defined in the Act (i.e., a person in a position exempted from the competitive service).[6] *All* legislative and executive branch agencies are included. Pending further clarification, it is assumed that individuals in the senior executive service are included under this definition.

Any lobbyist making an oral lobbying contact is required, on the request of the person being contacted, to state whether the organization he or she represents is registered, to identify the client, and to disclose whether any foreign interest is being represented. Somewhat similarly, a lobbyist discussing a matter with a member of an executive branch agency may ask the person with whom he or she is talking whether that person is a "covered executive branch official" as that term is defined in the Act and thus whether the communication would constitute a "lobbying contact."

Lobbying contacts include communications with regard to the formulation, modification, or adoption of federal legislation, including legislative proposals and potential nominees for Senate confirmation for appointed executive branch positions. Now also included are the formulation, modification, or adoption of a federal rule, regulation, executive order, or other policy of the U.S. government as well as the administration or execution of a federal program or policy, which includes the negotiation, award, or administration of a federal contract, a grant, loan, permit, or license.

Thus, the sweep of the Lobbying Disclosure Act is much broader than its title might suggest.

Specific exemptions are provided; "lobbying contacts" do not include:

(1) testimony given before a congressional committee, subcommittee, or task force;
(2) communications compelled by subpoena, civil investigative demand, statute, or regulation;
(3) request for meetings or for the status of an action or similar administrative requests if no attempt is made to influence a "covered official;"

(4) written information provided in response to a specific request by a "covered official;"

(5) comments submitted in response to a notice in the *Federal Register, Commerce Business Daily*, or similar publication;

(6) written comments filed on the record in a public proceeding;

(7) filings or proceedings that the government is required to maintain or conduct on a confidential basis;

(8) communications made concerning a judicial proceeding, criminal or civil enforcement inquiries, investigations or proceedings; and

(9) written petitions for agency action on the public record.

The initial and any supplemental registration must include the following information:

(1) the name, address, business telephone number, and a general description of the organization's business or activities;

(2) the name, address, and principal place of business of any organization that contributes more than $10,000 towards the lobbying activities of the registrant in a given semi-annual period *and* that has a major role in supervising or controlling the lobbying activities;

(3) a statement of the general issue areas in which the organization expects to engage in lobbying activities and the specific issues that have (as of the date of the registration) already been addressed or are likely to be addressed in lobbying activities; and

(4) the name of each employee of the registrant who has acted or who the registrant expects to act as a lobbyist.

The semi-annual reports must include the following information:

(1) the name of the registrant and any changes or updates to the information provided in the initial registration;

(2) for each general issue area in which lobbying activities took place during the filing period:

    (a) a list of the specific issues upon which a lobbyist employed by the registrant engaged in lobbying activities, including, to the maximum extent practicable, a list of bill numbers and references to specific executive branch actions;

    (b) a statement of the Houses of Congress and the federal agencies contacted by lobbyists employed by the registrant;

    (c) a list of the employees of the registrant who acted as lobbyists during that period; and

    (d) a description of the interest, if any, of any foreign entity in the specific issues listed; and

(3) a good faith estimate of the total expenses that the registrant and its employees incurred in connection with lobbying activities during the semi-annual filing period. (Note: estimates of amounts in excess of $10,000 are to be rounded to the nearest $20,000.)

Exhibit 1[7] provides a summary of the process to be used to evaluate whether an individual or an organization falls within the ambit of the Lobbying Disclosure Act.

Under the Byrd Amendment,[8] nonprofit organizations applying for federal contracts, grants, and loans are precluded from using those monies to lobby. Even if the organization has not used such monies for the lobbying referred to, the Lobbying Disclosure Act amends the Byrd Amendment to require any applicant or recipient of a federal contract, grant, or loan to name any registrant under the Lobbying Disclosure Act who had made lobbying contacts with regard to such contract, grant, or loan on behalf of the applicant. Applicants for Federal contracts, grants, and loans are also still required to certify that they had not lobbied for such contract, grant, or loan with appropriated funds.

Lobbying by Public Charities Act

The Lobbying by Public Charities Act, passed as part of the Tax Reform Act of 1976, specifically addressed lobbying as it affects section 501(c)(3) nonprofit organizations, and established limits on the amount of expenditures permitted to those organizations for lobbying. The implementing regulations can be found in the Internal Revenue Code. Simply stated, the tax code provides that charities risk losing their tax-exempt status—and the ability to assure supporters that their contributions are tax deductible—if they engage in "substantial lobbying."

The "Old" Rules. Under the rules in force prior to the enactment of this statute in 1976, the organization's continued tax-exempt status was in danger if lobbying expenditures were "substantial" (generally, if they exceeded five percent of the organization's total budget). In 1976, Congress provided that certain publicly supported section 501(c)(3) organizations (as described below) could elect to have their lobbying activities treated under the old "substantial" lobbying test or under the "new" 1976 rules to determine whether direct lobbying was a principal purpose of the organization.

The "New" Rules. Under the 1976 rules, a qualifying public charity[9] could elect to be treated under the "new" 1976 rules by notifying the secretary of the treasury of that decision by filing IRS Form 5768. Once an organization has elected treatment under the "new" rules, the election becomes effective for all tax years ending after the date of election until revoked by the organization, but such revocation is effective only for tax years beginning after the date of the revocation. For those electing to be covered by the "new" 1976 rules, the permitted annual level of expenditures for lobbying is twenty percent of the first $500,000 of the organization's exempt purpose expenditures[10] for the year, fifteen percent of the second $500,000, ten percent of the third $500,000 and five percent of any additional expenditures. In no one year can the amount permitted for lobbying exceed $1 million. Within these limits, a separate limitation is placed on "grassroots" lobbying.[11] Grassroots lobbying entails attempting to influence any legislation through an attempt to affect the opinion of the general public or any segment thereof. The grassroots permitted amount is twenty-five percent of the permitted lobbying amount. An organization that exceeds the general limitation or the grassroots limitation in a taxable year is subject to an excise tax of twenty-five percent on its expenditures in excess of the limitation.

An organization may elect to be covered by either the "old" rules or the "new" rules. There is a significant advantage, however, of electing to come under the 1976 "new" rules because the amounts of lobbying acceptable are clearly defined—organizations that continue under the pre-1976 "substantial" lobbying test are subject to what the IRS deems to constitute "substantial" for any given organization, and such determination may vary from time to time.

Revenue Reconciliation Act of 1993

The Revenue Reconciliation Act of 1993, which was part of the 1993 Omnibus Budget Reconciliation Act, limits deductions that organizations and individuals can take from their dues to tax-exempt organizations for lobbying activities. It provides that any portion of the dues paid to a tax-exempt organization that is spent to "influence legislation" will not be allowable as a deduction to the organizations and individuals paying those dues. As written, the statute does not apply to gifts or other income the tax-exempt organization might receive—the statute only applies to "dues or other similar amounts paid" (e.g., a special assessment) by a taxpayer to a tax-exempt organization and the proportion of those dues that is spent on "lobbying" as defined in the statute.

"Influencing legislation" is defined very broadly to include communications with any member or employee of a legislative body or with any government official or employee who may participate in the formulation of legislation if the purpose of those communications is to influence legislation. Expenses incurred for research and for the preparation, planning, and coordination of any activities associated with influencing such legislation are considered to be part of the effort to influence legislation and are also not deductible.

As a result, it is critical for each tax-exempt organization that participates in lobbying activities to determine what amount of its expenditures and the time and labor of its staff are spent on lobbying-related activities. Generally, an activity whose purpose is to "attempt to influence legislation" will constitute lobbying. To be considered lobbying, the communication must refer to specific legislation and must reflect the individual's or the organization's view on such legislation. Thus, meeting with a member of Congress to discuss the general state of an industry or to encourage support of a charitable cause would not constitute lobbying as long as those discussions are not related to specific pending legislation. Other exemptions are provided for:

(1) making available the results of a nonpartisan analysis or research on an issue;
(2) responding to the request of a governmental body for information;
(3) testifying before a congressional committee or in an agency administrative proceeding;
(4) communications with an organization's members (unless the communication urges members to contact their elected representatives);
(5) lobbying any local council or similar governing body; and
(6) any communication compelled by subpoena or by federal or state law.

Congress enacted a separate limitation on "grassroots lobbying," which are activities intended by an individual or organization to influence the general public, or segments thereof, with respect to legislative matters, elections, or referendums. These expenditures are nondeductible. There is no limit on an organization's communications to its members about pending legislation or other subjects; only those communications to the general public or a targeted segment thereof are limited. The proportion of membership dues of a tax-exempt organization that is attributable to grassroots lobbying is not allowed as a deduction to a tax-exempt organization's members.

In addition, no deduction is allowed for costs incurred in connection with any direct communication with a "covered executive branch official" that is intended to influence the official actions or positions of such governmental official, whether or not it pertains to "influencing legislations." "Covered executive branch officials" include the president and the vice president, cabinet members and their immediate deputies, the two most senior officers of each agency within the executive office of the president and any employees of the executive office of the president. Contrary to the comparable costs associated with influencing legislation, amounts paid for research and analysis associated with preparing positions used in those direct communications with a covered executive branch official *are* allowed as deductible expenses. For those activities, only the cost directly attributable to the direct communication, whether in person, by telephone, or otherwise, with a covered executive branch official is not deductible, but note that those communications need not be associated with legislation to constitute lobbying of those members of the executive branch.

Reporting Requirements

Tax-exempt organizations are required to include in their annual federal tax return (IRS Form 990) a report of the total expenditures for lobbying activities and the total amount of dues paid to the organization. Each tax-exempt organization must also, at the time of assessment or payment of dues, provide the payer with "a reasonable estimate" of the portion of the dues that is allocable to lobbying expenditures, because that portion is not tax deductible.

The "Proxy Tax"

If a tax-exempt organization fails to, or chooses not to, provide the information described above to its dues-paying members, it must pay a tax equal to the highest rate of tax imposed on corporations (currently thirty-five percent of its taxable income) for that tax year. This is frequently referred to as the "proxy" tax because the tax-exempt organization is paying the tax that otherwise would be paid by the organization's dues-paying members on the portion of the dues that are not deductible. Further, if a year's actual lobbying and political expenditures exceed the allocable amount that had been estimated, the organization is required to pay the "proxy" tax on the amount by which its actual expenditures exceeded the estimated amount.

Many organizations choose to pay the proxy tax to avoid the need to do the complex accounting described above and so that its members' dues to the tax-exempt organization are fully deductible by its members. Other organizations may choose to set up a separate subsidiary, which would be separately funded, to conduct all of the organization's lobbying activities, as a way to simplify the accounting required and to be able to satisfy reporting requirements more easily.

Conclusion

The three statutes described above, and associated IRS regulations, provide the framework in which tax-exempt organizations, including charities, are allowed to participate in lobbying activities. Although the statutes vary in reach, and the terms used are not necessarily consistent, tax-exempt organizations must comply with all three statutes.

Notes

1. U.S. Const. amend. I.

2. Pub. L. No. 104-65, 109 Stat. 692 (codified as amended in scattered sections of 2 U.S.C. and 5 U.S.C.).

3. At the time of preparation of this guidebook, definitive guidance has not been developed by the Clerk of the House and Secretary of the Senate. A number of ambiguities and inconsistencies will need to be resolved, and the U.S. Comptroller General is required by statute to recommend resolution by March 31, 1997.

4. 5 U.S.C. § 7511(b)(2) (1994).

5. Levels I–V of the executive schedule are codified in 5 U.S.C. §§ 5312-16 (1994), in a listing of executive schedule level by agency. It includes cabinet officers, assistant secretaries, and other senior members of the executive branch. Individuals filling positions in the executive schedule are appointed by the president and required to be confirmed by the Senate.

6. A general guide to confidential, policy-determining, policymaking, or policy-advocating positions is published at four-year intervals by the House Committee on Government Reform and Oversight and Senate Committee on Government Affairs, *Policy and Supporting Positions.* Informal guidance from the Office of Personnel Management states that all "Schedule C" positions (i.e., political appointees) are within the category of "covered executive branch officials." OPM has not made a final determination as to which additional positions fall within this category.

7. In addition, under the new legislation, a 501(c)(4) organization that engages in lobbying is not eligible to receive federal funds constituting an award, contract, grant, loan, or support in any other form.

8. 31 U.S.C. § 1352 (1994).

9. A "qualifying public charity" includes educational institutions, hospitals and medical research organizations, organizations supporting government schools, organizations publicly supported by admissions or sales, and organizations publicly supported by charitable contributions (the "typical" 501(c)(3) organization, for example)—but not churches, integrated auxiliaries of a church or association of churches, or private foundations.

10. "Exempt purpose expenditures" refers to a tax-exempt organization's activities that "contribute importantly" to the accomplishment of the tax-exempt purpose(s) the organization was created to accomplish.

11. *See* I.R.C. § 4911.02 (1994).

Bibliography

Boyce, Katherine R. and Thomas Hale Boggs, Jr. *Corporate Political Activity.* New York: Matthew Bender & Co., 1984.

Fitzpatrick, James F. and Martha Cochran. "The Federal Lobbying Disclosure Act of 1995." Presentation before the American Society of Corporate Secretaries, New York Chapter, New York, April 24, 1996.

House Conference Report. 103d Cong. (1993).

Overton, George, editor. *Guidebook for Directors of Nonprofit Corporations*. Chicago: American Bar Association, 1993.

Speigman, Rick. "Organizations Exempt under 501(c)(4) that Lobby Are Restricted from Receiving Federal Funds." *KPMG Management Issues for Not-for-Profits* (February 1996): 1.

Exhibit 1
Lobbying Disclosure Act of 1995

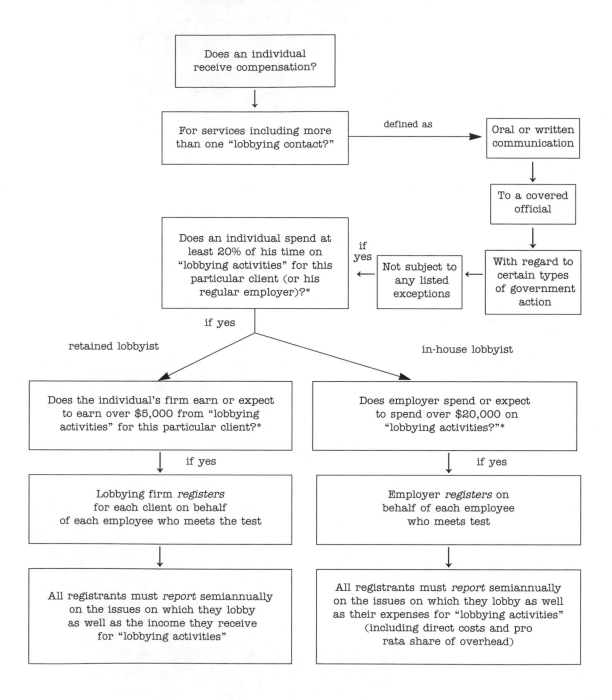

---

*In the applicable 6-month reporting period.
Exhibit 1 is reprinted with the permission of Arnold & Porter, Washington, D.C.

Fund Raising: The Roles of the Board and the Staff

Fisher Howe

This chapter addresses the fund-raising activity of nonprofit organizations in terms of where responsibility lies, what a board member's role is, how to deal with capital campaigns, and the board's general oversight responsibility in relationship to staff. Two often-asked questions are addressed.

In almost all that board members of nonprofit organizations do, they are *deliberating* and *deciding*; in fund-raising they *participate*. Note this distinction well because fund-raising calls upon you as a board member to play a more active part than in most other board responsibilities.

To understand the board member's role in fund-raising, one needs to be clear first about where the *responsibility* lies, and then about what a board member can *do*. In addition, a board member should be alert to the special problems associated with raising *capital* funds, and be mindful of *oversight responsibilities* that go with fund-raising.

Who Is Responsible

Responsibility for attracting resources lies with the board. In fund-raising as with all other aspects of the organization the board selects and supports the executive director, puts the budget in place to do the job and oversees and evaluates performance. Although responsibility for management is delegated, a governing board in the final analysis is answerable for the success or failure of the whole organization. In fund-raising particularly the board cannot *pass on to anyone else the responsibility for attracting the resources to sustain the programs*—not to the staff, not to a committee, not to an outside consultant or agent.

It is true that some health care and educational institutions create foundations or separate organizations to raise contributed funds, usually in order to separate contributed money from government appropriations or from other non-donated sources that may be earned from a gift shop or the income from an endowment. In the end, however, the board of the institution stands responsible for the success or failure of the organization's fund-raising effort.

This having been said, however, it is equally important to recognize that the board must have strong staff support in order to fulfill its responsibilities. Rarely, if ever, can a board by itself raise all the money required to support the programs.

Recognize and accept therefore that fund-raising must be a *partnership* of board and staff. In no other way can it work. Neither the board nor the staff can succeed without the other. Accordingly, the key is to put attention on the role of each, defining what the staff and what the board should do in the fund-raising effort.

The staff must always keep the files, records, and mailing lists. The staff does the research so essential to successful fund-raising and prepares correspondence, acknowledgments of donations, and proposals that seek the support of foundations, corporations, or government agencies. Fund-raising, as any program, needs to be planned. Preparing thorough plans for raising money is also clearly part of the staff role.

Above all, the staff, whether the executive director, a development officer, or volunteers acting as staff, must *supply the initiative*, constantly generating ideas that will move the fund-raising forward and motivate board members' action. Indeed, a significant part of the staff initiative function is the motivating of board members, especially those who have demonstrated a reluctance about fund-raising. Although a strong board president or chair will get members to do their fund-raising job, much of the burden falls on the executive or development officer; he or she must take a major part in stimulating directors' participation. Such an officer can engage directors in simple projects, one project at a time, small tasks before large ones, and can make each task specific and limited. If directors are asked *individually* to carry out a particular job, rather than appealed to generally in a board meeting, they will respond. Directors are no different from other people: they need to be individually stimulated, instructed, encouraged, and thanked profusely. And they want to be given the credit.

This motivating task is not easy for the executive and staff, but successful fund-raising depends upon its being fulfilled.

What a Board Member Can Do in Fund-raising

It is commonplace for board members to be reluctant, sometimes even resistant, to participate in fund-raising. Many people associate fund-raising with preying on friends, with begging; others fear being turned down. Some will say their contribution to the organization is in the program, or administration, not in fund-raising. Others will claim they were not told that fund-raising was part of being a board member. Even if board members accept, in principle, their responsibility to participate, when it comes to action they frequently fall short in fulfilling commitments, and procrastination is always present.

Directors need to understand some fundamentals. To be successful in asking for contributions one needs first to know *why people give*.

(1) People give money—board members themselves give money—because they *want to do so*. In raising money, directors do not need to "twist arms," or beg.
(2) People want to give money to worthy and successful endeavors that are *making a difference*. Directors must believe their organizations do make that difference.
(3) People give money to people. The *personal relationship* that underlies most contributions, especially in major gifts, must remain in sight.

Without acceptance of these truths, money will not be raised.

In order to overcome reluctance, one can show a director the many activities that assist the fund-raising effort but that don't actually involve asking for money. Many directors, even those who most want to help, do not realize these opportunities exist. A director can materially assist the fund-raising effort *without actually asking for a donation* in the following ways.

(1) **Contribution.** Every director, without exception, should make an annual, personal contribution to the organization. Regardless of the donations a director

may have helped to secure from other sources, this personal contribution is an essential act of commitment, no matter how small. No organization can expect others to invest in it if its leaders do not do so first. That investment starts with annual giving by board members. Many funding sources demand assurance that this stricture is fulfilled.

(2) **Strategic planning.** Institutional planning is important for the governance and the management of an organization; it is critical to successful fund-raising. A director must participate because strategic planning determines the funding needs, and is the basis for setting out the case why people should contribute.

(3) **Development plans.** Fund-raising itself, as any program, needs to be planned. Preparing thorough program plans for raising money is clearly a staff role but board members, as part of their oversight responsibility, should review and approve such plans.

(4) **Mailing list.** The mailing list is at the core of the whole fund-raising program. The names directors add to that list are more valuable than those drawn from any other source.

(5) **Prospect identification and evaluation.** Directors are the peers of important prospective donors—individuals, officials of companies, and foundations. They know them, and their help in evaluation is invaluable.

(6) **Cultivation of prospects.** A director who becomes identified with the organization can speak out in the community and can help interest prospective donors.

(7) **Introductions.** The most difficult part of a solicitation may be gaining the first introduction, especially to corporations and foundations. Directors, because of their familiarity with corporations and their standing in the community, can make the all-important introductions.

(8) **Annual appeal letters.** When directors append personal notes to appeal letters, the success rate will increase significantly. Appeals preceded or followed by phonathons give further opportunity for valuable director participation.

(9) **Supporting letters.** Organizations seeking support from a government agency, foundation, or company usually must submit a formal proposal. A separate supporting letter from a director does much to assure a favorable reading.

(10) **Special events.** Special benefit events are not only sources of money, they also help heighten the exposure of the organization; they are a form of public relations, of cultivation. Certainly board members will attend these events, but in addition it is particularly appropriate for board volunteers to manage them. This ensures that the event will not divert staff from their program responsibilities—a common problem.

(11) **Acknowledgments.** Letters of thanks for a donation are the first step toward obtaining repeat contributions. When a director adds an acknowledging thank you, it is particularly effective.

(12) **Accompanying on a solicitation.** When a director accompanies the executive, a staff member, or another director in making a solicitation, it adds great weight. Moreover, it is the best way for a director to become familiar with the process of asking for funds.

Directors can evaluate their performance, collective or individual, in carrying out these fund-raising actions by using the checklist set out in Exhibit 1. Each director can score his or her own performance, or that of the board as a whole, on the different participating actions in order to reveal areas where improvement can be sought.

Raising Capital Funds

A whole new dimension of board participation comes into play when an organization turns to raising *capital* funds for buildings or endowment, or when it seeks capital donations through *planned giving*.

Planned giving is a structured form of contributing assets. The recipient institution receives the donation only after an intervening period, often many years, during which time the donor and a beneficiary may retain the use of the property or the lifetime right to receive its income. Such gifts, closely associated with estate planning, can be in the form of bequests, insurance, real property, or securities.

Capital fund-raising is not to be undertaken lightly. Donations in capital drives for buildings or endowment are of a different magnitude from regular contributions for operating funds. A lot of care must go into preparing to raise capital funds and a major commitment from directors is requisite to success.

In particular, directors must be confident the organization is ready for a capital drive. Has strategic planning adequately identified realistic funding needs? Is the support constituency—the body of regular givers—strong? That is where the major donors to a capital campaign will be found. Is the leadership really prepared to get involved in the drive? Often an organization finds it prudent to employ an outside consultant to advise on this critical *readiness* factor through a development audit.

Additionally, to be on a sound footing before embarking on a capital drive, an organization must also call on professional assistance to evaluate the *potential*—whether the money and interest in the organization is out there—through a feasibility survey of the constituency.

Campaigns to raise capital funds, including planned giving programs, demand the full commitment and participation of the board. Capital donations, because they are large, involve board members directly in the identification, evaluation, cultivation, and solicitation of donors.

Oversight Responsibilities

The foregoing discussion elaborates what a director can and should do to *participate* in the development effort. But it is important also to note the special demands put upon the board in watching over the fund-raising effort. Two areas in particular warrant directors' attention: *ethics* and *costs*.

Through innocence or unrestrained aggressiveness, organizations can easily overstep the bounds of acceptable practice in seeking funding support. One clear ethical misstep to guard against is any fund-raising carried out on a commission basis. Unlike the practice of law, rewarding a fund-raiser with a percentage of the money received, while not illegal, is considered professionally unethical—a fact that may not be understood by board members unfamiliar with unscrupulous fund-raising agents.

It is also considered unethical to pay finders' fees to those who are in a position to help people with their estate planning for steering bequests or major gifts to an organization the donor may not have shown any interest in supporting. The donor's wishes to make the contribution to a specific organization should be the dominant motivation.

The expense of a fund-raising program should not be excessive in relation to the amount raised. Determining reasonable fund-raising costs, however, is by no means simple. Costs, figured in terms of the dollars spent to achieve dollars received, will vary widely with the size of the organization and the type of fund-raising. For example, the costs of soliciting corporations, foundations, and individuals who are part of the organization's own constituency are unlikely to be worrisome. Large national, high-profile organizations, however, depend heavily on mass mail techniques, which can be very expensive.

Direct mail should be used cautiously. It is important to distinguish between appeals to the organization's own mailing list—constituency mailing—and mass mailings to lists purchased, leased, or exchanged, where the purpose is to acquire contributors who will become regular donors and thus become part of the constituency. While the costs of constituency mailings tend to be modest, mass mail is expensive, with the return generally not covering costs in the first year or two.

Directors may be exposed to other problems in the oversight of a fund-raising program, such as public unhappiness with overly repetitive mail appeals, aggressive phone solicitations, and indiscriminate sales and exchanges of mailing lists. Several leading national philanthropic associations developed a donor "Bill of Rights" to serve as a reasonable guide (see Exhibit 2).

Fund raising will be one of the board's major preoccupations. Directors will need to understand its ramifications and participate wholeheartedly in order to do their jobs well.

Frequently-Asked Questions

Is it reasonable to set a level of financial contribution for all board members?

Clearly every board member should, as an act of commitment, make an annual personal contribution; everyone is capable of giving something, no matter how small. Many organizations, however, call upon every board member to give, or get others to give, a *prescribed amount*. This is sometimes described as a "give, get, or get off" policy.

The subject is controversial; strong views are held both for and against.

The principal argument for setting a contribution level is that board members will be stimulated into giving at a higher level than they otherwise would and a larger total board contribution will be realized.

There are several arguments against setting a contribution level. First, by setting a figure, the nonprofit presents a ceiling. Donors are inclined to give the suggested amount. Even if donors are asked to give *at least* the set figure, larger gifts may still be missed.

Second, a specific contribution level assumes a general equality in board members' capability to give and ability to attract contributions from others. Not only is there inevitably a wide disparity among members in both capability and ability, but the policy also runs at cross purposes to the need to achieve diversity in gender, age, race, occupation, skills on the board and among the nonprofit's constituency.

Third, the policy is difficult to enforce. The inevitable exceptions and compromises can be troublesome and bring into question the validity of the policy itself and the board's consistency.

And finally, the basic spirit of the board is changed when a monetary value is put on membership.

Overall, setting a contribution level would seem to work against other objectives of the nonprofit. Boards will want to recruit some members who can make major financial contributions and attract others to contribute in a similar manner. Members should not all be expected to fall into this category.

What can board members, or trustees, do when the organization is having trouble raising funds?

The first step is to seek to understand the underlying situation.

(1) Fees, contracts, tuitions, tickets, and reimbursements are earned *revenues*; fund-raising is limited to *contributions*—donations and grants. Increasing revenues may be important but should not be confused with fund-raising.

(2) Fund-raising is not only a *partnership*, it is also a *process*. It is not a series of single ideas for raising money. Nor is it mounting an expensive public relations campaign, or putting on a fancy fund-raising benefit. Rather it is *continuous work by staff and board members* taking action in accordance with an agreed-upon place with target goals.

(3) Fund-raising takes time. It is illusory to think an organization can suddenly raise $15,000, $50,000, or $100,000 to meet a shortfall or cash flow crunch. Whether seeking contributions from individuals, foundations, corporations, or government agencies, *it can take months, if not years, before a significant amount of money is raised.*

Then these actions may be taken.

(1) **Strategic plans.** The board, with staff support, undertakes comprehensive institutional planning, setting out (a) the vision of what the organization wants to be in the coming years; (b) the *programs* that will fulfill that vision; (c) the *priorities* among the programs; and (d) the *funding* needs for those programs. What emerges is a comprehensive understanding of the purposes for which one will be asking support.

(2) **The case.** The staff, in cooperation with the board, prepares the case, a persuasive statement of why people should support the organization. Unlike the mission, but based on it, the case looks at the organization through the eyes of the donor; it is a prospectus for investment.

Often the case—the core of a strong fund-raising program—is best expressed in a brief one and a half page memorandum. It is a *concept* to be used throughout the fund-raising effort, but is particularly designed to attract the initial attention and interest of prospects.

The most persuasive case statements *start* with an identification of the need in the community or the nation—what is missing, WHY the organization exists. Only after that does it describe WHAT the organization does, HOW it does it, and WHO the organization is. People give money to make a difference, to make a change for the good, so the organization should first *point out the problem that needs remedy before explaining what the organization does to correct the problem.* If the community need is to help the homeless, one might point out the number of homeless and how desperate they are. The community also needs to know what will happen if nothing is done for the homeless, and then what it is the organization does.

Most organizations have mission statements; few have an adequate statement of the case (see Exhibits 3 and 4).

(3) **Support constituency.** Staff and board together must make plans to solicit prospects in each category—government agencies, companies, foundations, other nonprofit organizations, and individuals—and establish priorities among them so that the effort is focused where the prospects are best.

(4) **Annual giving.** Those who make regular annual contributions, including "members," are the underlying strength of most nonprofit organizations. Pay a lot of attention to them. The *mailing list*—constantly increased and maintained—is the backbone of successful annual giving.

(5) **Special events.** Beware of diverting attention to, or relying on, benefits and fund-raising events. Ideas for such events are a dime a dozen but the competition is staggering. Mounting events is labor intensive—with the work too often put upon a busy staff. The first step for a gala or auction is to find a volunteer who can and will run it. If no one is willing to organize the event, the organization should seek other means of raising funds.

If the organization takes these five steps—strategic plans, the case, support constituency, annual giving and, guardedly, special events—it is on its way to successful fundraising.

Exhibit 1
Checklist
Board Participation in Fund-Raising

Score each item for yourself and for the board as a whole.
(1 = lowest; 5 = highest)

		self	*board*
1.	Board members make personal contributions	____	____
2.	Participation in strategic planning	____	____
3.	Understand and endorse development plans	____	____
4.	Add names to the mailing list	____	____
5.	Help identify and evaluate prospects —individuals, foundations, corporations, religious institutions, service clubs	____	____
6.	Share in cultivation of key prospects	____	____
7.	Make introductions to prospects	____	____
8.	Write notes on annual appeal letters	____	____
9.	Participate in phonathons	____	____
10.	Write supporting letters	____	____
11.	Help manage fund-raising events	____	____
12.	Write thank-you letters	____	____
13.	Accompany others on a solicitation	____	____
14.	ASK for a contribution	____	____

* * *

ALSO

15.	Actually DO what undertake to do	____	____
16.	Do not procrastinate	____	____

Exhibit 2
A Donor Bill of Rights*

Philanthropy is based on voluntary action for the common good. It is a tradition of giving and sharing that is primary to the quality of life. To assure that philanthropy merits the respect and trust of the general public, and that donors and prospective donors can have full confidence in the not-for-profit organizations and causes they are asked to support, we declare that all donors have these rights.

I.

To be informed of the organization's mission, of the way the organization intends to use donated resources, and of its capacity to use donations effectively for their intended purposes.

II.

To be informed of the identify of those serving on the organization's governing board, and to expect the board to exercise prudent judgment in its stewardship responsibilities.

III.

To have access to the organization's most recent financial statements.

IV.

To be assured their gifts will be used for the purposes for which they were given.

V.

To receive appropriate acknowledgment and recognition.

VI.

To be assured that information about their donations is handled with respect and with confidentiality to the extent provided by law.

---

* Developed by: American Association of Fundraising Counsel (AAFRC); Association for Healthcare Philanthropy (AHP); Council for Advancement and Support of Education (CASE); and National Society of Fundraising Executives (NSFRE). Endorsed by: Independent Sector; National Catholic Development Conference (NCDC); National Committee on Planned Giving (NCPG); National Council for Resource Development (NCRD); and United Way of America.

VII.

To expect that all relationships with individuals representing organizations of interest to the donor will be professional in nature.

VIII.

To be informed whether those seeking donations are volunteers, employees of the organization or hired solicitors.

IX.

To have the opportunity for their names to be deleted from mailing lists that an organization may intend to share.

X.

To feel free to ask questions when making a donation and to receive prompt, truthful and forthright answers.

Exhibit 3
Washington Area Council on Alcoholism and Drug Abuse
Case Memorandum

Every day, young Washingtonians take drugs for the first time ever. Drug peddlers, in their drive to claim turf, terrorize our streets and kill not only each other but also innocent passersby. The lives of tens of thousands of Washingtonians are spinning out of control as chemicals compromise their ability to make judgments; the destructive force of their actions harms our children and tears at the fabric of our family lives. The city's population includes 80,000 problem drinkers, 16,000 to 20,000 heroin addicts, and 60,000 users of cocaine, PCP, and marijuana. With an estimated population of 625,000 persons, the portion of the populace suffering from substance-related problems has wreaked havoc on the whole city.

All indicators suggest this critical problem is not abating.

Addiction poses an array of complex social, psychological, and physical problems, but these problems are not insoluble. Practitioners and researchers are gathering a wealth of experience and information about prevention and treatment strategies which work. Positive outcomes in substance abuse-related problems are possible, even probable, when trained professionals address them with clinical expertise and rigorous interventions.

WACADA has assembled a multidisciplinary team of health educators, prevention specialists, and addictions counselors. These professionals educate the community, stop high risk youth from using drugs before they get started, and treat indigent addicts from throughout the area. WACADA is spearheading its commitment to solid prevention and treatment interventions with the on-going exploration of state-of-the-art techniques.

The city does not confront the drug epidemic without any defenses; the seeds to solving this crisis are being sown quietly every day.

WACADA's programs include:

- *Crack Cocaine Education, Counseling, and Monitoring*—heightening community awareness and reducing the incidence of crack cocaine use in the District.
- *Outpatient Aftercare Program*—helping recovering addicts to adjust to abstinent living.
- *DWI Alcohol Education Program*—evaluating, assessing, educating, and counseling for persons who are convicted of driving while intoxicated.
- *Center For Addiction Training And Education*—responding to the need for professional education and training programs for alcohol and drug abuse service providers.

- *Alcohol/Drug Hotline*—providing alcohol and drug intervention and referral through a 24-hour-a-day, seven-days-a-week telephone service.
- *Substance Abuse Prevention in High-Risk Youth*—coordinating comprehensive substance abuse prevention, intervention, and rehabilitation for high risk youth.
- *Community Parent Organizing*—organizing concerned parents and assisting them to develop and implement strategies to combat substance abuse.

* * *

The Washington Area Council on Alcoholism and Drug Abuse (WACADA) is a non-profit organization which has served the Washington, D.C. metropolitan area with alcohol and drug abuse education, prevention, and treatment since 1949. WACADA is the area's oldest and most respected community-based organization addressing substance abuse-related issues. Because WACADA seeks no profit and is committed to only the community's betterment, making treatment resources available to the indigent of the community uniquely fulfills WACADA's forty year mission.

Exhibit 4
Institute for Circadian Physiology
Attacking the Problem of Human Error
Case Memorandum

The modern world of technology and automation, for all its benefits and rewards, holds major risks we have not clearly recognized or come to grips with. The human race has been catapulted into a 24-hour society where we must rely, as never before, on key people in strategic places to stay awake and alert around-the-clock. They watch over manufacturing plants and oil refineries; they take care of the critically ill; they defend the nation.

But the human body was not designed to be alert and productive at night, nor to cope with irregular schedules of work and rest. Biological (circadian) clocks in the human brain are programmed to a regular schedule of night-time sleep and daytime activity. Disrupting that pattern leads to fatigue, reduced productivity, human error, accidents, ill-health and impaired quality of life.

We would not consider operating a machine beyond its specifications, yet we do it to the bodies of men and women who work at critical jobs. We suffer the consequences: Chernobyl, Three Mile Island, Bhopal, Exxon Valdez, the Korean airplane shot down. All occurred between midnight and 5 a.m. In each, human error played a key role.

Scientific research must meet that challenge, must seek solutions to the problem of human error.

Recent research advances now enable us to understand how alertness, vigilance and performance are regulated by the human biological clock. For the first time we can address systematically the human limitations in round-the-clock life-styles. It is now possible to reset the biological clock for time-zone changes and work shifts so that natural sleep and optimal alertness can be obtained at any time of day or night. Practical methods are being developed to keep people alert day or night in the airplane cockpit, the truck driver's seat, the control room of a nuclear plant, the nurse's station.

At the Institute for Circadian Physiology multidisciplinary teams conduct basic research on how the biological clock works and applied research on how to optimize human safety, performance and health twenty-four hours a day. The Institute's HUMAN ALERTNESS RESEARCH CENTER (HARC) is designed to simulate for the first time round-the-clock workplaces—power plants, truck cabs, and airplane cockpits. Residential and workplace simulators control environmental conditions to which operators are exposed. Innovative techniques are developed for enhancing alertness and performance 24 hours-a-day.

Reliable "human" systems are finding their way into workplaces; human error is being lessened, lives are being saved.

The Institute's present and projected programs include:

- *Utility Industry Human Alertness Program*—reducing human error and improving safety in nuclear power plants and similar facilities.
- *Driver Alertness Program*—preventing highway accidents due to falling asleep behind the wheel.
- *Shiftworker Health and Performance Program*—improving the safety, productivity and health of the 20 million people who work shifts around-the-clock.
- *Sleep Disorders Program*—developing new techniques to help obtain good quality sleep.
- *Biological Time Regulation Program*—learning how to reset the body clock in the most effective and safe way.
- *Health Care Provider Alertness Program*—devising ways to reduce fatigue and improve alertness in doctors, nurses and other hospital staff.
- *Aircrew Alertness Program*—reducing human errors caused by fatigue in pilots and in air-traffic controllers.
- *Spaceflight Adaptation Program*—helping space travelers adapt to long-term missions.

* * *

The Institute is an independent nonprofit (501(c)3) research center which was spun-off in 1988 from a 15-year research program at Harvard Medical School. The Director of the Institute, Dr. Scott Campbell, a pioneer in both basic research on biological clocks and in the industrial applications of circadian physiology, heads an international team of distinguished investigators. The Institute includes basic research laboratories and the Human Alertness Research Center. In its ten years of operation the Institute has built a broad base of support from Federal research grants and contracts (NASA, NRC, NIH, USAF and Army), and from contributions from corporate sponsors including Liberty Mutual, Exxon, Mobil, Amoco, Alcan, Monsanto, Boston Edison and Foxboro.

The Organization's Risks

George W. Overton

This chapter examines the risk exposures of the nonprofit and how the officers and directors should respond to them.

Introduction

In any examination of the nonprofit organization's risks, certain assumptions must be made about the structure of the organization itself. In this chapter, we are writing about a wide variety of nonprofit entities: charities, trade associations, health care providers, and condominium associations, to mention a few. We are, however, making certain assumptions common to all of them; we write for organizations with the following characteristics.

(1) An active board of directors monitors and guides the activities, and receives reports and information from the management of the organization. To emphasize this assumption, we draw the model of a board that meets regularly, and reviews and discusses various reports.

(2) A staff, including an executive director or secretary (or other designated officer performing such functions) and a risk manager, manages day-to-day activities.

(3) A legal counsel, paid or unpaid, advises both board and staff on the legal requirements for the organization and has some continuing responsibility for this function—*i.e.*, the legal counsel does not simply await a request for specific services, but is expected to act on her or his own initiative.

As to the board, our assumption excludes entities which are mere shells—e.g., real estate title-holding entities whose directors seldom have occasion to meet, and which simply respond to the needs of some parent entity.

As to management staff, our assumptions will apply both to an organization with only one individual serving as staff and to a large entity with a central bureaucracy of dozens of men and women. For the sake of clarity, however, we shall write as though the organization has the following paid executives:

(1) an executive director, having overall management responsibility;

(2) a secretary, or other designated officer, responsible for defining the issues to be faced, recording decisions thereon, and communicating the same to all relevant parties; and

(3) a risk manager, who must analyze and advise on the issues described hereinafter, who examines and maintains all insurance records, indemnity contracts, and the like. This function may be (in our assumptions) performed by legal counsel.

As to legal counsel, we assume that a lawyer performs the functions described below. The lawyer may be a volunteer on the board, a volunteer supplied by a nonprofit legal service corporation which serves charitable entities, a paid staff counsel, or regular outside counsel (paid or unpaid).

We write as though this counsel regularly reviews the legal exposures and needs of the organization. Our assumption is that this is done on some schedule of assumed need—not just in response to a crisis.

We will make these assumptions for all the entities described above, whether large or small. We may appear to describe a number of separate people, but many a small organization will have staff consisting basically of only *one* person, or one person possibly assisted by a part-time secretary borrowed from some other body. We write for them just as much as for an institution with a staff of dozens.

In the case of an entity having only one executive, we assume that one person consciously divides his or her time into segments as though each segment were the activity of a specified individual. Thus, if the executive director and sole employee is named Brown: for part of each day, Brown becomes "Smith," the secretary; and, for part of each day, he or she becomes "Jones," the risk manager. Each of these separate personalities will be assumed on some minimum schedule so the tasks that we will outline will be performed on a regular continuous program, and so the executive does not simply lurch from one crisis to another.

All suggested activities can be performed by one person and in many organizations, that will be exactly the size of the organization and how it handles its affairs. The functions to be performed, however, are not different because the organization has only one staff member, in contrast to what would be required by an organization that might have an entire department for each of the functions involved. Those organizations large enough to have separate officers and separate departments will doubtless operate with somewhat greater efficiency, as full-time assignments will always be somewhat more efficient than a division of each day of a single officer trying to cover several fronts at once. This is all the more reason for the formal organization of an executive's time if he or she must cover a wide variety of functions.

The executive staff should be aware of the risk exposures of the organization; should study how to avoid or reduce any losses arising from risk; and see that there are in place appropriate policies and procedures to meet these problems, making recommendations to the board where appropriate.

All organizations are exposed to risks such as risks of lost assets, risks of injured employees or members of the public, risks of interruption of programs, and risks of litigation of all kinds.

The leadership of a nonprofit organization must be conscious of risk exposure, and guide management and the board toward the solution thereof. The problem we are now addressing involves insurance. We emphasize that insurance is a *solution* to many problems of risk and, for many organizations, for *all* such problems. The task of management and the board, however, is risk; until *risk* is identified and evaluated, any inquiry into insurance is premature.

We will readily admit that in this chapter we are suggesting procedures and concerns that are not always observed, even in fairly large nonprofit entities. We do so for the reasons that nonprofit organizations face a new world of duties. Thus, there is a need to strengthen all of the duties. We feel these steps are practical, even if relatively new to many of our readers.

We repeat our basic assertion: risks surround every nonprofit activity, large or small, and the leadership should be aware of that exposure and what methods are available to deal with it.

Prudent directors and officers will also be aware of the risks of litigation against themselves, and will seek insurance covering directors' and officers' (D&O) liability (see p. 131). This chapter, however, deals only with the organization's exposure. This exposure is partially one of internal losses, such as the destruction of a physical asset by fire, and partially an external one, such as the risk of litigation or administrative proceedings against the entity. Internal and external risks are discussed together because the available solutions for avoidance, mitigation, or elimination of loss are much the same.

The Analysis of Risks

The organization's leadership should periodically catalog and evaluate the risks to which the organization is normally exposed. Every nonprofit entity should periodically examine what kinds of events could impose a loss or impairment of the organization's mission. The list might start with the following:

(1) destruction of property by fire or accident;
(2) serious illness of the executive director;
(3) legal action by a governmental agency;
(4) embezzlement of funds;
(5) litigation brought by employees or former employees;
(6) a lawsuit arising from an automobile accident; and
(7) a refusal of a funding source to continue support for the organization.

A director or officer will note that some of the risks in the foregoing sample list can be transferred to an insurance company by a conventional form of insurance. Some of the above can be transferred by reorganization (leasing the premises instead of owning them, for example) and some cannot be transferred because they are risks inherent in the mission of the organization. The entity, in short, may not be able to eliminate all its risks, but it can minimize them by advance planning. Some realistic program of minimization is something which leadership, as a matter of good practice, should schedule and assign.

Analyzing risk potential is largely a management function. Few of the steps included here will be undertaken by the board directly, but all are matters of which the board should be informed as part of its governance responsibility.

We suggest that the more significant risk exposures be periodically listed and then analyzed from three standpoints:

(1) probability of occurrence;
(2) materiality of damage resulting from occurrence; and
(3) involvement of parties outside the organization in the event of an occurrence.

The foregoing considerations will determine what response should be made to these exposures.

Dealing with These Risk Exposures

Once the leadership has identified and evaluated its risk exposures, it should then choose one of four methods to deal with them. Insurance is perhaps the most obvious of these methods.

Additional common methods include reduction of risks by reorganization, indemnification, and bearing a risk inherent in the mission.

Reduction of Risks by Reorganization. The board and staff should periodically examine whether a risk may be avoided by simple reorganization of a function. This may mean leasing the premises rather than owning them—transferring the basic risk of fire loss to the owner, although continuing to bear the risk of interruption of function in the event of fire. In other cases, it may be possible to subcontract part of an organization's functions to other operators or suppliers, and thus transferring to such contractors the various employment and accident risks involved. This may or may not be appropriate, but should be evaluated in the decision concerning whether a given function should be performed directly or performed in part by third parties under contract.

Indemnification. The board and staff should examine whether, by contractual arrangements, possible losses can be indemnified by outside parties. Certain high risk activities may be transferable to vendors by contracts calling for indemnification and requiring the vendor to provide insurance to fund that commitment. For example, exposures connected with a large meeting or convention may be assumed by the hotel or convention center site and insurance carried by the entity providing the premises.

Insurance. Of course, risks can be assumed by an insurance company under various types of policies. We will expand upon these alternatives later in this chapter, but we note that it is only one of the four alternatives.

Bearing a Risk Inherent in the Mission of the Organization. Often a portion of the risk exposure cannot be reduced by reorganization, transferred to an indemnifying party, or to an insurer. Some part of the exposure may be inherent in the nature of the organization's mission; some part may be an exposure of all activities conducted in the organization's geographic area; some part may be of a type so new that insurers are not ready to offer coverage. For example, a public welfare entity operating a youth center in a poverty-ridden slum may find no insurer or indemnitor willing to cover the risk; therefore, many of the entity's risks must be accepted as a cost of its mission. A public action organization, promoting or opposing some legislative program, may decide to bear the risk of litigation against it as a necessary cost of its mission. Any analysis of risk will be bound to uncover substantial areas of uncertainty which cannot be transferred by any of the three methods outlined above. A decision to bear such risks must be a conscious one, and as this chapter indicates, leadership's duty is to minimize the area of untransferable risks.

Standards of an Insurance Program

We turn to the principle beginning this chapter: the problem is risk, not insurance. Insurance is a possible solution. In order to fulfill a program with regard to risk, the board and officers must be familiar with the insurance underwriting available to their organization. Usually, this will be a relatively routine task; but in some situations, the problem is complicated and technical. It may be complicated by the high cost of insurance for certain activities or even the lack of any kind of insurance for the activity. The size and nature of the problem is further complicated by the fact that the insurance industry is cyclical and at times has been extremely volatile. Because of these difficulties (caused by the inherent uncertainties in underwriting risks where the event insured against may not take place until years after the policy is issued), the risk manager cannot presume the continuity of any insurance program.

Insurance Programs Should Begin with Conventional and Easily Procurable Policies. Coverage for general liability, such as property damage, automobile liability, and other standard risks can usually be obtained from conventional sources without difficulty.

Special Coverages. Beyond the conventional insurance indicated above, the organization should explore more difficult coverages, such as business interruption, life and health coverage of key employees, coverage for volunteer activities, coverage of profit-making subsidiaries, if any, and earthquake and tornado damage where these risks, generally excluded from property insurance, are evident.

The Procurement of Insurance. Except for those organizations large enough to have a full time risk manager, the board and management are generally going to rely on an insurance broker for counsel, advice, and the procurement of insurance. The board and officers should understand that in doing so, they will be relying upon a supplier of a commodity who may have some conflict of interest in the transaction. Most obvious, of course, is the question of alternatives between different premium levels for the same type of coverage when one is dealing with special coverages which may not be readily procured on the standard market. Also, in many cases, the broker's ability to deliver a special type of coverage will be affected by his or her bargaining position with the suppliers of insurance and the degree to which a given broker is willing to exercise influence on behalf of the specific insured. No solution to this last problem is offered here, but the organization leadership should be aware that the problem exists.

The Insured Entity Itself. The insured organization itself plays a critical role in the procurement and maintenance of effective insurance coverage.

The Application for Insurance is a Part of the Policy. A vital part of any insurance program or insurance policy is the insured's application and any other communications by the insured. These are important documents, which should be prepared by the risk manager; they are not clerical details. Not only should the documents be truthful and complete, but the very questions asked may suggest alternatives which could reduce risk exposures. The organization may thus appear more attractive to a balky insurer, or may receive a lower premium. For example, past convenience may have led to handling bill payments through a one-signature checking account whereas a fidelity insurer may be more comfortable if the organization requires two signatures on its checks.

The Risk Manager Should Periodically Review All Coverage. The risk manager should periodically assess the coverages obtained, additional coverages needed, and what is available in the insurance marketplace. Any policy provisions containing exceptions or special definitions should also be reviewed annually.

This review should include reading of the insurance binders, the policies, and all applications, examination of appropriate limits, accuracy of names and addresses of the insureds, and a check of the coverages, warranties, and exclusions. File maintenance of insurance coverage is sometimes neglected. The original terms of a policy, however, may be varied by single page addenda issued in later years, and assembling a clearly complete document defining the organization's coverage requires a surprising degree of care in record keeping.

If the organization's market position gives it a choice of insurance companies, the risk manager may wish to learn the rating and reputation of each of the insurers. This information should be checked at each renewal. All insurance companies are rated by various agencies. The most universally regarded is the so-called Best's rating which the insurance supplier should be able to provide and explain.

Implicit in the foregoing is a vital function of the risk manager: he or she must read all policies. This is not a simple task. Apart from the technical complexity of much of the language, there is the frequent difficulty of defining which original policies, renewal certificates, amendments, etc., constitute the current and binding contract of the insurer. The physical separation and identification of the currently binding material should be a continuing function of the risk manager.

The Role of the Insurance Company and the Insurance Broker. Insurance companies should be requested to make "audits" of the insureds. The companies are often keen to do this because it reduces their potential liability, and the audits are often helpful. Insurance brokers can be similarly helpful in auditing the organization and in pointing out types of available coverages.

Bibliography

Tremper, Charles and George Babcock. *The Nonprofit Board's Role in Risk Management: More Than Buying Insurance.* Washington, D.C.: National Center for Nonprofit Boards, 1990. (A good general survey of this field.)

Risk Management for Nonprofits. 2d ed. Washington, D.C.: National Center for Community Risk & Management Insurance, 1992.

Lai, Mary et al. *Am I Covered For?* 2d ed. Consortium for Human Services, Inc., 1992.

Exhibit 1
Suggested Questions Concerning the Organization's
Risk and Insurance

1. What risks does the organization face?
2. Has the risk manager listed and defined those risks?
3. With respect to the exposures faced, how probable is the occurrence of a loss resulting therefrom?
4. What would happen to the organization's activities and interests if such a loss were incurred?
5. Who outside the organization would be affected by such an event?
6. Of those risks, which could be avoided by reorganizing the organization's activities?
7. Which risks could be reduced by indemnification?
8. Is that party financially responsible?
9. Is the indemnification adequately documented?
10. Where we are relying upon insurance of third parties (e.g., owners' insurance of automobiles used in the organization's business), have we information concerning this coverage?
11. Of the risks that cannot be reorganized or indemnified, which ones can be transferred to an insurer?
12. Which risks cannot be transferred or avoided?
13. What kinds of insurance policies does the organization carry?
14. Do they cover all insurance risks?
15. What are the dollar limits of the various policies? Are they enough? Or are they unnecessarily high?
16. Does the insurance cover just the organization, or does it cover parties collaterally at risk as well, such as directors, officers, employees, volunteers or third parties injured with or without fault?
17. If those policies do not cover such parties, can riders be obtained to do so?
18. Have the insurance applications been reviewed to see:
    a. If they were truthful and accurate when made? or
    b. Would they be truthful and accurate if applied to the present situation?
19. Does the risk manager read every insurance policy? How often? Does he or she know the Best's rating of the various insurance companies? When does the board of directors receive a report of such scrutiny?
20. Where does the organization buy insurance? What qualifications does this source have?

Strategic Planning

Carl T. Hagberg

This chapter describes the importance of having a formal strategic plan in place and of reviewing and revising it periodically. It includes a broad outline for a first-time planning session, or for a review of existing plans and a checklist for the board secretary to assure that all necessary logistical arrangements are made.

Introduction

A formal strategic planning process helps every organization meet the needs of its clients, its employees, and the community at large in an ever-changing world.

In many respects, the planning process is as important as the plan itself. An effective process—one that taps into the know-how, the creativity, and the commitment of officers, directors, employees, and other key contributors—will inspire and invigorate the entire organization and repay, many times over, the considerable effort that a good plan requires.

The Role of the Secretary

The secretary has several vital roles to play in the planning process: helping the chair and the board to set a focused yet flexible agenda, selecting suitable sites and dates for the "kickoff meeting" and for the follow-up and subcommittee meetings that invariably follow and, of course, providing minutes that will summarize and help to track the variety of action plans successful planning sessions generate. In addition, because the secretary is a key member of the board and management team at most nonprofits, he or she also needs to be an active *participant* in the planning process.

Planning to Plan

In the ideal world, the chair has already recognized the value of having a strategic planning process in place. He or she will actively lead the planning process and will foster an atmosphere that not only taps the technical and practical expertise of the staff and the board as a whole, but engages their enthusiasm, their energy and, most important, their creative juices.

Sometimes, however, the impetus for a formal planning process comes from the ground up, or at the urging of one or more directors, or in the least ideal situation, in the face of a crisis.

In any event, the chair will need to feel comfortable with the overall agenda, with the kind of information that needs to be presented, with the presenters and other attendees; in short, with the overall gameplan.

Most chairpersons are quite adept at leading such meetings and obtaining enthusiastic and useful participation from board members and key staff. Nonetheless, it is often worthwhile to consider using a professional meeting facilitator. This can help minimize the possibility that one or two strong personalities will dominate or over-influence discussion and fosters a more democratic process that will maximize creative give-and-take between directors and staff. Alternatively, any number of participants can be asked to present in their areas of expertise or to moderate specific meeting segments.

With these issues settled, the secretary can prepare the preliminary agenda, noting the presenters or facilitators for each session, and begin to consult with them, and the chair, on the amount of time and the number of sessions that will be required and the kind of setting that will be most appropriate. See Exhibit 1 for a checklist of organizational and logistical considerations and remember that advance planning and attention to detail are the keys to a successful planning session, just as they are to a successful plan.

There is a great deal to be said for taking the meeting away from the organization's typical environment, at least for the very first session. It underscores the importance of the meeting, minimizes distractions, and the less formal atmosphere can help to free creativity. It also presents a wonderful team-building opportunity. If board members are a bit "starchy," or if board and staff members do not really know one another, this is a chance to forge and kindle team spirit (see p. 51).

Building a high level of involvement and maintaining momentum are among the most important considerations. The sessions should be scheduled with this very much in mind. Based upon the time and resources available, a very productive format, in a hotel or resort setting, would begin with a late afternoon kick-off discussion of broad objectives and goals followed by dinner, where attendees can exchange ideas informally. A very early start the next morning so that participants need to race the clock a bit can help to produce a very full day, a strong sense of urgency, and a high rate of closure as participants lay out the business environment in detail, identify the most critical issues, agree on follow-up actions, and set a second meeting date before adjourning.

A Sample Agenda

The eight-step outline presented in the next section is designed to give a broad overview of the business environment. It zooms in for increasingly microscopic looks at the organization itself, as seen from several different angles, then steps back again to reexamine and, if necessary, reformulate goals and strategies in light of the likely environment two, three and five years ahead. Finally, and this will normally require one or more follow-up sessions, it focuses very minutely on specific strategies and tactics that will help the organization deal more proactively with the future.

While in an optimum arrangement participants will have to spend up to two and one-half days on intensive, high-quality time to lay out the broad strategic outlines of the plan, it will be *their plan* when they are done; one they are really committed to achieving.

Planning Session Outline

Review of the Business Environment

The Economic Environment. Focus not only on the national economy, but on the likely outlook for the regions and even the specific neighborhoods served. Try to look two, three, and five years into the future. Think of the likely impact of various economic scenarios on sources and uses of funds and the way that rising or falling economies are likely to affect the total demand for the products and services offered. It is important to note, for example, that most charitable organizations are counter-cyclical: demand rises in bad times, while revenues fall.

Social and Demographic Trends. Changing income levels, changing tastes, changing neighborhoods, and changing lifestyles can have profound effects on the current mix of products and services. Think, for example, of the abandoned churches and synagogues seen in many older neighborhoods—but also of the large number that have been successfully recycled or even revitalized by alert management.

Regulatory Issues. Regulatory or tax changes or landmark legal decisions can suddenly and dramatically affect the way one needs to do business. Do not always think of them as threats. Sometimes they create terrific opportunities for nimble organizations.

Technology. Rapid technological change can make current products and services obsolete. In the case of health care, for example, failure to invest in new technology will not only make services less desirable but less safe. Technology can also help to deliver service in new ways and to entirely new audiences, witness art history via CD-ROM, supertitles at the opera, and televangelism.

The Competitive Source

Thinking that nonprofits are somehow above and beyond the hurly-burly competitive world can be a lethal mistake. Ask the following.

(1) Who *are* our competitors? (A wide-ranging review of the economic, social and technological scene often yields some totally unexpected answers.)
(2) Who are the most and least successful—and why?
(3) Are there any acquisition or divestiture opportunities out there? Might we ourselves be devoured by the competition?

Customers

Many organizations tend to think only of end-users as customers. For many nonprofits, present and potential *donors* are really among their most important "customers." Many nonprofits, like many for-profit organizations are, sad to say, *not* customer-driven. Are customer needs fully understood and fully met? Are more customers becoming "regular customers?" If so, why? Have customers and other important constituencies been surveyed? Are there potential new kinds of customers or new *markets* to serve?

Opportunities and Threats

While most of these will probably be identified during the review of the general business environment, it is important that the organization pause to consider, sum up the opportunities and threats and perhaps uncover some items that might have been missed. It is especially important to consider what its *future* opportunities might be and to remember that every threat is an opportunity for *someone.*

Objective and Goals

This outline intentionally postpones the discussion of objectives and goals, and especially the mission statement, until the full environmental scan is complete. The idea is to prevent a rush to judgment before all the evidence is in. Now is the time to ask the following questions.

(1) What *is* the shared vision of where the organization would like to be in three to five years?
(2) What are the commitments to constituents . . . and to other members?
(3) How does our newly-reviewed "vision" relate to our current mission statement and to the way that we have been communicating our objectives and goals to constituents at large?
(4) What are the organization's most significant strengths and weaknesses now?
(5) What are the *critically important* factors in achieving—or failing to achieve—our vision?
(6) What resource gaps need attention?
(7) Is more information needed about any of the issues on the table now?
(8) What do we most need to do and who will do it?

One way to *really rethink* one's objectives and goals is to imagine that the entire organization has been destroyed, and it must be rebuilt from scratch. If starting over, would things be done the same way, or differently?

At this point, one hopes that most participants will be mentally and physically exhausted, but even so, full of enthusiasm for working on. If participant schedules permit, plan to continue working into the evening or through lunch the next day.

Another excellent way to tackle these issues—which are the most difficult and also the most important—is to reconvene after a week's reflection, and to begin "brainstorming" about the possible strategies and tactics that come to mind. Matching potential strategies and tactics to each area of the environmental review is a simple way to organize the ideas in the final three steps.

Strategic Action Plan

Begin to list the *kinds of things* the organization needs to do, with particular reference to its strengths and weaknesses. Some examples follow.

(1) "We need to capitalize better on our unique collection of . . . too few people know about it."
(2) "We need to make a major investment in a computer system to inventory and track our holdings."
(3) "We need to correct the misperception that we are purely a research institution."
(4) "We need to interest and involve more young people in our work."

Two kinds of "strategic action plans" seem to be emerging from the considerations in these examples: the need for some kind of PR/awareness/advertising/outreach campaign and the need for computerization.

The Tactical Action Plan

Begin to list the *very specific programs* to deal with future opportunities and threats, including:

(1) *who* will carry out each action?

(2) *what exactly* is to be accomplished and *exactly when do we hope to finish*?

(3) *where, when,* and *how* are the needed funds to be obtained and *roughly* how much money is to be budgeted for each planned action?

(4) *who* will measure and report on progress?

The Finishing Touches (This, believe it or not, is the easiest part!)

(1) Critique and prioritize the list of strategies and their associated tactical actions.

(2) Estimate the timeframe and budget for each action that is agreed upon as precisely as possible.

(3) Assign a specific individual to be accountable for each action plan.

Carefully consider whether the board itself is too large or too small—and whether the *staff* is too large or too small, in light of existing and planned activities.

(4) Reduce the entire strategic plan to writing.

(5) Develop a formal program to communicate the strategic plan and "vision" to all constituents, clients, referral sources, staff, volunteers, financial supporters, prospective supporters and the community at large.

(6) Formally review progress at board and committee meetings. Make mid-course corrections as required.

(7) Review the entire plan, and especially the assumptions that underlie the plan *in detail* at least once each year.

Bibliography

Howe, Fisher. *A Board Member's Guide to Strategic Planning.* San Francisco: Jossey-Bass, 1997.

Exhibit 1
Checklist for a Strategic Planning or Offsite Meeting

Who's Invited . . . and Who's Not?

- The entire board and the board secretary, of course, but which key staffers should attend?
- Should we consider outside facilitators, moderators, speakers, or presenters?
- Should all invitees be there the entire time?
- Who'll mind the store while they're away?
- Are there any other inside or outside presenters who are affiliates with the organization who might make a contribution?
- What about those who *haven't* been invited?

An "A" and "B" list might be a useful tool for discussion with the chair and for keeping track of who's invited, who's attending and who may still be on the fence.

Site Selection

A venue that will accommodate the group comfortably, that is reasonably convenient for the majority of attendees, not unduly posh, but not too spartan.

- Make up a list of three to five possible venues for discussion with the chair (visit them first, if at all possible).
- Get cost estimates from each for meals, meeting rooms, audio/visual support, overnight accommodations, etc.

Transportation

- How many of the prospective attendees can drive, carpool, or use public transportation?
- Is there a need for any special transportation arrangement, such as airport service or a van from a central location?
- Do any of the potential sites provide transportation from airports, rail, or other connections?

Coordination

As the agenda takes shape, someone needs to *coordinate* with each of the moderators and presenters and with the chair.

- Who will provide briefing and background information to any outsiders?
- How long is each session expected to take?
- Any need for "icebreaking" or breakout sessions?
- What are the logical times for breaks?
- Will there be handouts or materials to be reviewed in advance?
- Audio/visual requirements?

Finalizing the Arrangements

- Agenda
- Amenities (reception, meals, breaks and snacks, message center/ phones, recreation (?), special dietary needs (?), transportation
- Contracts
- Materials to be distributed in advance
- Materials needed at the meeting site (audio/visual equipment, handouts, nametags and placecards (?), other supplies)
- Tentative dates and sites for follow-up meetings

Social Events

- Will there be time for social events (e.g. informal fun, lunch, cocktail reception, dinner or other "icebreaker" event) to build esprit de corps, board sociability, teamwork and thus lead to better board planning?
- If so, what will such event(s) be?
- When will they take place?

Total Quality Management in Nonprofit Organizations

Susan Sommer Futter

This chapter explains the basic principles of Total Quality Management and describes ways in which they may be applied to nonprofit organizations. The executive director, corporate secretary, and board of directors are critical to the process by providing leadership and driving the initiative throughout the organization.

In the late 1980s, a large university-affiliated hospital found itself in severe financial difficulty.[1] Staff morale was at an all-time low and patient complaints at an all-time high. The hospital's new president, secretary, and board knew that the hospital's very survival depended on radically changing the way things were being done.

The group decided to adopt a Total Quality Management (TQM) philosophy in order to change the direction of the organization. The first step was to conduct an intensive assessment to determine where the hospital was doing well and where it was ailing. Next, the board and senior management group met to confront the difficult data they had collected and to make a plan for turning the organization around.

After communicating the plan to the entire hospital staff, twenty-four employees received instruction as facilitators to provide training to the entire organization in quality awareness, problem-solving, and team-building. Managers participated in strategic leadership workshops to provide them with the skills they needed to empower their employees to make decisions that would have a positive impact on their departments. Following the initial training, many employees at all levels participated in cross-functional and departmental teams to tackle the problems that were plaguing the hospital.

The results of this effort have been phenomenal. The hospital has completely turned around its financial condition, employee satisfaction is higher than it has ever been, and patient complaints are now a rarity. Some specific examples of team results include the following:

(1) The billing group team reduced billing "rework" from between thirty and fifty percent to less than one percent. In addition, a new billing system provides improved auditing and greatly reduced turnaround time;

(2) Patient registration time has been reduced from more than twenty minutes per patient to approximately ten minutes per patient; and

(3) The nursing department reduced its float staff from over thirty to five, thereby reducing its annual budget by more than $300,000.

These are tough times for many organizations—public, private, and nonprofit. Economic conditions have forced many organizations to reexamine the way they operate in order to maintain their competitiveness and organizational activities and maximize scarce resources. In response to the current business environment, many organizations have turned to the managerial concepts of service quality and continuous improvement (often referred to as Total Quality Management, or TQM) in order to facilitate change.

When understood and used properly, the principles of service quality and continuous improvement can be used to facilitate an organizational transformation within nonprofit organizations. The transformation comes about as the organization as a whole begins to shift its thinking on a number of dimensions: organizations which have adopted a total quality attitude are service-oriented as opposed to product-oriented; they emphasize prevention of errors rather than detection of errors; they balance short-term priorities with long-term priorities; they make quality the responsibility of everyone within the organization; and they rely on teams at all levels to solve problems rather than just those at the top of the organization.

Many organizations have developed their own catchy phrases to describe their service quality initiatives including, for example, "Service First," "Service Excellence," and "Team Spirit." The health care industry has adopted "Continuous Quality Improvement" (CQI) to describe its efforts. No matter how disparate the titles, however, the concepts and fundamentals behind the processes are fairly constant across industries and companies.

History of Total Quality Management

The quality concept is not new. In fact, the current "quality epidemic" has its roots in post-war Japan when a couple of American managers, not finding support for their ideas in the United States, took their message abroad to more receptive ears. While it is not necessary to memorize the teachings of these early quality pioneers, it is helpful to understand the sources of our current philosophies towards quality because some of these fundamentals are still used in many corporations today. It is important to note that while the original quality principles were applied primarily to manufacturing firms, they are now also widely accepted and used in service organizations and nonprofit organizations, notably health care providers.

Three experts are often cited as the "gurus" of the quality movement. These three are W. Edwards Deming, Joseph Juran and Philip Crosby. Perhaps the most renowned of the quality gurus is the late W. Edwards Deming, who is closely identified with the statistical process control approach to TQM.

Shortly after World War II, Dr. Deming, as a consultant to the State Department, was sent to Japan to conduct a national census of the war-torn country. A self-proclaimed quality expert, Dr. Deming began to spread his beliefs to eager managers in Japan. Companies who follow Deming's philosophy adhere to Deming's Fourteen Points.[2]

Another quality "guru" is Joseph Juran. Juran, a contemporary of Deming, was also a key player in Japan's post-war industrial revolution. Juran's philosophy is based on his belief that managers must shoulder the responsibility for building quality into a process through planning, rather than relying on the traditional inspection-and-rejection method that many organizations use. Juran has divided quality managerial processes into three parts, known as the "quality trilogy": quality planning, quality control, and quality improvement.[3]

A third notable expert in the field of quality, and one whose quality journey cannot be traced to post-war Japan but rather to the halls of ITT, is Philip Crosby. In his widely read book, *Quality is Free*, Crosby recommends that organizations locate themselves on a quality management grid (grid) which lists five measurement categories and five stages of maturity, ranging from Stage I: Uncertainty to Stage V: Certainty.[4]

Once an organization has determined where it falls in the grid, Crosby recommends the implementation of a quality process using his fourteen-step program.[5] Crosby defines quality as "conformance to [the] company's own quality requirements."[6]

Key Components of a Successful Total Quality Process

Although the details and emphasis of a continuous improvement process will vary depending on the consultant whose methodology is used, the experts do agree on several key components which must be present in any quality effort.

Top-Down Commitment and Leadership

A commitment to service quality cannot be delegated. A commitment to quality involves fundamental change in the culture of the organization. For this change to take hold, top management must recognize the need for a commitment to quality and be willing to demonstrate behavior that will facilitate the change. The executive director and senior management must also communicate the change at every opportunity. Organizations that have been truly successful have had the benefit of strong leadership at the outset. In addition, successful organizations have sought the commitment and involvement of their boards from the very beginning.

Customer Focus

Many organizations define quality as meeting or exceeding customer requirements. Indeed, without customers most organizations would be out of business. The customer concept applies to all organizations, public, private, and nonprofit. Customers can be internal or external. Any time an individual or organization performs a service or provides a product to another, the recipient of the service or product is a customer. Total quality organizations continually ask the following questions.

(1) Who are our customers?
(2) What are our customers' requirements?
(3) How are we doing relative to our customers' requirements?
(4) What do we need to do differently to consistently meet or exceed our customers' requirements?

Core Processes

Once an organization has identified its customers and their needs, the organization must examine its processes to determine whether or not they are meeting the customers' requirements. Some processes may need "tweaking," while others may require a comprehensive reengineering effort, which starts with a clean sheet of paper and the question, "What must we do to ensure that this process meets our customers' requirements?" Regardless of the degree of change required, the organization must have an institutionalized problem-solving methodology.

Employee Focus

Most organizations launching a quality initiative recognize the need to drive decision-making and problem-solving down through all levels of the organization. The process of delegating decision-making to lower levels is often referred to as "empowerment" or, in many health care organizations, "shared governance." Regardless of what it is called, organizations must ensure that their employees are provided with the proper tools and the resources they will need to solve problems and make decisions. Areas that are affected by the move to an empowered organization and that must be addressed early in the effort include performance management, rewards and recognition, education and training, and teamwork.

Implementing a Total Quality Process

Develop a Plan

The quality planning process is really where "the rubber hits the road." Too many organizations have made the mistake of jumping feet first into a quality implementation process without really taking the time to develop a plan for identifying and achieving goals. As the saying goes: "If you don't know where you are going, you will probably wind up someplace else."[7] Planning for building quality into the organization is not unlike planning a trip. There are many key issues to be addressed early in the process, including:

(1) where are we going?
(2) how will we get there?
(3) who is going with us?
(4) how much money do we want to spend? and
(5) how will we know when we arrive?

Part of the secret of success of post-war industrial Japan was a result of the Japanese approach to product (and project) management. Of the total time invested in a project, the Japanese spend approximately seventy percent planning and thirty percent executing. In the United States, these percentages are reversed, leading to poorly planned projects and much rework.

Ideally, the executive director should integrate the quality planning process with the organization's strategic planning process from the outset. The vision, mission, and values of an organization should reflect the organization's emphasis on quality. Stretch goals, measures, and tactics that reflect the organization's focus on quality should be included in the organization's strategic plan.

Gather Customer Data

No matter what the organization does, it is extremely important to gather actionable customer data continuously. The information collected must be specific enough to drive changes in the organization's processes.

The method for gathering this data is simple: just ask. There are three major ways of asking for customer input: one-on-one interviews, focus groups, and surveys. The method chosen depends on the organization's customer base, style, and access to its customers.

One-on-one interviews tend to be the most time-consuming because they accommodate only one customer at a time. This method, however, may generate the most information, particularly if the interviewer is skilled in questioning techniques. Always keep in mind that the object of any data-gathering technique is to obtain actionable data. A skilled interviewer will "peel the onion" in an interview to determine the customer's true needs.

Focus groups are a good method of gathering specific information in a shorter period of time than one-on-one interviews. This technique has traditionally been used by consumer product companies to gather data on customer requirements. Focus groups are meetings of eight to ten people for the purpose of gathering information on a specific topic. The information gleaned from focus groups and one-on-one interviews tends to be qualitative as opposed to quantitative. Again, the goal is to obtain actionable data and the individual conducting the focus group must be skilled at probing the respondents for specific information.

Surveys are perhaps the most widely used customer data-gathering technique. They also provide excellent quantitative information when used properly. For this reason, many organizations employ market research or other survey organizations to construct statistically valid survey instruments. It is possible, however, to develop an effective and low-cost survey instrument in-house if certain principles are kept in mind.

First, it is always advisable to conduct interviews with a group of the customers *before structuring the survey* in order to ensure that the questions reflect their needs. Secondly, the survey should ask respondents not only *how well* the organization is doing in a certain dimension, but *how important* that dimension is to them. Many organizations ask their customers the first question but neglect the second. The results from this type of survey will help determine where to focus the initial process improvement efforts. For example, a dimension which consistently ranks low in performance and high in importance should be an early target of the process improvement initiative.

Institutionalize Process Improvement and Problem-Solving

Surprisingly few organizations have institutionalized an effective problem-solving methodology. Even organizations which have teams in place often neglect to provide the teams with the resources and tools they need to achieve results, erroneously believing that, because the team members are intelligent and familiar with the process, they will be able to work through a problem without structure or guidance.

Outlined below is an eight-step process improvement methodology, variations of which are used by many successful organizations. Often these eight steps are depicted in a circle to illustrate the concept of continuous improvement.

(1) Select the area of opportunity for improvement
(2) Identify customers, users, suppliers, and outputs of the process
(3) Establish customer or user requirements and expectations
(4) Describe and analyze the current process
(5) Identify the "gaps" between the current process and customer requirements
(6) Generate a list of possible solutions
(7) Test and implement one solution
(8) Continually measure and monitor the process

An integral part of any process improvement methodology is a set of "tools" which are utilized by teams as they progress through the steps. Many books on quality and problem-solving describe and explain in detail how to use the "tools." One such work is *The Team Handbook* by Peter Scholtes and others.

Launch the Effort with One or Two Key Projects

Nothing will get people's attention faster than success. Therefore, many organizations begin their quality improvement efforts with one or two highly visible projects, the successful results of which will have a positive impact on the organization. Clearly, it is extremely important to structure and manage these initial projects in such a way so as to ensure their success and impact on the organization.

Members chosen to serve on these initial teams should be familiar with the process chosen for improvement and should have a vested interest in the outcome. The presence and active participation on each team of at least one senior manager will send a very positive message to the organization.

The teams should be headed by a leader or facilitator who is familiar with the process and trained in the problem-solving methodology. Team members should be given an overview of the methodology and tools which they will be using as they progress through the problem.

The processes or areas chosen for these initial projects should be selected according to the following criteria. The project should

(1) be aligned with the organization's mission and strategies (it should have an organizational improvement goal);
(2) have enough priority to secure the necessary commitment of time to improve it;
(3) be repetitive, not a one-time or infrequently occurring event;
(4) be recognized by the organization and the user as needing change and improvement;
(5) be actionable (the team has at least partial control over the outcome);
(6) be of a manageable size (resolution can be reached within ten to twelve weeks); and
(7) not have obvious solutions for improvement.

Educate

The purpose of any training effort within an organization is to bridge the gap between the current performance of the organization as a whole, and individuals within the organization, and the customer's requirements both now and in the future. Therefore, a "training needs analysis" that addresses the following questions should be conducted as an organization launches its quality effort.

(1) What are the new skills, abilities, and knowledge sets people will need in order to be effective in meeting future customer and organizational needs?
(2) What skills, abilities, and knowledge sets do people within our organization currently have?
(3) What are the gaps between what we have and what we need?
(4) What education/training can best fill these gaps?

Training in problem-solving and process improvement is a necessity for an organization focused on continuous improvement. Within the realm of quality, some additional areas in which employees and managers may need training include quality awareness; influence skills; leadership; performance management; policy deployment; and measurement.

Communicate

Like education, communication is a key to garnering employee commitment and involvement. For a continuous improvement effort to be truly successful, the senior managers must "talk the talk" and encourage employees to do the same. At the very beginning of the effort, senior managers should elicit the help of employees in developing and communicating the organization's vision, mission, goals, and strategies. As the effort progresses, a strategy should be put in place for recognizing and communicating team efforts. Customer input should be accumulated and disseminated on a regular basis. Last, but not least, employees should be given a vehicle for communication. Often this takes the form of a formal suggestion system, and when possible, regular meetings between employees and senior management.

In developing a communication strategy, the organization should keep in mind how its employees typically give and receive information. Some organizations are comfortable celebrating their process improvements with balloons and banners, while others rely only on e-mail. Still others publish regular quality newsletters which contain information on teams, customers, and employees.

Reward and Recognize

Many organizations make continuous improvement and customer satisfaction a priority but fail to reward behaviors that support these priorities. It is a well-known management axiom that "what gets rewarded will get repeated."[8] By linking performance management to the achievement of quality objectives, organizations will greatly enhance their chances of reaching their goals.

Once an organization has identified its customers and their requirements, the performance management system should be aligned to ensure that the performance that is rewarded is centered around the customers' requirements. It is important to note that rewards and recognition can be either financial or non-monetary.

Conclusion

The principles of TQM have their roots in post-war Japan's industrial revolution. Although manufacturing companies were the first to embrace the fundamentals of TQM in the United States, many organizations in all industries, including nonprofits, are now using the concepts of TQM to facilitate organizational change.

When understood and used properly, the principles of TQM can help nonprofit organizations meet their goals. Successful quality implementations are implemented from the top down and emphasize a focus on customer requirements, employee involvement and a commitment to continuous improvement.

This chapter provides executive directors and the board of directors with guidelines for implementing a TQM process within their organizations. Although the concepts are fairly simple, many organizations choose to use outside consulting help in order to facilitate the implementation.

Notes

1. Derived from client case studies of Organizational Dynamics, Inc.
2. Andrea Gabor, *The Man Who Discovered Quality.*
3. V. Daniel Hunt, *Quality in America: How to Implement a Competitive Quality Program* (1992), 67.
4. Phillip B. Crosby, *Quality is Free* (1979), 32–33.
5. V. Daniel Hunt, *Quality in America,* 55–56.
6. Ibid., 79.
7. Attributed to Yogi Berra and others.
8. Jim Clemmer, *Firing on All Cylinders, The Service/Quality System for High-Powered Corporate Performance* (1991), 209.

Bibliography

Clemmer, Jim. *Firing on all Cylinders: The Service/Quality System for High-Powered Corporate Performance.* Toronto: Macmillan of Canada, 1991.

Crosby, Philip B. *Quality is Free.* New York: Mentor Books, 1979.

Crosby, Philip B. "Does Training Pay Off?" *Across the Board (The Conference Board Magazine)* (June 1996): 38.

Dobyns, Lloyd and Clare Crawford-Mason. *Quality or Else: The Revolution in World Business.* Boston: Houghton, Mifflin Company, 1991.

Gabor, Andrea. *The Man Who Discovered Quality.* New York: Times Books, 1990.

Hunt, V. Daniel. *Quality in America: How to Implement a Competitive Quality Program.* Homewood, Illinois: Business One Irwin, 1992.

Juran, J. M. *Juran on Leadership for Quality: An Executive Handbook.* New York: The Free Press, 1989.

Labovitz, George, Y.S. Chang and Victor Rosansky. *Making Quality Work: A Leadership Work: A Leadership Guide for the Results-Driven Manager.* New York: Harper Collins Publishing, 1993.

Scholtes, Peter R. *The Team Handbook: How to Use Teams to Improve Quality.* Madison, Wisconsin: Joiner Associates Inc., 1988.

The Records Management Program

Lucy S. Binder

Records are a resource on which the organization bases its decisions and documents transactions. This chapter covers records retention from two aspects: records related to the board of directors and records related to the organization as a whole.

Board Records

Boards of directors require permanent records of meetings. The secretary must assure that the records are filed, protected, indexed, up-to-date, accessible, usable, and retained in accordance with applicable laws and regulations and sound organizational practice. The board and board committee minute books are the permanent records of the organization and are kept in active, protected status in the office of the secretary or, to the extent not actively used, in another location under the secretary's charge.

As the organization and its records expand, the use of microfilm or microfiche may be used to reduce the mass of records generated. At such time as this documentation is changed to inactive status, if ever, it may be moved to a central storage area. Duplicate copies of such records or electronically coded records are to be stored offsite in safeguarded facilities as the back-up for the permanent records—for example, the minute books. Back-up documentation for board and board committee meetings are often treated in this manner.

The secretary may find it more convenient to work from a duplicate set of meeting documents rather than the originals. One set of confidential meeting materials should be retained with the records of the meeting. All other copies of those materials should be destroyed following board or committee meetings. Some organizations require that confidential material in board mailings be returned to the secretary for destruction following the meeting. The secretary's notes, from which minutes are prepared, should also be destroyed following approval of the minutes.

Records to Be Retained

The organization should retain the following records.

(1) Minutes, which should be kept in books of strong construction
(2) Back-up documentation of meetings
    (a) meeting notices and records of their mailing
    (b) agendas
    (c) exhibits and other documents brought before the board or committees and not filed as part of the minutes
(3) Historical records of the organization
    (a) charters or articles of incorporation

       (b) bylaws
       (c) certifications
    (4) Other documentation (as applicable)
       (a) membership records
       (b) contribution records and related correspondence
          (i) corporate
          (ii) foundation
          (iii) individual
          (iv) other
       (c) estate gift records
       (d) tax records and returns, exemption rulings such as Internal Revenue Service application (Form 1023) for 501(c)(3) status, and annual IRS Tax Form 990 filings
       (e) licenses
       (f) contracts, agreements, deeds, leases
       (g) insurance policies
       (h) bank records

Organizations need a standardized policy covering the length of time each document or microfilm or microfiche copy is to be retained. Some organizations may have an employee act as a records manager to work with and carry out a retention policy. Records management really provides a database for an organization and is therefore extremely valuable. Removal and elimination of duplicate file copies of material can also reduce expenditures in time, money, staff, and save space occupied by filing cabinets.

Filing systems evolve in all organizations, often resulting in the retention of numerous copies of individual paper documents at a rather large cost to the budget. Filing systems may be different in each section of the organization. Paper documents amount to ninety to ninety-five percent of recorded information. When the organization takes into consideration rental of office space and staff overheads, the cost of records stored in one active file drawer for one year can be substantial. Organizations should be very cognizant of this cost and seek to reduce it. Not only does this save space and money, it will serve to eliminate records which might be burdensome in litigation.

The fact that eighty percent of documents filed are not referred to again lends credence to a program to establish a standardized records retention program. The process requires:

(1) agreement by the organization's leadership to establish the program;
(2) a policy statement to be adhered to by all sections within the organization;
(3) a records management or oversight committee (in larger organizations), which includes representatives of the various sections;
(4) establishment of retention guidelines; and
(5) a records management manual which includes a system for enforcing the destruction/retention guidelines.

Following agreement on the need for the program and a policy statement, the organization must establish administrative guidelines for the program. The following outline suggests the issues to be addressed.

(1) Determine what the records retention program will cover
    (a) types of records to be retained
    (b) design of an inventory form (see Exhibit 1)
    (c) identify active and inactive records by inventory
    (d) categorize the inventory
    (e) determine which records are vital, important, useful

(2) Establish retention guidelines based on
    (a) ordinary organizational needs
    (b) federal, state or municipal regulations
    (c) comparable organization practices
    (d) consultation with legal and tax advisors
    (e) consultation with records retention specialists

(3) Determine the policy and process under which records can be destroyed based on
    (a) a routine schedule defining
        (i) how and when destruction will occur
        (ii) when to purge files of unnecessary duplicate copies and other unneeded materials
    (b) a determination that there are no future substantial needs of any user, legal, historical, or for other purpose
    (c) destruction process
        (i) confidential materials—shredding or incineration
        (ii) non-confidential matters—tearing or simply dropping in wastebasket

(4) Determine where records will be retained
    (a) in the office
    (b) in a vault or fire-safe
    (c) in a safe deposit box (microfilm/microfiche)
    (d) in a central storage area
    (e) in a secure, offsite storage facility for inactive, but necessary records

(5) Communicate and implement guidelines throughout the organization

(6) Select and install the standardized filing system for use by the entire organization

Organization-wide records management programs provide advantages that include the opportunity to eliminate unneeded duplicate copies and reduce required file space; paper processing in a standard, consistent, cost-effective manner; the availability of documentation as required by legal and/or tax advisors; and production of a records management manual, an orientation and reference source for employees.

A sample records management policy of a general industry association is attached as Exhibit 2. The exhibits are offered as examples only and should be reviewed with the organization's counsel in light of federal, state, and local regulations.

It is prudent to maintain any records that have an impact on the financial statements of an organization. At the time that records are no longer needed because their impact on financial statements has ended, the records should only be maintained from that year forward to the end of the statute of limitations for any organization or regulatory authorities which may require those records.

Electronic Records

With the expanded usage of personal computers, it is vital that consideration be given to electronic storage on disks. A prime advantage of electronic records is the savings generated by the minimal usage of storage space. Depending upon the organization's system, disk backup may be on a daily, weekly, or monthly basis. The data generated on these disks is considered an information asset, is normally essential to the survival of the organization, and must be protected.

The organization must determine what electronic information need not be retained and what must be protected and to what degree, examining:

(1) sensitivity to destruction;
(2) sensitivity to disclosure;
(3) recovery plans for essential applications, including:
    (a) definition of requirements;
    (b) plan preparation and support;
    (c) protection of vital records;
    (d) usage of offsite backup system;
    (e) usage of offsite storage facility; and
    (f) annual testing of program; as well as
(4) proper destruction of unneeded electronic media.

To be effective, a program for the maintenance of electronic information also requires support from the organization's management and leadership; and user responsibility to comply with guidelines. Exhibits 1 and 2 to this chapter illustrate a typical records inventory and analysis worksheet and a records management program (including a detailed records retention schedule) which also covers electronic files.

Resources

American Society of Corporate Secretaries, Inc.
Records Management Report
1270 Avenue of the Americas, New York, NY 10020; 212-765-2620

Business Laws, Inc.
Guide to Records Retention
11630 Chillicothe Road, Chesterland, OH 44026; 216-729-7996

Office Systems Magazine
941 Danbury Road, Georgetown, CT 06829; 205-544-9526

The Records Management Group
Encyclopedia of Records Retention by Clark
540 Frontage Road, Suite 345
Northfield, IL 60093; 847-446-3222

Association of Information and Image Management (AIIM)
Silver Spring, MD; 301-587-8202

Association of Records Managers and Administrators (ARMA)
Post Office Box 8540, Prairie Village, KS; 800-422-2762

Business Forms Management Association (BFMA)
Portland, OR; 503-227-3393

Exhibit 1
Records Inventory and Analysis Worksheet

INVENTORY DATA	**Location:**	**Department/Section:**	**Building/Floor/Room:**

Record Series Name:

DESCRIPTION OF FILES/USE AND PURPOSE:

Physical Form/Media:
☐ Hardcopy   ☐ Computer Printout   ☐ Aperture Card
☐ Roll Film   ☐ Microfiche
☐ Other:_____

Volume:	Inclusive Dates:	Present Retention:
Office of Origin:	Office of Record:	

Other Offices Receiving Copies:

Analyst Name/Date:

RECORD ANALYSIS AND APPRAISAL	Legal Requirements:

Preliminary Retention Recommendation:	Final Retention Recommendation:
Office:	Office:
Records Center:	Records Center:
Remote Site:	Remote Site:
Total:	Total:

Analyst Name/Date:

DEPARTMENT INTERVIEW	
Operational Value:	Expires After:
Audit Requirements:	Expires After:
Potential Legal Value:	Expires After:
Historical/Archival Value:	
Other Comments/Recommendations:	

Interviewee Name/Date:	Interviewee Name/Date:	Tax Name/Date:
Interviewee Name/Date:	Accounting Name/Date:	Audit Name/Date:

Exhibit 2
Records Management Program

Sample General Association

Date Prepared: _____

Date Revised: _____

Prepared by: _____

        Secretary/Records Manager/General Counsel

Approved by: _____

        Chair/Executive Director

Purpose

The purpose of this policy is to establish organization procedures for the retention, maintenance, and destruction of records.

Policy

Certain organization records must be maintained in order to comply with federal, state, and local regulations. This includes the certificate/articles of incorporation/charter, bylaws, and minutes of meetings of the board of directors and board committees. In addition, other organization-related records must be retained for specified periods.

With respect to other records there are basic principles to be achieved:

1. Documents should be retained as necessary to provide a record of significant events and the conclusion reached in a particular issue, consistent with the need to ensure that the costs associated with record retention in terms of space and maintenance are not disproportionate to the value of retaining the records.
2. Document files, both hard and electronic copy, should be reviewed periodically to ensure that only required documents are retained, and that unneeded superseded drafts are destroyed.

Policy Implementation

Goals can best be achieved through the disciplined implementation of this policy. Each segment of the organization is responsible for ensuring that suitable records are retained in accordance with this policy and are disposed of when no longer required. The following Records Retention Schedule for hard and electronic files provides general guidelines.

Each segment is responsible for retaining the official file for those issues within its areas of responsibility. Questions concerning the appropriate disposition of records not listed in the Records Retention Schedule or any questions about application of the policy in specific circumstances should be directed to the corporate secretary.

Any correspondence or records that are relevant or related to or involved in any currently pending or threatened litigation or in any proceeding before any regulatory agency should promptly be brought to the attention of the general counsel or secretary.

Records Retention Schedule

CATEGORY OF DOCUMENT: **RETENTION PERIOD:**

CORPORATE RECORDS: Life of corporation
   Certificate/articles of incorporation;
   bylaws; minutes of meetings of the
   board of directors and board committees;
   backup files for board and committee meetings

ACCOUNTING RECORDS:
   General book of accounts   Life of corporation
   Accounts payable and receivable   Seven years
   Budgets   Four years
   Bank reconciliation and cancelled checks Seven years
   Depreciation records   Life of asset
   Tax returns   Life of corporation
   Year-end financial statements and   Life of corporation
      audit reports
   FICA and FUTA payroll records   Seven years

CONTRACTS AND AGREEMENTS: Completion/termination date of
                                                contract, plus six years

INSURANCE POLICIES: Life of corporation

LEASES AND DEEDS: Completion date of lease or
                                                ownership and property plus
                                                ten years

DRAFTS OF ANY DOCUMENTS: Destroyed on execution of the
                                                final document except in
                                                special circumstances

PERSONNEL RECORDS: Period of employment plus six
                                                years
   Applications for employment   One year
   (including resumes)

ANNUAL REPORTS: Life of corporation
Correspondence related to the foregoing should be filed with the documents.

ELECTRONIC RECORDS:

DISPOSITION:

SYSTEM FILES:

Retain on-line with an updated tape backup in secure storage

WORKING DOCUMENT FILES:

Documents currently in process should remain on-line until approved for hard copy

ARCHIVE DOCUMENT FILES:

1. Documents no longer required to be on-line, but for which immediate access is probable, should be transferred from the computer files to a diskette
2. Documents required to be maintained as corporate records, but for which no immediate use is anticipated, should be transferred to a tape backup established for the particular computer name

Documents on electronic file need only be maintained and readable for periods similar to those for the same records stored in paper form. Any document not required to be retained should be deleted.

PART IV
Taxes and Accounting

In this section we address areas of specific legal and technical concern. It is essential that both the board and staff of a nonprofit understand the basic structure of the federal tax provisions affecting nonprofits, even though, as our authors recommend, the organization should use outside professionals in many of these areas. We treat here the "charity," exempt as a private foundation or otherwise, and the basic systems of accounting in use by nonprofits. Furthermore, while this area of the law is always subject to change, the issues discussed here are likely to survive specific changes, and accordingly the subject should command the reader's attention.

What an Executive Director of a Charity Needs to Know about Tax Law

Gilbert H. Jacobson[1]

Many attempts have been made to enumerate those aspects of federal tax law that executive directors of charities without a background in tax should know. The author's experience, in serving as a legal consultant to executive directors and fund-raisers for many years, is that people who are not "tax-oriented" turn off when they are inundated with the provisions of the Internal Revenue Code, the regulations promulgated thereunder, and the minutia contained therein. This chapter will cover only those items with which an executive director should be familiar.

Introduction

An executive director should develop sufficient familiarity with the issues discussed in this chapter to know when it is appropriate to seek guidance. It is crucial that staff of nonprofit organizations have a qualified tax advisor familiar with these topics with whom they can consult when the occasion arises.

This chapter focuses on Section 501(c)(3)[2] charitable organizations and provides a brief introduction to some other commonly encountered tax-exempt organizations. The discussion set forth herein should not be relied on without review by legal counsel. There may have been changes in the law since it was written, or the reader may be facing a situation which differs in some significant respect from that referred to here.

Exemption from Federal Income Tax

Because a corporation is a nonprofit does not mean that the corporation is exempt from income tax. Tax-exempt status is not a right. It is a privilege conferred on an organization which meets, and continues to meet, certain requirements set out by the Code. Most organizations seeking exemption under Section 501(c)(3) (i.e., charitable, educational, and religious organizations) and other types of tax-exempt organizations must obtain Internal Revenue Service (IRS) approval of their tax-exempt status by filing an application for recognition of exemption (Form 1023) and receiving a favorable determination letter from the IRS.

Churches and synagogues, their integrated auxiliaries, conventions or associations of churches and synagogues, and organizations having gross annual receipts normally not more than $5000 that are not private foundations are not required to file Form 1023.

There are currently twenty-five types of tax-exempt organizations set forth in Section 501(c). Donors to most of these types of organizations may not deduct gifts made to them. Gifts are generally only deductible if the organization qualifies under Section 501(c)(3). Sometimes payments to other types of tax-exempt corporations may be deductible by the donor if the payment qualifies as a trade or business expense.

Obtaining Tax-Exempt Status

Section 501(c)(3) Organizations. A charitable organization has the burden of showing that it falls within the statutory parameters of the exemption it claims. Organizations wishing to apply for tax-exempt charitable status generally must file a Form 1023, Application for Recognition of Exemption under Section 501(c)(3), with the IRS. Form 1023 requires every applicant organization to notify the IRS of the basis on which it is entitled to section 501(c)(3) status and whether it should be treated as a private foundation. A copy of the organization's governing documents, including the articles of incorporation and bylaws, must be attached to the Form 1023. Detailed financial information is also required.

The filing of the Form 1023 is a one-time obligation. It usually takes several months for the IRS to act on the application. Exempt status is granted retroactively, beginning with the date of the filing of the organization's articles of incorporation, if Form 1023 is filed within twenty-seven months from the end of the month in which the organization was created. If not, it will begin when notification is received from the IRS. A Form 1023 will be returned without being processed if the appropriate user fee is not enclosed.

The IRS must be notified if any information originally provided on Form 1023 substantially changes.

Section 501(c)(3) organizations must make a copy of their application for exemption (Form 1023) and the annual information returns (Form 990) available for public inspection during normal business hours at the organization's principal office. The names of contributors need not be disclosed.

Other Tax-Exempt Organizations. Although Section 501(c)(3) organizations are the most common tax-exempt organizations, there are many other types of exempt organizations. Generally, the distinguishing feature of tax-exempt organizations is their pledge to serve the welfare or convenience of a wide class of individuals or organizations, and to avoid the enrichment of individuals running the organizations, such as employees or shareholders. Tax-exempt organizations other than Section 501(c)(3) organizations include civic leagues and broad social welfare organizations (Section 501(c)(4)), labor, agricultural, or horticultural organizations (Section 501(c)(5)), business leagues, chambers of commerce, real estate boards, and boards of trade (Section 501(c)(6)), social clubs (Section 501(c)(7)), fraternal beneficiary societies (Section 501(c)(8)), and various other organizations entitled to tax-exempt status under the provisions of Section 501(c) of the Code. Organizations other than 501(c)(3) organizations generally may file a Form 1024, Application for Recognition of Exemption under Section 501(a). In many respects, the Form 1024 is similar to the Form 1023.

Annual Tax Filings

Generally, all exempt organizations are required to file yearly tax returns (Form 990). Tax exemption may be lost if the return is not filed. There are different versions of the Form 990, and the type of Form 990 that must be filed depends upon the classification of the charitable organization under section 501(c) of the Code.

A tax-exempt organization, whether exempt under section 501(c)(3) or another provision of the Code, must file an annual information return on Form 990 on or before the fifteenth day of the fifth month following the close of its accounting period with the IRS Center identified on the Form 990 instructions. The fact that corporations are exempt under Section 501 also does not excuse them from the requirement for filing information returns under Section 6041 of payments of salary, interest, annuities, etc. or from withholding requirements. Tax-exempt corporations are required to file information returns and withhold tax at the source in the same manner as other corporations.

Churches and synagogues, their integrated auxiliaries, conventions or associations of churches and synagogues, and organizations other than private foundations that normally have gross receipts in each tax year of not more than $25,000 are generally not required to file Form 990.

Section 501(c)(3) Organizations

Section 501(c)(3) deals with organizations which are "organized and operated exclusively for religious, charitable, scientific, testing for public safety, literary, or educational purposes, or to foster national or international amateur sports competition (but only if no part of its activities involve the provision of athletic facilities or equipment), or for the prevention of cruelty to children or animals." No part of the net earnings of a Section 501(c)(3) organization may inure to the benefit of any private individual or shareholder and no substantial part of its activities may consist of the carrying on of propaganda or otherwise attempting to influence legislation. In addition, Section 501(c)(3) organizations are absolutely prohibited from participating in or intervening in any political campaign on behalf of, or in opposition to, any candidate for public office.

A Section 501(c)(3) organization can operate a trade or business, even if the operation does not further its exempt purposes, as long as this is an "insubstantial" part of its activities, and taxes are paid on any income earned. The organization, however, would then be subject to the tax imposed under Section 511 of the Code on unrelated business income. If the unrelated trade or business activities become too substantial, the organization risks losing its tax-exempt status, because its primary purpose would be to engage in the unrelated trade or business rather than to perform its charitable purposes.

Organizational and Operational Tests

In order to be exempt under Section 501(c)(3), an organization must be organized and operated exclusively for one or more of the purposes mentioned above. If an organization fails to meet either the organizational test or the operational test described below, it is not exempt.

Organizational Test. The organizational test requires that the legal documents creating the entity provide that all assets are dedicated exclusively to one or more of the purposes mentioned above. It is essential that these documents contain a clause which ensures that, should the entity cease to exist, all assets will continue to be used for one of these exempt purposes (see p. 191).

Operational Test. In order for an organization to be regarded as operated exclusively for one or more exempt purposes, it must engage primarily in activities which accomplish one of these exempt purposes. As mentioned above, if more than an insubstantial part of its activities are not in furtherance of an exempt purpose, an organization will not meet this test. A part of the operational test will include the following.

Private gain. If an organization is operated for private gain or purposes, it will be denied exempt status. Private gain includes excessive compensation, below market or interest-free loans, gifts, lease arrangements, and other forms of remuneration to directors. Private gain is permitted if it is only incidental to the exempt purposes of the organization.

Commensurate test. An organization whose principal activity consists of raising funds must carry on charitable activities commensurate in scope with its financial resources. There is no fixed percentage of income that a public charity must pay out for charitable purposes. The facts and circumstances must be considered. Low distribution levels, however, will invite IRS scrutiny.

Insurance activities. Generally, a Section 501(c)(3) organization is tax-exempt only if no substantial part of its activities consists of providing commercial-type insurance.

Lobbying. An organization will not qualify under Section 501(c)(3) if it devotes a "substantial part" of its activities to lobbying, propaganda or attempting to influence legislation. "Substantial" is generally thought for this purpose to be 5%. This figure, however, cannot be relied on with certainty. The "substantial part" test is based on the particular facts and circumstances of the organization and is, therefore, inherently vague.

Section 501(h) of the Code provides a safe harbor for certain organizations that regularly engage in some lobbying and wish to elect out of the more general "substantial part" test. Such organizations may instead elect the "expenditure" test. Permitted lobbying expenditures for a year are 20% of the first $500,000 of the charity's exempt purpose expenditures for the year, plus 15% of the second $500,000, plus 10% of the third $500,000, plus 5% of any additional expenditures. Under no circumstances may amounts spent on lobbying exceed $1 million for any year. Within these limits, attempts to influence the general public on legislative matters ("grassroots" lobbying) are permitted up to 25% of the permitted lobbying amount.

Although Section 501(h) clarifies the scope of permitted lobbying activities, it can impose strict penalties on the organization and its directors if these safe harbor limits are exceeded. Persistent lobbying in excess of that permitted by Section 501(h) may result in a loss of the organization's tax-exempt status. In addition, penalty taxes may be imposed on any officer, director, or responsible employee of the organization involved. All charitable organizations should closely monitor all direct and indirect lobbying expenditures.

Political campaigns. An organization will lose its status under Section 501(c)(3) if it participates or intervenes, directly or indirectly, in any political campaign on behalf of or in opposition to any candidate for public office. Unlike lobbying, this is an absolute prohibition. Candidates for public office include those involved in national, state, or local campaigns. Activities which constitute participation or intervention in a political campaign on behalf of or in opposition to a candidate include, but are not limited to, the publication or distribution of written or printed statements or the making of oral statements on behalf of or in opposition to a candidate. Intervention in an election should be distinguished from attempts to influence legislation, as discussed above.

Public policy. The purpose of a Section 501(c)(3) organization cannot be illegal or contrary to public policy. Discrimination on the basis of race, for example, is clearly contrary to public policy, and would likely result in the revocation of Section 501(c)(3) status.

Unrelated Business Taxable Income

Exempt organizations, including Section 501(c)(3) organizations, are subject to tax on income generated by their involvement in regularly carrying on a trade or business unrelated to their exempt purposes.

Examples of unrelated trade or business activities have been: the sale of computer time to the public; profits received by the American Bar Endowment by providing group insurance to members with a stipulation that members assign refunded dividends back to it; income that an exempt cemetery corporation received from a covenant not to compete granted in relation to the sale of its mortuary subsidiary; an exempt medical college's income from the sale of advertising in its professional journal; the income a state university received from forty-five professional entertainment events; and pet grooming services provided by a society for the prevention of cruelty to animals.

The IRS imposes a three-part test in determining whether an activity generates unrelated business taxable income: first, whether the activity constitutes a trade or business; second, whether the activity is regularly carried on; and, third, whether the activity is related to the organization's exempt purposes.

Rates. An incorporated tax-exempt organization that has unrelated business taxable income pays tax at the regular corporate tax rates. In 1995, for example, taxable income of $50,000 or less was taxed at 15%; between $50,000 and $75,000 the marginal rate was 25%; between $75,000 and $100,000, 34%; between $100,000 and $335,000, 39%; and between $335,000 and $10,000,000, 43%.

Debt-Financed Property. Income from debt-financed property (real or personal) is subject to the unrelated business income tax. Debt-financed income property is property acquired by incurring debt, retained to produce income, and unrelated to the organization's exempt purposes. Examples of debt-financed property are a certificate of deposit bought with borrowed funds, or a building with a mortgage that is rented to an unrelated third party.

Acquisition Indebtedness. A factor in determining whether unrelated debt-financed income exists is whether there is any acquisition indebtedness. The term "acquisition indebtedness" means the unpaid amount of any debt:

(1) incurred in acquiring or improving the property;
(2) incurred before acquiring or improving the property, if the indebtedness would not have been incurred but for the acquisition or improvement; or
(3) incurred after the acquisition or improvement, provided the indebtedness would not have been incurred but for the acquisition or improvement, and the incurring of indebtedness was reasonably foreseeable at the time of the acquisition or improvement.

Mortgage indebtedness on property received under a will or, under certain conditions, by gift may not be acquisition indebtedness. If mortgaged property is received under a will, the mortgage is not treated as an acquisition indebtedness for a period of ten years from the date of acquisition. This exception does not apply if the organization either assumes and agrees to pay all or part of the indebtedness secured by the lien, or makes any payments for the equity owned by the decedent, other than a payment for certain annuities.

The ten-year rule is also applied to gifts if the mortgage was placed on the property more than five years before the date of the gift and the property was held by the donor for more than five years before the gift. Unless acquisition indebtedness falls under one of these exceptions, it will result in the property being considered debt-financed property.

Promotion of Sponsors. Payments received by exempt organizations from corporate sponsors are not subject to unrelated business income tax, if there is no expectation that the organization will provide a substantial return benefit to the donor. The IRS has issued proposed regulations which state that an exempt organization's recognition of corporate sponsorship in a yearbook, program, or other material related to, and primarily distributed in connection with, a specific sponsored event results in unrelated business income if the recognition is considered to be advertising, but not if it is considered to be an acknowledgment of the sponsor. An acknowledgment merely recognizes a sponsor. Advertising is any activity, message, or other programming material that is broadcast, published, displayed, or distributed for compensation in order to promote or market a company, service, facility or product.

Deductions from Gross Income. In determining its unrelated business taxable income, an exempt organization may deduct costs directly connected with the carrying on of the business from gross income.

Exceptions. The unrelated business income tax does not apply to any trade or business conducted largely by volunteers without compensation, or to the sale of donated goods.

The following items, and any deductions directly connected with them, are excluded from unrelated business taxable income, unless such income is debt-financed: dividends; interest payments with respect to securities, loans and annuities; royalty income; most rents from real property; rents from personal property leased with real property if they are an incidental amount not exceeding ten percent of the total rents from all property leased; and capital gains and losses, with certain exceptions. Gains or losses are included in the computation of unrelated business income, however, if they result from the sale, exchange, or other disposition of stock in trade or other property that would be included in inventory and property held primarily for sale to customers in the ordinary course of a trade or business.

Specific Deduction. A $1,000 deduction is allowed in computing the tax on unrelated business taxable income. This deduction is not allowed for computing net operating loss. For a diocese, a province of a religious order, or a convention or association of churches or synagogues, each parish, individual church or synagogue, district, or other local unit may claim a specific deduction of the lower of $1,000 or the gross income derived from any unrelated business regularly carried on.

Partnerships. An exempt organization that is a general or limited partner of a partnership conducting a trade or business must report as unrelated business taxable income the exempt organization's share in the partnership gross income which, with respect to the exempt organization, is income from the unrelated trade or business. It may also apply its share of the deductions attributable to this gross income.

Exchanges and Rentals of Membership or Donor Lists. Generally, unrelated trade or business does not include the exchange with another charitable organization of the names and addresses of members or donors to that charity, or the renting of such names and addresses.

Final Word on Unrelated Business Income. This analysis of the unrelated business income tax has merely scratched the surface of this topic. Consult with a knowledgeable attorney when faced with an actual situation that might trigger an unrelated business income tax consequence.

Charitable Contribution Substantiation and Quid Pro Quo Disclosure

A large number of charities receive substantial funding through public contributions. Although donors ideally would give irrespective of tax benefits, the reality is that tax benefits drive charitable contributions. As a result, a recipient charity has an interest in assisting the donor in complying with the requirements affecting the deductibility of the donor's contribution. One such requirement involves proper substantiation of the deduction.

Benefits (i.e., goods or services) provided in return for contributions reduce the allowable charitable deduction. For gifts exceeding $75 where there is a *quid pro quo* (donor benefit), the solicitation materials, or a receipt furnished to the donor, must advise that the charitable deduction is limited to the contribution in excess of the value of the benefits received, and furnish a good faith estimate of those benefits.

Note that it is not a difference of more than $75 between the amount given by the donor and the value of the object received by the donor that triggers disclosure. The amount actually paid by the donor is what matters.

Subsequent to January 1, 1994, for gifts of $250 or more, a donor must have a written receipt from the donee charity. Charities may give this receipt at the time of the gift or may give a year-end statement tallying all payments and benefits received. A cancelled check is not sufficient to document gifts.

The statement should set forth the amount of cash contributed and a description, but not the value, of any property other than cash contributed. If the charity provides any goods or services in consideration of the gift, the receipt should so state, together with a description and a good faith estimate of the value of such goods or services. If no goods or services were given to the donor, the receipt must so state. The statement must also inform the donor that the charitable deduction is limited to the amount of the payment in excess of the value of the goods and services provided. Fine print disclosure on tickets or promotional material will not suffice, because disclosure must be made in a manner that is reasonably likely to come to the donor's attention. For purposes of determining the $250 threshold, separate payments made at different times of the year for separate fund-raising events generally will not be aggregated.

If a donor makes a gift of $250 or more to a religious organization and receives in return solely an intangible religious benefit that generally is not sold in commercial transactions outside the donative context, the religious benefit may be disregarded. Even though the necessity for a description and good faith valuation is waived, however, a statement to the effect that such benefits were provided must be made.

Donee Reporting

If the claimed value of all noncash property contributions to a charity exceeds $500, regardless of their individual values, the donor must file Form 8283 (Noncash Charitable Contributions) and attach it to his or her income tax return.

Gifts of property (other than cash and publicly traded securities) require an appraisal when the claimed or reported value of the property exceeds $5000. For this category of gifts, Form 8283 must be signed and dated by the charitable donee.

The IRS requires charities to file Form 8282 (Donee Information Return) if they sell or transfer property for which an appraisal was required, within two years of receipt. This return includes: the donee's name, address, and employer identification number; the donor's name, address, and taxpayer identification number; a description of the property; the contribution date; the amount received on the disposition; and the date of disposition.

Dispositions after two years need not be reported. The donee must furnish a copy of the Form 8282 to the donor.

Potential Traps for the Unwary

Executive directors of charitable organizations need to be particularly aware of the ways in which their own conduct might give rise to potential risks to the tax-exempt status of their charitable organizations. In particular, two areas require careful scrutiny. First, any transaction between the executive director and the organization itself or between the organization and any other member of the staff or the executive director's relatives or affiliates needs to be carefully scrutinized to avoid claims of self-dealing or private benefit. Second, the executive director and the charitable organization need to carefully scrutinize the executive director's compensation, taking into account all of the various benefits provided to him or her, in order to avoid any claims that the compensation paid to the executive director is unreasonable or excessive.

The charitable organization itself needs to scrutinize any transaction it enters into in order to make sure that the terms of the proposed transaction are consistent with the language in its charter and bylaws and to avoid any claims that its conduct in entering into the transaction would constitute a "substantial" business activity unrelated to its exempt purposes. Each transaction, also, needs to be scrutinized to ensure that no private inurement or benefit other than what is incidental to the exempt purposes of the organization will be granted to any insider, such as a board member or officer, or to a substantial contributor. In addition, the charitable organization needs to monitor carefully the extent and scope of any activities that could be characterized as "political" in nature to ensure that the prohibition against political activity and the restrictions with respect to lobbying activity are being observed. Finally, the organization needs to maintain proper records, including minutes of all meetings of the board of the organization and its various committees, to ensure that all required tax filings are made and to follow state and local fund-raising registration and reporting rules.

What This Chapter Does Not Cover

There are several important areas with which an executive director of a charitable organization should be familiar, but which are beyond the scope of this chapter.

Each state, and sometimes each municipality or local subdivision, has laws which govern charities and charitable fund-raising. An executive director should be familiar with the rules of his or her state and locality.

An executive director should also familiarize himself or herself with laws concerning charitable giving, as well as what qualifies and what does not qualify as a charitable deduction. An executive director should have access to an accountant who is familiar with the special rules that are applicable for tax-exempt organizations.

It is also important for an executive director to be familiar with various planned giving techniques, such as charitable lead trusts, charitable remainder trusts, and charitable gift annuities.

Notes

1. The author gratefully acknowledges the careful review of this chapter by, and the many helpful suggestions from, W. Donald Sparks of Richards Layton & Finger, P.A.

2. I.R.C. § 501(c)(3) (1994). All references herein, unless otherwise noted, are to the Internal Revenue Code of 1986, as amended (Code), *id.* §§ 1-9722 (1994).

Private Foundations

W. Donald Sparks, II[1]

Many, if not most, public benefit nonprofits are classified for tax purposes as private foundations, and subject to important restrictions imposed by that classification. This chapter outlines the classification and its consequences.

Introduction

"Private foundation" is a technical term of tax law, applicable to many nonprofits. This chapter summarizes the provisions of the Internal Revenue Code, as amended (Code) governing private foundations, and explains their importance.

More than twenty-five years have passed since the Tax Reform Act of 1969[2] was enacted. That law contained the basic provisions that govern the conduct of private foundations today. It was passed in response to perceived abuses by donors and charitable organizations with respect to both the charitable deduction taken by the donor and the lack of public accountability of private foundations. Many commentators at the time predicted the demise of private foundations because of the harsh restrictions and sanctions imposed by Congress. With historical perspective, it is possible to observe, like Mark Twain upon hearing reports of his death, that reports of this demise were greatly exaggerated. Today, private foundations are alive and well. They have weathered three major Congressional reviews and strict Internal Revenue Service (IRS or Service) scrutiny and remain a significant force in the exempt organizations community.

General Background

Definition

A private foundation is a section 501(c)(3)[3] charity that does not meet the "public support" test or qualify as a public charity on the basis of the other categories set forth in sections 170(b)(1)(A)(i) through (vi) and 170(b)(1)(A)(viii) of the Code. Private foundations may be "operating" or "non-operating." Typically private foundations are privately funded and controlled and operated to make grants to other charities for the active conduct of their programs. There are large, well endowed, grant-making foundations with large staffs and well defined programmatic fields of interest for their grant-making. There are also, however, many modestly funded foundations that operate with little or no staff in areas of charity consistent with their major contributors' philanthropic interests.

Purpose

Private foundations are designed to provide a flexible and efficient vehicle for the charitable giving of its donor or donors. A private foundation's flexibility, however, is limited by the rules on the income-tax deductibility of gifts to a private foundation and by restrictive excise taxes imposed on private foundations as part of the regulatory scheme of the federal tax law.

The two major reasons for creating a private foundation are privacy and control. A private foundation permits the donor's philanthropic activity and philosophy to continue after death. Although it need not be, a private foundation typically is controlled by a self-perpetuating board of directors or trustees that were originally appointed by the foundation's major donor. There is nothing in the foundation rules that prohibits the donor, the donor's family, or business associates from completely controlling and operating a foundation so long as they act in their fiduciary capacities as trustees or directors with respect to the foundation.

Foundations Typically Hold Their Assets as Endowment

Out of the endowment and the income thereon, private foundations satisfy the requirement that they spend or distribute annually a minimum amount to accomplish their charitable purposes through direct expenditures or through grants. The establishment of the endowment and the utilization of ongoing grant-making by the foundation provide the flexibility and the resources necessary to meet changing charitable needs and conditions that are not generally present in one-time gifts to specific charities.

Foundations Are Not Required, under Federal Tax Law, to Diversify Their Assets

As long as they observe the general "business judgment" standard in managing their assets, foundations are not required to diversify their assets. Foundations, however, may be subject to certain state laws, such as those applicable to trustees of charitable trusts, that are more strict than the federal standards.

The Endowment Structure of Private Foundations Permits the Donor to Provide for the Future by Having Assets Invested with Minimal Tax Effects

A private foundation will generally have an endowment with earnings that escape the traditional income tax. Section 4940,[4] however, imposes a two percent excise tax on the private foundation's investment income.

Private Foundations as Distinguished from Public Charities

Basic to the regulatory scheme of the Tax Reform Act of 1969 is the dichotomy adopted by that legislation between private foundations, on the one hand, and public charities, on the other. Furthermore, Congress established the presumption that every charitable organization described in Section 501(c)(3) is a private foundation unless a statutory exception could be found for the organization to qualify as "not a private foundation."[5] The categories of public charities include the following.

"Traditional" Public Charities

Pursuant to Sections 509(a)(1) and 170(b)(1)(A)(i)-(vi) of the Code, "traditional" public charitables include: churches; schools; hospitals and medical research organizations; development foundations for state universities; governmental units; and publicly supported organizations, those normally receiving at least one-third of their annual support from governmental units or from direct or indirect contributions from the general public, or those meeting a ten percent facts and circumstances test.

The IRS has been issuing rulings to newly created exempt organizations under special rules if the organization establishes that it can reasonably be expected to be publicly supported. Under such a ruling, an organization is treated as publicly supported, and not as a private foundation, for its first two years and the organization and its grantors and contributors may rely on that ruling for the two-year period. The reliance period may be further extended until the IRS makes a final determination of the organization's foundation status if the organization submits, within ninety days after the organization's second tax year ends, information needed to determine whether it meets the requirements for publicly supported status for its first two years.

Publicly Supported Organizations Described in Section 509(a)(2)

Section 509(a)(2) organizations are organizations (similar to organizations previously described, and yet different in certain ways) that receive more than one-third of their annual support from gifts, grants, contributions, or members' fees and not more than one-third of their annual support from investment income and unrelated business income.

In determining whether the organization meets the annual support test, investment income is to include the excess (if any) of the amount of unrelated business taxable income over the amount of unrelated business income tax imposed on such income. Further, in determining whether the organization meets the annual support test, the investment income of the organization includes payments (dividends, interest, fees, income from collateral security, and income from investment of collateral security) received by the organization in connection with securities that it has loaned to brokers. "Investment income" includes interest, dividends, payments with respect to securities, loans and annuities, income from notional principal contracts, and other substantially similar income from ordinary investments, but only to the extent that it is not subject to the unrelated business income tax. "Support" includes gifts, grants, contributions, membership fees, gross receipts from admissions, and other related activities and net income from unrelated activities whether or not carried on as a business.

Affiliated Supporting Organization Described in Section 509(a)(3)

Unlike public charities described in Section 509(a)(1) and (2), a Section 509(a)(3) organization is often privately endowed and is rarely dependent on public support. Its public charity status is not dependent on the nature of its support, but on its activities and its relationship with one or more public charities. A Section 509(a)(3) supporting organization may also support organizations that are described in Sections 501(c)(4), (5), and (6). The Section 509(a)(3) supporting organization is preferred by donors who wish to avoid the restrictions applicable to private foundations, but who are willing to give up some degree of control. The IRS has imposed a complex set of standards an organization must meet before qualifying for this status.

Community Foundation

A community foundation attracts larger donations from donors in a specific geographic area, pools these funds, and makes distributions to public charities within the area. The community foundation may be composed of various component funds, donor-advised funds, and Section 509(a)(3) support organizations. In this structure, the donors yield control over the funds to the community foundation, which in turn is controlled by a representative group of citizens from the community.

Types of Private Foundations

The Independent Foundation

This category is the most common, comprising over 44,400 of the total 45,628 private foundations classified by the IRS as of February 28, 1991. It is frequently established and referred to as a "family foundation." Most of these foundations are organized as nonprofit corporations, but some are trusts. The corporate structure is preferred because of the ease of amendment and to preclude individual liability. Independent foundations generally have an endowment feature and are managed by their own trustees or boards of directors who frequently are family members. They are generally grant-making organizations as distinguished from private operating foundations described hereinafter.

The Corporate Foundation

A corporate foundation is a private foundation supported by a particular business organization. There is no legal distinction between a corporate foundation and an independent foundation, and they are generally treated the same by the IRS. There are distinct advantages that a company can obtain through a corporate foundation over a general corporate contribution program. The corporate foundation: allows for the buildup of an endowment that provides consistent financial resources despite fluctuation in corporate earnings; establishes a structure to take advantage of tax benefits in a shifting economic climate; separates the charitable decision-making from business decision-making, with the potential of professionalizing the charitable function; provides a planning program and a commitment to charitable giving; and provides a vehicle for deductible, charitable giving (in areas such as foreign grants and grants to individuals) not available to a contribution program.

The Conduit or Pass-through Foundation

Described in Section 170(b)(1)(E)(ii), this type of foundation is favored by donors who wish to make large charitable gifts after death. The conduit or pass-through foundation is used to establish the family foundation during the donor's lifetime and, upon death, to fund it fully. Donors to this type of foundation receive the fifty percent maximum charitable contribution deduction and favorable treatment of contributions of appreciated property.

Pooled Common Fund Foundation

Described in Section 170(b)(1)(E)(iii), this organization resembles the Section 509(a)(3) support organization except that the donor retains control. While classified as a private foundation, the donor can utilize all the favorable rules for any charitable deductions to it. The foundation, however, must meet the following requirements: it must be the affiliate of one or more public charities; the income must be distributed to public charities no later than two and one-half months after the end of the year; and the donor or spouse may designate annually recipients of income attributable to the donor's contribution and must direct by deed or will the distribution of the corpus one year after the death of donor or spouse.

Operating Foundation

An operating foundation is distinguished from a private foundation because it is not a grant-making foundation. Instead, it carries out its own charitable programs directly. It has the advantage of providing its donors with the same sort of favorable tax treatment with respect to contributions that donors to public charities receive. An operating foundation, however, must expend substantially all of its net investment income currently and directly for the active conduct of its exempt activities. Section 4942(j)(3) sets out the various requirements that must be satisfied to obtain this status. Congress recognized that certain operating foundations were, in substantial respects, functioning like public charities and, in 1984, excepted these foundations from the excise tax on net investment income and permitted them to make grants to other private foundations without exercising expenditure responsibility.

Specific Rules for Private Foundations

The basic scheme of regulation applied to private foundations as a result of the Tax Reform Act of 1969 is, with the exception of Section 4940, the imposition of a series of punitive excise taxes. Authority for the IRS to impose these taxes is based solely on the occurrence or nonoccurrence of specific actions on the part of foundations, and intent, reasonableness of conduct, or, indeed, benefit to the foundation or other charitable beneficiary will not prevent taxation.

Section 4940: Excise Tax on Investment Income

Originally justified as the means to finance the costs of IRS auditing compliance by private foundations with the excise tax regime, the excise tax on foundation investment income was set initially at the rate of four percent. It soon became apparent that this tax generated revenues in excess of the Service's costs for auditing not only private foundations, but all tax-exempt organizations. Accordingly, the rate was cut in half to two percent for tax years beginning after September 30, 1977.

This tax is imposed on "net investment income"—comprised of dividends, interest, rents, royalties, certain payments from securities-lending transactions, and capital gains on the sale of property used for the production of such income. Both long- and short-term capital gain income are subject to the tax. The basic rate of the tax may be reduced to one percent for any year in which the foundation meets certain additional charitable payout requirements. Deductions allowable against investment income in arriving at "net investment income" are, generally, limited to the expenses of producing such income or holding property for its production. As a result of the Tax Reform Act of 1986, private foundations now must make quarterly estimated tax payments each equaling twenty-five percent of the required annual payment.

Section 4941: Excise Tax on Self-Dealing

The "self-dealing" proscription aims to rule out most transactions between private foundations and their "disqualified persons" as defined in Section 4946(a) (substantial contributors, officers, directors, trustees, related parties, and certain others). The Code defines self-dealing to include a number of specific transactions between private foundations and disqualified persons (sale or exchange of property, lending of money, furnishing of goods or facilities, payment of compensation, etc.), and then concludes with a broad, catch-all clause sweeping in any "transfer to, or use by or for the benefit of, a disqualified person of the income or the assets of a private foundation."[6] The statute specifies a number of exceptions to this general rule—the most common allowing foundation payment of reasonable, non-excessive compensation for the performance of personal services—but the fundamental congressional purpose here was to build a wall between private foundations and their closely-related parties.

An excise tax of five percent is imposed under Section 4941(a)(1) on each act of self-dealing between a disqualified person and a private foundation. The tax is based on the amount involved with respect to the act of self-dealing and is paid by each disqualified person involved in the act of self-dealing.

An excise tax of two and one-half percent is imposed under Section 4941(a)(2) on any foundation manager, defined in Section 4946(b), who knowingly participates in an act of self-dealing, unless such participation is not willful and is due to reasonable cause. The maximum aggregate excise taxes collectible from all foundation managers with respect to a single act of self-dealing is limited to $10,000. Participation by foundation managers ordinarily will not be considered knowing or willful and will be considered due to reasonable cause, if the manager relied on an opinion of legal counsel, after full disclosure of the factual situation, that an act is not an act of self-dealing.

A second-tier tax of two hundred percent of the amount involved is imposed by Section 4941(b)(1), if an act of self-dealing is not corrected within the taxable period. Section 4941(b)(2) similarly imposes a tax of fifty percent of the amount involved on the foundation managers who refuse to agree to part or all of the correction of the act of self-dealing. Whenever more than one person is found liable for any tax under Section 4941(a) or (b), all are jointly and severally liable. The maximum aggregate amount of second-tier taxes on foundation managers is limited to $10,000.

Section 4942: Taxes on Failure to Distribute Income

Foundations, other than operating foundations, generally, must pay out five percent of their net endowment value each year for their charitable purposes. The law gives foundations the benefit of a one-year lag to make the required payout. Thus, foundations may choose to make the required charitable distributions by the end of the year following the year for which the five percent computation is made, although many, perhaps most, foundations make their required charitable distributions on a current-year basis. The fundamental payout rule is subject to a number of exceptions, qualifications and special conditions, such as treatment of "set-asides," grants to "pass-through" organizations and certain other items, but the basic intent of this provision is to mandate annual charitable distribution by private foundations of five percent of their assets. On this point, the Council on Foundations has recently advised its members:

> Some commentators have suggested that the minimum total return on investment [must be] at least 9.5 percent or higher if a foundation is to maintain the

purchasing power of its assets over time. This figure is determined by adding 5 percent payout to a median 0.5 percent for investment management costs plus annual inflation of at least 4.0 percent since 1950.

Section 4943: Excess Business Holdings

The statute establishes a percentage ceiling on the aggregate amount of stock that a foundation by itself, or when its holdings are aggregated with those of its disqualified persons, may own in a business enterprise. Generally, the law has three provisions.

(1) The principal limitation on permitted holdings is twenty percent of the voting stock in an incorporated business enterprise. If a disqualified person has an interest in the same business, the foundation's permitted holdings are reduced by the amount owned by the disqualified person. A higher percentage limitation may apply if the foundation and disqualified persons do not own more than thirty-five percent of the voting stock of an incorporated business enterprise and effective control of the corporation is in one or more persons who are not disqualified.

(2) The ceilings are subject to an across-the-board de minimis rule permitting a private foundation to own up to two percent of a business enterprise, no matter what the holdings of its disqualified persons are.

(3) There are exceptions and transition rules, the most important of the latter permitting foundations to hold business interests above the ceiling for five years when the holdings are received by gift or bequest.

Section 4944: Jeopardizing Investments

The statute imposes restrictions on certain types of investments that would jeopardize the ability of the foundation to carry out its exempt purposes. Essentially, the standard imposed is that of the prudent investor. The statute, however, does provide an exception for program-related investments so that foundations may assist charities through taking financial positions in investments that would not otherwise be considered appropriate.

Section 4945: Taxable Expenditures

As with other private foundation sanctions, Congress was concerned that the pre-1969 Tax Reform Act sanction of loss of tax-exempt status for a private foundation engaging in prohibited activities, such as lobbying, election campaigns for candidates for public office, and spending amounts for other than charitable purposes, was both ineffective and too harsh. Thus, it created a tiered excise tax system that penalizes certain expenditures by private foundations ("taxable expenditures").

A taxable expenditure is an amount spent by a foundation to: influence legislation; influence the outcome of any public election, or to carry on any voter registration drives; make a grant to an individual for study or travel unless the IRS approves, in advance, the grant-making procedures; make grants to organizations that are not public charities unless the foundation exercises "expenditure responsibility"; or make grants for other than charitable, educational, and similar broadly charitable purposes specified in Section 170(c)(2)(B).

The excise tax is applied as follows. (1) A foundation generally is subject to a ten percent tax on the amount of the taxable expenditure, and an additional tax of one hundred percent if the expenditure is not corrected within the taxable period. (2) A two and one-half percent tax is assessed on the foundation manager, if the manager agreed to the expenditure knowing it was a taxable expenditure, "unless such agreement is not willful and is due to reasonable cause." An additional tax of fifty percent, with a limit of $10,000, is imposed if the manager refuses to agree to the correction, in whole or in part.

Reporting Requirements

Private foundations must file an annual return with the IRS on Form 990-PF reporting the following:

(1) gross income for the year;

(2) expenses attributable to such income;

(3) a balance sheet showing assets, liabilities, and net worth as of the beginning of the year;

(4) disbursements within the year for exempt purposes;

(5) total contributions and gifts received, and the names and addresses of all substantial contributors;

(6) names, addresses, and compensation of officers, directors, and highly compensated employees;

(7) an itemized statement of securities and all other assets at the close of the year;

(8) an itemized statement of all grants made or approved for future payment, including the name and address of each grantee and the purpose and amount of each grant; and

(9) the address of the principal office of the foundation and, if different, the place where its books and records are kept.

Finally, each private foundation must make its return available for public inspection at the principal office of the foundation during regular business hours, upon a request made within 180 days after the date of publication of the notice of its availability. Such publication must be made no later than the day required for filing the return with the IRS, and the notice, including the foundation's telephone number, must be published in a newspaper having general circulation in the county of the principal office of the foundation.

Conclusion

Despite the sometimes complex and convoluted regulatory scheme outlined above, the private foundation community continues to grow and distribute significant amounts for charitable purposes. Reporting in 1994 on foundation activities in 1992, the Foundation Center noted that the more than 6700 large foundations, holding assets of $162 billion, made grants in excess of $9 billion. While, as indicated above, private foundations have special rules to be aware of and a few problems to be attentive to, new challenges and opportunities await the private foundation community in, among other things, assisting in the rebuilding of the

American economy and the emerging democracies throughout the world. The private foundation is clearly an attractive vehicle for many donors to carry forward their philanthropic objectives and a unique approach to bringing to bear private decision-making in matters of public interest.

Notes

1. The author gratefully acknowledges the substantial contribution of J. Warren Wood, III, vice-president, general counsel, and secretary of the Robert Wood Johnson Foundation, to this chapter. Mr. Wood's work constituted the basis for much of what appears herein.

2. Pub. L. No. 91-172, 83 Stat. 487 (1969).

3. I.R.C. § 501(c)(3) (1994).

4. All statutory references herein are to the Internal Revenue Code of 1986 as amended. All references to regulations are to the Treasury Regulations in effect under that Code.

5. See 26 I.R.C. § 509(a) (1994).

6. Id. § 4941(d)(1)(E).

Bibliography

Blazek, Jody. *Tax Planning and Compliance for Tax-Exempt Organizations.* 2d ed. New York: John Wiley & Sons, 1993.

U.S. Treasury Department. Internal Revenue Service. *Exempt Organizations Continuing Professional Education Technical Instruction Program Textbook.* Washington: Government Printing Office. Prepared annually.

———. *Tax-Exempt Status for Your Organization.* Publication no. 557.

———. *Tax Information for Private Foundations and Foundation Managers.* Publication No. 578.

Edie, John A. *First Steps in Starting a Foundation.* Washington, D.C.: Council on Foundations, 1987.

Hill, Frances R., Barbara L. Kirschten, et al. *Federal and State Taxation of Exempt Organizations.* Boston: Warren, Gorham & Lamont, 1994.

Hopkins, Bruce R., *The Law of Tax-Exempt Organizations.* 6th ed. New York: John Wiley & Sons, 1992.

Basic Nonprofit Accounting Terms, Methods, and Operations

Robert Kornreich and David C. Ashenfarb

This chapter presents a brief overview of the accounting methods and operations used by nonprofit organizations in accounting for the resources received and the use of the resources for program services.

Introduction

Several different types of organizations are organized as nonprofit entities. Such diverse organizations as membership clubs, trade associations, certain schools, churches, civic associations and charities are examples of the various types of nonprofit entities. While each type of nonprofit organization has unique accounting methods, there are many similarities which are common to all nonprofit organizations.

Revenues, also known as support, can be in the form of contributions from the public, foundations, and corporations; grants from governmental entities; and dues or non-dues revenues. Contributions from the public can come to the organization in a variety of ways including responses to direct mail solicitations, through special events such as telethons and walkathons, and sponsorship of special events (i.e., annual dinners, silent auctions, and art shows). Contributions received from the general public are usually solicited for the operation of the nonprofit organization as a whole rather than for any specific program run by the organization.

Contributions from foundations, corporations, and governmental units are also called grants and each are solicited from the grantor in a similar manner. There are several publications (e.g., the *Foundation Directory* and the *Foundation 1000* published by the Foundation Center) which list foundations, corporations, and government entities which have funds available for grants to nonprofit organizations. To apply for these grants the nonprofit generally completes a grant request as specified by the grantor.

These requests for grants require the nonprofit to describe its operations generally, how it expects to use the proceeds of the proposed funding and how it has used similar funding in the past. If the nonprofit is successful in obtaining the grant, it is generally subject to periodic reporting to the grantor. Such reporting includes a comparison of actual expenses incurred to those projected in the grant application as well as a statement concerning accomplishments of the programs funded by the grant.

The prior discussion centered on charitable organizations. There are other nonprofits, however, which are not charities. Trade associations, for example, would receive support from their members, which operate in a similar industry. Such support, in the form of dues, are assessed on various bases. A trade association could base its annual membership dues on a variety of factors, such as the length of time a member has been in business, number of employees of the member, or the volume of product shipped by the member. Schools receive a major portion of their support in the form of tuition, the amount of which is generally determined by the board of directors.

While the activities of nonprofits are generally exempt from income tax, there are certain items of income, which may be received by a nonprofit, that are not exempt. Such nonexempt income is known as unrelated business taxable income and is subject to income tax. Unrelated business taxable income is generally defined as the conduct of a trade or business which is substantially unrelated to the organization's exempt purpose. The fact that the proceeds generated from the activity are used to further the exempt purpose does not govern.

The rules covering unrelated business taxable income are very complex. Given the taxing authorities' desire to increase tax revenues through strict compliance, any new activity contemplated by a nonprofit should be reviewed by a professional advisor to ensure the organization does not run afoul of these complex rules (see p. 297).

Examples of what would be considered related and unrelated income follows:

Related Income (not subject to tax)	Unrelated Income (subject to tax)
The operation of a cafeteria which is available for use only by employees of the organization	The operation of a cafeteria which is available for employees and the general public (i.e., hospitals, museums)
Gift shop sales of merchandise by a museum, etc.	Sale, to other entities, of the customer list of the gift shop
	Advertising income

Funds

Both commercial and nonprofit entities incur expenses for salaries, rents, telephone, etc. The commercial enterprise spends these funds to support its commercial activities. In a nonprofit organization, such expenditures are made in support of the nonprofit's purpose. For example, if a nonprofit was organized to educate the public about the environment, then costs, such as those described above, incurred in encouraging recycling are in support of the organization's goals. These expenditures are called program services.

In order to establish stewardship over its resources and measure the degree of success a nonprofit has achieved in support of its stated goals, most nonprofits use fund accounting. This method of accounting segregates resources received into what is known as funds. Each fund is used to account for different aspects of the operations of the entity.

Operations

Now that we are familiar with the basic accounting in a nonprofit environment, we should turn our attention to how the organization operates on a day-to-day basis. Most nonprofit organizations are headed by an executive director. The executive director is ultimately responsible for the operations of the organization. This includes insuring that program services are provided and resources expended in a manner consistent with the goals of the organization; that accounting procedures are implemented so contributions received and resources expended are properly reported, and to solicit sources of funding to ensure the organization has sufficient funds to provide future program services. Typically the executive director delegates these tasks, respectively, to a business manager or financial controller and a director of development.

A business manager is generally responsible for the accounting function. This includes setting up procedures and financial controls which ensure that all transactions are properly recorded in the books and records and that there are adequate safeguards over organization assets. If a museum has a gift shop, for example, certain procedures can be instituted to achieve control over cash received as follows: the gift shop cash register should be totalled on a daily basis and reconciled to the cash in the register. This cash should be deposited in the bank daily to safeguard it from theft.

Another control procedure would require separate persons to process contributions received, to process checks to vendors, and to perform bank reconciliations. In small organizations it is not always economically feasible to have those functions performed by three different individuals. In many small organizations, in fact, these tasks are performed by the same person. To mitigate this apparent control weakness, the business manager should sign all checks and receive the bank statement directly from the bank so he or she can review the enclosures for any suspicious items. Checks in excess of a specified amount should generally be required to have two signatures.

The business manager is also responsible for preparation of the annual operating budget of the organization. The budget process is important since it provides the organization with a means of assessing how actual operating results measure up to the organizational goals. The business manager develops the current year budget by reviewing variances between the prior year budget and actual operating results, by discussing new programs or changes in existing programs with appropriate organization personnel and by working with the director of development to ascertain if there are any new funding sources or, conversely, decreases in prior sources of funds. The budget, once developed, becomes the tool to evaluate the operating effectiveness of the organization. If, for example, it becomes apparent that the projected contributions will not reach the budgeted amounts, the organization may decide to reduce or eliminate some program service(s) in order to compensate for the reduced revenues.

The director of development is responsible for pursuing funding for the organization. This is accomplished by the director seeking out those funding organizations which provide grants in support of the nonprofit activities as well as seeking funding from other sources. Typically the development officer makes contacts at the funding organization, develops a proposal for how grant monies would be spent and completes a formal application for grant. If the funding body approves the application, the funds are granted and generally the recipient organization is required to report on the progress of the program funded by the grant and how the funds are expended.

As the executive director is responsible for the day-to-day running of the organization, the board of directors generally oversees the overall direction of the organization. The board sets the goals and monitors the effectiveness of the organization. It is the board which provides the executive director and other officers with the directions and goals the nonprofit is to achieve. The board, through monitoring of the budget and actual results of operations, advises, reinforces, and, in some cases, modifies the direction the executive director and his or her officers are steering the nonprofit.

Accounting

The Financial Accounting Standards Board (FASB) has issued statement No. 116, Accounting for Contributions Received and Contributions Made (the "Contributions Statement"), and Statement No. 117, Financial Statements of Nonprofit Organizations (the "Display Statement"). These statements were enacted to provide nonprofit organizations with standards that will help the financial statements look more consistent with those of their peers.

It is essential that the affected areas of the organization, such as accounting, development, and board, become familiar with these statements in order for an efficient and orderly transition leading to their adoption by the organization.

FASB No. 116: Contributions Statement

Statement 116 establishes accounting standards for entities that receive contributions from donors. Contributions, which are considered unconditional transfers of cash and other assets, are required to be recognized as revenues in the period received. In addition, unconditional promises to give (including multiyear promises) are required to be recognized by both donee and donor(s) at fair value in the period during which the promise is made. Conditional promises to give are recognized as income when the conditions are substantially met. The statement also formulates new rules on when contributions of services should be recorded and suggests types of footnote disclosures to help the reader understand the significance of volunteer time.

The effect on the timing of contributions under Statement 116 could be significant for some organizations. Prior to the adoption of Statement 116, organizations recorded unconditional contributions at the time the promises were fulfilled (when the cash was received or the restriction was satisfied). Under Statement 116, if a foundation or other donor makes a multi-year unconditional commitment, the nonprofit organization would be required to recognize the full amount of the promise in the year the promise was made. If the restricted purpose of the contribution has not been fulfilled, the unspent money will create temporarily restricted net assets. For a further discussion on the classes of net assets, see the discussion on FASB Statement 117 which follows.

It is important to note that while unconditional promises to give are recorded as revenue immediately, appropriate documentation to affirm the validity of promises must be on hand. Therefore, an organization should take measures to establish controls, including formalized policies and procedures, over the preparation and retention of documentation to substantiate promises made.

Contributions of services and volunteer hours are recorded as income and expense only when: (1) they would have been purchased at fair value on the open market had they not been contributed and they require specialized skills that are provided by individuals possessing those skills, or (2) they create or enhance non-financial assets.

Receipt of contributions of works of art should generally be recorded at fair market value. An exception to this rule exists when the work of art is held for public exhibition, is preserved and protected, and is subject to an organizational policy that requires any proceeds from the sale of the work of art to go towards purchasing additional collectibles.

Statement 116 lists professional services such as those provided by lawyers, accountants, architects, doctors, and engineers as the types of services that should be recorded. Other contributed services that do not meet the above criteria should not be recognized as income and expenses. While there is no requirement to record volunteer services that do not meet this requirement, organizations are encouraged to disclose information about those services, such as number of hours served and the programs to which they apply.

FASB Statement No. 117: Display Statement

Statement No. 117 was issued to enhance the understandability and comparability of financial statements issued by nonprofit organizations. In the past, organizations reported their financial status in formats that differed from one to another. The new standards emphasize reporting information for the organization as a whole; in the past, many organizations reported information by fund groups only. This display statement establishes broad standards for consistency of external financial statements for all nonprofit organizations.

The display statement also requires nonprofit organizations to provide a statement of financial position (in lieu of a balance sheet); a statement of activities (in lieu of a statement of revenues, expenses, and change in fund balances); and a statement of cash flows. A statement of functional expenses is required for voluntary health and welfare organizations and is encouraged for other nonprofit organizations. The statements must show results for the entity as a whole and their separate classes of net assets (if applicable).

Under FASB No. 117, the grouping of similar funds takes on a new concept. The traditional fund groups used in financial statements were:

1) restricted;
2) unrestricted;
3) endowment; and
4) plant.

The new statement divides the fund groups into separate net asset groups as follows:

1) Permanent Restriction—A donor-imposed restriction stipulating that resources be maintained permanently but permitting the organization to use all or part of the income currently.
2) Temporary Restriction—A donor-imposed restriction, which expires either by the passage of time or by actions of the organization, stipulating that the organization use the donated assets as specified.
3) Unrestricted—All other transactions not covered by the definition of permanent restriction or temporary restriction.

Statements 116 and 117 were issued simultaneously and are usually adopted by organizations simultaneously as well. The following example is an illustration of the theory of the application of both statements.

An organization with a year ending December 31, 19X1 receives a three-year unconditional commitment for $9,000 to be used evenly during years 19X1 through 19X3. Payments will be made to the nonprofit organization on December 1, 19X1, 19X2, and 19X3. Since the promise is considered unconditional, the organization should recognize the full $9,000 as a contribution in 19X1. But the contribution specified certain time restrictions which have not been satisfied as of December 31, 19X1, so $6,000 would remaining as a temporarily restricted class of net assets (formerly termed fund balance). During 19X2 and 19X3, these net assets would be released from restrictions and reduce the net assets until there is no balance remaining.

Under the rules that existed prior to Statements 116 and 117, the nonprofit organization would have recorded contributions of $3,000 per year, without any fund balance being created. The following excerpts of the financial statements reflect the above-mentioned activity under both methods. The changes made by FASB Statements 116 and 117 are further illustrated in Exhibits 1-4.

Before Statements 116 and 117

	19X1	19X2	19X3
Contributions	$3,000	$3,000	$3,000
Expenses	3,000	3,000	3,000
Surplus/Deficit	$ 0	$ 0	$ 0

After Adoption of Statements 116 and 117

19X1

	Unrestricted	Temporarily Restricted	Total
Contributions	$0	$9,000	$9,000
Net assets released from restrictions (1)	3,000	(3,000)	0
Total revenues	3,000	6,000	9,000
Expenses	3,000	0	3,000
Net increase/(decrease) in net assets	0	6,000	6,000
Net assets—beginning of year	0	0	0
Net assets—end of year	$0	$6,000	$6,000

19X2

	Unrestricted	Temporarily Restricted	Total
Contributions	$0	$0	$0
Net assets released from restrictions (1)	3,000	(3,000)	0
Total revenues	3,000	(3,000)	0
Expenses	3,000	0	3,000
Net increase/(decrease) in net assets	0	(3,000)	(3,000)
Net assets—beginning of year	0	6,000	6,000
Net assets—end of year	$0	$3,000	$3,000

	19X3		
	Unrestricted	Temporarily Restricted	Total
Contributions	$0	$0	$0
Net assets released from restrictions (1)	3,000	(3,000)	0
Total revenues	3,000	(3,000)	0
Expenses	3,000	0	3,000
Net increase/(decrease) in net assets	0	(3,000)	(3,000)
Net assets—beginning of year	0	3,000	3,000
Net assets—end of year	$0	$0	$0

(1) Under the rules of Statement 117, as a donor-imposed restriction expires by either passage of time or other satisfaction of the restriction (performing the stated objectives of the restriction by spending the money for the stated purpose), a transfer is made from the temporarily restricted class of net assets to the unrestricted class of net assets. An example of this is shown in years 19X2 and 19X3.

Assumptions

The key to any financial statement is the assumptions on which it is based. If the assumptions are not sound, in whole or in part, then the financial statement will be suspect. It therefore behooves the executives and the directors of nonprofits to examine carefully and to understand the assumptions on which its financial statements are based. This is particularly the case where the statements involve budgets of future operations. Is the projected increase in membership (and therefore dues revenues) sound? What is the source of the expected increase in contributions? Is the expected increase in postal rates reflected in the expenses? A typical set of assumptions is attached as Exhibit 5.

Bibliography

Bryce, Herrington, J. *The Nonprofit Board's Role in Establishing Financial Policies*. Washington, D.C.: National Center for Nonprofit Boards, 1996.

Coopers & Lybrand. *Financial Reporting and Contributions: A Decision Making Guide to FASB Nos. 116 and 117*. 1994.

Coopers & Lybrand. *Financial Reporting and Contributions: Guidance for Implementation of FASB Nos. 116 and 117*. 1995.

Exhibit 1
Typical Nonprofit
Sample Statement of Financial Position
June 30, 19X1 and 19X0

	19X1	19X0
Assets:		
Cash and cash equivalents	$358,275	$389,310
Accounts and interest receivable	17,955	0
Prepaid expenses (Definition 2)	35,264	77,141
Contributions receivable (Definition 1)	32,764	40,748
Land, building and equipment (Definition 3)	2,848,009	2,942,339
Long-term investments	839,785	645,383
Total assets	4,132,052	4,094,921
Liabilities and net assets:		
Accounts payable (Definition 4)	3,026	14,927
Refundable advance (Definition 5)	74,803	3,198
Other	66,381	62,485
Total liabilities	144,210	80,610
Net Assets: (Definition 6)		
Unrestricted	3,688,971	3,764,311
Temporarily restricted	48,871	0
Permanently restricted	250,000	250,000
Total net assets	3,987,842	4,014,311
Total liabilities and net assets	$4,132,052	$4,094,921

Notes and Observations

General
—June 30, 19X1 represents current year.
—June 30, 19X0 represents previous year.

Statement of Financial Position—reports on the assets, liabilities, and net assets (previously fund balances) of an organization.
—Net assets ($3,987,842) on the Statement of Financial Position equals total assets minus total liabilities.
—Net assets ($3,987,842) on the Statement of Financial Position will correspond to net assets at end of year on Statement of Activities (Exhibit 2).

Definitions

1) Contributions Receivable—Unconditional pledges or promises by another entity to make a voluntary and non-reciprocal transfer of cash or assets to the organization.

2) Prepaid Expenses—Unexpired or unused portion of an expenditure that will benefit future periods.

3) Land, building and equipment—Long-lived assets acquired or donated for use in the operation of the organization net of accumulated depreciation.

4) Accounts Payable—Liabilities arising from purchase of goods or services.

5) Refundable advance—The remaining balance of assets received that are not considered contributions under the rules of Statement 116, i.e., government grants. This would include reciprocal or conditional transfers of cash which the condition has not been met.

6) Net Assets—

Unrestricted—The portion of net assets that does not contain any donor restrictions.

Temporarily Restricted—The portion of net assets that results from contributions whose use is limited by donor-imposed restrictions that will either expire by time or satisfaction of the program restriction.

Permanently Restricted—The part of net assets that results from contributions that contain donor-imposed restrictions that stipulate that resources be maintained permanently.

Exhibit 2
Typical Nonprofit
Sample Statement of Activities
Years Ended June 30, 19X1 & June 30, 19X0

	Unrestricted	Temporarily Restricted	Permanently Restricted	Total 19X1	Total 19X0
Revenues, gains, and other support:					
Contributions	$1,467,335	$84,621	$0	$1,551,956	$1,239,892
Fees	95,717			95,717	92,199
Rents	320,293			320,293	331,811
Other investment income	53,105			53,105	54,222
Net unrealized and realized gains on long-term investments	23,317			23,317	16,344
Other	3,982			3,982	2,011
Net assets released from restrictions:					
Satisfaction of program restrictions	2,000	(2,000)		0	0
Total revenues, gains, and other support	1,965,749	82,621	0	2,048,370	1,736,479
Expenses and losses:					
Program A	1,508,617			1,508,617	1,248,714
Program B	118,713			118,713	123,901
Program C	73,755	33,750		107,505	47,795
Management and general	220,102			220,102	265,703
Fund raising	119,902			119,902	86,488
Total expenses	2,041,089	33,750	0	2,074,839	1,772,601
Change in net assets	(75,340)	48,871		(26,469)	(36,122)
Net assets at beginning of year	3,764,311	0	250,000	4,014,311	4,050,433
Net assets at end of year	$3,688,971	$48,871	$250,000	$3,987,842	$4,014,311

Notes and Observations

1) This financial statement represents minimum requirements. Each class of net assets above (unrestricted, temporarily restricted, and permanently restricted) may be broken into subcategories as long as the total of the net asset group is shown.

General
—June 30, 19X1 represents current year.
—June 30, 19X0 represents previous year.

Statement of Activities—Reports information about an organization's change in net assets.
—Total 19X1 represents the current year totals of unrestricted, temporarily restricted, and permanently restricted columns.
—Change in net assets represents the difference between total revenues, gains, and other support ($2,048,370) and total expenses of ($2,074,839).
—Expenses and losses are categorized by program (Programs A, B, and C), management and general, and fund raising. These are further categorized and the totals for these items are the same as those shown on the Statement of Functional Expenses (Exhibit 4).

Definitions

Contributions—The unconditional transfer of cash or other assets by another entity in a voluntary non-reciprocal transfer to the organization.
Satisfaction of Program Restriction—Records the expenditure of funds in satisfaction of program-restricted funds.

Exhibit 3
Typical Nonprofit
Sample Statement of Cash Flows
Years Ended June 30, 19X1 & June 30, 19X0

	19X1	19X0
Cash flows from operating activities:		
Change in net assets	($26,469)	($36,122)
Adjustments to reconcile change in net assets to net cash used by operating activities:		
Depreciation	123,608	122,994
(Increase) in accounts & interest receivable	(17,955)	0
Decrease in prepared expenses	41,877	(47,632)
Decrease in contributions receivable	7,984	(13,703)
(Decrease) in accounts payable	(11,901)	(6,606)
Increase in refundable advance	71,605	554
Increase in other	3,896	0
Net cash provided by operating activities	192,645	19,485
Cash flows from investing activities:		
Purchase of equipment	(29,278)	(57,599)
Proceeds from sale of investments	294,203	39,366
Purchase of investments	(488,605)	(58,195)
Net cash used by investing activities	(223,680)	(76,428)
Net decrease in cash and cash equivalents	(31,035)	(56,943)
Cash and cash equivalents at beginning of year	389,310	446,253
Cash and cash equivalents at end of year	$358,275	$389,310

Notes and Observations

General
—June 30, 19X1 represents current year.
—June 30, 19X0 represents previous year.

Statement of Cash Flows—reports the net increase and decrease in cash and cash equivalents.
—Change in net assets ($26,469 & $36,122) on Statement of Cash Flow reconciles with total changes in net assets from Statement of Activities (Exhibit 2).
—Net decrease in cash and cash equivalents ($31,035) is the difference in cash provided by operating activities ($192,645) and cash used ($223,680) by investing activities.
—Cash and cash equivalents at end of year ($358,275 and $389,310) will agree with cash and cash equivalents on the Statement of Financial Positions (Exhibit 1).

Exhibit 4
Typical Nonprofit Sample Statement of Functional Expenses
For the year ended June 30, 19X1
(With comparative totals for June 30, 19X0)

| | Program Services | | | | Supporting Services | | | Total All Funds | Total 6/30/X0 |
	Program A	Program B	Program C	Total	Management and General	Fund Raising	Total		
Salaries	$740,259	$94,574	$86,613	$921,446	$95,261	$64,988	$160,249	$1,081,695	$933,569
Payroll taxes and fringe benefits	123,544	22,263	20,892	166,699	22,977	15,675	38,652	205,351	194,792
Total personal service expenses	863,803	116,837	107,505	1,088,145	118,238	80,663	198,901	1,287,046	1,128,361
Consultants	53,897			53,897	7,575		7,575	61,472	39,882
Occupancy	2,400			2,400	9,000		9,000	11,400	0
Utilities	86,151			86,151	0		0	86,151	71,900
Insurance	21,104			21,104	11,032		11,032	32,136	30,891
Contract services	39,339			39,339	0		0	39,339	49,939
Food	246,123			246,123	3,359		3,359	249,482	152,381
Supplies	45,447	938		46,385	12,665	3,398	16,063	62,448	46,989
Communications	12,079	129		12,208	4,241	6,710	10,951	23,159	19,108
Minor equipment	15,060	607		15,667	0		0	15,667	25,575
Repairs and maintenance/ equipment	27,164			27,164	715		715	27,379	35,723
Travel	1,838			1,838	3,361		3,361	5,199	3,702
Fund raising expenses				0		28,820	28,820	28,820	33,687
Dues, subscriptions and other	11,563	202		11,765	8,957	511	9,268	21,033	11,469
Total expenses before depreciation	1,425,968	118,713	107,505	1,652,186	179,143	119,902	299,045	1,951,231	1,649,607
Depreciation	82,649			82,649	40,959		40,959	123,608	122,994
Total expenses	$1,508,617	$118,713	$107,505	$1,734,835	$220,102	$119,902	$340,004	$2,074,839	$1,772,601

329

Notes and Observations

General

—June 30, 19X1 represents current year.

—June 30, 19X0 represents previous year.

Statement of Functional Expenses—reports expense classification by program and supporting services (management and fund raising).

The totals of each activity are brought forward to the Statement of Activities (Exhibit 2).

Exhibit 5
Assumptions—Proposed Budget

April 1, 1995—March 31, 1996

Starting with a general discussion of basic assumptions and financial prospects with the Budget Committee in January, the planning process then began in earnest when each of the seven staff members with direct cost and/or revenue responsibility prepared detailed cost center budgets for the coming year based on services planned in conjunction with the appropriate committee liaisons. The proposed budget was then compiled and reviewed by senior staff for recommendation to the Budget Committee.

The staff has operated under the primary goal of producing quality educational programs, publications and research services to meet the perceived needs of the _____ members while working to increase membership and operate an efficient National Office.

(1) The proposed budget assumes that 2,655 of the assumed 3,215 dues-paying regular members at April 1, 1995 will pay $_____. It is further assumed that 350 such members will join during the year and 325 will resign or be terminated for a net gain of 25 to 2,680.

Accordingly, the proposed budget assumes that 560 of the assumed 3,215 dues-paying regular members at April 1, 1995 will pay $_____. It is further assumed that 100 such members will join during the year and 50 will resign or be terminated for a net gain of 50 to 610.

Associate Members stay flat at 125, but 17 Quarter-Century Club members pay reduced associate dues of $_____.

No change in Entrance Fees ($_____) or Associate Dues ($_____); entrance fee discounting to $50 Oct. and Nov. only.

(2) National Conference Income/Expense:

The National Conference at _____ in June 1995 will attract 375 member registrants (675 attendees) and 25 exhibitors.

No fee changes except the upcharge for all couples is increased by $25, i.e. early member single registrants will continue to pay $_____ but early member couples will pay $_____ rather than $_____, etc.

Budgeted speaker fund subsidy of $_____ underwriting of the opening reception and full absorption of printing/mailing services by financial printers help to reduce the high _____ charges for speaker/staff rooms, audiovisual aids, and all meals and services not covered under the _____ there.

Exhibit 5 is reprinted with the permission of the American Society of Corporate Secretaries.

(3) Seminar Income/Expense:

No changes in the following rate structure: members pay $550 for 1 1/2-day programs and $595 for 2-day programs, non-members pay $625 for the short programs and $675 for the long programs, and each additional registrant from a corporation pays $395 for the short programs and $450 for the long programs. For _____, which has many concurrent sessions, each additional registrant pays $300.

For FY96:	Oct.	(100 registrants)	$
	Nov.	(120 registrants)	$
	Jan.	(100 registrants)	$
	March	(100 registrants)	$ _____
			$

A Videoconference II is planned for the winter of 1996 and will be priced to break even, but no revenue or expense for the program is included in the proposed budget.

(4) Publication Sales:

Includes sales of 1995 _____ Report and a full _____ Book (both published once every two years) plus a new _____ Guidebook.

(5) Other Services Income:

Increased based on the past few years' volume of library services, _____, sales, and _____ sales. No change in fees charged.

(6) Interest Income:

Cash outlays for new office equipment, leasehold improvements and security deposits decrease opening portfolio balances but are partially offset by the free office rent period until January 1996 and rates holding at current levels.

(7) Salaries:

Staffing at 13 with anniversary date merit raise pool of ____%. Includes annual $_____ of part-time file clerk/typist/data input support. Projected actuals for current year include limited use of temporary help, lower total increases than projected and periods of lower personnel costs during staff changes.

(8) Payroll Taxes:

No tax rate changes except FICA cap increases and slightly lower state unemployment charges. Projected actuals include unbudgeted payroll taxes on bonuses accrued in March 1995 but not paid until April 1995.

(9) FAS 87 Pension Cost:

Actuarially determined; no change in pension assumptions as recommended by the _____ Audit Committee.

(10) Other Benefits:

Reflects the new comprehensive coverage with lower premiums due to higher copays and deductibles adopted in September 1994. Continued employee contributions to dependent health coverage to the extent premiums for such additional coverage increase. Assumed 10% coverage premium increase at policy anniversary in September 1995.

(11) Publications:

Continued use of selective distribution with an assumption that _____ expanding desktop publishing resources help to hold printing costs. Projected   actuals reflect budgeted committee publications not yet ready for issuance.

(12) Postage:

Office postage volume flat, selective distribution of publications continues and the January 1995 postal rate increase is included.

(13) Board and Committee:

Includes costs of all Board events, committee meetings held in conjunction with National and fall conferences, _____, committee conference calls and special mailings to members. The _____ hosts the _____, in January 1996. Current year projected actuals are lower due to timing—the spring Board meeting is in April rather than March as planned.

(14) Occupancy:

Reflects the _____ March 25 move to new offices with lower rent over a 13-year lease. The total lease cost, including the free rent allowance until January 1996, is amortized over the 12 years and eight months the _____ will occupy the premises. _____ has leased the _____ current offices as of April 1, relieving our obligation for the remaining four months on the lease which expires July 31.

(15) Office Services:

Holding the line with recent positive change in long-distance carrier and slightly higher maintenance costs at the new office. Current year projected actuals include the March moving expenses.

(16) Equipment Rental/Maintenance:

Reflects lower maintenance costs of new equipment with various warranty periods.

(17) Depreciation/Amortization:

Total depreciation (furniture and equipment) and amortization (leasehold improvements) has returned to the _____ customary level for years prior to FY94 when the last major office equipment purchases were fully depreciated. Includes computer upgrade to Windows environment on Novell network with Compaq hardware, H-P and Lexmark laser printers, data/fax modems and scanning equipment; copier upgrade to Xerox 5385; and new Executone phone system. Also reflects the purchase of new and refurbished office furniture/files for entire new office and leasehold improvements there in excess of the construction allowance.

(18) Auditors/Consultants:

Includes annual audit fee of $_____ and new initiatives cost of $_____ for market research study of non-member public corporations. Current year projected actuals include legal fees for the new office lease negotiations.

(19) Other Operating Expenses:

Includes chapter meeting and conference fees, professional dues and development, office hospitality and ongoing computer support/training. The increase in the proposed budget from current year projected actuals is primarily due to staff training for the new computer system.

About the Authors

David Ashenfarb, of Schall & Ashenfarb, P.C., certified public accountant, is a former manager at Ernst & Young, LLP. Mr Ashenfarb is a certified public accountant in the state of New York, who currently sits on the not-for-profit committee of the New York State Society of CPAs. He is a frequent speaker at the Council of Senior Centers and Services and advises clients in a variety of nonprofit matters.

David M. Bardsley is a consultant with Financial Markets International (USAID). He has conducted seminars on the organization, operation, and regulation of mutual funds in Romania. In Kyrgyz Republic, Central Asia, he conducted seminars and workshops for owners and managers of newly privatized companies on corporate structure, management, and governance. Mr. Bardsley also served as senior counsel to The Mutual Life Insurance Company of New York, and handled corporate work for major public companies at Rosen & Reade. He has contributed to publications by the American Society of Corporate Secretaries for nonprofit organizations.

Carol M. Barker is secretary of the corporation and vice president for associational affairs at the College Board. Prior to her appointment as secretary in 1987, she served for five years as deputy secretary with primary responsibility for membership policy and services. From 1969–82, she was a member of the research staff and, eventually, associate director for research of the Twentieth Century Fund, a nonprofit public policy research foundation. She earned her B.A. from Radcliffe College and her M.A. and Ph.D. in political science from Columbia University. In addition to her professional positions in nonprofit organizations, she has served as secretary and as president of the Radcliffe Club of New York City and is currently president of Pathways for Youth, Inc., a nonprofit community-based organization in New York City.

Lucy S. Binder was formerly secretary, PECO Energy Company.

Robert W. Bishop is vice president, general counsel and secretary of Nuclear Energy Institute, Inc. His previous responsibilities have included serving as corporate secretary of a variety of nonprofit organizations and of a major publicly-traded corporation.

William G. Bowen states: "Much of the raw material for [a recent book] consists of lessons I have learned while serving on a reasonably wide variety of corporate and nonprofit boards. These include, in the for-profit sector, American Express, Merck, NCR (before it was taken over by AT&T), Readers Digest, and Rockefeller Group Inc. (the owner of Rockefeller Center); in the nonprofit sector, Denison University, the Center for Advanced Study in the Behavioral Sciences, the Public Broadcast Laboratory, the Smithsonian Institution, the Sloan Foundation, Princeton University and The Andrew W. Mellon Foundation."

William H. Cox is a member of the firm of Herzfeld & Rubin, P.C. and has had substantial experience in forming and counseling nonprofit organizations.

Joan Elise Dubinsky is senior legal counsel for the MITRE Corporation of McLean, Virginia, specializing in all aspects of employment, labor, individual rights, ethics and corporate compliance. Ms. Dubinsky received her undergraduate degree in religious philosophy from the University of Michigan in 1974 and her doctor of jurisprudence from the University of Texas in 1979. Before joining MITRE's legal office, Ms. Dubinsky was the corporate secretary, associate general counsel and ethics officer for the American Red Cross, and assistant city attorney for the city of Austin, Texas. Ms. Dubinsky has developed a special interest in business ethics and corporate compliance, and is a well-known speaker and writer in this area.

Frank W. Evans is vice president and secretary of Junior Achievement.

Philip A. Faix, Jr. is an adjunct professor of law at Duquesne University's School of Law in Pittsburgh, Pennsylvania. Mr. Faix was general counsel and corporate secretary of Medusa Corporation and serves on diverse nonprofit boards.

Susan Sommer Futter works with organizations to design and implement organization change and management training programs. As a consultant, Ms. Futter was instrumental in helping a large, regional nonprofit health organization implement its highly successful Total Quality initiative. Ms. Futter began her career as a special education teacher and has been involved in numerous volunteer activities. She is currently serving as a committee officer with the New York Junior League, where she has facilitated team-building and problem-solving sessions. She received a masters degree in education and an MBA from the University of Virginia.

Victor Futter is chair of the ad hoc committee on nonprofits of the American Society of Corporate Secretaries. Mr. Futter was vice president and secretary of Allied Corporation (now Allied-Signal Inc.); general counsel and secretary of the board of trustees of Fairleigh Dickinson University; secretary of Nova Pharmaceuticals Corporation, and is of counsel to Sills, Cummis, Zuckerman, Radin, Tischman, Epstein & Gross. He is currently on the boards of Greenwich House (senior vice-chair) and the Justice Resource Center. He has served as president of the Columbia College Alumni Association; chair of the Senior Lawyers Division of the American Bar Association; chair of the Columbia College Fund; chair of the parents committee, Mount Holyoke College; and on the boards of the Academy of Political Science, Corod Foundation, the American Society of Corporate Secretaries (president, New York Chapter), The New York Chapter of the National Association of Corporate Directors (president), The National Association of Local Arts Agencies; Board of Directors Port Washington Community Chest (chairman Fund Drive); and Deputy Mayor, Village of Flower Hill (Nassau County, N.Y.). He also teaches seminars in corporate governance at both Columbia and Hofstra schools.

Carl T. Hagberg is the chairman of Carl T. Hagberg and Associates, a strategic marketing and investor services consulting firm. He holds a B.A. in economics from New York University and an M.S. in business policy from Columbia University Graduate School of Business. He is a member of the American Arbitration Association, the American Society of Corporate Secretaries (former New York Chapter president, former national treasurer), the National Investor Relations Institute and Securities Transfer Association (special advisor to the board). He is a director of The Minerva Fund, Inc. and is also the publisher of *The Shareholder Services Optimizer*.

Regina E. Herzlinger is the Nancy R. McPherson Professor of Business Administration at the Harvard Business School in Boston, Massachusetts, and the senior author of *Financial Accounting and Managerial Control for Nonprofit Organizations* (Cincinnati: South-Western, 1993).

Fisher Howe is a consultant for nonprofit organizations with the firm of Lavender/Howe and Associates with offices in Washington, D.C. and Ojai, California. A former foreign service officer, he has had management experience as an assistant dean at Johns Hopkins University School of Advanced International Studies and with Resources for the Future, a Washington, D.C. research organization. He serves on several local and national boards. His book, *The Board Member's Guide to Fund Raising* (Jossey-Bass, 1991) has been widely acclaimed.

Gilbert H. Jacobson is director, Endowment Foundation of the United Jewish Community of Bergen County, New Jersey.

Kenneth P. Kopelman is an attorney in private practice in New York City. He also serves as corporate secretary of Liz Claiborne, Inc.

Robert Kornreich is a certified public accountant, Phillips Gold and Company, LLP.

George W. Overton is of counsel, Wildman, Harrold, Allen & Dixon, Chicago; co-chair, subcommittee on *Guidebook for Directors of Nonprofit Corporations* of the American Bar Association and, as such, editor and principal author of the *Guidebook*. He writes frequently on the problems of nonprofit corporations.

Leonard M. Polisar is a member of the firm of Herzfeld & Rubin, P.C. He serves as an officer, director or trustee of several nonprofit organizations, including The Mental Health Association of New York City and Union Temple of Brooklyn. Mr. Polisar also serves on the advisory councils of both the Business Council for the United Nations and Business Executives for National Security.

David B. Rigney is counsel to Lankenau Kovner & Kurtz in New York City. He practiced with Sullivan & Cromwell in New York City from 1972-79, and from 1979-89 was general counsel and vice chancellor for legal affairs of The City University of New York.

Robert L. Seaman is an attorney engaged primarily in the practice of corporate and securities law in New York City, New York. He has been an active participant on the boards of several nonprofits over the last 20 years. His roles include serving as secretary of the board of Friends Academy, a private secondary school in Locust Valley, New York. He also served as chairman of the board of Friends World College, located in Lloyd Harbor, New York and as interim head of that institution. He is an experienced arbitrator and mediator as well as being a writer and lecturer in the field of institutional governance.

W. Donald Sparks, II is a director in the firm of Richards, Layton & Finger, P.A. in Wilmington, Delaware, specializing in the field of tax law. He received his B.A. degree from Dartmouth College and his J.D. from Yale Law School. He clerked for Judge Caleb Wright of the U.S. District Court for the District of Delaware and practiced for three years with the firm of Ballard, Spahr, Andrews & Ingersoll of Philadelphia, Pennsylvania, before joining Richards, Layton & Finger. He is a member of the American Bar Association, the Pennsylvania Bar Association and the Delaware Bar Association. He is a member of the Real Property and Trusts Section of the Pennsylvania Bar and the Tax and Estates and Trusts Sections of the American Bar and Delaware Bar Associations. He is a past chairman of the Delaware Bar Association Section of Taxation and has appeared as a speaker on numerous occasions on various tax-related topics.

Sally P. Trabulsi was formerly secretary of Mount Holyoke College.

Cherry S. White is the regional director of corporate affairs at Allegheny Health, Education and Research Foundation, a nonprofit academic health care system located in Pennsylvania, comprising nine hospitals, a continuing care center, two medical universities, and a research institute.

Order additional copies of
NONPROFIT GOVERNANCE
The Executive's Guide
(PC # 5070305)

Please send me:

_____copies @ $79.95 each (1-3 copies)

_____copies @ $59.95 each (4-10 copies)

_____copies @ $49.95 each (11+ copies)

$_____Subtotal

$_____Tax (DC residents add 5.75%, IL residents add 8.75%, MD residents add 5%)

$__5.95__Handling

$_____Total

Payment:

☐ Bill me   ☐ Check enclosed payable to the ABA   ☐ VISA   ☐ MasterCard

Acct #_____ Exp.Date_____

Signature_____

Name_____

Firm/Org_____

Address_____

City/State/Zip_____

Phone number (in case we have a question about your order)_____

Mail to: American Bar Association, Publication Orders,
P.O. Box 10892, Chicago, IL 60610-0892

Or Phone: 800-285-2221

Or Fax: 312-988-5568   source code: BOOK